Employee Reward Structures

Aidan Langley

Spiramus

Published August 2006 by

Spiramus

Spiramus Press Ltd
The Boathouse Office
57a Gainsford Street
London SE1 2NB
Telephone +44 20 7357 0861
www.spiramus.com

This publication is based upon the law as at 24 July 2006

ISBN

1 904905 26 9	Book
1 904905 27 7	CD ROM
1 904905 28 5	Set

Printed and bound in Great Britain by Biddles, King's Lynn, Norfolk
Cover design: David Shaw and associates

Acknowledgements

I would like to thank the following colleagues at PricewaterhouseCoopers LLP for their help in reviewing this second edition: Sue Wilson, Jonathan Fice, Paul Scarborough, Brian Edwards, Tim Sexton and Iain Selfridge. I would also like to thank Fiona Aikman of Berwin Leighton Paisner LLP, a sharp-eyed reader of the first edition, who drew my attention to some errata.

Contents

List of abbreviations

FA 2005 etc.	Finance Acts
ICTA 1988	Income and Corporation Taxes Act 1988
IHTA 1984	Inheritance Tax Act 1984
ITEPA 2003	Income Tax (Earnings and Pensions Act) 2003
ITTOIA 2005	Income Tax (Trading and Other Income) Act 2005
SSCBA 1992	Social Security Contributions and Benefits Act 1992
TCGA 1992	Taxation of Capital Gains Act 1992
TMA 1970	Taxes Management Act 1970
VATA 1994	Value Added Tax Act 1994
HMRC	Her Majesty's Revenue & Customs
CA 1985	Companies Act 1985
ERA 1996	Employment Rights Act 1996
FSMA 2000	Financial Services and Markets Act 2000
NIA 1965	National Insurance Act 1965
SCSOA 2001	Social Security Contributions (Share Options) Act 2001
WRPA 1999	Welfare Reform and Pensions Act 1999
SSCR 2001	Social Security (Contributions) Regulations 2001

1. Introduction

This is a practical guide written by two employee compensation practitioners, to be read by accountants, lawyers and other advisers to unquoted businesses.

Alison Haynes, who has written the section on employment status, is a partner in the Employer Solutions group at Deloitte & Touche LLP, advising on employment tax matters.

Aidan Langley, who has written the remainder of the book, has practised as a solicitor and is now a director in the HR Services Group at PricewaterhouseCoopers LLP, advising smaller companies on the design and implementation of short and long-term reward plans.

Tax law in this area is in a period of substantial change, with new rules on share plans being introduced in 2003 and significantly amended in 2004, and an entirely new pensions regime introduced in 2006. Some previous regimes have been repealed entirely; others have been grandfathered and remain applicable in particular circumstances. More than ever, this area is a minefield for the practitioner who does not deal with it regularly.

The authors recognise that clients will present different problems: designing a package for a new hire; introducing a new all-employee benefit plan; determining the tax effects of an existing plan. Therefore, each chapter of the book provides a different entry point from which the user can drill down to the relevant text.

The glossary defines key terms, which are then used in a consistent manner throughout the book. Clicking on any key term in the CD-ROM version will immediately bring up the definition of that term. In the hard copy version, defined terms are shown in **bold text**.

This book gives general practitioners instant access to expert knowledge so as to serve their clients more effectively.

2. Recruiting a New Executive

2.1. Employment Status

The question of employment status is an absolutely critical one which must be determined correctly by any organisation using the skills of workers. Failure to categorise correctly the employment status of its workers can have a catastrophic impact on the financial good health of an organisation irrespective of its size or sector group.

Most businesses are heavily reliant on their workers, not only for their financial prosperity, but indeed for their very existence. For a good many businesses the costs associated with their workers comprise the largest item of annual expenditure. It is therefore very important for businesses to identify the status of their workers correctly and to ensure that where appropriate tax and national insurance contribution (NIC) costs are correctly calculated and paid. Clearly, the issue of being an employee or a self-employed person is of great importance to an individual; and it is no less so for the business making use of their services. Where a worker is used by a business in an employed capacity, the employer has a duty to calculate the tax and NIC due in respect of the earnings and to pay them over to HM Revenue & Customs on a timely basis. This obligation is always the employer's and failure either to identify their employees correctly, or to account for the correct amounts of tax and NIC under PAYE can be very costly for a business.

Although most businesses regularly consider the status of their workers, this issue usually comes into sharp focus when it becomes the subject of dialogue with HM Revenue & Customs. The question of status is always to be determined by proper evaluation of the facts, but frequently engagers struggle with the proper weight to place on the various elements comprising the contract under consideration. HM Revenue & Customs recognise these endeavours and in December 2005 they launched their Employment Status Indicator tool. This tool is aimed, primarily, at the businesses who engage workers as opposed to the individual workers. HM Revenue & Customs have stressed that the tool is intended to give an indication of employment status and is not a legally binding opinion. This tool can be of assistance to employers, particularly in helping them to focus on some of the circumstances and tests which need to be considered, but it should never be used as a substitute for a clear and thorough evaluation of the appropriate tests, which we will consider later in this chapter. The tool can be found at http://www.hmrc.gov.uk/calcs/esi.htm.

There are two main categories of employment status: employed or self-employed, although further in this chapter we will also consider workers covered by the IR35 legislation, office-holders and certain types of worker who are deemed to be employees for tax and/or NIC purposes.

Most of the issues which are dealt with in this book are described and prescribed by statute and in many instances a specific question will be answered just as specifically by statutory reference. This is not so with employment status. Certainly there are consequences of being either an employee or a self-employed worker which are laid down by statute, but in general the principles determining status have been laid down over many centuries and have been primarily formulated and codified, by case law rather than statute.

2.2. Why is the distinction between being employed or self-employed important?

Many workers enjoy being employed earners because of the many and varied benefits associated with employment status. In particular, the security of knowing that for the duration of the contract, or until they either give notice or are given notice by their employer, that they will be offered work for a certain number of hours every week or month, and in return will receive a set salary or wage, is extremely attractive. In addition, employees benefit from the security of knowing that they are within the remit of the employment law legislation which affords many protections to employees, including the right not to be unfairly dismissed and in most instances, the right to some form of statutory compensation or redundancy payment in the event that the business down-sizes. Some employees also appreciate the fact that their employer is obligated to calculate and withhold tax and NIC under the PAYE system, ensuring that the pay they receive is net of tax and NIC costs, which relieves them of the burden of having to calculate their tax and NIC liability and of having to budget for paying such costs. Employees also benefit from paid holidays, statutory sick pay and frequently from additional benefits such as participation in an employer's pension scheme.

In contrast, self-employed individuals do not generally have job security, nor do they seek it. Rather, a self-employed worker will enjoy seeking out opportunities and contracts, will work for a variety of different businesses each and every year and will have the opportunity of charging for their services at the prevailing market rate, giving them the opportunity of charging rather more in good times and having to accept lower rates when prevailing market conditions dictate. However, self-employed workers are accountable to HM Revenue & Customs for their own taxes and NIC costs; they do not have the employment law benefits afforded to employees, nor do they share in any of the benefits provided by employers, such as statutory sick pay.

The taxation and NIC treatments attaching to either employment or self-employment are also very different. Employees are taxable on the income they receive for acting as an employee less expenses which have been incurred wholly, exclusively and necessarily in the course of their duties [ITEPA 2003, s336] or necessarily incurred in the case of travel expenses [ITEPA 2003, s337]. On the other hand, a self-employed worker is taxable on the gross receipts from acting as a self-employed person less any expenses incurred wholly and exclusively in the course of their trade or profession [ITTOIA 2005, s34]. The absence of the word 'necessarily' in the requirements for self-employed workers means that frequently they can claim business expenses against their taxable income for acting as a self-employed worker which would not be tax deductible if expended by somebody in employment.

The NIC position for employees is also different from that which applies to self-employed workers. Employees are subject to Class 1 NIC, of which primary NIC is payable by the employee and secondary NIC by the employer. In contrast, self-employed workers pay Class 2 and 4 NIC.

Table 1: NIC Rates sets out the rates of Class 1 NIC applicable to employees and of Class 2, 3 and 4 NIC which could be applicable to self-employed workers.

Table 1: NIC Rates

Weekly Rates and Limits	**2006-07**
Lower earnings limit, primary Class 1	£84
Upper earnings limit, primary Class 1	£645
Employee and employers' earnings threshold	£97
Employees' primary Class 1 rate between earnings threshold and upper earnings limit	11%
Employees' primary Class 1 rate above upper earnings limit	1%
Employees' contracted-out rebate on earnings between the lower and upper earnings limit	1.6%
Employers' secondary Class 1 rate above employers' threshold	12.8%
Employers' contracted-out rebate on earnings between the lower and upper earnings limit, salary-related schemes	3.5%
Employers' contracted-out rebate on earnings between the lower and upper earnings limit, money-purchase schemes	1%
Class 2 rate	£2.10
Class 3 rate	£7.55
Class 4 lower profits limit	£5,035 per year
Class 4 upper profits limit	£33,540

	per year
Class 4 rate between lower profits limit and upper profits limit	8%
Class 4 rate above upper profits limit	1%

2.3. Pros and Cons of being an employed earner

Advantages/Rights

For the employee

- Certainty and security including the hours to be worked and the rate of pay for the job.
- Benefits provided to employee – such as participation in employer's pension scheme, life insurance scheme etc.
- Employment law protections.
- Statutory benefits such as maternity rights.
- Smooth cashflow and less administration - relevant tax and NIC will have been deducted at source.
- No material business costs – tools, equipment, uniforms etc.
- Ability to expect all rights granted under the contract of employment.

For the employer

- Control over the way in which tasks are performed.
- Certainty of resource – particularly of the number and quality of employees.
- Exclusivity – particularly knowing that key workers must work exclusively for the employer and are not available to his competitors.
- Ability to enforce his contractual rights and obligations from the employee.

Disadvantages/obligations

For the employee

- Less flexibility in varying or opportunity to change the terms of the contract (other than by negotiation or at annual review dates).
- A higher rate of NIC and a more limited capacity for taking a tax deduction for expenses against the employment income.
- An obligation to exert themselves for the advancement of their employer rather than on their own account.
- An obligation to work under the employer's direction and control.
- Unable to leave without giving either a statutory notice period or such period as is provided for in the contract of employment.

For the employer

- A requirement to provide the infrastructure and organisation of dealing with employees, including to deduct and pay over to HM Revenue & Customs the tax and NIC on behalf of each and every employee in addition to paying the secondary NIC.

- A requirement to provide all relevant equipment, tools and uniforms.
- An obligation to ensure that the premises on which their employees work and all equipment and tools meet all legal standards of health and safety etc to fulfil their contractual obligations to their employee, including providing the appropriate statutory notice period or such longer period as is provided for in the contract.
- The additional cost of secondary NIC.

2.4. Pros and cons of being a self-employed worker

Advantages/Rights:

For the self-employed worker

- Greater flexibility and control over working, when and how they choose.
- Ability to benefit from the lower rates of NIC and more generous tax deductions for expenses of business.
- Ability to react to market forces and charge more for their services when the market allows.
- No obligation to perform the services themselves, but to use a substitute.
- The cashflow advantage of not having to pay over their tax and social security to HM Revenue & Customs on a monthly basis.

For the engager

- No obligation to offer work on a regular or frequent basis – a great benefit in quiet times.
- Fewer or no employment law costs, requirements or considerations.
- None of the administration or infrastructure necessary for employing workers.
- No requirement to withhold tax under PAYE or account for NIC.
- No requirement to pay employer's NIC – in many cases this can mean a lower cost for the contract.
- Reduced or eliminated need to provide employment related benefits such as sick pay, pensions or holiday pay.

Disadvantages/obligations

For the worker

- Increased risk – no job security or entitlement to redundancy pay.
- No employment style benefits – sick pay, participation in employer's pension scheme.
- Little or no employment law protection.
- A requirement to bear costs of being in business.
- A requirement to put right poor quality work at own cost.

For the engager

- No control over when and who undertakes tasks.

- No ability to require the worker to undertake any tasks or projects.

Although outside the scope of this book, the National Minimum Wage legislation and Working Time Directive (with particular regard to the rights of workers to have paid holidays each year) should be considered as the term "workers" for the purpose of these pieces of legislation can in certain circumstances include self-employed workers.

2.5. Contract of service/contract for services

The question of whether an individual is performing duties as an employee or a self-employed individual is fundamentally determined by the nature of the relationship between engager and worker. Essentially does the relationship constitute a contract of employment or a contract 'for services'? The phrase 'contract of service' is synonymous with contract of employment and indicates that the duties have actually to be performed by the individual in question and that there is a degree of control or master/servant relationship between the employee and the employer. In contrast, a contract for services indicates the services which will be provided under the contract, but is not specific as to whether the holder of the contract has to provide them themselves, or whether they may use suitably qualified individuals to perform them on their behalf.

Differentiating between 'a contract of service' and 'a contract for services' is a complex area which is not always easy to determine and has been the subject of much litigation over the years. Whilst there are various indicators which may point towards a contract for services, there are always two criteria which must be present for a contract of service:

- Firstly, there must be a mutuality of obligation between the employer and the employee.
- Secondly, the employee must be obligated to perform the services himself.

The case of *Express and Echo Publications Limited v Ernest Tanton* [1999] EWCA 1050 demonstrates the need for the employee to be obligated to perform the services himself. The facts of the case were these:

Express and Echo Publications Limited had employed Ernest Tanton for a period until he was made redundant in 1995. Later in 1995 he was re-engaged to work for them under a new agreement. The company intended that under this agreement Mr Tanton would be self-employed and apparently at this stage Mr Tanton agreed with this intent but subsequently changed his mind. Furthermore, in July 1997 he applied to an industrial tribunal complaining of what he described as a breach of contract. At this point, whilst Mr Tanton maintained that he was employed by the company, the company's view was that he was a self-employed contractor. It was therefore necessary to consider the contract between the parties. There were various factors not in dispute, which included that Mr Tanton's duties were to pick up and deliver newspapers as part of a fixed run in the order dictated by the company. Mr Tanton had to wear the company uniform, drove a vehicle provided by the company, and was paid a fixed fee for the journey. Mr Tanton received no sick pay and no holiday pay. The clause in the contract which was to prove pivotal was clause 3.3 which provided:

"In the event that the contractor was unable or unwilling to perform the services personally, he shall arrange at his own expense entirely for another suitable person to perform the services."

However, it ultimately appeared that there was at least one occasion on which Mr Tanton had been obligated to perform the services personally as the company deemed the substitute he provided to be unacceptable. On the quoted occasion, Mr Tanton had been on sick leave and only able to get about on crutches, but nevertheless performed the duties himself as he believed he was obligated to under the contract.

This case was important in showing that whilst on previous occasions Mr Tanton had supplied a substitute and indeed had paid that substitute himself, this ultimately was not the deciding factor. What was important was that the company clearly under the contract had the right to refuse the substitution and insist that Mr Tanton undertake the duties himself. Nevertheless, the Court of Appeal held that Mr Tanton was not an employee.

This case can be considered alongside *Hall v Lorimer* [1994] STC 23, described in more detail below, in which the right of substitution was not the deciding factor and established that self-employment could exist even where an engager required an individual's personal service.

2.6. Employment tests

The two criteria mentioned in section 2.5, namely mutuality of obligation and the obligation to perform the service personally, whilst critical for the purposes of determining whether an employment may be able to exist, are not of themselves necessarily sufficient to prove that an employment actually does exist. There are many and various factors which can be taken into account when determining whether an employment relationship actually exists and generally these are broken down into six headings:-

- Mutuality of obligation.
- Personal service/substitution.
- Control/supervision – sometimes referred to as the master/servant test.
- Employment Benefits
- Financial risk.
- Provision of equipment.

In addition to the above six usual tests there are two further points which must be considered. First, does the contract reflect the substance of the relationship and secondly has that substance changed through the passage of time? Indeed, sometimes it may be necessary to apply the tests and all objective criteria separately to the documentation surrounding the contract and to the reality of how the engagement is undertaken. The principle of substance over form is absolute and regularly has to be considered when determining a worker's status. It is irrelevant how clear and carefully constructed a contract between two parties may be in specifying that the arrangement is a contract for services, if the reality is quite different.

However, where the appropriate tests and considerations for whether an employment exists or not are of equal weight, then the intention of the parties can be a useful indicator. This is most commonly found to be helpful where the nature of the engagement was clearly documented at the outset and either time or circumstances have necessitated a change in behaviour. Clearly, however, well documented stated intentions will be irrelevant if it is quite obvious when considering the facts that they support the opposing position.

Let us now examine each of the potentially relevant tests in rather more detail:-

2.6.1. Mutuality of obligation

In essence this means that where the engager is obliged to offer work, the individual is obliged to accept the work and undertake it personally at which point the engager is obliged to pay. Where over a period of time work has regularly been offered to an individual, which has always been accepted and performed by the individual personally, this would usually be a strong indicator that an employment relationship may subsist. It is not essential that a worker always accepts work when offered it by an engager, and indeed occasional refusals may be synonymous with an employee taking annual holiday. This test is at least task or project focussed and will usually be based around whether, once an individual has been offered a piece of work and accepted it, they have the obligation to see it through.

The mutuality of obligation concept can be applied further in assessing the obligation of an engager to offer work and of a worker to accept work that is offered. An employee is required to accept and undertake work and tasks provided by his employer. In most cases, engagers of self-employed workers have no obligation to offer work on a regular or frequent basis and the worker has no obligation to accept that work. However, there have been instances where there has been a break either in work being offered by an engager or accepted by an individual but that over a period of time there has been a pattern of work being offered and accepted. In such instances it is possible to conclude that a mutuality of obligation exists and a series of short-term employments between the engager and the individual have taken place.

2.6.2. Personal service/substitution

Under an employment contract it is clear that an individual is required to provide his or her services personally. It is therefore important to determine whether or not an individual could provide a replacement worker or substitute at their own volition.

Where it is understood or explicitly agreed between the engager and the individual that a suitably qualified or skilled person can be substituted at the worker's discretion, this will usually be a very strong indicator towards self-employment. It is important however to consider whether any substitution can be effected entirely at the worker's volition or whether there has to be any degree of approval by the engager, and if so to what extent this approval is necessary, and the impact on the engagement were it refused. In *Express and Echo Publications Limited v Ernest Tanton*, although Mr Tanton was contractually permitted to provide "another suitable person" to substitute for him where necessary, there was, on at least one occasion, a substitute of Mr Tanton's choosing who was not deemed to be suitable by the engager to the extent that Mr Tanton was obliged to undertake the services himself.

Another case worthy of note was *Glasgow City Council v MacFarlane and Skivington* EAT/1277/99 where an Employment Appeal Tribunal ruled that as the engager would only accept a substitute provided they had already been approved by the Council and were on an approved list of individuals, the engagement bore the hallmarks of employment as opposed to self-employment. Accordingly it can be seen that the importance of the personal service/substitution test is not merely whether in fact a substitute ever stands in for the individual, but whether such substitution is entirely at the discretion of the individual or requires the agreement or acquiescence of the contractor.

2.6.3. Control/ supervision

The degree of control placed on an individual by the engager is a very important test in determining the employment status of the contract. If the engager can control what an individual does, how he does it and when he does it then there is a strong indication that employment exists. Furthermore when an individual is expected to work set hours each day, to attend the same premises and to conform to standards of behaviour or dress expected of others within the working environment then this will also be an indicator of employment status. Conversely a self-employed person will usually have the ability to determine when and how they work although there will be certain types of contract when it is essential for a self-employed worker to be on their engager's premises and in some instances they will also be asked to conform to patterns or standards of behaviour normally associated with employees such as being asked to observe a dress standard whilst on the engager's premises or the engager's client's premises.

2.6.4. Employment benefits

Where the engager provides the individual with amenities or benefits usually associated with employment, these may suggest that an employment relationship exists. Benefits frequently provided to employees such as pensions, bonuses, private medical insurance, company cars etc would normally not be provided to a self-employed worker and the receipt of them would usually be a strong indicator that an employment relationship existed. Care should be taken with holidays and holiday pay however as the Working Time Directive can sometimes apply to self-employed workers. The absence of such benefits, however, is not quite such a strong indicator of self-employment as their presence is of employment status.

In addition to benefits associated with employment, there can be other factors which are also important in determining whether an employment relationship exists. For example, does the individual perform services similar to or substantially the same as those performed by an employee; is the individual sufficiently integral within the organisation to have a defined role or indeed to be recognised in documents such as the internal telephone directory? In short, is the individual part and parcel of the organisation either because of the nature of the contract, the way in which they personally have performed the contract, or indeed because the nature of the duties are such that the perception of an outsider would be that they would be integral to the organisation? The example frequently quoted for this test is that of a surgeon. Clearly, to function effectively, a hospital requires surgeons and yet in terms of the master/servant relationship it is hard to envisage who, from a technical perspective, could supervise a surgeon at the top of his field.

2.6.5. Financial risk

Where an employee is engaged to undertake services, to the extent that there is any financial risk, that risk is held by the business and not by the employee. In principle an employee is paid an agreed rate of pay for a specified period of time. If his employer is short of work, the employee will still be paid even though there may be insufficient work to keep him fully occupied. Additionally, if an employed worker's performance is below standard, any remedy to the task already performed will generally be undertaken at the employer's cost not the individual's. This is not the case for the self-employed worker. Where an individual uses their own money to meet the running costs of an engagement and takes on the associated financial risks whilst also having the opportunity to achieve a greater profit as a result of their exertions, this is an indicator of self-employment.

Financial risk, or indeed the opportunity to make a profit or loss as a result of the actions of the individual, is both important and may be considered on several different levels. The financial risk borne or carried by an individual in business on his own account will include, but not necessarily be limited to, the following areas:

- the risk of not being paid for work deemed to be of an inferior standard by the engager;
- late payment for whatever reason by the engager and possibly in some circumstances even the absence of payment leading to the issue of bad debts.

An individual in business on their own account will also usually have to carry work in progress sometimes for a considerable period of time before being able to render an account. In the meantime that individual will be incurring overheads and expenses and there may be costs which need to be incurred irrespective of whether the work is won or not, most notably the bidding for or proposing for engagements. Usually a business will incur a certain level of expenditure irrespective of whether client engagements are being undertaken. At one extreme these may include substantive costs such as the rental of premises and staff costs but might be limited to expenses such as telephone costs, stationery, postage, advertisements seeking engagements.

In some instances, it is possible to show that an individual has more opportunity to make a profit by being in business on their own account even if they also have an ability to make a loss. Whilst HM Revenue & Customs rarely regard the ability to make a greater profit as being as persuasive as the ability to make a profit or loss, the ability to make a profit or a greater profit nevertheless denotes a degree of control over finances which would be unusual for an employed earner and therefore merits consideration.

2.6.6. Provision of equipment

This test is closely tied to the above test of financial risk. Where an individual provides equipment and, if appropriate, materials in order to complete the contract, this would be regarded as a strong indicator of self-employment. This will be particularly so where the individual has specialist equipment which the engager relies upon the individual to provide.

2.7. Office-holders/non-executive directors

When considering whether an individual worker should be regarded as an employee or a self-employed worker, it can be important to consider whether the individual is holding an office. For practical purposes, where a person is employed by a business they may also be an office-holder within that business and, practically speaking, the two roles may be contractually intertwined. This will present no practical problems from a tax and NIC perspective but this would not be the case if a self-employed individual were to undertake a position which is defined as an "office". When considering the definition of an office, a good starting point is the statement made by Rowlatt J in 1920 in *Great Western Railway Co v Bater* 8 TC 231 as "an office or employment which was a subsisting, permanent, substantive position, which had an existence independent from the person who filled it, which went on and was filled in succession by successive holders". Although this quotation is attributed to Rowlatt J, this was apparently a definition put to him during the course of this case by Counsel appearing before him. The Great Western Railway case was concerned primarily with the interpretation of the phrase "public offices and employments of profit" which, under current legislation no longer require defining, but this quotation is nevertheless helpful today in providing an indication of what might be regarded as an "office" as opposed to an employment. Clearly it would be appropriate to construe a Companies Act director as being an office-holder and the payment therefrom being attributable to the holding of that office. Subsequent opinions and judgments have refined opinion upon what exactly an office is deemed to be in this context but, broadly speaking, the current view accords with the words of Harman LJ in *Mitchell and Edon v Ross* [1962] AC 813 as "an office is a position or post which goes on without regard to the identity of the holder of it from time to time".

These two definitions provide us with the concept of an office being distinct from the identity of the person who is the current holder.

For tax purposes, the holding of an office within an organisation (for example, being a director of company) is always regarded as an employment [ITEPA 2003, s5]. The payment to an office-holder for fulfilling that office will always fall to be taxed as employment income and cannot be regarded as part of a self-employed practice. In some instances it can be possible to demonstrate that an engager is paying an office-holder for different duties, and although the initial presumption would be that all duties for which an engager pays an office-holder will be in respect of the office it can be possible to show the converse is true. For example, a financial director had for many years a small business as a magician and children's entertainer. One year he was engaged independently and coincidentally by the company for whom he was a finance director to entertain the employees' children at a Christmas party. The fee he received for acting as the children's entertainer was received in a different capacity from the earnings he received for acting as a finance director. It was therefore appropriate to determine the nature of those duties totally distinctly from the nature of the duties of being finance director and to conclude that in relation to this contract the individual was self-employed.

Particular attention should be paid to non-executive directors (NEDs). A NED is not an employee but is, nevertheless, the holder of an office for the purpose of tax legislation which means that PAYE and NIC must be deducted from any payments if the director is remunerated as an individual.

It is not unusual for NEDs to be appointed by or on behalf of third parties. For example, the director of one company may be invited to sit as a NED for another organisation. In such cases, it is not unusual for the remuneration which would otherwise have been paid to the NED to be paid to the business upon whose behalf the NED is sitting on the board. ESC A37 broadly provides that where the fees payable for or in respect of the NED's duties are taken into account in determining the total level of remuneration from the primary business or partnership employing the NED then PAYE and NIC do not need to be deducted.

However, care needs to be taken if NED services are provided through a personal service company (PSC) or other intermediary which can frequently be the case. Since the introduction of the personal service company legislation, usually referred to as "IR35", which applies where the individual would have been an employee of the engager but for the existence of an intermediary (usually in the form of a PSC), in such a case the intermediary, not the engager, has the responsibility to account for PAYE and NIC. However, as NEDs are office-holders for the purpose of tax legislation they do not fall under the jurisdiction of IR35. Consequently for PAYE purposes, where the individual's only relationship with the engager is as a NED, IR35 will not apply for tax purposes even where the NED's services are provided through a PSC. Strangely, the converse is true for NIC purposes. The legislation that introduced the IR35 rules for NIC did not draw a distinction between office-holders and employees and can therefore apply to cases in which a NED's services are provided by an intermediary.

2.8. Deemed employed worker

Certain workers, irrespective of their employment or tax status, are deemed by Social Security regulations to be employed earners for NIC purposes. This is set out in the Social Security (Categorisation of Earners) Regulations 1978. Occupations covered by these rules include office cleaners, telephone apparatus cleaners, lecturers, teachers, instructors, ministers of religion and certain types of entertainer. Where an individual carries on one of the occupations referred to in these regulations, then, even though for tax purposes they may be regarded as a self-employed worker and taxed accordingly, they and their "employer" will have an obligation to account for Class 1 NIC on the basis that they are an employed earner within the regulations. An illustrative case which focuses on these regulations is *St John's College School, Cambridge v The Secretary of State for Social Security* (unreported but mentioned in HMRC Manual ESM7230[1]). This case was particularly interesting as it considered the circumstances of two peripatetic music teachers providing individual music lessons to pupils of St John's College School.

---

[1] http://www.hmrc.gov.uk/manuals/esmmanual/esm7230.htm

Generally speaking, teachers are not self-employed individuals in that they usually work under a strong degree of supervision and control, they will work with the tools and equipment provided by the school and they work to set hours and conditions. Furthermore, they have to provide personal service and cannot choose to send a substitute. On the few occasions that a teacher is absent any substitution will be arranged by the school, certainly not by the teacher themselves. However, there are a few instances where teachers, even within a school environment, may be held to be self-employed and these may include visiting or peripatetic teachers providing individual tuition in subjects such as music and drama. For these teachers to be brought within the ambit of Class 1 NIC as an employed earner the following criteria have to be established:

- they need to be engaged as a teacher within an educational establishment;
- they must be teaching in a face to face situation i.e. not engaged in remote learning; and finally
- the earnings from such teaching must be paid by or on behalf of the person providing the education.

Where these three factors are present, Class 1 NIC will be due as if the teacher were employed rather than self-employed. In the case of St John's College School, it was found that the teachers were providing individual music lessons to pupils of the school, on school premises and with payment being made by the school to the teachers albeit on behalf of the parents.

A difficult area to consider is where an individual is clearly engaged in a trade or profession during the course of which a variety of engagements may be entered into. Although it is perfectly possible to conclude that none of the engagements themselves has a distinct identity and that they all form part of the self-employed earnings, it is also possible to conclude that certain of the engagements have a distinct identity and should be viewed separately from the general self-employed activity carried out by the individual. Once again, Rowlatt J has made some interesting and pertinent remarks. In particular, in the case of *Davies v Braithwaite* 18 TC 198, he said "it seems to me that where one finds a method of earning a livelihood which does not contemplate the obtaining of a post and staying in it, but essentially contemplates a series of engagements and moving from one to the other – and in the case of an actor's or actress's life it certainly involves going from one to the other and not going on playing one part for the rest of his or her life, but in obtaining first one engagement, and then another, and a whole series of them – then each of those engagements could not be considered an employment, but is a mere engagement in the course of exercising a profession....".

In a subsequent case, *Fall v Hitchin* 49 TC 433, the individual sought to rely on Rowlatt J's statement in *Davies v Braithwaite*. However, in this case, the courts deemed the engagement to be one of employment rather than self-employment, possibly based on the length of the engagement. The effect of these two cases left the acting profession in an uncertain position but the Revenue (as it then was) introduced a concession in 1990 allowing certain performers to retain self-employed status. The Revenue's approach to the status of actors was changed further when Alec McCowen and Sam West successfully appealed to the Special Commissioners that they should have self-employed status.

In recent years HM Revenue & Customs' Special Film Industry and TV Unit has published a list of specific roles in the industry which they are prepared to accept should be treated as self-employed for tax purposes.

Whilst there are many cases on the subject of employment status, there are several that stand out not only because of the conclusions, or perhaps not even because the conclusions, but because of the particular facts of the case upon which judgment rested. One of the most notable cases in this category is *Hall v Lorimer*. Mr Lorimer had been employed as a vision mixer in the TV business. In 1985 he left full time employment as he felt he could earn more money by going "freelance". It was accepted that being a vision mixer was a highly skilled occupation and one in which it was usually necessary to use the client's equipment. Mr Lorimer organised an office at home with his wife assisting him with administration. He prepared a cv and wrote to many companies within the TV industry seeking engagements, telephoned and visited some prospective clients. Over the years his client list grew and although in most years he worked on a small nucleus of clients, these were different year from year. From 1 February 1985 he was VAT registered. In early 1989, he used the services of an agent but only for a short time as the agent only introduced existing clients to Mr Lorimer. Mr Lorimer's engagements were usually of short duration, normally of one or two days, and the longest of up to ten days. Engagements were accepted on a "first come, first served" basis. On one occasion it was noted that Mr Lorimer had provided the services of a substitute rather than himself to one of his clients, making a profit upon that engagement as the amount he paid to the substitute was less than he billed to the client.

Whilst Mr Lorimer clearly bore the costs of seeking clients and engagements and running the office, he also carried the risk of real financial loss. For example, he could and did lose money when a client became insolvent and some of his clients were bad payers, resulting in considerable delay in him receiving payment. The summing up by the Special Commissioner, cited by Nolan LJ in the Court of Appeal, is extremely pertinent in analysing factors that provide contrary indications of employment status, whilst drawing an overall conclusion:

"It is said that Mr Lorimer provides no equipment (i.e. he has no tools), he provides no "workplace" or "workshop" where the contract is to be performed, he provides no capital for the production, he hires no staff for it. No he does not. But that is not *his* business. He has his office, exploits his abilities in the marketplace, he bears his own financial risk, which is greater than that of one who is an employee, accepting the risk of bad debts and outstanding invoices and of no or an insufficient number of engagements. He has the opportunity of profiting from being good at being a vision mixer, according to his reputation, so there will be a demand for his services for which he will be able to charge accordingly. The more efficient he is at running the business of providing his services, the greater is his prospect of profit.

"I find that the activities of Mr Lorimer in the years under appeal bear the hallmarks of a man who is in business on his account and they outweigh substantially such factors as may be thought to militate against my conclusion that Mr Lorimer was in business on his own account in those years" – D A Shirley (Special Commissioner). Although the Crown appealed against the Special Commissioner's decision both to the High Court and the Court of Appeal, the Courts upheld the judgement of the Special Commissioner.

In *Bank Voor Handel En Scheepvaart N V v Slatford* [1952] 2 All ER 956, Denning LJ said "the test of being a servant does not rest nowadays on submission to orders. It depends on whether the person is part and parcel of the organisation".

Certain appointments, such as being an auditor, are strictly offices but where these appointments are held by practising accountants, or similar appointments are held by solicitors, it would be acceptable to include the payments arising therefrom in the business profits of the profession. Equally, fees from directorships held by members of professional partnerships may also be included in the partnership profits, provided that the directorship is being carried out as part of the normal professional practice and that the fees form only a small part of the professional partnership income.

Employment includes any employment under a contract of service or apprenticeship or in the service of the Crown [ITEPA 2003, s4]. Unless otherwise indicated, the provisions apply equally to any "office" which in particular includes any position which has an existence independent of the person holding it and may be filled by successive holders [ITEPA 2003, s5].

2.9. IR35

In 1999 the Inland Revenue published a press release setting out proposed new legislation that would transform the employment status landscape for individuals trading via personal service companies and other intermediaries (including partnerships). The legislation was subsequently introduced from 6 April 2000 and has become popularly known by the number of the original press release "IR35" but is also known as "the intermediaries legislation". It was introduced to counter perceived tax and NIC avoidance in a number of industries. Individuals wishing to be treated as self-employed would set up a company through which businesses could engage the individual's personal services. In a number of cases, individuals were working in a manner that was identical to that of an employee had it not been for the imposition of a personal service company between the engager and the individual. The imposition of this personal service company (PSC) in the contractual chain hindered HM Revenue & Customs' ability to pursue perceived avoidance; in particular it facilitated the avoidance of secondary Class 1 NIC.

The intermediaries legislation was introduced in FA 2000 for tax purposes (now consolidated into ITEPA 2003, Part 2, Chapter 8 and in the Social Security Contributions (Intermediaries) Regulations 2000). The effect of this legislation is to construct a concept of a deemed employment in situations where one or more intermediaries are placed in the contracting chain between the engager and the worker and where, had it not been for the intermediary, the relationship would have been an employment relationship.

The tests applied in determining if a deemed employment exists for the purposes of the intermediaries legislation are therefore identical to those described in earlier paragraphs. Where the relationship between the engager and the worker has the hallmarks of employment, all payments made by the engager to the intermediary are broadly treated as employment income of the worker. In this case the intermediary is treated as a deemed employer and is required to operate PAYE and account for NIC.

2.10. Agency Workers

The tax and NIC treatment of agency workers is relatively straightforward in the majority of cases, and can be important when considering employment status. Agency workers are essentially treated as employees of the agency supplying them to the engager. The agency supplying workers to an engager is required to operate PAYE and account for NIC where that supply is under an agency contract and no employment contract exists directly between the worker and the business to which their services are provided.

The definition of an agency worker for these purposes is set out in ITEPA 2003, Part 2, Chapter 7 and broadly requires the worker to be providing personal services and be subject to the right of supervision, direction and control in the way their services are provided. These tests reflect some of the important factors in considering employment status generally but are distinguished by the fact that they are set out in primary legislation rather than being reliant on case law.

2.11. Practical Points

Inevitably there are a number of practical points to consider in addition to (and sometimes in priority to) employment status. HM Revenue & Customs' approach to reviewing status depends very much on the scenario. As well as reviewing the tax affairs of self-employed persons and personal service companies, they also consider status during employer compliance reviews.

Their approach and focus will vary from situation to situation but generally in the context of employer compliance reviews, they will be concerned with establishing whether an employer is engaging any workers on a self-employed basis. Some employers have sought to minimise their risks in relation to employment status by only engaging self-employed workers who operate via a personal service company. By doing so they seek to ensure that the PAYE and NIC risks are borne by the worker's personal service company rather than the employer business. Using this approach can be very effective for engagers to the extent that any costs and risks of retrospective status reclassification can be avoided. However, a policy of this nature is only successful to the extent that the practical and contractual relationships are properly constructed. It is important that contracts demonstrate that the engager is contracting with the intermediary for the provision of services. Absence of a written contract or a contract between the worker and the engager provides little protection for the engager, even if the intermediary business invoices for services provided.

Recent case law reviews these "triangular"employment relationships. In *Dacas v Brook Street Bureau Ltd* [2004] EWCA Civ 217, the Court of Appeal considered a case where an individual had obtained a job with a local authority through an employment agency. The employment agency actually paid the individual, out of funds provided by the local authority. The local authority had day-to-day control over the individual's activities. The Court of Appeal held that the individual was not actually employed by the employment agency. It did not hold that the individual was employed employed by the local authority, as it was not asked to consider that question. However, Mummery LJ said: "Employment Tribunals should not determine the status of the applicant without also considering the possibility of an implied contact of service and making findings of fact relevant to that issue".

In *Cable &Wireless PLC v Muscat* [2006] IRLR 354, an employment tribunal inferred that an employment relationship existed between Cable & Wireless and Mr Muscat, even though the legal documentation said that Mr Muscat was employed by a personal services company which in turn contracted with Cable & Wireless. The Court of Appeal supported this view, and held that the tribunal had properly applied the principles of *Dacas*.

Some commentators have suggested that this line of cases may ultimately make IR35 unnecessary, by allowing HM Revenue & Customs to infer an employment relationship into a wider range of situations.

2.12. Golden Hellos

2.12.1. Description

A golden hello is a bonus payment made to a new recruit to induce him to join the business. Although simple in concept, there are important practical issues to be addressed, particularly when and how the payment should be made.

Frequently, the employer will not want to pay the golden hello up-front, but will want to wait to see if the new recruit serves out his or her probationary period. The employer may want to be able to claw back the golden hello if the recruit leaves within, say, two years. However, the recruit will want security that the payment will eventually be made to him or her.

In either of these circumstances, it may be better to defer payment, or pay the money into an escrow account. This will of course need to be negotiated with the prospective employee. It is particularly important to avoid a situation whereby the employee is taxed on a golden hello that he receives but subsequently forfeits by leaving within the agreed retention period. It will be difficult for the employee to secure a refund of the tax paid, or for the employer to recover the secondary NIC from HM Revenue & Customs.

If the recruit is not a director, it may be appropriate to lend the bonus money to him and then write the loan off at the end of the agreed retention period. This should defer his income tax liability until the employer writes off the loan (see section 16.3).

2.12.2. Disclosure

See section 3.1.2.

2.12.3. Tax Treatment of Employee

The tax treatment of the recruit will generally be as set out in section 3.1.3. As described in 2.12.1 above, it may be sensible for the employer to lend the money to an employee who is not a director if there is to be an agreed retention period. The tax treatment of cheap loans to employees is set out in section 16.3.

Note that a golden hello is taxable even if a third party provides it to the employee [HMRC Manual EIM00700[2]].

2.12.3.1. PAYE

See section 3.1.3.2.

---

[2] http://www.hmrc.gov.uk/manuals/eimanual/EIM00700.htm

2.12.3.2. NIC

See section 3.1.3.3.

2.12.3.3. Reporting

See section 3.1.3.4.

2.12.4. Tax Treatment of Employer

The same PAYE, NIC and reporting consequences, and, for the employer, corporation tax and accounting treatment, will apply as for cash bonuses, described in the next chapter.

2.12.4.1. Corporation Tax Deductibility

See section 3.1.4.1.

2.12.4.2. NIC

See section 3.1.3.3.

2.12.4.3. Reporting

See section 3.1.4.3.

2.12.5. Accounting Treatment

See section 3.1.5.

3. Designing and Implementing New Reward Plan for Senior Executives

There are several ways to reward and motivate senior employees. The choice between them will depend on the company's financial status, its intentions as regards an exit, and the relative importance it attaches to cashflow, reported earnings and its balance sheet.

In summary, the following kinds of plan have the following characteristics:

A cash bonus plan (see section 3.1) is simple to explain and operate. However, it has no tax benefits and will usually be the most expensive choice, both in terms of the impact on earnings and on cashflow.

A phantom share plan (see section 3.2) is a form of cash bonus plan. Its advantage is that payments from the plan are closely linked to the creation of shareholder value. Careful drafting is necessary to ensure that the plan is self-financing; there should be no risk that the growth in the amount payable to the employee outstrips the company's ability to pay it.

An executive pension scheme (see section 3.3) provides the employee with an opportunity for long-term wealth planning. It is tax-effective for the employer in that there is no secondary NIC liability in relation to contributions to **registered pension schemes**.

The company can give the employee free shares, or the opportunity to invest in shares (see section 3.5). However, an employee is not likely to want to become a long-term shareholder unless the shares have a high dividend yield. Therefore, unless there is an exit, the company may ultimately have to finance the cost of providing an opportunity for the employee to sell the shares, perhaps back to the company for cancellation or to an employee benefit trust ("EBT").

A share option plan (see section 3.7), like a share investment plan, can provide effective motivation if there is an exit. However, even where there is no exit, a **CSOP** or **EMI option** plan can be tax-effective in the sense that the tax deduction for the employer can be higher than the tax borne by the employee.

3.1. Cash Bonus Plans

3.1.1. Description

A cash bonus plan is simple and straightforward to establish and operate. It can be discretionary or contractual.

In a discretionary plan, the employer reviews performance at the end of a period of time and decides whether to reward that performance by paying a bonus.

In a contractual plan, the employer sets targets at the beginning of the year. The employer promises to pay a fixed bonus for achieving those targets – this is called the "on-target" bonus.

Often there will be a target range of performance, perhaps varying between 80% and 120% of the median. The on-target bonus is payable for performance at the median of the target range; there is no bonus if the performance is below the bottom of the range, and the maximum bonus is achieved at the top of the range.

The choice of performance targets needs to be carefully thought through. The targets must be achievable to be meaningful. It is also important that they should not encourage the employee to ignore other responsibilities in the pursuit of the target. The author has seen examples of badly-designed bonus plans where some employees were so focused on achieving their targets that they neglected other duties, with the result that other employees could not achieve their own targets. This led to disputes and an overall decline in performance.

A cash bonus plan should ideally also be self-financing, meaning that the achievement of the targets should generate at least enough cash to pay the bonus. Again, the author has seen bonus plans where this was not considered in advance, with the result that the employer was unable to meet its commitments.

3.1.2. Disclosure

A bonus payable to a director does not have to be separately disclosed but will form part of the aggregate of his emoluments, which must be disclosed in the notes to the annual accounts [CA 1985, Sch6, para 1(1)(a)].

3.1.3. Tax Treatment of Employee

3.1.3.1. Receipts Basis

The tax treatment of an employee in relation to a bonus differs subtly from that of a director.

A bonus payable to a UK **resident, ordinarily resident** and domiciled employee will always be taxable in the year in which it is received [ITEPA 2003, s15].

A cash bonus is deemed to be received on whichever of the following events occurs first:

- the bonus is actually paid to the employee, or the employer makes a payment on account of the bonus (see section 3.1.3.1.1);
- the employee becomes unconditionally entitled to payment of the bonus, or to a payment on account of the bonus – see section 3.1.3.1.2;
- if the employee is a director, the company credits the bonus in its accounts (see section 3.1.3.1.3);
- if the employee is a director, and the amount of the bonus is calculated before the end of the performance period, the last date in the performance period (see section 3.1.3.1.4);

- if the employee is a director, and the amount of the bonus is calculated after the end of the performance period, the date it is calculated (see section 3.1.3.1.5).

[ITEPA 2003, s18].

3.1.3.1.1. Actual Payment or Payment on Account

Actual payment of the cash bonus is clearly a receipt by the employee. For examples of actual payments, see HMRC Manual EIM42270[3].

A payment on account of a bonus needs to be carefully distinguished from an advance of the bonus. If the employer makes an advance of the bonus, this means that the employee has the use of the money but the employer has the right to recover it from him. If, instead, the employer makes a payment on account of the bonus, the employer retains no right of recovery [HMRC Manual EIM42280[4]].

If a director has a drawings account with the company, amounts drawn from that account during the year will not normally be payments on account [HMRC Manual EIM42280[5]].

3.1.3.1.2. Unconditional Entitlement to Payment

It is important to distinguish between being unconditionally entitled to a bonus, and being entitled to payment of the bonus. The terms of the bonus plan might specify that the employee becomes entitled to the bonus at the end of the performance measurement period, but it will not be paid until a later date. Although the employee is entitled to the bonus at the end of the performance period, he is not entitled to payment of it until later, and therefore does not receive it for income tax purposes until the later date [HMRC Manual EIM42290[6]].

3.1.3.1.3. Crediting the Bonus in the Accounts

A director is deemed to receive a bonus when it is credited to an account in the company's books, even if he is not free to draw on that account. This does not mean, however, that the director is taxed on the bonus while it is still contingent, or that he is taxed just because the company prudently makes a provision against future payment. The rule only applies where the bonus itself is credited to the account [HMRC Manual EIM42320[7]].

---

[3] http://www.hmrc.gov.uk/manuals/eimanual/EIM42270.htm

[4] http://www.hmrc.gov.uk/manuals/eimanual/EIM42280.htm

[5] http://www.hmrc.gov.uk/manuals/eimanual/EIM42280.htm

[6] http://www.hmrc.gov.uk/manuals/eimanual/EIM42290.htm

[7] http://www.hmrc.gov.uk/manuals/eimanual/EIM42320.htm

3.1.3.1.4. Bonus Determined Before End of Performance Measurement Period

Sometimes the amount of the bonus to be paid to a director in respect of a period will be determined before the end of that period. That in itself does not mean that he has received the bonus for tax purposes, but he will be deemed to receive it at the latest on the last day of the period [HMRC Manual EIM42330[8]].

3.1.3.1.5. Bonus Determined Following End of Performance Measurement Period

Sometimes the amount of the bonus to be paid to a director cannot be determined until after the end of the period. For example, the bonus might be a percentage of profits above a certain amount. In this case, the bonus cannot be calculated before the profits have been calculated [HMRC Manual EIM42350[9]].

3.1.3.2. PAYE

PAYE is due on a cash bonus when it is treated as received [ITEPA 2003, s686(1)].

3.1.3.3. NIC

Primary NIC is due on a cash bonus when it is received [SSCR 2001, reg 2].

3.1.3.4. Reporting

The employee should include the amount of the bonus in his total employment income if he is required to file a self-assessment tax return.

3.1.4. Tax Treatment of Employer

3.1.4.1. Corporation Tax Deductibility

A bonus payment will generally be deductible for corporation tax purposes, unless there is some ancillary reason for making it, such that it fails the "wholly and exclusively" test [HMRC Manual BIM45451[10]]. It should be paid within nine months of the end of the accounting period in which it is charged in order to be deductible for that period [FA 1989, s43] (see section 17.2).

3.1.4.2. NIC

Secondary NIC is due on a cash bonus when it is received [SSCR 2001, reg 2].

3.1.4.3. Reporting

At the end of the tax year the employer must report to HM Revenue & Customs the total remuneration paid to the employee, and the tax and primary NIC withheld on Form P14 (the summary year end statement for each employee). Form P14 must be submitted to HM Revenue & Customs by 19 May following the end of the tax year.

The employee's copy of Form P14, Form P60, must be provided to each employee by 31 May following the end of the tax year.

---

[8] http://www.hmrc.gov.uk/manuals/eimanual/EIM42330.htm

[9] http://www.hmrc.gov.uk/manuals/eimanual/EIM42350.htm

[10] http://www.hmrc.gov.uk/manuals/bimmanual/BIM45451.htm

In addition, Form P35 (the Employer's Annual Return) is a summary of total income tax and employer's and employees' NIC paid in the tax year for all employees. Form P35 must be submitted to HM Revenue & Customs by 19 May following the end of the tax year. A specimen copy of Form P35 can be downloaded from HM Revenue & Customs' website at http://www.hmrc.gov.uk/employers/e10-p18.pdf

3.1.5. Accounting Treatment

See section 19.2.

3.1.6. Matrix Summary of Advantages and Disadvantages of Cash Bonus

Feature	Advantage	Disadvantage
Availability	Available to any company	
Flexibility	Wholly flexible	
Limits	No limits	
Accounting (p/l)		Bonus charged to profit and loss account
Corporation Tax	Deduction, generally for year of payment	
Income Tax and NIC		Bonus fully subject to PAYE and NIC
Capital Gains Tax	N/A	

3.2. Phantom Share Plans

3.2.1. Description

A phantom share plan or phantom share option plan gives the employee a contractual right to a bonus. The bonus is equal to the value, or the growth in value, of a number of real shares. It can also be based on a formula designed to replicate the value of a shares, such as three times the last year's earnings per share.

Phantom share plans are often used where it is not possible or desirable to use real shares. An example is where the shares are tightly controlled by particular shareholders.

Other names for a phantom share plan include: "shadow share plan"; "synthetic share plan"; "equity appreciation rights plan" and "share appreciation rights plan".

A phantom share plan should ideally also be self-financing, meaning that the achievement of the targets should generate at least enough cash to pay the award.

3.2.2. Disclosure

A phantom share plan is a form of **long term incentive scheme**. Therefore, the aggregate of the amount of money payable to directors under the phantom share plan must be disclosed in the notes to the accounts [CA 1985, Sch6, para 1(1)(c)(i)]. For an unquoted company, the notes should also state the number of directors who received payments under the plan [CA 1985, Sch6, para 1(2)(b)(ii)].

3.2.3. Tax Treatment of Employee

HM Revenue & Customs take the view that a phantom right is not an **employment-related security** or **securities option**. This view is published on their website at http://www.hmrc.gov.uk/shareschemes/news/phantom-share-plans.htm. At the time of writing, a contrary view is expressed in the Employment-Related Securities Manual, but it is understood that the Manual will be corrected [HMRC Manual EIM01600[11]]. The consequence of this is that employees are taxed on the cash actually received on the receipts basis.

3.2.3.1. PAYE

The same as for cash bonuses (see section 3.1.3.2.)

3.2.3.2. NIC

The same as for cash bonuses (see section 3.1.3.3).

3.2.3.3. Reporting

The same as for cash bonuses (see section 3.1.3.4).

3.2.4. Tax Treatment of Employer

3.2.4.1. Corporation Tax Deductibility

The same as for cash bonuses (see section 3.1.4.1).

3.2.4.2. NIC

The same as for cash bonuses (see section 3.1.3.3).

3.2.4.3. Reporting

The same as for cash bonuses (see section 3.1.4.3).

3.2.5. Accounting Treatment

The same as for cash bonuses (see section 19.2).

3.2.6. Matrix Summary of Advantages and Disadvantages of Phantom Share Schemes

Feature	Advantage	Disadvantage
Availability	Available to all companies	
Flexibility	Entirely flexible	
Limits	None	

---

11 http://www.hmrc.gov.uk/manuals/eimanual/EIM01600.htm

Feature	Advantage	Disadvantage
Accounting (p/l)		Payment charged to profit and loss account
Corporation Tax	Deductible usually in year of payment	
Income Tax and NIC		Subject to income tax and NIC
Capital Gains Tax	N/A	

3.3. Executive Pensions (Approved / Registered Schemes)

Contributions to tax-qualified pension schemes are very tax-efficient. From the employer's perspective, the contributions are free from secondary NIC.

From the employee's perspective, there are several advantages. First, tax is deferred until the employee starts to draw an income from the pension fund; in the meantime the funds can grow in a tax-free environment. Second, the employee can take a proportion of the pension fund as a tax-free lump sum. Third, employer contributions are free from primary NIC.

However, there are disadvantages to a tax-qualified pension scheme. Amongst these are the following:

It is difficult to get access to the funds before **normal minimum pension age**.

There are restrictions on how the funds can be invested, although these have been liberalised since 5 April 2006.

There are limitations on how much money can be invested in the pension scheme on a tax-favoured basis in any tax year and there are limitations on the proportion of the fund that is tax-free at **retirement**.

This chapter describes the regime that came into existence on 6 April 2006. A different regime applied before that date.

3.3.1. Description

There are two kinds of pension arrangement: **registered pension scheme**s, which have certain tax reliefs associated with them, and **employer-financed retirement benefits scheme**s, which benefit only from tax deferrals (see section 3.4).

There are three basic types of **registered pension scheme**: **cash balance plan**s; **money purchase plan**s; and **defined benefits plan**s. There are hybrid plans that combine elements of two or more of the three basic types.

Registered pension schemes can be occupational pension schemes, meaning that they are established by an employer to provide benefits to its employees. Alternatively, they can be established by insurance companies or other financial institutions.

Smaller companies are generally likely not to establish occupational pension schemes, because of the regulatory and compliance burdens associated with these plans.

However, there may be circumstances where a smaller company chooses to establish an occupational pension scheme, for example if it wants to borrow money from the scheme or control the scheme's investment policy.

Smaller companies are not likely to establish **defined benefits plan**s because it is difficult to control the costs of such plans.

Instead, the least onerous and costly route is likely to be to offer a stakeholder plan to all staff, and to make contributions on behalf of employees to the external **money purchase plan**s that they nominate. In this way, the pension provider is responsible for the regulatory issues, and the employer has no risk.

3.3.2. Disclosure

The aggregate amount of contributions made to a **money purchase plan** on behalf of directors must be disclosed in the notes to the accounts [CA 1985, Sch6, para 1(1)(d)]. The company should also disclose the number of directors who are accruing benefits under any company-sponsored pension plan [CA 1985, Sch6, para 1(1)(e)].

3.3.3. Regulatory Treatment

Very often, an unlisted company will appoint an external administrator for its pension plan, who will be responsible for ensuring compliance with applicable regulations. For more information see *Dealing With Pensions by Robin Ellison and Grant Jones [Spiramus Press 1 904905 06 4].*

3.3.4. Tax Treatment of Employee

This section contains an overview of the most common tax issues that are likely to affect smaller businesses and their employees. It does not purport to be a thorough review of pensions taxation.

Smaller businesses are unlikely to set up new **defined benefits plan**s, so this section deals only with issues relating to **money purchase plan**s.

Other areas of complexity relate to:

- employees who accrue rights under overseas pension plans, or who have income arising abroad;
- pension sharing orders or provisions made under the Welfare Reform and Pensions Act 1999.

These areas are beyond the scope of this book, and this section assumes that the employee is a **relevant UK individual**.

The scheme of pensions taxation that started on 6 April 2006 has the following main features:

- a single annual monetary limit replaced the previous limits on annual contributions as percentages of salary. In theory, an employee can contribute his entire salary to a **registered pension scheme** and claim tax relief (see section 3.3.4.1). If the annual allowance is exceeded in any year, the excess tax relief will be clawed back through an annual allowance charge (see section 3.3.4.2);
- the employee's pension fund is valued when he starts to withdraw money from it. If the value of the fund exceeds the lifetime limit, he will be taxed on the excess (see section 3.3.4.3). Up to one quarter of the fund within the lifetime limit can be drawn as a tax-free lump sum.

3.3.4.1. Tax Relief on Contributions

The employee is entitled to income tax relief on any contributions he makes to a **registered pension scheme** [FA 2004, s188(1)]. The maximum relief in any tax year is limited to the higher of:

- his **relevant UK earnings** which are chargeable to income tax during that tax year; and
- (in relation to contributions to personal pension arrangements) the basic amount, which is £3,600 for the year 2006/7 [FA 2004, s190(4)].

If the amount of the contributions causes the employee to exceed the higher of these amounts, or to exceed the annual allowance, the excess relief will be clawed back through an annual allowance charge (see section 3.3.4.2).

Generally, there are two ways in which the relief is given: relief at source (see section 3.3.4.1.1); and relief given through net pay arrangements (see section 3.3.4.1.2). In some circumstances, however, it is necessary for the contributions to be paid gross and tax relief to be given through self-assessment (see section 3.3.4.1.3).

From a planning perspective, however, it is better if the employee does not contribute directly to the pension scheme. This is because there is no relief for primary or secondary NIC in relation to salary that an employee contributes to a pension scheme.

The more cost-efficient route is for the employee to contribute through salary sacrifice. In other words, the employee agrees to a reduced salary and higher employer pension contributions. This creates NIC savings for both the employer and the employee (see section 3.3.4.1.4).

3.3.4.1.1. Relief at Source

Relief is given at source where the employee is contributing to an external pension scheme, e.g. one run by an insurance company.

Example:

- *The employee wants to contribute a gross amount of £10,000 to the scheme, and the basic rate is 22%.*
- *The employee actually pays £7,800 to the scheme administrator [FA 2004, s192(1)].*
- *The scheme administrator is bound to accept this as a contribution of £10,000 [FA 2004, s192(2)].*
- *HM Revenue & Customs pay £2,200 to the scheme administrator [FA 2004, s192(3)].*
- *If the employee is a higher-rate taxpayer, his basic rate limit is increased by £10,000, thereby reducing the amount of income on which he pays higher rate tax [FA 2004, s192(4)*].

3.3.4.1.2. Relief under net pay arrangements

The net pay arrangements are only available for members of an occupational pension scheme where all contributions from employees are treated in the same way [FA 2004, s191(3)].

Under the net pay arrangements, the employer in effect reduces the employee's salary by the amount of the contribution.

Example:

- *The employee wants to contribute a gross amount of £10,000 to the scheme.*
- *The employee's salary is reduced by £10,000 [FA 2004, s193(2)].*
- *The employer pays £10,000 to the scheme administrator [FA 2004, s193(2)].*

3.3.4.1.3. Gross Payments

Sometimes it will be necessary for the employee to pay a gross contribution and obtain the tax relief through the self-assessment tax return [FA 2004, s194]. For example, this may be necessary where the employee continues making payments under a pre-1989 retirement annuity contract [FA 2004, Sch36, para 40].

3.3.4.1.4. Employer Contributions

The employee does not pay income tax on any contributions that his employer makes to a **registered pension scheme** [ITEPA 2003, s308].

Moreover, there is no primary or secondary NIC payable in relation to employer's contributions to approved personal pension arrangements [SSCR 2001, Sch3, Part VI, para 2].

This means that there can be NIC savings for both employer and employee if the contributions are made through salary sacrifice. In other words, the employee should not contribute directly to the **registered pension scheme** but should instead agree to a reduced salary and enhanced employer pension contributions. See section 4.4.2 for more discussion of salary sacrifice.

3.3.4.1.5. Transfers from SIP and SAYE

Where an employee exercises an **SAYE** option (see section 4.3) or receives a transfer of shares from a **SIP** (see section 4.2.4), he can transfer those shares into a **registered pension scheme** within 90 days [FA 2004, s195]. He will be eligible for tax relief on the value of the shares, usually through relief at source (see section 3.3.4.1.1).

3.3.4.2. *Annual Allowance Charge*

The annual allowance charge is a special charge to income tax. Its purpose is to regulate the amount of tax relief given in any year in relation to a **registered pension scheme**. This is achieved by setting an annual allowance and measuring the total pension input amount (see below) for all the individual's pension schemes against it.

The annual allowance charge is not payable in the year in which the employee dies or crystallises all his remaining benefits under the scheme [FA 2004, s229(3)]. Effectively, therefore, the only limits on the amount the employee can contribute tax-free in the tax year of his **retirement** are the lifetime limit and the amount of his **relevant UK earnings**.

Similarly, there is no annual allowance charge in any tax year after the employee dies. So if, for example, the employee dies on 5 April 2007, the employer can augment the lump sum death benefit in 2007/8 without an annual allowance charge.

The annual allowance for 2006/7 is £215,000 [FA 2004, s228(1)].

The annual allowance charge is actually paid by the employee [FA 2004, s227(2)] and the rate is 40% [FA 2004, s227(4)].

The amount subject to the annual allowance charge is the amount by which the "total pension input amount" for the tax year exceeds the annual allowance [FA 2004, s227(1)].

The total pension input amount is the aggregate of the pension input amounts for the "pension input period" for each scheme of which the employee is a member [FA 2004, s229(1)].

The pension input period is a period selected by the employee (in relation to money purchase plans) or by the scheme administrator in accordance with FA 2004, s238. There must be a pension input period ending in every tax year, but apart from that the period can be chosen to suit the scheme or, in some cases, the member.

The way in which the pension input amount is measured varies depending on the nature of the **registered pension scheme**.

3.3.4.2.1. Pension Input Amount for a Cash balance plan

The pension input amount for a **cash balance plan** is effectively the amount by which the employee's rights increase in value during the pension input period, after adjusting for the cost of living.

It is calculated by deducting the opening value of the employee's rights from the closing value of the rights [FA 2004, s230(2)].

The opening value is the value of the employee's rights at the beginning of the pension input period [FA 2004, s230(4)]. However, it is increased by at least 5%, or by the growth in the RPI over the pension input period, if this is higher [FA 2004, s231(2) and (3)].

The closing value is the value of the employee's rights at the end of the pension input period, after adjusting for transfers in and out of the scheme from/to other pension schemes [FA 2004, s232].

3.3.4.2.2. Pension Input Amount for a Money purchase plan

This section sets out the pension input amount for a **money purchase plan** that is not a **cash balance plan**.

It is the total of the tax-relieved contributions made by the member and by the employer during the pension input period [FA 2004, s233].

Therefore, the growth in value of the fund, if any, is ignored.

3.3.4.3. Lifetime Allowance Charge

As stated above, the annual allowance charge controls the amount by which a member's rights under a **registered pension scheme** can grow in any pension input period. In relation to a money purchase plan, this excludes growth derived from investment returns.

The lifetime allowance charge, in contrast, controls the total amount that is available to provide **retirement** benefits.

In the simplest, and probably most common, of circumstances, the employee will participate in a **money purchase plan** and choose to take all his benefits at once.

Such an employee will have a lifetime allowance available to him, which, for 2006/7, is £1.5 million [FA 2004, s218(2)].

If the total value of his rights in the **registered pension scheme** is more than the lifetime allowance, there is a lifetime allowance charge on the excess [FA 2004, s215].

The employee can choose to take the whole of the excess as a lifetime allowance excess lump sum, in which case the lifetime allowance charge will be 55% of the lump sum amount [FA 2004, s215(2)(a)]. The lump sum amount is the lump sum itself plus any gross-up payment [FA 2004, s215(5) and (6)].

If the employee chooses not to take the excess as a lump sum, the lifetime allowance charge will be 25% of the retained amount [FA 2004, s215(2)(b)]. Since the retained amount must be paid out as income, and assuming it is taxed at 40%, the effective rate of tax is also 55%.

More complicated situations arise where:

- the employee chooses not to take all his benefits at once (see section 3.3.4.3.1);
- the employee has made an election for primary or enhanced protection (see section 3.3.4.9); or
- the scheme is a defined benefits scheme, which is outside the scope of this book.

The lifetime allowance charge is normally a joint and several liability of the scheme administrator and the employee [FA 2004, s217(1)]. However, if the liability arises on payment of a **lump sum death benefit**, then the liability is that of the recipient [FA 2004, s217(2)].

3.3.4.3.1. More than One Benefit crystallisation event

The employee may not wish to take all his benefits from the **registered pension scheme** at once. In these circumstances, there will be a sequence of **benefit crystallisation events**.

On the first **benefit crystallisation event**, the whole of the lifetime allowance is normally available[12] [FA 2004, s219(2)].

Example: the employee retires in 2006/7, when the lifetime allowance is £1,500,000.

He draws a lump sum of £300,000 and uses £900,000 to purchase an annuity. He has therefore used £1,200,000, or 80%, of his lifetime allowance.

On a second or subsequent **benefit crystallisation event**, the employee needs to determine how much of the lifetime allowance remains available. This is done by multiplying the amount that has already been crystallised by an adjustment factor. The adjustment factor is the current year's lifetime allowance divided by the lifetime allowance for the year in which the last **benefit crystallisation event** occurred [FA 2004, s219(5)].

Example: in 2008/9 the lifetime allowance is £1,650,000. The adjustment factor is 1,650,000 / 1,500,000 = 1.1. Therefore the employee's previously used amount is £1,200,000 x 1.1 = £1,320,000 and the remaining lifetime allowance for 2008/9 is £330,000.

Eventually, the lifetime allowance will be completely used up. Once this has happened, the lifetime allowance charge will apply to the whole of the amount

---

[12] Note that the whole of the lifetime allowance will not be available if the employee already has a pension in payment since before 6 April 2006 [FA 2004, Sch36, para 20]

crystallised on any subsequent **benefit crystallisation event** [FA 2004, s214(3) and s215(4)(b)].

3.3.4.4. *Lump Sum Payments*

Once an employee has reached **normal minimum pension age**, or the **ill health condition** applies, the scheme administrator can pay a lump sum from the **registered pension scheme**.

In most circumstances, a lump sum payment from a **registered pension scheme** will be exempt from income tax [ITEPA 2003, s636A(1)] up to the lifetime allowance [ITEPA 2003, s636A(2)].

There are five kinds of authorised lump sum payment, which are always exempt from tax to the extent that they are covered by the member's available lifetime allowance. They are:

- Pension Commencement Lump Sums (see section 3.3.4.4.1);
- Serious Ill-Health Lump Sums (see section 3.3.4.4.2);
- Refund of Excess Contributions Lump Sums (see section 3.3.4.4.3);
- Defined Benefits **lump sum death benefits** (only payable from **defined benefits plans** and therefore outside the scope of this book); and
- Uncrystallised Funds **lump sum death benefits** (see section 3.3.4.4.5),

Transfer **lump sum death benefits** are always income tax-free (see section 3.3.4.4.7).

There are other kinds of lump sum payment that are chargeable to tax. They are:

- Trivial Commutation Lump Sums and death benefits (see section 3.3.4.4.8);
- Winding Up Lump Sums (see section 3.3.4.4.6);
- Lifetime Allowance Excess Lump Sums (see section 3.3.4.4.9);
- Short Service Refund Lump Sums (see section 3.3.4.4.4);
- Pension Protection **lump sum death benefits** (only payable from **defined benefits plans** and therefore outside the scope of this book);
- Charity **lump sum death benefits** (see section 3.3.4.4.10);
- Annuity Protection **lump sum death benefits** (see section 3.3.4.11); and
- **Unsecured pension fund lump sum death benefits** (see section 3.3.4.4.12).

3.3.4.4.1. *Pension Commencement Lump Sums*

A pension commencement lump sum is tax-free [ITEPA 2003, s636A(1)(a)] within the lifetime allowance [ITEPA 2003, s636A(2)]. It is the most commonly found form of lump sum in practice.

3.3.4.4.1.1 Date of Payment

All three of the following conditions must be met:

- It is paid within three months of the date the employee becomes entitled to any of: **income withdrawal**; a **lifetime annuity**; or a **scheme pension**; as part of the same arrangement [FA 2004, Sch29, paras 1(a), 1(c) and 3].

- It is paid after the employee has reached **normal minimum pension age**, unless the **ill health condition** applies [FA 2004, Sch29, para 1(d)].
- It is paid before the employee's 75th birthday [FA 2004, Sch29, para 1(e)].

3.3.4.4.1.2 Excluded Lump Sums

A lump sum will not be exempt from tax if it is payable in connection with a pension that will reduce when the employee becomes entitled to **state retirement pension** [FA 2004, Sch29, para 1(4(a)] and if the sole or main purpose of providing the related pension is to increase the employee's entitlement to a tax-free lump sum [FA 2004, Sch29, para 1(4)(b)].

A lump sum may be an **unauthorised member payment** if it is "recycled", i.e. reinvested in the pension scheme [FA 2004, Sch29, para 3A].

3.3.4.4.1.3 Limit on Tax-Free Lump Sum

The amount that the member can take as a tax-free lump sum is limited to the lower of:

- the available portion of the member's lump sum allowance (i.e. 25% of the available lifetime allowance); and
- the applicable amount (see below) [FA 2004, Sch29, para 2(5)].

FA 2004, Sch29, paras 2(6), (7) and (8) explain the mechanism for determining how to calculate the available portion of the member's lump sum allowance. Essentially, this is exactly the same as the mechanism for calculating the available lifetime allowance (see section 3.3.4.3.1) except that the available portion of the member's lump sum allowance is one quarter of the available lifetime allowance.

FA 2004, Sch29, para 3 explains how to calculate the applicable amount. Essentially this is one quarter of the aggregate of (a) the lump sum itself and (b) the funds used to provide the corresponding pension.

3.3.4.4.2. Serious Ill-Health Lump Sums

A serious ill health lump sum is tax-free [ITEPA 2003, s636A(1)(b)] within the lifetime allowance [ITEPA 2003, s636A(2)]. It is payable only when all the following five conditions are met:

- the member has a life expectancy of less than one year [FA 2004, Sch29, para 4(1)(a)];
- the member has not utilised all his lifetime allowance [FA 2004, Sch29, para 4(1)(b)];
- there has been no previous **benefit crystallisation event** in relation to the particular scheme from which the lump sum is paid [FA 2004, Sch29, para 4(1)(c) and (2)];
- it extinguishes the member's rights under that scheme [FA 2004, Sch29, para 4(1)(d)]; and

- it is paid before the member's 75th birthday [FA 2004, Sch29, para 4(1)(e)].

3.3.4.4.3. Refund of Excess Contributions Lump Sums

If the employee contributes more to a **registered pension scheme** in any tax year than the maximum relief he is entitled to for that year, there is an annual allowance charge for that year (see section 3.3.4.2) [FA 2004, s227].

The excess can be paid back to the employee as a refund of excess contributions lump sum [FA 2004, Sch29, para 6]. It is tax-free [ITEPA 2003, s636A(1)(c)].

There are provisions in FA 2004, Sch29, para 6(2) to (6) to prevent double-counting where more than one refund of excess contributions lump sum is made in a tax year.

3.3.4.4.4. Short Service Refund Lump Sums

An occupational pension scheme can pay a lump sum to a member who terminates pensionable service before **normal minimum pension age** and is not entitled to short service benefit [FA 2004, Sch29, para 5(1)(a) and (b)]. The payment must be made before the member's 75th birthday, and before any **benefit crystallisation event** occurs in relation to the member and the pension scheme [FA 2004, Sch29, para 5(1)(c) and (e). It must extinguish his entitlement to benefits under the scheme [FA 2004, Sch29, para 5(1)(d)].

A short service refund lump sum cannot be more than the aggregate of the member's contributions to the scheme [FA 2004, Sch29, para 5(2)].

The scheme administrator has to pay tax on the short service lump sum [FA 2004, s205(1) and FA 2004, s205(2)]. The tax rate is 20% on the first £10,800 and 40% on any excess [FA 2004, s205(4)].

3.3.4.4.5. Uncrystallised Funds Lump sum death benefits

An uncrystallised funds **lump sum death benefit** is tax-free [ITEPA 2003, s636A(1)(e)] within the amount of the lifetime allowance [ITEPA 2003, s636A(2)].

It applies where a member dies before crystallising all the funds in his **money purchase plan**, and it cannot be more than the amount or value of the relevant uncrystallised funds [FA 2004, Sch29, para 15(3) and (4)]. The relevant uncrystallised funds are whatever remains in the pension scheme that has not been used to purchase a **scheme pension**, a **lifetime annuity**, a **dependants' scheme pension** or a **dependants' annuity**, or designated for the payment of **unsecured pension** [FA 2004, Sch29, para 15(2)].

It is paid within two years of the member's death [FA 2004, Sch29, para 15(1)(c)]. The member must have been under 75 when he died [FA 2004, Sch29, para 15(1)(a)].

3.3.4.4.6. Winding-Up Lump Sum and Death Benefits

A winding-up lump sum is taxable pension income of the employee who receives it [ITEPA 2003, s636B(2)]. However, if the member has not previously been entitled to any benefits under the scheme, the amount of taxable pension income is reduced by 25% [ITEPA 2003, s636B(3)].

Similarly, if it is paid after death in the form of a winding-up **lump sum death benefit**, it is taxable pension income of the recipient [ITEPA 2003, s636C(2)].

A winding-up lump sum is paid to a member of an occupational pension scheme when it is being wound up [FA 2004, Sch29, paras 10(1)(a) and (b)]. The employer must have made contributions to the scheme in respect of the member in the past, and must undertake not to make any further contributions in respect of the member to any other registered scheme for at least a year [FA 2004, Sch29, para 10(3)].

A winding-up lump sum must be less than 1% of the standard lifetime allowance on the payment date [FA 2004, Sch29, para 10(2)].

The lump sum must be paid to the member before his 75th birthday [FA 2004, Sch29, para 10(1)(f)]. It must extinguish his rights under the pension scheme in question [FA 2004, Sch29, para 10(1)(e)] and he must have lifetime allowance available [FA 2004, Sch29, para 10(1)(d)].

Winding-up **lump sum death benefit** is paid to a **dependant** when a scheme is being wound up [FA 2004, Sch29, para 21(1)(a)]. The **dependant** must otherwise have been entitled to receive **pension death benefit** in respect of the deceased member [FA 2004, Sch29, para 21(1)(b)] and the payment must extinguish the **dependant**'s right to receive **pension death benefit** and **lump sum death benefit** [FA 2005, Sch29, para 21(1)(c)].

Winding-up **lump sum death benefit** cannot be more than 1% of the standard lifetime allowance on the day it is paid [FA 2004, Sch29, para 21(2)].

3.3.4.4.7. Transfer Lump sum death benefits

A transfer **lump sum death benefit** is free of income tax [ITEPA 2003, s636A(1)(f)]. However, it will form part of the member's estate for IHT purposes [IHTA 1984, s151A].

The circumstances where transfer lump sum death benefit becomes payable are:

- where a member dies on or after his 75th birthday, without any **dependants** [FA 2004, Sch29, para 19(1)(a) and (b)]. The member must have been entitled to **income withdrawal** at the date of his death.
- where **dependant**'s **income withdrawal** is being paid to the **dependant** of a member, and the **dependant** dies on or after his 75th birthday, leaving no other **dependants** of the member [FA 2004, Sch29, para 19(2)(a), (b) and (c)].

In these circumstances the remaining funds can be applied for the benefit of other members of the scheme. The member, or **dependant**, can nominate the recipients before his death, or the scheme administrator can make a nomination afterwards [FA 2004, Sch29, para 19(1)(d) and (2)(e)].

The transfer lump sum death benefit cannot be more than the amount or value of the member's, or **dependant**'s **alternatively secured pension fund** [FA 2004, Sch29, para 19(4) and (5)].

3.3.4.4.8. Trivial Commutation Lump Sum and Death Benefit

A trivial commutation lump sum is taxable pension income of the employee who receives it [ITEPA 2003, s636B(2)]. However, if the member has not previously been entitled to any benefits under the scheme, the amount of taxable pension income is reduced by 25% [ITEPA 2003, s636B(3)].

Similarly, if it is paid after death in the form of a trivial commutation **lump sum death benefit**, it is taxable pension income of the recipient (but there is no 25% reduction) [ITEPA 2003, s636C(2)].

A trivial commutation lump sum is paid to a member of a **registered pension scheme** when the value of his pension rights is so small as not to be worth using to buy a pension. This is the case where the value of his pension rights is less than 1% of the standard lifetime allowance on the date he nominates [FA 2004, Sch29, para 7(1)(b) and (4)].

The method of calculation of the value of the member's pension rights is set out in FA 2004, Sch29, paras 8 and 9.

The lump sum must be paid to the member between his 60th and 75th birthdays [FA 2004, Sch29, para 7(1)(e)]. It must extinguish his rights under the pension scheme in question [FA 2004, Sch29, para 7(1)(d)] and he must have lifetime allowance available [FA 2004, Sch29, para 7(1)(c)].

A trivial commutation **lump sum death benefit** is paid to a **dependant** of a member who dies before reaching the age of 75 [FA 2004, Sch29, para 20(1)(a)]. The **dependant** must otherwise have been entitled to receive **pension death benefit** in respect of the deceased member [FA 2004, Sch29, para 20(1)(b)] and the payment must extinguish the **dependant**'s right to receive **pension death benefit** and **lump sum death benefit** [FA 2005, Sch29, para 20(1)(d)]. It must actually be paid before the deceased member would have been 75 [FA 2004, Sch29, para 20(1)(c)].

A trivial commutation **lump sum death benefit** cannot be more than 1% of the standard lifetime allowance on the day it is paid [FA 2004, Sch29, para 20(2)].

3.3.4.4.9. Lifetime Allowance Excess Lump Sum

As explained in section 3.3.4.3, once the lifetime allowance has been used up, the balance can be paid to the member as a lifetime allowance excess lump sum [FA

2004, Sch29, para 11(a)]. It will be taxed at 55% [FA 2004, s215(2)(a)], but will otherwise not be taxable [ITEPA 2003, s636A(5)].

However, it will not be a lifetime allowance excess lump sum if it is a short service refund lump sum or a refund of excess contributions lump sum (see sections 3.3.4.4.3 and 3.3.4.4.4) [FA 2004, Sch29, para 11(b)].

It will not be a lifetime allowance excess lump sum if it does not reduce or extinguish the member's pension entitlement [FA 2004, Sch29, para 11(c)]. It must be paid after **normal minimum pension age**, unless the **ill health condition** is met, and before the member's 75th birthday [FA 2004, Sch29, para 11(d) and (e)].

The member cannot take a lifetime allowance lump sum if the member has elected for enhanced protection (see section 3.3.4.9.2).

3.3.4.4.10. Charity Lump sum death benefit

A charity **lump sum death benefit** can be paid where a member dies on or after his 75th birthday, without any **dependants** [FA 2004, Sch29, para 18(1)(a) and (b)]. The member must have been entitled to **income withdrawal** at the date of his death.

It can also apply where **dependant**'s **income withdrawal** is being paid to the **dependant** of a member, and the **dependant** dies on or after his 75th birthday, leaving no other **dependant**s of the member [FA 2004, Sch29, para 18(2)(a), (b) and (c)].

In these circumstances the remaining funds can be paid to charity. The member, or **dependant**, must nominate the charity before his death [FA 2004, Sch29, para 18(1)(d) and (2)(e)].

It cannot be more than the amount or value of the member's, or **dependant**'s **alternatively secured pension fund** [FA 2004, Sch29, para 18(4)].

3.3.4.4.11. Annuity Protection Lump sum death benefits

When a member takes out a **scheme pension** or a **lifetime annuity**, the amount of the annuity will be based on his life expectancy. If in fact he dies earlier than expected, then the annuity provider makes a windfall gain.

It is possible to protect against this by providing that, if the member dies before his 75th birthday, the unpaid balance of the annuity is paid out as a **lump sum death benefit**.

This is an annuity protection **lump sum death benefit**. It can only be paid in relation to a member who dies before his 75th birthday [FA 2004, Sch29, para 16(1)(a)]. It must be paid in relation to a **scheme pension** or a **lifetime annuity** to which the member was entitled when he died [FA 2004, Sch29, para 16(1)(c)].

The amount of an annuity protection **lump sum death benefit** is limited to the amount that was originally crystallised to acquire the pension, less the total amount of pension actually paid between the crystallisation and the death of the member [FA 2004, Sch29, para 16(3)].

When the scheme administrator pays an annuity protection **lump sum death benefit**, there is an income tax charge on the administrator [FA 2004, s206(2)]. The rate of tax is 35% [FA 2004, s206(4)].

3.3.4.4.12. Unsecured pension fund Lump sum death benefits

An **unsecured pension fund lump sum death benefit** can be paid where a member dies before his 75th birthday [FA 2004, Sch29, para 17(1)(a)]. The member must have been entitled to **income withdrawal** at the date of his death [FA 2004, Sch29, para 17(1)(b)].

It can also apply where **dependant**'s **income withdrawal** is being paid to the **dependant** of a member, and the **dependant** dies before his 75th birthday [FA 2004, Sch29, para 17(2)].

In these circumstances, the remainder of the member's, or **dependant**'s **unsecured pension fund** can be paid out as a **lump sum death benefit**.

When the scheme administrator pays an annuity protection **lump sum death benefit**, there is an income tax charge on the administrator [FA 2004, s206(2)]. The rate of tax is 35% [FA 2004, s206(4)].

3.3.4.5. Pensions and Income withdrawal

Once an employee has reached **normal minimum pension age**, or the **ill health condition** applies, the member can crystallise the fund, either all at once or in stages, in return for a pension.

There are several different ways in which income can be provided, depending on the age of the member, the type of scheme and the way in which he wants to crystallise his entitlement.

The types of income available are:

- **Scheme pension** (see section 3.3.4.5.1); and
- **Lifetime annuity** (see section 3.3.4.5.2);
- Short-Term Annuity (see section 3.3.4.5.3); and
- **Income withdrawal** (see section 3.3.4.5.4).

3.3.4.5.1. Scheme pension

A **scheme pension** cannot be paid before the member reaches **normal minimum pension age**, unless the **ill health condition** applies [FA 2004, s165(1) rule 1].

A **scheme pension** is taxable pension income [ITEPA 2003, s579B].

A **scheme pension** cannot be paid unless the member has been given an opportunity to select a **lifetime annuity** instead [FA 2004, s165(1) rules 4 and 6].

A **scheme pension** will be paid by the scheme administrator or by an insurance company selected by the scheme administrator [FA 2004, Sch28, para 2(2)].

A **scheme pension** is usually paid until the member's death. However, a **scheme pension** can be arranged to run until the later of: the member's death and the end of a fixed period of up to ten years. This enables the member to continue to benefit his **dependants** in the event of his dying within ten years of first drawing the **scheme pension** [FA 2004, Sch28, para 2(3)(a)]. The **scheme pension** will still be regarded as being for a fixed term if it terminates when the **dependant** marries, reaches the age of 18, or ceases full-time education [FA 2004, Sch28, para 2(6)].

A **scheme pension** cannot normally be reduced [FA 2004, Sch28, para 2(3)(b)]. However, there are several circumstances when it can be reduced:

- if the **ill health condition** applied when the member first became entitled to the pension, but the member recovers to the extent that he is no longer entitled to the pension [FA 2004, Sch28, para 2(4)(a)];
- if all the **scheme pensions** payable from the scheme are reduced in the same way – for example because the scheme is no longer able to pay the pensions at the original rate [FA 2004, Sch28, para 2(4)(b)];
- if the **scheme pension** is reduced when the member becomes entitled to **state retirement pension**, and the reduction is not more than 125% or 250% of the basic state pension for contracted out and contracted in members respectively [FA 2004, Sch28, para 2(4)(c)];
- if the **scheme pension** is reduced by virtue of a court order, a pension sharing order or provision, or it is reduced or forfeited under HM Revenue & Customs regulations [FA 2004, Sch28, para 2(4)].

If the **scheme pension** is reduced in other circumstances, this may be treated as an unauthorised payment to the member [FA 2004, Sch28, para 2A].

3.3.4.5.2. Lifetime annuity

A **lifetime annuity** cannot be paid before the member reaches **normal minimum pension age**, unless the **ill health condition** applies [FA 2004, s165(1) rule 1].

A **lifetime annuity** is taxable pension income[13] [ITEPA 2003, s579B].

A **lifetime annuity** must be paid by an insurance company that the member has an opportunity to select [FA 2004, Sch28, paras 3(1)(a) and (b)].

A **lifetime annuity** is usually paid until the member's death. However, a **lifetime annuity** can be arranged to run until the later of: the member's death and the end of a fixed period of up to ten years. This enables the member to continue to benefit his **dependants** in the event of his dying within ten years of first drawing the **lifetime annuity** [FA 2004, Sch28, para 3(1)(c)]. The **lifetime annuity** will still be

---

[13] This is because it is a "pension under a registered pension scheme" [ITEPA 2003, s579D(1)(a)] and therefore ITEPA 2003, s579A applies to it.

regarded as being for a fixed term if it terminates when the **dependant** marries, reaches the age of 18, or ceases full-time education [FA 2004, Sch28, para 3(2)].

The amount of a **lifetime annuity** either cannot decrease, or is determined in accordance with HM Revenue & Customs regulations [FA 2004, Sch28, para 3(1)(d)].

3.3.4.5.3. Short-Term Annuity

A short-term annuity cannot be paid before the member reaches **normal minimum pension age**, unless the **ill health condition** applies [FA 2004, s165(1) rule 1].

A short-term annuity is taxable pension income[14] [ITEPA 2003, s579B].

A short-term annuity must be paid by an insurance company, that the member has an opportunity to select [FA 2004, Sch28, paras 6(1)(b) and (c)].

A short-term annuity cannot have a term that is longer than five years, and it must end before the member's 75th birthday [FA 2004, Sch28, para 6(1)(d)]. The amount of a short-term annuity either cannot decrease, or is determined in accordance with HM Revenue & Customs regulations [FA 2004, Sch28, para 6(1)(e)].

A short-term annuity is a form of **unsecured pension** [FA 2004, Sch28, para 4(a)]. It must be paid from the member's **unsecured pension fund** [FA 2004, Sch28, para 6(1)(a)].

3.3.4.5.4. Income withdrawal

Income withdrawal is where the member draws income from his pension fund without actually purchasing a lifetime or short-term annuity or a **scheme pension**.

Income withdrawal is taxable pension income[15] [ITEPA 2003, s579B].

A member might not want to use his pension fund to purchase an annuity or provide a pension because, for example, he hopes that annuity rates will increase. He may nevertheless want or need to draw an income from the fund, and this is provided through **income withdrawal**.

The rules are different depending on whether the member is under 75, or 75 or over.

3.3.4.5.4.1 Member is aged under 75

If the member is under 75, **income withdrawal** is a form of **unsecured pension** [FA 2004, Sch28, para 4(b)]. It must be paid from the member's **unsecured pension fund** [FA 2004, Sch28, para 7(a)].

---

[14] This is because it is a "pension under a registered pension scheme" [ITEPA 2003, s579D(1)(a)] and therefore ITEPA 2003, s579A applies to it.

[15] This is because it is a "pension under a registered pension scheme" [ITEPA 2003, s579D(1)(b)] and therefore ITEPA 2003, s579A applies to it.

There is a limit on the amount of **unsecured pension** that can be paid out in any year. This is 120% of the basis amount for that year [FA 2004, s165(1) rule 5].

The basis amount is the annual amount of a hypothetical "relevant annuity" that could have been purchased with the member's **unsecured pension fund** at a nominated date in the year [FA 2004, Sch28, para 10(2), (4) and (6)]. The relevant annuity is itself calculated on the basis of regulations issued by HM Revenue & Customs [FA 2004, Sch28, para 14].

The basis amount must be recalculated if part or all of the **unsecured pension fund** is used to purchase a **scheme pension** or annuity, or if additional funds are designated for the payment of **unsecured pension**, or a pension sharing event occurs [FA 2004, Sch28, paras 10(4) to (8)].

3.3.4.5.4.2 Member is aged 75 or more

If the member is aged 75 or more, **income withdrawal** is **alternatively secured pension** [FA 2004, Sch28, para 5]. It must be paid from the member's **alternatively secured pension fund** [FA 2004, Sch28, para 7(b)].

There is a limit on the amount of **alternatively secured pension** that can be paid out in any year. This is 70% of the basis amount for that year [FA 2004, s165(1) rule 7].

The basis amount is the annual amount of a hypothetical "relevant annuity" that could have been purchased with the member's **alternatively secured pension fund** at a nominated date in the year [FA 2004, Sch28, para 13(1) and (2)]. The relevant annuity is itself calculated on the basis of regulations issued by HM Revenue & Customs [FA 2004, Sch28, para 14].

3.3.4.6. Death Benefits

When the member dies, the assets of the fund can be used to provide either **pension death benefits** or **lump sum death benefits**.

There are four forms of **pension death benefit**:

- **Dependants' scheme pension** (see section 3.3.4.6.1);
- **Dependants' annuity** (see section 3.3.4.6.2);
- **Dependants**' Short-Term Annuity (see section 3.3.4.6.3); and
- **Dependants' income withdrawal** (see section 3.3.4.6.3).

There are nine forms of **lump sum death benefit**:

- Defined Benefits **Lump sum death benefits** (generally only payable from **defined benefits plans** and therefore outside the scope of this book);
- Pension Protection **lump sum death benefits** (generally only payable from **defined benefits plans** and therefore outside the scope of this book);
- Uncrystallised Funds **Lump sum death benefits** (see section 3.3.4.4.5);
- Annuity Protection **Lump sum death benefits** (see section 3.3.4.4.10);

- **Unsecured pension fund Lump sum death benefit**s (see section 3.3.4.4.12).
- Charity **Lump sum death benefit**s (see section 3.3.4.4.10);
- Transfer **Lump sum death benefit**s (see section 3.3.4.4.7).
- Trivial Commutation **Lump sum death benefit**s (see section 3.3.4.4.8); and
- Winding Up **Lump sum death benefit**s (see section 3.3.4.4.6).

3.3.4.6.1. Dependants' scheme pension

A **dependants' scheme pension** may only be paid to a **dependant** of the member [FA 2004, s167(1) rule 1].

A **dependants' scheme pension** is taxable pension income [ITEPA 2003, s579B].

A **dependants' scheme pension** cannot be paid unless the **dependant** has been given an opportunity to select a **dependants' annuity** instead [FA 2004, s167(1) rules 3 and 5].

A **dependants' scheme pension** will be paid by the scheme administrator, or by an insurance company selected by the scheme administrator [FA 2004, Sch28, paras 16(2)].

3.3.4.6.2. Dependants' annuity

A **dependants' annuity** must be paid by an insurance company, that either the member or the **dependant** had an opportunity to select [FA 2004, Sch28, paras 17(1)(a) and (b)]. It is purchased either together with a **lifetime annuity** payable to the member or after the member's death [FA 2004, Sch28, para 17(1)(za)].

A **dependants' annuity** is taxable pension income[16] [ITEPA 2003, s579B].

If the **dependant** is not the member's child, the **dependants' annuity** is paid either until the **dependant**'s death; or until the earlier of the **dependant**'s death or marriage [FA 2004, Sch28, para 17(1)(d)].

If the **dependant** is the member's child, the **dependants' annuity** is paid either until the earlier of the **dependant**'s death or ceasing to be a **dependant**, or until the earliest of the **dependant**'s death, marriage, or ceasing to be a **dependant** [FA 2004, Sch28, para 17(1)(e)].

The amount of a **dependants' annuity** either cannot decrease, or is determined in accordance with HM Revenue & Customs regulations [FA 2004, Sch28, para 17(1)(c)].

3.3.4.6.3. Dependants' Short-Term Annuity

A **dependants**' short-term annuity must be paid by an insurance company, that the **dependant** had an opportunity to select [FA 2004, Sch28, paras 20(1)(b) and (c)].

---

[16] This is because it is a "pension under a registered pension scheme" [ITEPA 2003, s579D(1)(a)] and therefore ITEPA 2003, s579A applies to it.

A **dependants**' short-term annuity is taxable pension income[17] [ITEPA 2003, s579B].

A **dependants**' short-term annuity cannot have a term that is longer than five years, and it must end before the **dependant**'s 75th birthday or earlier death [FA 2004, Sch28, para 20(1)(d)]. The amount of a **dependants'** short-term annuity either cannot decrease, or is determined in accordance with HM Revenue & Customs regulations [FA 2004, Sch28, para 20(1)(e)].

A **dependants**' short-term annuity is a form of **unsecured pension** [FA 2004, Sch28, para 18(a)]. It must be paid from the **dependant**'s **unsecured pension fund** [FA 2004, Sch28, para 20(1)(a)].

3.3.4.6.4. Dependants' income withdrawal.

Dependants' income withdrawal is where the **dependant** draws income from his pension fund without actually purchasing a lifetime or short-term annuity or a **scheme pension**.

Dependants' income withdrawal is taxable pension income[18] [ITEPA 2003, s579B].

The rules are different depending on whether the **dependant** is under 75, or 75 or over.

3.3.4.6.4.1 Dependant is aged under 75

If the **dependant** is under 75, **dependants' income withdrawal** is a form of **unsecured pension** [FA 2004, Sch28, para 18(b)]. It must be paid from the **dependant**'s **unsecured pension fund** [FA 2004, Sch28, para 21(a)].

The **dependant**'s **unsecured pension fund** consists of the money and assets held in the fund, which have been designated for payment of **dependants' unsecured pension**, and have not been applied towards the provision of a **dependants' scheme pension** [FA 2004, Sch28, para 22(1)].

There is a limit on the amount of **dependants**' **unsecured pension** that can be paid out in any year. This is 120% of the basis amount for that year [FA 2004, s167(1) rule 4].

The basis amount is the annual amount of a hypothetical "relevant annuity" that could have been purchased with the **dependant**'s **unsecured pension fund** at a nominated date in the year [FA 2004, Sch28, paras 24(2), (4) and (6)]. The relevant annuity is itself calculated on the basis of regulations issued by HM Revenue & Customs [FA 2004, Sch28, para 14].

---

[17] This is because it is a "pension under a registered pension scheme" [ITEPA 2003, s579D(1)(a)] and therefore ITEPA 2003, s579A applies to it.

[18] This is because it is a "pension under a registered pension scheme" [ITEPA 2003, s579D(1)(b)] and therefore ITEPA 2003, s579A applies to it.

The basis amount must be recalculated if part or all of the **dependant**'s **unsecured pension fund** is used to purchase a **dependants' scheme pension** or annuity, or if additional funds are designated for the payment of **dependants**' **unsecured pension** or a pension sharing event occurs [FA 2004, Sch28, paras 24(4) to (8)].

3.3.4.6.4.2 Dependant is aged 75 or more

If the **dependant** is aged 75 or more, **dependants' income withdrawal** is **alternatively secured pension** [FA 2004, Sch28, para 19]. It must be paid from the **dependant**'s **alternatively secured pension fund** [FA 2004, Sch28, para 21(b)].

The **dependant**'s **alternatively secured pension fund** consists of the money and assets which were held in his **unsecured pension fund** immediately before his 75th birthday, and which have not been applied towards the provision of a **dependants' scheme pension** [FA 2004, Sch28, para 25(2)]. The **dependants**' **alternatively secured pension fund** also includes any amount which became held in the **dependant**'s fund on or after his 75th birthday [FA 2004, Sch28, para 25(3)].

There is a limit on the amount of **dependant**'s **alternatively secured pension** that can be paid out in any year. This is 70% of the basis amount for that year [FA 2004, s167(1) rule 6].

The basis amount is the annual amount of a hypothetical "relevant annuity" that could have been purchased with the **dependant**'s **alternatively secured pension fund** at a nominated date in the year [FA 2004, Sch28, para 26(1) and (2)]. The relevant annuity is itself calculated on the basis of regulations issued by HM Revenue & Customs [FA 2004, Sch28, para 14].

3.3.4.7. Unauthorised Payments

A **registered pension scheme** is authorised to make only certain types of payment [FA 2004, s160(1)]. They include the types of benefit listed in sections 3.3.4.4, 3.3.4.5 and 3.3.4.6, as well as transfers to certain other pension schemes, payments under pension sharing orders or provisions, and other payments prescribed in regulations [FA 2004, s164].

This section describes the unauthorised payments that a **registered pension scheme** can make, and the consequences of making them.

3.3.4.7.1. Unauthorised member payments

There are eight types of **unauthorised member payment** in relation to money purchase plans (other than cash balance plans): payments to or in respect of a member (including a pensions commencement lump sum that is "recycled" – see section 3.3.4.4.1); assignments or surrenders of benefit by a member (see section 3.3.4.7.1.1); the provision of benefits to a member or his family or household (see section 3.3.4.7.1.); increases in rights of a connected person on the death of a member (see below); allocation of unallocated employer contributions (see below);

value-shifting (see section 3.3.4.7.1.); and an investment in certain kinds of property called "taxable property" [FA 2004, s174A].

FA 2004, s172B provides that there is an unauthorised member payment if a member dies and, as a consequence, there is an increase in the pension rights of another member who was a **connected person** of the deceased member. There are exceptions, e.g. transfer lump sum death benefits.

FA 2004, s172C provides that there is an unauthorised member payment if an employer makes a contribution to a **registered pension scheme**, the contributions are at first unallocated, then later allocated for the provision of benefits to a member, and the amount so allocated exceeds the maximum amount of relief to which the member is entitled, and the member is a **connected person** of the employer or someone connected with the employer.

The consequences of making an **unauthorised member payment** are that the member or recipient will be liable to pay the unauthorised payments charge and possibly also the unauthorised payments surcharge (see section 3.3.4.7.2).

3.3.4.7.1.1 Assignments of Benefit

If a member assigns his rights to any benefit or right under a **registered pension scheme**, this is an unauthorised payment [FA 2004, s172(1)]. This does not include an assignment under a pension sharing order or provision [FA 2004, s172(2)]. It does not include a situation where a pension continues to be paid for a limited period following the member's death [FA 2004, s172(7)].

The same applies if the assignment is made, not by the member, but by someone who has a right to a benefit in respect of the member, such as a **dependant** [FA 2004, s172(3) and (4)].

The same also applies if the member or any other person surrenders or agrees to surrender any benefit or right under the **registered pension scheme** [FA 2004, s172A].

The amount of the unauthorised payment is the consideration received for the assignment or, if greater, the consideration that would have been received on an arm's length transaction [FA 2004, s172(5)].

3.3.4.7.1.2 Provision of Benefits

There is an unauthorised payment if the **registered pension scheme** uses an asset to provide a benefit to a member or someone in the member's family or household [FA 2004, s173(1)]. The same applies after the member's death [FA 2004, s173(4)]. This includes a loan to the member or any connected person of the member.

However, this does not apply if the member was not in **excluded employment** [FA 2004, s173(2) and (6)].

Even if the member was in **excluded employment**, this section only applies to benefits provided from an occupational pension scheme, where the member is a director of the sponsoring employer with a **material interest** in the sponsoring employer [FA 2004, s173(3) and (7)], and only to benefits to which Chapter 6 or Chapter 10 of the benefits code would apply.

The amount of the unauthorised payment will generally be the cash equivalent of the benefit under the benefits code, but HM Revenue & Customs may issue regulations prescribing a different value [FA 2004, s173(8)].

3.3.4.7.1.3 Value-Shifting

There is an unauthorised payment where a **registered pension scheme** enters into a transaction that is not at arm's length, and, as a result, value is shifted out of the pension scheme to, or for the benefit of, a member. FA 2004, s174 sets out in full the circumstances where this can apply.

The amount of the unauthorised payment is the amount by which the value of the pension scheme falls, over and above what would have happened in an arm's length transaction [FA 2004, s174(4)].

3.3.4.7.2. Unauthorised Payments Charge and Unauthorised Payments Surcharge

If a **registered pension scheme** makes an unauthorised payment, there is a tax charge called the unauthorised payment charge [FA 2004, s208(1)]. The tax is payable by the member or recipient in the case of an **unauthorised member payment** and by the sponsoring employer in the case of an unauthorised employer payment [FA 2004, s208 (2)].

The rate of tax is 40% [FA 2004, s208(5)]. The effect therefore in the case of an **unauthorised member payment** is to charge tax at the same rate as the tax relief already given. But in the case of an unauthorised employer payment, the tax charge is at a higher rate than the original tax relief.

However, if the percentage of the pension fund used up for that member by making **unauthorised member payment**s is more than 25% in a 12-month period, there will be a surchargeable **unauthorised member payment**, giving rise to an unauthorised payments surcharge [FA 2004, s209 and s210]. This is charged at an additional 15%, making a total of 55%. This is the same rate of tax as the lifetime allowance charge (see section 3.3.4.3), so the effect is to reduce the ability of a member to avoid the lifetime allowance charge at 55% by receiving **unauthorised member payment**s taxed at 40%.

Similarly, if the percentage of the pension fund used up for that member by making unauthorised employer payments is more than 25% in a 12-month period, there will be a surchargeable unauthorised employer payment, giving rise to an unauthorised payments surcharge [FA 2004, s213]. Since the original relief was only given at 30%, a tax charge at 55% is very unattractive.

3.3.4.8. *Authorised Employer Loans*

It is possible for any **registered pension scheme** to make a loan to the sponsoring employer of up to 50% of the fund value [FA 2004, s179(1)(a)]. The loan must be at or above the prescribed rate of interest [FA 2004, s179(2)(a)] and be properly secured on an asset of adequate value [FA 2004, s179(1)(b)]. It must have a maximum term of five years [FA 2004, s179(2)(b)], but this can be extended once for a further period of up to five years [FA 2004, s179(3)].

The prescribed rate of interest is the average of the rates of leading banks and is determined in accordance with the Pension Schemes (Prescribed Interest Rates for Authorised Employer Loans) Regulations 2005 [SI 2005/3449].

FA 2004, Sch30 sets out in detail the rules for authorised employer loans.

If the loan is not authorised, or ceases to meet the requirements of an authorised employer loan, then there is an unauthorised employer payment. FA 2004, Sch30, paras 5 to 16 set out how the amount of the unauthorised employer payment is calculated.

3.3.4.9. *Transitional Rules*

The introduction of the new pension rules on 6 April 2006 had adverse effects on some people, in particular people whose funds were already worth more than the lifetime allowance.

There are two forms of protection that those people can elect for: primary protection, and enhanced protection.

In order to rely on either primary or enhanced protection, the individual must give notice to HM Revenue & Customs before 6 April 2009 [Pension Schemes (Enhanced Lifetime Allowance) Regulations 2006].

3.3.4.9.1. *Primary Protection*

Primary protection works by increasing the lifetime allowance by a lifetime allowance enhancement factor. This means that the lifetime allowance at the time of a subsequent **benefit crystallisation event** is increased [FA 2004, s218(4)].

If the accrued lump sum on 6 April 2006 was greater than £375,000, then the permitted maximum pension commencement lump sum is increased by what is effectively the same factor [FA 2004, Sch36, para 24 and para 28]. Hence primary protection often does not increase the tax free cash above 25% of the smaller of the fund and the standard lifetime allowance.

The enhancement factor is (RR – £1.5 million) / £1.5 million, where RR is the value of the member's rights (whether uncrystallised or crystallised) under the pension scheme at 5 April 2006 [FA 2004, Sch36, para 7(3)].

If the member is already drawing a pension, this is valued by multiplying the annual pension rate by 25 [FA 2004, Sch36, para 10].

Example:

On 5 April 2006, the member has retirement annuity contracts and personal pension plans worth £1.3 million. He is already drawing a pension of £20,000, which is therefore valued at £500,000.

The lifetime allowance enhancement factor is therefore 0.2 (£1.8 million - £1.5 million) / £1.5 million.

In 2007/8, the standard lifetime allowance is £1,600,000. After increasing by the lifetime allowance enhancement factor, the member has an enhanced lifetime allowance of £1,920,000.

The effect of primary protection is therefore to tax any growth in the value of the pension fund over and above the rate of growth in the lifetime allowance.

3.3.4.9.2. Enhanced Protection

If the member elects for enhanced protection, he is exempt from the lifetime allowance charge [FA 2004, Sch36, para 12(3)].

Furthermore, the permitted maximum pension commencement lump sum will not be reduced by reference to the lifetime allowance [FA 2004, Sch36, para 29, amending FA 2004, Sch29, para 3] (see section 3.3.4.4.1.3).

In order to elect for enhanced protection, the member must agree to freeze the pre-6 April 2006 arrangements. He cannot make any further contributions to any money purchase scheme; neither can his employer make any contributions on his behalf [FA 2004, Sch36, para 14].

Under enhanced protection, it will still be necessary for any pension commencement lump sum to meet the rule that at least part of the lifetime allowance is available at the time the lump sum is drawn (see section 3.3.4.4.1).

If he is a member of a **defined benefits plan** or a **cash balance plan**, his rights cannot be allowed to grow by more than indexation [FA 2004, Sch36, para 15]. Indexation for these purposes means the highest of: salary growth for that plan's employment, 5% per annum, and the RPI.

3.3.4.10. NIC Issues

There is no "NIC relief" for employee contributions to a **registered pension scheme** in the same way that there is tax relief. Therefore, it is more efficient for an employee to waive salary in return for enhanced employer contributions to the scheme. An employee does not pay NIC in relation to employer contributions [SSCR 2001, Sch3, Part VI].

3.3.4.11. *Inheritance Tax*

An employee's rights under an approved or **registered pension scheme** are not generally taken into account in determining the value of his estate for inheritance tax purposes on his death [IHTA 1984, s151(2)]. However, there is a potential inheritance tax charge if an **alternatively secured pension fund** is not exhausted by the time of the member's death or if a member omits to exercise his pension rights.

There is no transfer of value for inheritance tax purposes when a spouse or **dependant** becomes entitled to an annuity from an approved or **registered pension scheme** as a result of an election by the deceased member of the scheme [IHTA 1984, s152].

However, if a member dies aged under 75, and has omitted to exercise any of his pension rights, the omission can be a transfer of value, but only where the member made another disposition of his rights under the pension scheme within two years before his death (ignoring a disposition that was not intended to confer gratuitous benefit) and at the time he made the disposition he had reason to believe that he would die within two years [IHTA 1984, s12(2B)]. Even then, there will not be a transfer of value if the effect of the omission is to confer a **lump sum death benefit**, or a **pension death benefit**, on a relevant **dependant**, or to make a payment to charity [IHTA 1984, s12(2D)].

If an **alternatively secured pension fund** is not exhausted by the time of the member's death, there are several things that can be done with the remaining fund:

- It can be retained in the scheme and used to provide benefits to other members but in these circumstances it will fall into the estate of the member for inheritance tax purposes;
- It can be paid back to the employer company as an authorised surplus payment – however, in these circumstances it will be treated as part of the member's estate for IHT purposes and will also be charged to income tax in the hands of the employer at 35% [FA 2004, s207];
- It can be paid to charity, in which case it will be free from inheritance tax;
- It can be used to provide benefits for the member's spouse, civil partner, or other person who is financially dependent on the member, in which case it will be free from inheritance tax;
- It can be used to provide benefits for some other **dependant**, in which case it will form part of the member's estate for inheritance tax purposes [IHTA 1984, s151A].

If any funds still remain once the member's spouse, civil partner, or **dependant**, has died or ceased to be eligible for benefit, then they will usually form part of the member's estate for inheritance tax purposes [IHTA 1984, s151B]. However, they may form part of the **dependant**'s estate if the member originally died before 75 [IHTA 1984, s151C].

3.3.4.12. Reporting

See section 3.3.6.7.

3.3.5. Summary of Benefits Payable from Registered Money Purchase Pension Schemes

3.3.5.1. Member has not reached Normal minimum pension age

The following benefits are available before the member reaches **normal minimum pension age**: winding up lump sums; refund of excess contributions lump sums; and short service refund lump sums. In addition, an employee who had protected rights existing before 6 April 2006 may be able to receive benefits before **normal minimum pension age**.

All the other benefits listed in **Table 2** are available where the **ill health condition** applies, but not otherwise.

3.3.5.2. Member has reached Normal minimum pension age but is under 75

Table 2

Description of Benefit	Features	Availability	Limit	Tax Treatment	Cross-reference
Scheme pension	Payable until death or until later of death and end of a fixed term of up to ten years	In accordance with scheme rules or at choice of member	Amount that can be purchased with value of fund	Taxable Pension Income	3.3.4.5.1
Lifetime annuity	Payable until death or until later of death and end of a fixed term of up to ten years	In accordance with scheme rules or at choice of member	Amount that can be purchased with value of fund	Taxable Pension Income	3.3.4.5.2
Short-Term Annuity	Maximum five year life; must end before 75th birthday or member's earlier death	In accordance with scheme rules or at choice of member	Amount that can be purchased with value of **unsecured pension fund**	Taxable Pension Income	3.3.4.5.3
Income withdrawal		In accordance with scheme rules or at	120% of hypothetical annuity	Taxable Pension Income	3.3.4.5.4.1

Description of Benefit	Features	Availability	Limit	Tax Treatment	Cross-reference
		choice of member	purchased with **unsecured pension fund**		
Pension Commencement Lump Sum	Linked to **income withdrawal**, a **lifetime annuity**, or a **scheme pension**	Within three months of becoming entitled to **income withdrawal**, a **lifetime annuity**, or a **scheme pension**	Lower of (a) 25% of available lifetime allowance or (b) 25% of fund	Tax-free	3.3.4.4.1
Serious Ill-Health Lump Sum	Must extinguish member's entitlement to benefits	Member has life expectancy of less than one year	The value of the fund	Tax-free	3.3.4.4.2
Refund of Excess Contributions Lump Sum		Member has contributed more than the annual allowance	The excess over the annual allowance	Tax-free	3.3.4.4.3
Short Service Refund Lump Sum		Member terminates pensionable service before normal pension age with no right to scheme benefits	The amount of the member's contributions	20% on first £10,800 and 40% on any excess	3.3.4.4.4
Trivial Commutation Lump Sum		Fund is worth 1% or less of the lifetime allowance	The value of the fund	Taxable Pension Income (but possible 25% reduction)	3.3.4.4.8
Lifetime		Value of fund	The excess	Taxed at	3.3.4.4.9

Description of Benefit	Features	Availability	Limit	Tax Treatment	Cross-reference
Allowance Excess Lump Sum		exceeds lifetime allowance	over the lifetime allowance	55%	
Winding-Up Lump Sum	Only where scheme is being wound up	Fund is worth 1% or less of the lifetime allowance	The value of the fund	Taxable Pension Income (but possible 25% reduction)	3.3.4.4.6

3.3.5.3. Member is Over 75

Table 3

Description of Benefit	Features	Availability	Limit	Tax Treatment	Cross-reference
Scheme pension	Payable until death or until later of death and end of a fixed term of up to ten years	In accordance with scheme rules or at choice of member	Amount that can be purchased with value of fund	Taxable Pension Income	3.3.4.5.1
Lifetime annuity	Payable until death or until later of death and end of a fixed term of up to ten years	In accordance with scheme rules or at choice of member	Amount that can be purchased with value of fund	Taxable Pension Income	3.3.4.5.2
Income withdrawal		In accordance with scheme rules or at choice of member	70% of hypothetical annuity purchased with **alternatively secured pension fund**	Taxable Pension Income	3.3.4.5.4.2

3.3.5.4. *Benefits Payable On or Following Death of Member*

Table 4

Description of Benefit	Features	Availability	Limit	Tax Treatment	Cross-reference
Continuation of Member's **Scheme pension** or **Lifetime annuity**	Must terminate within ten years of member first drawing the pension or annuity	Where pension or annuity originally issued on those terms		Taxable Pension Income	3.3.4.5.1 and 3.3.4.5.2
Dependants' scheme pension		In accordance with scheme rules or at choice of **dependant**	Amount that can be purchased with value of fund	Taxable Pension Income	3.3.4.6.1
Dependants' annuity (not payable to child)	Payable until death or until earlier of death and marriage	In accordance with scheme rules or at choice of **dependant**	Amount that can be purchased with value of fund	Taxable Pension Income	3.3.4.6.2
Dependants' annuity (payable to child)	Payable until (a) earlier of death or ceasing to be **dependant** or (b) earliest of death, marriage and ceasing to be **dependant**	In accordance with scheme rules or at choice of **dependant**	Amount that can be purchased with value of fund	Taxable Pension Income	3.3.4.6.2
Dependants' Short-Term Annuity	Maximum five year life; must end before 75th birthday or the dependant's earlier death	In accordance with scheme rules or at choice of **dependant**	Amount that can be purchased with value of **dependant's unsecured pension fund**	Taxable Pension Income	3.3.4.6.3
Dependants' income withdrawal		In accordance with scheme rules or at	120% of hypothetical annuity	Taxable Pension	3.3.4.6.4.1

Description of Benefit	Features	Availability	Limit	Tax Treatment	Cross-reference
(**dependant** under 75)		choice of **dependant**	purchased with **unsecured pension fund**	Income	
Dependants' income withdrawal (**dependant** 75 or over)		In accordance with scheme rules or at choice of **dependant**	70% of hypothetical annuity purchased with **alternatively secured pension fund**	Taxable Pension Income	3.3.4.6.4.2
Uncrystallised Funds **Lump sum death benefit**		Where member died aged under 75	Limited to uncrystallise d funds in pension scheme	Tax-Free within available lifetime allowance of member	3.3.4.4.5
Transfer **Lump sum death benefit**	Funds used for benefit of other members of scheme	Where member (or **dependant**) was receiving **income withdrawal** and died aged 75 or more leaving no more **dependants** of member	Amount in **alternatively secured pension fund**	Free of income tax but may be subject to inheritance tax	3.3.4.4.7
Trivial Commutation **Lump sum death benefit**		Where member died aged under 75 and fund is worth 1% or less of the lifetime allowance	The value of the fund	Taxable Pension Income	3.3.4.4.8
Charity **Lump**	Funds	Where	Amount in	Tax-free	3.3.4.4.10

Description of Benefit	Features	Availability	Limit	Tax Treatment	Cross-reference
sum death benefit	transferred to charity	member (or **dependant**) was receiving **income withdrawal** and died aged 75 or more leaving no more **dependants** of member	**alternatively secured pension fund**		
Annuity Protection **Lump sum death benefit**		Where member dies aged under 75 and pension or annuity was protected	Original cost of pension or annuity, less total amounts actually paid	35%	3.3.4.4.11
Unsecured pension Lump sum death benefit		Where member (or **dependant**) was receiving **income withdrawal** and dies aged under 75	Amount in **unsecured pension fund**	35%	3.3.4.4.12
Winding-Up **Lump sum death benefit**	Only where scheme is being wound up	Fund is worth 1% or less of the lifetime allowance	The value of the fund	Taxable Pension Income	3.3.4.4.6

3.3.6. Tax Treatment of Trustee/Scheme Administrator

3.3.6.1. Income Tax

A **registered pension scheme** is exempt from income tax on all forms of investment income, except income from investments and deposits held as a member of a **property investment LLP** [FA 2004, s186].

A **registered pension scheme** is not exempt from tax on trading income.

FA 2006 introduced the concept of an "investment-regulated pension scheme", which is effectively a pension scheme which invests in certain kinds of assets, such as residential property. Income and capital gains on taxable property held by an investment-regulated pension scheme will be taxed at 40%; the tax will be paid by the scheme administrator [FA 2004, s185A].

3.3.6.2. *Capital Gains Tax*

A **registered pension scheme** is exempt from capital gains tax [TCGA 1992, s271(1A)].

3.3.6.3. *Inheritance Tax*

The assets of an approved or **registered pension scheme** are not "relevant property" and are therefore not subject to the inheritance tax charges on settled property without a qualifying interest in possession [IHTA 1984, s58(1)(d)].

3.3.6.4. *Borrowing by a Money purchase plan*

3.3.6.4.1. *Authorised Borrowing*

A registered money purchase pension scheme is authorised to borrow funds worth up to 50% of its assets [FA 2004, s182]. It can use the borrowed money for any purpose in connection with the scheme.

3.3.6.4.2. *Unauthorised borrowing*

If a **money purchase plan** borrows funds worth more than 50% of its assets, the excess is **unauthorised borrowing** [FA 2004, s183]. The excess is a **scheme chargeable payment**, subject to the **scheme sanction charge** [FA 2004, s183(2)] (see section 3.3.6.5).

3.3.6.5. *Scheme sanction charge*

The unauthorised payments charge and unauthorised payments surcharge are payable by the member, recipient or employer (see section 3.3.4.7.2). By contrast, the **scheme sanction charge** is payable by the scheme administrator [FA 2004, s239(2)].

The **scheme sanction charge** is payable in respect of a **scheme chargeable payment** [FA 2004, s239(1)]. The rate of tax is 40% [FA 2004, s240(1)].

A **scheme chargeable payment** is an unauthorised payment, the result of **unauthorised borrowing** or taxable income or gains on taxable property held by an investment-regulated scheme [FA 2004, s241(1)].

There is a limited range of exclusions. These include the following:

- Where the **unauthorised member payment** was the use of a non-wasting asset to provide a benefit to the member (see section 3.3.4.7.1.2). In these circumstances, the asset still exists and remains in the pension scheme. So although there is an **unauthorised member payment**, there is no **scheme chargeable payment** [FA 2004, s241(2)(a)].
- Where it is a compensation payment (see section 3.3.7.1) [FA 2004, s241(2)(b)]
- Where it is paid pursuant to an actual or potential court order, or is of a description prescribed by HM Revenue & Customs [FA 2004, s241(2)(c), (d) and (e)].

Where the **scheme chargeable payment** is also an unauthorised payment, there is clearly scope for double taxation of both the scheme administrator, and the member, recipient or employer. There is a limited relief against double taxation. The amount of the **scheme chargeable payments** for the year is reduced by the lower of (a) 25% of the **scheme chargeable payments** on which tax has been paid and (b) the actual tax paid as an unauthorised payments charge.

Example: The scheme makes an ***unauthorised member payment*** *of £100,000, and this is the only* ***scheme chargeable payment*** *made during the tax year.*

The member pays an unauthorised payments charge of £40,000.

The ***scheme sanction charge*** *is £40,000, less the lower of (a) 25% of the* ***scheme chargeable payment****, i.e. £25,000 or (b) the tax paid of £40,000. Therefore, the* ***scheme sanction charge*** *is £15,000 (£40,000 - £25,000).*

This means that the total tax paid in relation to the payment is:

Unauthorised Payments Charge of £40,000

Scheme sanction charge *of £15,000, plus possibly*

Unauthorised Payments Surcharge of £15,000

This means an effective tax rate of 55% or possibly 70% if there is an unauthorised payments surcharge.

3.3.6.6. De-registration Charge

HM Revenue & Customs have power to de-register a scheme in limited circumstances [FA 2004, s157].

When this happens, there is a de-registration charge of 40% of the assets of the scheme [FA 2004, s242].

3.3.6.7. Reporting

There are extensive reporting obligations imposed on the scheme administrator by the Registered Pension Schemes (Provision of Information) Regulations 2006. Those obligations are not set out in this book since the scheme administrator will normally be independent from the company.

3.3.7. Tax Treatment of Employer

3.3.7.1. Unauthorised Employer Payment

Once the employer has made a contribution to a **money purchase plan**, there are very few ways in which funds can be returned to the employer. The authorised employer payments are set out in FA 2004, s175; any other payments to or for the benefit of the employer are unauthorised employer payments.

The consequences of making an unauthorised employer payment are that the sponsoring employer will be liable to pay the unauthorised payments charge and possibly also the unauthorised payments surcharge (see section 3.3.4.7.2).

The following are authorised employer payments:

- an authorised surplus payment [FA 2004, s177];
- a compensation payment, where the member commits a criminal, fraudulent or negligent act and incurs a liability to the employer [FA 2004, s178];
- an authorised loan to the employer (see section 3.3.4.8);
- a scheme administration employer payment, where the scheme makes an arm's length payment to the employer for its administration or management [FA 2004, s180].

3.3.7.2. *Corporation Tax Deductibility*

3.3.7.2.1. *General rules*

For accounting periods beginning on or after 6 April 2006, contributions to a **registered pension scheme** by an employing company are deductible [FA 2004, s196] provided they are made "wholly and exclusively" for the purposes of the trade. In January 2006, HM Revenue & Customs published draft text for the Business Income Manual, suggesting that they will look closely at the motives behind pension contributions, particularly those made by owner-managed businesses. If they consider that there is a duality of purpose, they may disallow all or a proportion of the contribution. At the time of writing, this text has not been finalised.

The deduction normally arises in the year of actual payment [FA 2004, s196].

There are anti-avoidance rules that HM Revenue & Customs can apply to restrict relief in relation to a member who may also receive benefits under an **employer-financed retirement benefits scheme** [FA 2004, s196A].

3.3.7.2.2. *Spreading of exceptionally large contributions*

The relief can be spread over two to four accounting periods if the contribution is exceptionally large. This will be the case if the contribution is both (a) more than 210% of the contribution paid in the immediately preceding period; and (b) at least £500,000 more than 110% of the contribution paid in the preceding period [FA 2004, s197(1), (2) and (3)].

Examples:

1. *The company contributes £100,000 to the pension scheme in 2006/7 and £250,000 in 2007/8. The whole contribution of £250,000 is allowed in 2007/8. Although the 2007/8 contribution is more than 210% of the 2006/7 contribution, the excess over 110% is only £140,000 [FA 2004, s197(3)(a)]*
2. *The company contributes £1 million in 2006/7 and £1.7 million in 2007/8. The whole contribution of £1.7 million is allowed in 2007/8, since the 2007/8 contribution is less than 210% of 2006/7 contribution [FA 2004, s197(1)(b)].*
3. *The company contributes £400,000 in 2006/7 and £1.2 million in 2007/8. The "amount of the relevant excess contributions" is £760,000 [FA 2004, s197(2)]. Since*

this is more than £500,000 but less than £1 million, the table in FA 2004, s197(5) specifies that relief for the amount of the relevant excess is spread over two years. Relief is given in 2007/8 for £820,000 (110% of the contribution plus one half of the amount of the relevant excess contributions) and for £380,000 in 2008/9.

4. *The company contributes £1 million in 2006/7 and £2.6 million in 2007/8. The "amount of the relevant excess contributions" is £1.5 million [FA 2004, s197(2). Since this is more than £1 million but less than £2 million, the table in FA 2004, s197(5) specifies that relief for the amount of the relevant excess is spread over three years. Relief is given in 2007/8 for £1.6 million (110% of the contribution plus one third of the amount of the relevant excess contributions) and for £500,000 in each of 2008/9 and 2009/10.*

The spreading does not apply to payments that are made to cover an increase in the cost of living of pensioner members, or to fund future service for new employees [FA 2004, s197(7)].

Appropriate adjustments are made where the two accounting periods are of different lengths [FA 2004, s197(8)].

3.3.7.2.3. Cessation of Business

If the employer ceases business before being able to claim relief for the whole of a pension contribution, because the contribution was spread under FA 2004, s197, then the employer can elect either (a) to take relief for the remainder of the contribution in the accounting period in which it ceases business or (b) to spread the relief evenly over the whole period beginning with the year in which the contribution was made and ending with the cessation of business [FA 2004, s198].

3.3.7.3. NIC

There is no secondary NIC payable in relation to contributions to **registered pension schemes** [SSCR 2001, Sch3, Part VI].

3.3.7.4. Inheritance Tax

A payment into a **registered pension scheme** is not a transfer of value for inheritance tax purposes [IHTA 1984, s12(2)]

3.3.7.5. Reporting

See section 3.3.6.7.

3.3.8. Matrix Summary of Advantages and Disadvantages of Registered Pension Schemes

Feature	**Advantage**	**Disadvantage**
Availability	Available to all companies	
Flexibility		Subject to statutory protections for members and restrictions on how funds can be invested and used for benefit of

Feature	Advantage	Disadvantage
		members
Limits		Subject to annual and lifetime limits
Accounting (p/l)		Contributions charged to profit and loss account
Accounting (balance sheet)		Not applicable for **money purchase plans**
Corporation Tax	Deductions generally available for contributions when paid	
Income Tax and NIC	No income tax or NIC on contributions. Investment returns free of income tax. 25% tax-free lump sum on **retirement**	
Capital Gains Tax	Growth in value of pension fund free of CGT	
Inheritance Tax	Value of pension fund usually free from IHT on death	

3.4. Executive Pensions (Employer-Financed Retirement Benefits Schemes)

3.4.1. Description

Before 6 April 2006 there were two kinds of unapproved retirement benefits scheme: funded unapproved retirement benefits schemes (FURBS) and unfunded unapproved retirement benefits schemes (UURBS). The two schemes each had a different tax treatment.

Now there are **employer-financed retirement benefits schemes**, which have the same tax treatment as previously applied to UURBS.

In summary, the rules are as follows:

- an employee is generally not taxed on contributions to an **employer-financed retirement benefits scheme** (see section 3.4.4.1.2.2);
- instead, the employee is taxed on benefits he receives from the **employer-financed retirement benefits scheme**, with relief for amounts already taxed (see section 3.4.4.2.3);
- the employer cannot deduct contributions to an **employer-financed retirement benefits scheme** until the employee receives benefits, and the deductions are limited to the lower of (a) the amounts originally contributed and (b) the benefits provided (see section 3.4.6.1);

- income and gains of an onshore **employer-financed retirement benefits scheme** are taxed at 40% (32.5% on dividends) (see sections 10.4.4 and 10.4.2);
- the value of an employee's interest in an **employer-financed retirement benefits scheme** is in the employee's estate for inheritance tax purposes, with relief under transitional rules for amounts already in a FURBS on 5 April 2006 (see section 3.4.4.4).

Therefore the one tax advantage of an **employer-financed retirement benefits scheme** lies in the fact that the employee's income tax liability is deferred until he actually receives benefits, while income and gains can usually accrue in an offshore **employer-financed retirement benefits scheme** free of UK taxation. However, note that there are possible UK tax charges on some overseas **employer-financed retirement benefits scheme** under FA 2004, Sch34.

3.4.2. Disclosure

See section 3.3.2.

3.4.3. Regulatory Treatment

This is covered in detail in *Dealing With Pensions* by Robin Ellison and Grant Jones *[Spiramus Press 1 904905 06 4].*

3.4.4. Tax Treatment of Employee

Income tax and NIC issues potentially arise for the employee when the employee actually receives a benefit from the scheme (see section 3.4.4.2).

The employee also needs to be aware of his inheritance tax position in relation to the assets of a FURBS.

3.4.4.1. Income Tax: Making or Promising a Contribution

A contribution made or promised to an **employer-financed retirement benefits scheme** on or after 6 April 2006, which is made with a view to providing relevant benefits to a particular employee, will not count as employment income of that employee.

However, making a contribution on or after 6 April 2006 to an **employer-financed retirement benefits scheme** that was funded before that date may have adverse income tax and inheritance consequences for the member (see sections 3.4.4.2.2.5 and 3.4.4.4.2).

3.4.4.2. Income Tax: Receipt of a Benefit

3.4.4.2.1. UURBS

The general rule is that the provision of any benefit to an individual from an UURBS gives rise to employment income for that individual [ITEPA 2003, s394]. The taxable amount is the cash payment, or, for a non-cash benefit, the higher of its money's worth value, or the cash equivalent calculated under the benefits code [ITEPA 2003, s398].

3.4.4.2.2. FURBS established and funded before 6 April 2006

To avoid double taxation, there is a complete or partial exemption for lump sum payments from a FURBS established on or before 6 April 2006. Since the employee will usually have paid tax on the contributions into the FURBS, it would be unfair to tax him again on the benefits provided.

3.4.4.2.2.1 Benefits Provided from Onshore FURBS on or after 6 April 2006 (no funding on or after 6 April 2006)

A lump sum paid from an onshore FURBS on or after 6 April 2006 will be wholly exempt if the employer has made no further contributions into the FURBS after 5 April 2006 [FA 2004, Sch36, para 54(2)].

3.4.4.2.2.2 Benefits Provided from Offshore FURBS on or after 6 April 2006

A lump sum paid from an offshore FURBS on or after 6 April 2006 will be partially exempt from tax. The taxable amount of the lump sum will be reduced by the aggregate of any employer contributions made before 6 April 2006 on which the employee was taxed, and any contributions the employee himself made to the FURBS at any time [FA 2004, Sch36, para 55]. However, note that if the FURBS was established before 1 December 1993 and has not been varied after that date, the lump sum may be totally exempt [FA 2004, Sch36, para 54(1)(b)].

3.4.4.2.2.3 Benefits Provided from Onshore FURBS on or after 6 April 2006 (further funding provided on or after 6 April 2006)

A lump sum paid from an onshore FURBS on or after 6 April 2006 will be partially exempt if the employer has made further contributions into the FURBS after 5 April 2006 [FA 2004, Sch36, para 54(3)].

The exempt amount will be the market value of the assets of the fund on 5 April 2006, uplifted for inflation since that date, plus any amounts contributed to the FURBS by the member after 5 April 2006 [FA 2004, Sch36, para 54(4)].

3.4.4.2.3. Employer-Financed Retirement Benefits Schemes established on or after 6 April 2006

The provision of any relevant benefit to an individual from an **employer-financed retirement benefits scheme** on or after 6 April 2006 gives rise to employment income for that individual [ITEPA 2003, s394]. The taxable amount is the cash payment, or, for a non-cash benefit, the higher of its money's worth value, or the cash equivalent calculated under the benefits code [ITEPA 2003, s398]. If the employee himself has contributed to the scheme, then these amounts are deducted from the taxable amount [ITEPA 2003, s395].

3.4.4.3. NIC

It is arguable that a payment into a FURBS is not subject to NIC, and support for this view is found in *Tullett & Tokyo Forex International Ltd v Secretary of State for Social Security* [2000] EWHC Admin 350. However, HM Revenue & Customs do not accept that this case applies to FURBS payments – see the article in *IR Tax Bulletin* 65[19]. The prudent approach is to account for NIC on the payment "under protest".

3.4.4.4. *Inheritance Tax*

3.4.4.4.1. *FURBS established and funded before 6 April 2006 (no funding on or after 6 April 2006)*

A FURBS is a sponsored superannuation scheme as defined in ICTA 1988, s624. Therefore the employee's interest in the FURBS is left out of account in determining the value of his estate assuming no further contributions are made after 5 April 2006 [IHTA 1984, s151(2)].

Similarly, the provisions of the inheritance tax legislation that deal with interests in possession under settlements do not apply to interests in FURBS assuming no further contributions are made after 5 April 2006 [IHTA 1984, s151(3)].

3.4.4.4.2. *FURBS established and funded before 6 April 2006 (more funding provided on or after 6 April 2006)*

If further contributions are made into a FURBS after 5 April 2006, then only a proportion of the value of the FURBS will be left out of account. That proportion is

(ACV / V) x 100

where ACV is the value of the funds on 5 April 2006, uplifted for inflation since that date, and V is the value of the funds on the date the inheritance tax charge arises.

This means that any real growth in value of the funds since 5 April 2006 will be within the charge to inheritance tax.

3.4.4.4.3. *Employer-Financed Retirement Benefits Schemes established on or after 6 April 2006*

An **employer-financed retirement benefits scheme** established on or after 6 April 2006 is within the scope of inheritance tax.

The member's interests in an **employer-financed retirement benefits scheme** form part of the value of his estate on death, since the exclusion in IHTA 1984, s151 is not available.

The exclusion in IHTA 1984, s152 for cash options does not apply.

3.4.5. Tax Treatment of Trustee

3.4.5.1. *FURBS – Income Tax*

The income tax treatment of a FURBS is identical to that of an EBT: see section 10.4.4 for onshore FURBS and section 10.4.5 for offshore FURBS.

---

[19] http://www.hmrc.gov.uk/bulletins/tb65.htm#f

3.4.5.2. FURBS – Capital Gains Tax

The capital gains tax treatment of a FURBS is identical to that for an EBT: see section 10.4.2 for onshore FURBS and section 10.4.3 for offshore FURBS.

3.4.5.3. Inheritance Tax

Property held in a FURBS is within the charge to inheritance tax. Therefore a right to an annuity or a pension may be a qualifying interest in possession to be aggregated with the member's estate on death.

Any funds in which a qualifying interest in possession did not exist might be subject to the special regime for employee trusts, depending on the terms of the FURBS. If so, the tax treatment would be as described in section 10.4.1.1.

In many circumstances, the FURBS will be taxed in the same way as any other discretionary trust. The ten-yearly charge will apply (see section 10.4.1.2).

3.4.6. Tax Treatment of Employer

3.4.6.1. Corporation Tax Deductibility

A contribution to an **employer-financed retirement benefits scheme** is an "employee benefit contribution" as defined in FA 2003, Sch24, para 1(2)(c) and therefore subject to the deferral of deductions described in section 17.3.

If the employer incurs expenses of providing benefits otherwise than by making contributions, these expenses are not deductible unless a person is chargeable to income tax on receipt of the benefits [FA 2004, s246].

If the employer incurs expenses or makes contributions to **employer-financed retirement benefits scheme** and there is a corresponding reduction in benefits payable under a **registered pension scheme**, then relief is denied except to the extent that it is just and reasonable [FA 2004, s246A].

3.4.6.2. NIC

See section 3.4.4.3.

3.4.6.3. Reporting

The trustee or manager of an **employer-financed retirement benefits scheme** is the "responsible person" in respect of the scheme [ITEPA 2003, s399A].

The responsible person must make a report to HM Revenue & Customs within three months following the date when the scheme comes into operation, i.e. the first occasion when an employer makes a contribution to the scheme, or benefits are provided to a member.

In addition, if relevant benefits are provided to a member during a tax year, the responsible person must report the details to HM Revenue & Customs by 7 July of the following tax year [Employer-Financed Retirement Benefits Schemes (Provision of Information) Regulations 2005]

3.4.7. Matrix Summary of Advantages and Disadvantages of Employer-Financed Retirement Benefit Schemes

Feature	Advantage	Disadvantage
Availability	Available to all companies	
Flexibility		Subject to statutory protections for members
Limits	No limits	
Accounting (p/l)		Contributions charged to profit and loss account
Accounting (balance sheet)		Not applicable for **money purchase plans**
Corporation Tax	Deductions generally available for contributions when benefits paid to members	
Income Tax and NIC	No income tax or NIC on contributions.	Investment returns taxed in same way as EBT
Capital Gains Tax		Subject to same rules as EBT
Inheritance Tax	Complete or partial exemption for FURBS established before 6 April 2006.	

3.5. Investment in Shares

3.5.1. Overview

One of the most common ways of rewarding employees is to allow them to acquire shares in the company. This aligns their personal financial interests with those of the shareholders of the company and therefore reduces some of the problems identified by agency theory, such as the difficulty of ensuring that the manager of a business acts in the best interests of the owners of the business, rather than acting in his own best interests.[20]

If the shares grow in value, the employee may be able to claim business asset taper relief from capital gains tax on the eventual disposal, giving an effective tax rate of 10% (see section 12.11.6).

If the shares fall in value, the employee may be able to claim income tax loss relief under ICTA 1988, s574(1) (see section 12.12).

In addition, shares in an unquoted company are "relevant business property" for inheritance tax purposes [IHTA 1984, s105(1)(bb)] unless the business the company

---

[20] For an academic discussion of agency theory, see Eisenhardt, K. 1989. Agency theory: An assessment and review. *Academy of Management Review*, 14(1): 57-74

carries on consists wholly or mainly in dealing in securities, land or buildings, or making or holding investments [IHTA 1984, s105(3)]. This means that there is effectively no inheritance tax on a transfer of shares that have been held for two years or more [IHTA 1984, s104 and s106].

This section describes some of the many ways in which shares can be provided to employees. These are:

- 3.5.3 Unrestricted Shares
- 3.5.4 Restricted Shares
- 3.5.5 Convertible securities
- 3.5.6 Nil-paid and Partly-paid Shares
- 3.5.7 Ratchet Arrangements
- 3.5.8 Value Freezing
- 3.5.9 Flowering Shares and
- 3.5.10Share Appreciation Rights.

Other ways of offering shares that are more appropriate for broad-based employee offers are described in section 4.2.

3.5.2. Company Law Issues

3.5.2.1. Financial Assistance

See section 18.7.

3.5.2.2. Loans to Directors

See section 18.11.

3.5.2.3. Disclosure

See section 18.9, paras 8, 10 and 13.

3.5.3. Unrestricted Shares

3.5.3.1. Description

The simplest way of providing shares to employees is to give them shares that are not **restricted securities** and which carry no special rights. However, this may not achieve the objectives of retaining and motivating the employees.

3.5.3.2. Tax Treatment of Employee

An employee who acquires unrestricted shares by reason of his employment will be subject to income tax on the difference (if any) between the **money's worth value** (see section 15.1) of the shares and the price he pays for them. Any subsequent growth in value should be subject to capital gains tax. If the employee makes a loss, he may be able to claim income tax relief (see section 12.12). There is a more detailed description of the employment income tax treatment in section 11.1.2 and of the capital gains tax treatment in section 12.11.5.

3.5.3.3. *Tax Treatment of Employer*

3.5.3.3.1. Corporation Tax Deductibility

See section 17.4.2.

3.5.3.3.2. NIC

See section 11.1.2.

3.5.3.3.3. Reporting

See section 11.1.2.

3.5.3.4. *Accounting Treatment*

See section 19.3.6.1.

3.5.3.5. *Sources of Shares*

See section 3.7.4.

3.5.3.6. *Matrix Summary of Advantages and Disadvantages of Employee Investment in Shares*

Feature	Advantage	Disadvantage
Availability	Available to all companies	
Flexibility	Entirely flexible	
Limits	No limits	
Accounting (p/l)		Value of shares charged to p/l
Effect on Shareholders		If new shares issued, dilution of shareholders' interests
Corporation Tax	Deduction may be available for value of shares **award**ed	
Income Tax and NIC		Yes, subject to PAYE and NIC if **readily convertible assets**
Capital Gains Tax	Business Asset Taper Relief may be available	
Inheritance Tax	Business Property Relief may be available	

3.5.4. Restricted Shares

3.5.4.1. Description

Often the employer will wish to impose restrictions on shares awarded to an employee. Typical restrictions include the following:

- if the employee leaves employment within a certain period, he has to offer his shares for sale at the price he originally paid for them. Such a restriction ties the employee to the employer for that period of time, because by leaving he forfeits the growth in value of the shares;

- if the company fails to meet certain performance targets within a certain period, the employee has to offer his shares for sale at the price he originally paid for them. This is a stronger version of the first restriction: it ensures that the shareholders only share the growth in value with the employees if the company achieves the objectives set by the shareholders.

3.5.4.2. *Tax Treatment of Employee*

The income tax and NIC treatment of the employee depends on the nature of the restrictions and the length of time for which they operate. The rest of this section only applies to employees who are **resident** and **ordinarily resident** in the UK on the **acquisition date** [ITEPA 2003, s421E(1)].

3.5.4.2.1. *Shares restricted but not forfeitable*

When an employee acquires shares that are **restricted**, but not **forfeitable**, there are two elections that he and the employer can jointly make: a **Section 431(1) election** or a **Section 431(2) election**. For the effect of making an election see section 22.2 and for details of the reporting see section 22.3.

3.5.4.2.1.1 No Election

On the **acquisition date**, the employee will be subject to employment income tax on the amount by which the **money's worth value** of the shares (taking account of all the restrictions) is greater than the **acquisition price** (if any) (see section 11.1.3).

When the restrictions are lifted, there will be a further employment income tax charge on a proportion of the subsequent growth in value (see section 12.3.4).

When the employee sells the shares, the remaining growth in value will be subject to capital gains tax (see section 12.11.3).

3.5.4.2.1.2 Section 431(1) election

The employee and employer can jointly make a **Section 431(1) election** to ignore all the restrictions on the shares. The employee will be subject to employment income tax on the amount by which the **unrestricted market value** of the shares is greater than the **acquisition price** (if any) (see section 11.1.3).

When the employee sells the shares, the remaining growth in value will be subject to capital gains tax (see section 12.11.3).

3.5.4.2.1.3 Section 431(2) election

The employee and employer can jointly make a **Section 431(2) election** to ignore some, but not all, the restrictions on the shares. The employee will be subject to employment income tax on the amount by which the **CGT value** of the shares, ignoring the specified restrictions, is greater than the **acquisition price** (if any) see section 11.1.3).

When the remaining restrictions are lifted, there will be a further employment income tax charge on a proportion of the subsequent growth in value (see section 12.3.4).

When the employee sells the shares, the remaining growth in value will be subject to capital gains tax (see section 12.11.3).

3.5.4.2.2. *Shares forfeitable for a period of less than five years*

When an employee acquires shares that are restricted and which are subject to forfeiture conditions that must expire within five years, there are three elections that he and the employer can jointly make: a **Section 425 election**, a **Section 431(1) election** (see section 3.5.4.2.1.2) or a **Section 431(2) election** (see section 3.5.4.2.1.3).

3.5.4.2.2.1 No Election

If the employer and employee make no election, there will usually be no employment income tax charge in relation to the acquisition (see section 11.1.4).

When the restrictions are lifted, there will be an employment income tax charge on a proportion of the subsequent growth in value (if any) (see section 12.3.4).

When the employee sells the shares, the remaining growth in value will be subject to capital gains tax (see section 12.11.3).

3.5.4.2.2.2 Section 425 election

The employer and employee can jointly make a **Section 425 election** to be taxed on the **money's worth value** of the shares. If they do, the employee will be subject to employment income tax, on the **acquisition date**, on the amount by which the **money's worth value** of the shares (taking account of all the restrictions) is greater than the **acquisition price** (if any) (see section 11.1.4).

When the restrictions are lifted, there will be a further employment income tax charge on a proportion of the subsequent growth in value (see section 12.3.4).

When the employee sells the shares, the remaining growth in value will be subject to capital gains tax (see section 12.11.3).

3.5.4.2.3. *Shares forfeitable for a period of more than five years*

The tax treatment of an employee who acquires shares that are forfeitable for a period of more than five years is the same as applies to shares which are restricted but not forfeitable (see section 3.5.4.2.1). HM Revenue & Customs have accepted in unpublished correspondence that a period of exactly five years should be treated as if it were less than five years.

3.5.4.2.4. *PAYE and NIC*

See section 12.3.5.

3.5.4.3. *Tax Treatment of Employer*

3.5.4.3.1. *Corporation Tax Deductibility*

If the shares are corporation tax deductible when the chargeable event occurs, the employing company should be able to claim a corporation tax deduction. The deduction will be for (broadly) the same amount and arise in the same year as the chargeable event for the employee (see section 17.4.4).

If the shares are not corporation tax deductible when the chargeable event occurs, the availability of tax relief will be determined using general principles (see section 17.1).

3.5.4.3.2. *NIC*

Secondary NIC will be due if the shares are **readily convertible assets** when the chargeable event occurs [SSCR 2001, reg 22(7)].

3.5.4.3.3. *Reporting*

See section 23.

3.5.4.4. *Accounting Treatment*

See sections 19.3.6.2 and 19.3.6.3.

3.5.4.5. *Sources of Shares*

See section 3.7.4.

3.5.4.6. *Matrix Summary of Advantages and Disadvantages of Restricted Securities*

Feature	**Advantage**	**Disadvantage**
Availability	Available to all companies	
Flexibility	Entirely flexible	
Limits	No limits	
Accounting (p/l)		Fair value of shares charged to p/l, spread over **vesting period** where shares are subject to forfeiture (see section 19.3.6.3
Effect on Shareholders		If new shares issued, dilution of shareholders' interests
Corporation Tax	Deduction may be available for value of shares on **award** or **vesting**	
Income Tax and NIC		Yes, subject to PAYE and NIC if **readily convertible assets**
Capital Gains Tax	Business Asset Taper Relief may be available	

Feature	Advantage	Disadvantage
Inheritance Tax	Business Property Relief may be available	

3.5.5. Convertible securities

3.5.5.1. Description

Sometimes the employer will award convertible shares or other securities to the employee. This is particularly likely to happen in a venture capital or private equity situation, where the employee may be awarded shares that initially have limited rights, but which convert into ordinary shares on certain events.

Convertible shares used to offer a tax-effective way of rewarding senior employees. However, the current tax treatment is not particularly favourable: any growth in value that results from the conversion is taxable as income, and the remaining growth in value is taxable as a capital gain.

3.5.5.2. Tax Treatment of Employee

There may be an income tax charge on the acquisition of the **convertible securities** – however, any value attributable to the conversion rights will normally be ignored (see section 11.1.2).

There will be a further income tax charge on the conversion of the **convertible securities**. This will be on the growth in value that results from the conversion. If the value of the conversion right is realised without a conversion taking place, e.g. by a sale of the securities prior to conversion there are mechanisms to tax the resulting gain also as income (see section 12.4.2).

3.5.5.2.1. PAYE and NIC

See section 12.4.5

3.5.5.2.2. Reporting

See section 12.4.6.

3.5.5.2.3. Capital Gains Treatment

There may be capital gains tax on the eventual disposal of the securities, or the shares into which they are converted (see section 12.11.3), but not on the conversion itself [TCGA 1992, s127 and s132].

3.5.5.3. Tax Treatment of Employer

3.5.5.3.1. Corporation Tax Deductibility

See section 17.4.4.

3.5.5.3.2. NIC

See section 12.4.5.

3.5.5.3.3. Reporting

See section 12.4.6.

3.5.5.4. *Accounting Treatment*

See section 19.3.2.

3.5.5.5. *Sources of Shares*

See section 3.7.4.

3.5.5.6. *Matrix Summary of Advantages and Disadvantages of Convertible Securities*

Feature	Advantage	Disadvantage
Availability	Available to all companies	
Flexibility	Entirely flexible	
Limits	No limits	
Accounting (p/l)		Fair value of shares charged to p/l
Accounting (balance sheet)		If new shares issued, dilution of shareholders' interests
Corporation Tax	Deduction may be available for gain on conversion and amount taxed on award	
Income Tax and NIC		Subject to PAYE and NIC if **readily convertible assets**
Capital Gains Tax	Business Asset Taper Relief may be available	
Inheritance Tax	Business Property Relief may be available	

3.5.6. Nil-paid and Partly-paid Shares

3.5.6.1. *Description*

Sometimes an employer will issue shares to an employee on a partly-paid or nil-paid basis. This means that the employee owns the shares, but has not yet paid for them in full.

If the share price goes up, this can be favourable to the employee, because he gets the benefit of the growth in value without actually having the cashflow cost of paying for the shares.

However, if the share price goes down, or the company becomes insolvent, the employee may remain contractually bound to pay the remainder due on the shares.

This is therefore a potentially disadvantageous structure if the value of the shares falls.

Note also that if one of the main purposes of issuing partly-paid shares is the avoidance of tax or NIC, then there are anti-avoidance provisions that can be disadvantageous to the employee (see section 11.1.6).

3.5.6.2. *Tax Treatment of Employee*

The employee will be treated as having received an interest-free loan of the unpaid amount of the purchase price of the shares (see section 12.8).

3.5.6.2.1. PAYE

See section 12.8.4.7.

3.5.6.2.2. NIC

See section 12.8.4.8.

3.5.6.2.3. Reporting

See section 12.8.4.9.

3.5.6.2.4. Capital Gains Treatment

See section 12.11.5.

3.5.6.3. *Tax Treatment of Employer*

3.5.6.3.1. Corporation Tax Deductibility

See section 17.1 – note that relief under FA 2003, Sch23 is not available in relation to charges under ITEPA 2003, Part 7, Chapter 3C.

3.5.6.3.2. NIC

See section 12.8.4.8.

3.5.6.3.3. Reporting

See section 12.8.4.9.

3.5.6.4. *Accounting Treatment*

See section 19.3.2.

3.5.6.5. *Sources of Shares*

See section 3.7.4.

3.5.6.6. *Matrix Summary of Advantages and Disadvantages of Nil-Paid and Partly-Paid Shares*

Feature	Advantage	Disadvantage
Availability	Available to all companies	
Flexibility	Entirely flexible	
Limits	No limits	
Risk		Employee at risk if share price falls, because tax charge based on notional loan
Accounting (p/l)		Fair value of shares charged to p/l

Feature	Advantage	Disadvantage
Accounting (balance sheet)		If new shares issued, dilution of shareholders' interests
Corporation Tax		No statutory deduction for amount taxed on employee
Income Tax and NIC		Income tax and Class 1A NIC potentially chargeable on cash equivalent of the benefit of notional loan. PAYE and NIC on write-off if **readily convertible assets**
Capital Gains Tax	Business Asset Taper Relief may be available	
Inheritance Tax	Business Property Relief may be available	

3.5.7. Ratchet Arrangements

3.5.7.1. Description

Ratchets have been for many years a typical way of arranging management participation in venture capital or private equity investments. The actual structure has evolved to cope with changing tax legislation.

Typically, a new company ("Newco") will be established to acquire a business or company. Newco may receive funding in several different ways, including senior debt, mezzanine debt, preference shares, shareholder loans, and ordinary share capital. The ordinary share capital will be highly geared, meaning that it has the potential to grow exponentially as the value of the company increases.

The ordinary share capital will be provided by the managers ("Management") and the venture capitalist ("VC").

The idea of a ratchet is that Management get a variable proportion of the value of Newco when the VC "Exits", usually through an initial public offering ("IPO") or trade sale.

With a ratchet, the proportion of Newco taken by Management will depend on the performance of Newco. The VC will be planning to receive a certain internal rate of return ("IRR") on its investment. Once it has achieved its IRR, the VC will be willing to share any excess returns with Management.

For example, Management might subscribe for 5% of the initial capital of Newco, but have the right to receive between 5% and 10% of the value on Exit. There are several ways to structure this.

3.5.7.1.1. Management Upwards Ratchet

This was the most usual structure for a ratchet for many years.

Management would subscribe for a class of convertible ordinary shares, which would convert into sufficient ordinary shares to deliver between x% and y% of the Exit proceeds, depending on performance.

This structure is not often used now, because Management will be taxed on the increase in value due to conversion, under the **convertible securities** rules (see section 12.4).

Example:

Newco is capitalised with equity share capital of £100,000. The VC subscribes £85,000 for 85,000 equity shares. Management subscribes £15,000 for 15,000 convertible ordinary shares that can deliver between 15% and 20% of the Exit proceeds.

Five years later Newco is sold in a trade sale for £1,000,000 and the ratchet delivers in full.

Management's shares convert into equity shares worth 20% of the revised share capital. Management sells the shares for £200,000, of which £50,000 represents the increase in value on conversion. This is taxable as employment income (see section 12.4.4.1).

The balance of the gain is £135,000 and this is taxed as a capital gain.

3.5.7.1.2. VC Downwards Ratchet

This structure became widely used for several years before the enactment of FA 2003, but is not common any more.

The VC would subscribe for a class of ordinary shares, some of which converted downwards into worthless deferred shares in order to give Management the correct return under the ratchet.

Example:

Newco is capitalised with ordinary share capital of £100,000. The VC subscribes £85,000 for 85,000 convertible equity shares that will deliver between 80% and 85% of the Exit proceeds. Management subscribes £15,000 for 15,000 ordinary shares.

Five years later Newco is sold in a trade sale for £1,000,000 and the ratchet delivers in full.

25,000 of the VC shares convert downwards into worthless deferred shares. This means the VC holds 60/75 of the share capital, ie 80% and management holds 20%.

HM Revenue & Customs believe that the conversion of the VC shares is a benefit to Management, which is taxable as employment income. This view is stated in HMRC FAQ 4(a)[21]. However, HMRC will not usually apply this to shares acquired before 16 April 2003 [HMRC FAQ 4(b)[22]]. Many practitioners do not believe that

[21] http://www.hmrc.gov.uk/shareschemes/faq_emprelatedsecurity-ch4.htm#a

[22] http://www.hmrc.gov.uk/shareschemes/faq_emprelatedsecurity-ch4.htm#b

HMRC's view would survive scrutiny by the courts; however, since FA 2003 most venture capital investments have been structured as management downwards ratchets (see section 3.5.7.1.3).

3.5.7.1.3. Management Downwards Ratchet (the Memorandum of Understanding)

On 25 July 2003, the Inland Revenue and the British Venture Capital Association jointly published a Memorandum of Understanding ("the MoU")[23], which sets out their joint understanding of a way in which Management investments can be structured to obtain capital gains tax treatment, rather than being taxable as employment income.

The MoU sets out the conditions that have to be satisfied in order for HM Revenue & Customs to accept that (a) no general earnings charge arises on the initial investment by Management and (b) no subsequent liability arises under ITEPA 2003, Part 7, Chapter 2, on the operation of the ratchet. The conditions are:

A. Managers must subscribe for ordinary capital [MoU, para 4.1(a)].

B. Any preference capital provided by other ordinary shareholders must be provided on commercial terms [MoU, para 4.1(b)]. This is taken to mean that the coupon or expected rate of return on the preference capital should not be less than the rate of interest on the most expensive external debt. The reason for this is that it would otherwise be possible for shareholders to lend money to Newco on "soft" terms, which could artificially inflate the value of Management's shares.

C. Management and the VC should acquire their shares in Newco at the same time [MoU, para 4.1(d)].

D. Management's shares should not have any features that enhance them in relation to the VC's shares [MoU, para 4.1(e)].

E. Management are fully remunerated on a commercial basis as employees [MoU, para 4.1(f)].

F. The ratchet must relate to the overall performance of Newco, or the VC's investment in Newco, and not to the performance of individual employees [MoU, para 6.2(a)].

G. The ratchet is in place when the VC invests in Newco [MoU, para 6.2(b)].

H. Management must pay a price per share that reflects their maximum economic entitlement [MoU, para 6.2(c)].

Note that Condition B does not address the issue of "thin capitalisation". In unpublished correspondence, HM Revenue & Customs have taken the position that there can be a liability under ITEPA 2003, s447 where a company has borrowed a greater amount from its investors than it could have borrowed on an

---

[23] http://www.hmrc.gov.uk/shareschemes/bvca_and_fb2003_managers.pdf

arm's length basis. They believe that returns to equity shareholders can be enhanced by such borrowing, and this represents a transfer of value from the lenders to the equity shareholders. In this particular case, the company involved complied in every other respect with the MoU. HM Revenue & Customs' position is being strongly challenged by the taxpayers and is likely to be heard by the Special Commissioners in due course.

Condition H is important to understand. In effect, it means that Management must pay for the maximum percentage that they can receive. If in fact the ratchet is not fully achieved, then Management will have paid for a greater proportion of the share capital than they eventually own.

Example:
Newco is capitalised with ordinary share capital of £100,000. The VC subscribes £80,000 for 80,000 convertible ordinary shares that will deliver between 80% and 85% of the Exit proceeds. Management subscribes £20,000 for 20,000 ordinary shares that will deliver between 15% and 20% of the Exit proceeds.

All the other conditions of the MoU are satisfied.

Scenario 1: Five years later Newco is sold in a trade sale for £1,000,000 and the ratchet is achieved in full.

No alteration to the share capital is necessary because Management already owns 20%.

HM Revenue & Customs will accept that Management's gain is entirely taxable as capital.

Scenario 2: Five years later Newco is sold in a trade sale for £150,000. The VC's IRR minimum target is not achieved. The Management shares convert downwards so that they receive only 15% of the Exit proceeds, i.e. £30,000. Management's gain is entirely taxable as capital.

3.5.7.2. *Tax Treatment of Employee*

This section describes the tax treatment that applies if all the conditions of the Memorandum of Understanding are satisfied in relation to Management's investment in Newco.

3.5.7.2.1. PAYE and NIC

No income tax should arise on the initial acquisition of shares or the subsequent disposal or lifting of restrictions. This is because HM Revenue & Customs will accept that Management acquire their shares for their **unrestricted market value**. Nevertheless, Management will often make protective **Section 431 elections**. One reason for making the election is to give reassurance to a prospective purchaser of the company that there is no latent liability to tax.

3.5.7.2.2. Reporting

There are no reporting obligations on the participant.

3.5.7.2.3. Capital Gains Treatment

See section 12.11.5.

3.5.7.3. Tax Treatment of Employer

3.5.7.3.1. Corporation Tax Deductibility

There is no statutory right to a corporation tax deduction in relation to the growth in value.

3.5.7.3.2. NIC

If the Memorandum of Understanding applies there should be no secondary NIC liability.

3.5.7.3.3. Reporting

The shares are **employment-related securities** and therefore the acquisition should be reported to HM Revenue & Customs on Form 42 by 6 July of the tax year following the acquisition date [ITEPA 2003, s421J and ITEPA 2003, s421K(3)(a).

3.5.7.4. Accounting Treatment

See section 19.3.6.4.

3.5.7.5. Sources of Shares

See section 3.7.4.

3.5.7.6. Matrix Summary of Advantages and Disadvantages of Ratchet Arrangements

See section 3.5.3.6.

3.5.8. Value Freezing

3.5.8.1. Description

Value freezing is a way in which to give employees a proportion of the growth in value of the company, while being taxed at the favourable capital gains tax rates.

One disadvantage is that it requires a reconstruction of the share capital of the company. Another is that employees must make an upfront investment, unless nil-paid shares are used.

The concept is for the company to have two classes of share capital. The first class are preference shares, which carry the right to receive the current value of the company on a winding-up and to receive a cumulative dividend equal to the company's current profits. The second class are ordinary shares, which, by deduction, carry only the future value of the company. Therefore, at the time of issue, the ordinary shares have hope value only. These shares can be issued to employees when they are created. It is clearly important to get the valuation of these shares right to avoid any income tax risk on acquisition.

3.5.8.2. *Tax Analysis*

3.5.8.2.1. *Restricted securities Rules*

If the ordinary shares are **restricted securities**, then employees should consider making a **Section 431(1) election** to be taxed on the (presumably low) **unrestricted market value** and therefore avoid any subsequent charge to income tax under ITEPA 2003, Part 7, Chapter 2 (see section 12.3.3.1).

HM Revenue & Customs have confirmed that shares are not to be considered **restricted securities** merely because their rights on a liquidation are deferred to other shares [HMRC FAQ 2(y)[24]].

3.5.8.2.2. *Convertible securities Rules*

The nature and description of the ordinary shares never changes, so the **convertible securities** rules in ITEPA 2003, Part 7, Chapter 3, should not be in point. This should be contrasted with flowering shares (see section 3.5.9) which HM Revenue & Customs consider can be **convertible securities**.

3.5.8.2.3. *Artificial Depression and Artificial Enhancement Rules*

The artificial depression and artificial enhancement rules in ITEPA 2003, Part 7, Chapter 3A and Chapter 3B should not apply. This is because nothing is done to reduce the value of the ordinary shares before issue to the employees and nothing is done to increase them afterwards. Their rights are deferred to the preference shares from the moment of issue.

3.5.8.2.4. *Special Benefit Rules*

The growth in value of the ordinary shares after issue cannot (in the author's view) be considered to be a special benefit to the shareholders. However, HM Revenue & Customs may seek to argue that the company is thinly capitalised, and that this in itself represents a transfer of value from lenders to equity shareholders.

Even if there is a special benefit, it is likely that one of the exemptions in ITEPA 2003, s449 will be available in many cases.

3.5.8.2.5. *Capital Gains Treatment*

Employees should benefit from capital gains tax treatment in relation to the growth in value of the ordinary shares.

3.5.8.3. *Matrix Summary of Advantages and Disadvantages of Value Freezing*

See section 3.5.3.6.

3.5.9. Flowering Shares

3.5.9.1. *Description*

"Flowering" shares are sometimes called "performance shares" or "blossoming shares". The concept is that they are a class of deferred ordinary shares. They have

[24] http://www.hmrc.gov.uk/shareschemes/faq_emprelatedsecurity-ch2.htm#y

no (or limited) rights until the happening of a pre-determined event, such as the achievement of a certain level of profits. From that time onwards they rank *pari passu* with the ordinary shares.

3.5.9.2. Tax Analysis

When FA 2003 was introduced, many advisers saw "flowering shares" as a way in which employees could invest and get capital gains tax treatment.

Unfortunately, HM Revenue & Customs believe that such shares can either be considered restricted or convertible [HMRC FAQ 3(e)[25]]. No technical justification is given for this position in the FAQs, but HM Revenue & Customs' position is believed to be as follows:

- the shares may be considered restricted if, say, they initially have limited voting or dividend rights;
- the "flowering", i.e. the eventual increase of rights, is a conversion into shares of a different description or a special benefit.

Neither of these views is easy to reconcile with the actual wording of the legislation. The temporary absence of dividend or voting rights at the time of issue is not a restriction within the meaning of ITEPA 2003, s423(2) or (3). Shares which were issued with dividend rights and/or voting rights that were subsequently temporarily taken away would be **restricted securities** by virtue of ITEPA 2003, s423(3)(c), because rights had been conferred on the shares and then restricted. However, if the shares never have voting rights or dividend rights, it is hard to see how those rights can have been conferred on the shares.

HM Revenue & Customs' view that the shares can be convertible is somewhat easier to understand: shares which have no voting rights would be described differently from shares that do have voting rights.

Therefore, it does seem that "flowering shares" may be taxable under the **convertible securities** rules in ITEPA 2003, Part 7, Chapter 3, but not, *pace* HM Revenue & Customs, under the **restricted securities** rules in Chapter 2 (see section 12.3).

3.5.9.3. Matrix Summary of Advantages and Disadvantages of Flowering Shares

See section 3.5.3.6.

3.5.10. Share Appreciation Rights

3.5.10.1. Description

A share appreciation right gives the employee a right to receive the growth in value of a number of shares at the end of a period of time.

---

[25] http://www.hmrc.gov.uk/shareschemes/faq_emprelatedsecurity-ch3.htm#e

This is similar in concept to a phantom share plan (see section 3.2). However, sometimes the share appreciation right can be settled by delivering shares rather than cash.

If the share appreciation right can only be settled by delivering shares, or the participant has the right to choose between shares and cash, then it is a **securities option** and the treatment in section 3.7 applies.

If the share appreciation right can only be settled in cash, or the employer has the right to choose to settle in cash or shares, then it should be treated in the same way as a phantom share option (see section 3.2).

3.5.10.2. *Matrix Summary of Advantages and Disadvantages of Share Appreciation Rights*

See section 3.2.6.

3.5.11. Capital Gains Tax and Business Asset Taper Relief

Where an employee holds securities of his employing company, or its parent, the securities will normally be eligible for business asset taper relief (see section 12.11.6). This can significantly reduce the effective capital gains tax rate on sale.

3.5.12. Loan Interest Relief

Loan interest relief may be available where an employee acquires shares in a **close company** (see section 16.5) or an **employee-controlled company** (see section 16.6).

3.6. Payments into Employee Benefit Trusts (EBTs)

3.6.1. Description

Another commonly used technique for rewarding senior employees is an EBT with sub-funds.

The advantage of this structure is that funds can be used for the benefit of the employee and his family without triggering employment income tax charges on the capital amount. The funds are outside the employee's estate for inheritance tax purposes and can be distributed free of income tax to his beneficiaries after his death.

The disadvantage of the structure is that the corporation tax deduction for the payment of the funds is deferred until the employee pays employment income tax in respect of the payment. This may mean that it is deferred indefinitely. This is therefore mainly of interest to companies that do not pay corporation tax, perhaps because of losses.

The structure works as follows:

- the employing company establishes an EBT for the benefit of all employees;
- the employing company makes a voluntary contribution of assets to the EBT;
- the Trustee establishes a sub-fund for the benefit of one particular employee and his family;

- the Trustee appoints the assets into the sub-fund; the appointment is revocable with the consent of the beneficiaries;
- the Trustee uses the assets in the sub-fund for the benefit of the employee and his family, perhaps by making loans or allowing the beneficiaries to occupy or use property or other assets.

3.6.2. Tax Analysis

3.6.2.1. Income Tax and NIC

The payment into the EBT and subsequent appointment into sub-funds does not itself cause any employment income tax or NIC charge to arise. As long as the sub-funds are discretionary, there is no benefit for the employee that can be converted into money's worth. It is important to ensure that the class of beneficiaries of the sub-fund is wider than the member's family and household, but it cannot be so wide that the EBT no longer satisfies IHTA 1984, s86 (see section 10.4.1.1).

The Inland Revenue unsuccessfully challenged this view before the Special Commissioners in *Dextra v MacDonald* [2002] STC (SCD) 413 and [2005] STC 1111. Although the Inland Revenue appealed against that decision on other grounds, they accepted that there was no employment income tax liability in relation to the payments into the EBT. The House of Lords has subsequently upheld the Revenue's appeal on other grounds.

If the Trustee provides benefits to the beneficiaries while the employee remains in the same employment, then the employee is taxed under the benefits code. See for example section 16.3 on the taxation of cheap loans.

In the tax year following the termination of the relevant employment and subsequent tax years, it is no longer possible for an employment income tax charge to arise under the benefits code. This is because a benefit can only be an employment-related benefit if it is provided to someone who holds that employment during the same tax year [ITEPA 2003, s201(4)].

Even after termination of employment, an actual payment to the employee or another beneficiary would be taxable as employment income. However, this does not apply to payments made after the employee's death.

It remains possible for an income tax charge to arise under ICTA 1988, s740. For this reason, the EBT should invest for capital gains rather than income.

3.6.2.2. Collection of NIC

A payment made to an employee by an EBT is treated for NIC purposes as if it had been made by the employer. The employer is entitled to withhold primary NIC from other payments made to the employee that year or in the following year [SSCR 2001, Sch4, paras 1(2), 4A, 7(3), and (8)].

3.6.2.3. *Capital Gains Tax*

If the company transfers an asset into the EBT, rather than paying cash, then it can claim exemption from capital gains tax under TCGA 1992, s239 (see section 10.2.3).

However, if the company is close, it is essential to exclude from benefit under the EBT anyone who is a **participator** in the **close company**, unless they can only benefit by receiving payments taxed as income.

It is sometimes suggested that a **participator** can receive a loan from an EBT. Any such loan must be on fully commercial terms; for example it must be appropriately secured and bear a commercial rate of interest. If this is not the case, the Trustee is committing a breach of trust.

3.6.2.4. *Inheritance Tax*

The EBT should comply with IHTA 1984, s86 in order to obtain the favourable tax treatment (see section 10.4.1.1). The appointments into sub-funds must be revocable to ensure that this treatment is not lost.

3.6.2.5. *Corporation Tax*

The payment into the EBT will be an employee benefit contribution; the corporation tax deduction may therefore be deferred under FA 2003, Sch24 (see section 17.3).

3.6.3. Disclosure

The EBT Trustee is connected with any director who is a beneficiary of the EBT [CA 1985, s346(2)(c)].

Therefore, contributions to the EBT must be disclosed as if they were emoluments payable to the director, although the disclosure can be footnoted to make it clear that the director has no personal entitlement to the funds in the EBT (see section 18.9, paragraph 1).

3.6.3.1. *Matrix Summary of Advantages and Disadvantages of Payments into EBTs*

Feature	Advantage	Disadvantage
Availability	Available to all companies.	Special care needed for close companies
Flexibility	Entirely flexible	
Limits	No limits	
Accounting (p/l)		Contributions charged to p/l when irrevocably allocated to employees
Corporation Tax		Deduction may be postponed until benefits delivered to employees

Feature	Advantage	Disadvantage
Income Tax and NIC	No income tax or NIC on contributions to EBT	
Capital Gains Tax	Offshore EBT is free from capital gains tax	
Inheritance Tax	Assets in EBT outside estate for IHT purposes	

3.6.4. Frequently Asked Questions on Employee Benefit Trusts

3.6.4.1. Can an EBT invest in employing company shares?

This is possible as long as the class of potential beneficiaries is limited to those people who could participate in an **employees' share scheme.** If the class of beneficiaries is wider, then the company cannot normally fund the EBT with the intention that the EBT will invest in its own shares, because this would be unlawful financial assistance. The only way this could be done would be to use the CA 1985, s155 "whitewash" procedure (see section 18.7.6).

3.6.4.2. Is there a capital payment where loans are made or assets are provided to beneficiaries following the termination of employment?

If a non-resident EBT Trustee makes interest-free loans repayable on demand to a beneficiary, this is the provision of a benefit from the trust within TCGA 1992, s97(4). This means that the value of the benefit is a capital payment for the purposes of the capital gains provisions relating to offshore trusts (*Cooper v Billingham* [2001] STC 1177).

However, these provisions apply only where there is a "settlement". HM Revenue & Customs accept that an EBT is not a settlement for these purposes since there is no element of bounty. However, it is treated as a settlement for other purposes.

3.6.4.3. If there is a capital payment, what is the quantum?

If HM Revenue & Customs seek to use the capital payment provisions in relation to an EBT, the value of the interest-free loan will be the difference between a commercial rate of interest and the actual interest paid on the loan.

If the beneficiary is allowed to occupy property rent free the taxable benefit will be the full open market rent.

Details of any capital payments should be reported to HM Revenue & Customs on form 50(FS).

3.7. Share Options

A share **option** plan is a very common way of rewarding and motivating senior employees.

A share **option** plan works in the following way: the employee is granted a right to acquire shares during an **exercise period**, which usually lasts for ten years. Sometimes the employee has to pay a fee or premium in order to be granted the **option** (the **grant price**). Typically the **optionholder** has to pay a price for the shares when he **exercises** the **option** (the **exercise price**); however sometimes there is no **exercise price** – such an **option** is called a "nil-cost" or "zero-cost" **option**.

Often, the **option** will be subject to a **vesting period**, e.g. the **optionholder** cannot **exercise** it for three years, or cannot **exercise** before an initial public offering ("IPO"). It may also be subject to performance conditions, e.g. the **optionholder** cannot **exercise** the **option** unless earnings reach a certain level.

The **optionholder** is therefore motivated to increase the value of the shares; he only benefits from the arrangement if he is able to **exercise** the **option** at a time when the value of the shares is higher than the aggregate of the **grant price** and the **exercise price**. He is also motivated to remain in employment until the end of the **vesting period** and/or the achievement of the performance conditions.

The **optionholder** has no "downside", other than the chance of losing any **grant price** he has paid. If the value of the shares falls to below the **exercise price**, he will not **exercise** the **option**.

Generally, an **optionholder** will not **exercise** the **option** unless he intends to sell the shares immediately. There is usually little point in incurring the cost of exercising the **option** and holding the shares, since the employee benefits from the growth in value anyway.

There are some circumstances where an **optionholder** might choose to **exercise** the **option** and hold the shares. One example would be if the **option** were on the point of expiry, perhaps because the end of the **exercise period** was approaching. Another example would be if the dividend yield on the shares was greater than the cost of financing the **exercise**. A third example would be if there were some particular reason why the **optionholder** wanted to become a shareholder, perhaps to exercise voting rights at a forthcoming meeting or to receive a special dividend.

The most tax-effective form of **option** for senior employees is an **EMI option**, described in section 3.7.6.

If the individual or the shares do not qualify for EMI, then consider establishing a **CSOP** (see section 3.7.8) although the benefits are more limited.

If the **options** can be made available on a non-discriminatory basis, consider establishing an **SAYE** Plan (see section 4.3).

If it is not possible or desirable to establish a **qualified** or **approved plan**, then consider establishing an unapproved option plan, described in section 3.7.5.

3.7.1. Key Features of Share Options

Feature	Comment	See Section
Profit and Loss Account	Theoretical value of **option** calculated and charged to profit and loss account over **vesting period**	19.3
Balance Sheet	Issue of new shares dilutes earnings per share	3.7.3.16
Benefit to Employee	Employee only benefits if able to **exercise** the **option** and obtain shares for less than **market value.**	
Shareholding	Unlikely to encourage employees to become shareholders	
Income Tax and NIC	Generally arises on **exercise**, but may be exempt if **EMI**, **CSOP** or **SAYE option**	3.7.6.8, 3.7.8.9, 4.3.2
Corporation Tax	Gain may be deductible under FA 2003, Sch23 or under general principles	17
Reporting	Annual reporting required	3.7.5.2.3

3.7.2. Company Law Issues

Before establishing a new share option plan, it is necessary to check the corporate procedures with which the company must comply.

3.7.2.1. Corporate Authority

Check that the company has the necessary power in its Memorandum of Association and check whether the directors need the consent of shareholders in order to exercise their power.

Check that the Board has enough members who will not be eligible to receive **options** in order to be able to authorise the establishment of the plan. Depending on the terms of the Articles of Association, a director who is eligible to receive **options** may not be able to vote or be counted in the quorum at the meeting (see section 18.12).

3.7.2.2. Notification to Auditors

The auditors must be notified if the share option plan is to be approved by a written resolution of shareholders [CA 1985, s381B] (see section 18.3).

3.7.2.3. Restrictions on Allotment of Shares

It is therefore important to ensure that the share option plan constitutes an "**employees' share scheme**" as defined in CA 1985, s743, so that the allotment of shares can take place without regard to pre-emption rights (see section 18.6).

3.7.2.4. Financial Assistance

If the **option** gives the **optionholder** the right to purchase shares from an existing shareholder, such as an EBT Trustee, then it is important that any financial assistance given to the **optionholder**, or to the third party shareholder, is legal (see section 18.7).

3.7.2.5. *Disclosure*

The Companies Act disclosure requirements for **option**s are set out in section 18.9, paragraphs 7, 10 and 14.

3.7.3. Designing a Share Option Plan and Drafting the Rules

Share **option**s are usually granted under a written set of Plan Rules. This is because for company law purposes it may be necessary to demonstrate that the **option** has been granted under an "**employees' share scheme**" and it is generally accepted that this requires a written framework of rules (see section 18.8.1).

The Rules of the Plan should set out the provisions that are common to all **option**s granted under the Plan. Any terms that are specific to the **optionholder** should be included in the option agreement or certificate that is issued to him.

There are specific issues to be addressed for **EMI**, **CSOP** and **SAYE** Rules. This section looks at the generic issues for all share **option** plans.

3.7.3.1. *Standard Definitions*

3.7.3.1.1. *Grant date*

The **grant date** or "date of grant" of the **option** is the day on which the **optionholder** acquires the legal rights inherent in the **option**. If the **option** is granted unilaterally by deed, this will be the date the deed is executed. If the **option** is granted following an invitation and acceptance procedure, this will be the day that the employee's acceptance is unconditionally accepted by the grantor of the **option**.

3.7.3.1.2. *Group Member / Participating Company / Constituent Company*

If the Plan is intended to extend to employees from a group of companies, then a definition is needed to determine which companies are capable of being included. The term used is often "Group Member" or "Member of the Group".

Normally, this will use the company law definitions of "**holding company**" and "**subsidiary**" from CA 1985, s736 and s736A.

In relation to the **scheme organiser**, the Group Members will be its **holding company** (if any), its subsidiaries, and any other subsidiaries of its **holding company**. The reason for this is to ensure that the Plan is an **employees' share scheme** as defined in CA 1985, s743 (see section 18.8).

It may be desirable to include a further definition of "Participating Company" or "**constituent company**", which is a Group Member nominated by the Directors to participate in the Plan. This is only necessary if the Company wants to include some Group Members but not others.

The term "Participating Company" may also include **jointly owned companies**, but note that, if it does, the Plan will not be an **employees' share scheme**.

For **EMI**, **CSOP** and **SAYE** purposes, there are further limitations on which companies are allowed to participate. For EMI purposes, only qualifying subsidiaries can be included (see section 3.7.6.3.2). For **CSOP** and **SAYE** purposes, the Plan should be limited to companies of which the **scheme organiser** has **Section 840 control**, and **jointly owned companies** (see sections 3.7.8.3 and 3.7.8.4.2).

3.7.3.1.3. Market value

The Plan may include a definition of **market value**. This definition is used for two purposes. The primary purpose is to feed into the definition of **exercise price**, because frequently the Plan will prohibit **option**s being granted with an **exercise price** which is less than **market value**. This is necessary for a **CSOP** in order for HM Revenue & Customs approval to be available (see section 3.7.8.8.1.7). For an unapproved plan or an **EMI** plan, it is not necessary for tax purposes but may be a requirement imposed by shareholders.

The secondary purpose relates to **option** rollovers. For an **option** rollover to be fair to both parties, the **CGT value** of the shares under the new **option** should be the same as the **CGT value** of those which were under the old **option**, measured at the date of release. This is necessary for the rollover to qualify for EMI purposes [ITEPA 2003, Sch5, para 43(6)] and for an approved rollover of a **CSOP** or **SAYE option** [ITEPA 2003, Sch3, para 39(4)(c) and Sch4, para 27(4)(c)].

If the definition of **market value** is being included for tax purposes, it should refer to TCGA 1992, Part VIII and (unless the shares are listed on a **recognised stock exchange**) will have to be agreed with HMRC Shares Valuation. If it is being included for other purposes, then it can be defined in any other way, perhaps by reference to a formula such as a fixed multiple of earnings.

If the Plan is intended to continue in operation following a flotation, then it should contain a definition of **market value** to be used from flotation onwards. This should refer to the listed price on the last business day before the **grant date**: if it refers to the listed price on the **grant date** itself then this creates the practical difficulty that the price cannot be determined until the market has closed. If the quoted price is volatile, it may be preferable to use an average, perhaps of the last three business days before the **grant date**, so as to smooth out peaks and troughs in the share price.

Note that for **CSOP** and **SAYE** purposes, HM Revenue & Customs will accept the listed price on the London Stock Exchange as being **market value**, but not the price on AIM since that is not a **recognised stock exchange** [HMRC Manual ESS25021][26].

3.7.3.1.4. Normal Retirement Age

If retiring employees are to be treated as "**good leavers**" (see section 3.7.3.8) then a definition of normal retirement age should be included. Note that, for **CSOP** and **SAYE** purposes, this has to be the same for both men and women and cannot be less than 55 (see section 3.7.8.8.1.11).

It is potentially discriminatory under the Employment Equality (Age) Regulations 2006 to define "retirement" by reference to reaching a particular age. The concern is that this discriminates against younger employees who choose to retire from the labour market. One solution is to define "retirement" as ceasing to engage in gainful economic activity, at whatever age.

3.7.3.1.5. Option

The term **option** should be defined as a right to acquire, or purchase, or subscribe for, shares.

If the word "purchase" is used, then the **option** can only be satisfied by the transfer of existing shares, whereas if the phrase "subscribe for" is used, the **option** can only be satisfied by the issue of new shares. Using the word "acquire" is usually preferable, because it allows the company flexibility to satisfy the **option** using either method.

It is important to determine whether the **option** does in fact give the **optionholder** a legal right to have shares delivered to him, even though that right may be conditional. If the company can choose to satisfy the **option** by delivering cash to the **optionholder**, then it will not be a "**securities option**" and therefore not be within the scope of ITEPA 2003, Part 7, Chapter 5 (see section 8.1.1).

3.7.3.1.6. Share

It is usual to include a definition of a "share", particularly if the company has more than one class of share capital, so as to set out which class (or classes) of share can be used in the Plan.

Note that for EMI purposes, the shares used must be **ordinary share capital** (see section 3.7.6.3.6). For **CSOP** and **SAYE** purposes, the shares must satisfy the tests described in sections 3.7.8.3.1 to 3.7.8.3.5 inclusive.

---

[26] http://www.hmrc.gov.uk/manuals/essumanual/essu25000/essu25021.htm

3.7.3.1.7. Exit

If the company is being prepared for a shareholder exit, it may be sensible for the Rules to provide that the exit changes the status of the **option**s in some way, probably by allowing some or all of them to become **exercisable**. If so, a definition of "Exit" needs to be included. This will probably define Exit as either a Listing or a Sale. "Listing" will be defined as the admission of the company's shares to dealing on a regulated market such as AIM or the London Stock Exchange. "Sale" needs to be carefully defined so that it does not include a change of control arising from a group reorganisation, perhaps preparatory to a flotation.

3.7.3.1.8. Eligible Employee

The Rules should contain a definition of "Eligible Employee", which says who is eligible to receive and **exercise option**s under the Plan.

If the Plan is to be an **employees' share scheme**, then it must exclude people who are not employees, such as consultants (see section 18.8.4).

Note that there are special rules for eligibility under EMI (see section 3.7.6.4), **CSOP** (see sections 3.7.8.5.1 and 3.7.8.5.2) and **SAYE** (see section 4.3.1.4).

3.7.3.2. *Grant of Options*

3.7.3.2.1. Who has Power to Grant Options

The Rules should state who has power to grant **option**s. Normally this will be the Board of Directors, but it may have delegated this power to the Remuneration Committee.

If the **option**s are to be granted over shares held by a third party, such as an EBT, then it may be necessary to provide that the third party has to agree in advance to the grant of **option**s.

3.7.3.2.2. Who can Receive Options

The Rules should provide that **option**s can only be granted to eligible employees (see section 3.7.3.1.8).

3.7.3.2.3. When can Options be Granted

It may be desirable to provide that **option**s can only be granted at certain periods in the year, perhaps following the auditing of the accounts. However, this is not necessary for an unlisted company, which is more likely to want the flexibility to be able to **grant option**s to new hires as and when they join.

3.7.3.2.4. How is an Option Granted

An **option** should be a legally binding obligation of the grantor. If the grantor is a company incorporated in Great Britain, this usually means that it is executed as a deed in accordance with CA 1985, s36A and s36B.

Alternatively, the **option** could be granted using an "invitation and acceptance" procedure, whereby the company offers the **option** to the employee who accepts by paying the **grant price**.

SAYE options are always granted by invitation and acceptance (see section 4.3.1.8.1.4).

3.7.3.3. *Exercise price*

The **exercise price** is usually fixed on the **grant date**. However, it can be variable, perhaps depending on a formula, although this is unusual since it is difficult to communicate to employees and therefore diminishes the incentive effect of the Plan.

The Rules should either state that the **exercise price** cannot be less than the nominal value of the shares, or set out what is to happen if an employee **exercises** an **option** and pays an **exercise price** which is less than the nominal value of the shares.

The issue here is that a company cannot issue shares for less than their nominal value [CA 1985, s100] (see section 18.4).

One way around this is for the company to capitalise sufficient distributable profits on the **exercise date** to pay the difference between the **exercise price** and the nominal value – it can then credit the shares as **fully paid up**. However, this is of course only possible if it has sufficient distributable profits at that time.

Another possibility is for the company not to issue shares but instead to arrange for the **optionholder** to purchase existing shares from another shareholder (see section 3.7.3.17).

3.7.3.4. *Performance Conditions*

The company should consider making the **options** subject to the achievement of performance conditions. Normally, the Rules will contain the power to impose performance conditions, but the detailed terms of those conditions will be set out in the **option** agreement or certificate. This gives the Directors power to tailor the performance conditions to particular **optionholders** without amending the Rules.

Ideally, performance conditions should relate to the tasks that the Directors want the company, or the individual **optionholder**, to achieve within the **vesting period**. For example, if the company is aiming for a flotation, the performance conditions should relate to the company achieving the necessary level of performance for a successful flotation to occur.

It is usual to provide that performance conditions must be objective and to limit the Directors' power to make subsequent changes to them. This is particularly important for a **CSOP** (see section 3.7.8.8.1.5).

Note that there is a difference in accounting terms between market-based and non-market-based performance criteria (see section 19.3.5).

3.7.3.5. Individual Limits

The Plan Rules will often contain a limit on the size of **option**s that can be **grant**ed to any individual employee. This is not a tax or legal requirement, but is included to reflect the terms upon which shareholders have authorised the Plan.

The limit will usually be expressed as a multiple of salary, but could be expressed as a fixed number or value of shares. Shareholders may require **option**s that have been **exercise**d, or which have been cancelled or renounced, to continue to count against the limits.

In addition, the Rules of a **CSOP** or **SAYE** Plan must contain limits on individual participation (see sections 3.7.8.5.3 and 4.3.1.5.4).

There are limits on the size of awards that can be made under an **EMI** Plan (see sections 3.7.6.5.1.2.1 and 3.7.6.5.1.2.2). There is no obligation to include these limits in the Plan Rules; but in practice many companies do so.

3.7.3.6. Overall Limits

The Plan Rules will often contain a limit on the overall number of **option**s that can be granted through the Plan. As with the individual limits, this is not a tax or legal requirement, but is included to reflect the terms upon which shareholders have authorised the Plan.

The limit will usually be expressed as a percentage of share capital, but could be expressed as a fixed number of shares. Normally, shareholders will require **option**s that have been **exercise**d to count against the limits, but not **option**s that have lapsed or been cancelled.

There is a limit on the overall value of shares that can be put under **option** through an **EMI** Plan (see section 3.7.6.5.1.2.3). There is no obligation to include this limit in the Plan Rules; but in practice many companies do so.

3.7.3.7. Vesting period

The Rules will usually include a **vesting period** on **option**s. The length of the **vesting period** should depend on the company's needs in relation to the particular employee or group of employees who will receive **option**s. If the company is trying to lock in the employees to perform a particular task or achieve a particular goal, then it may be sensible to link the **vesting period** to the expected time for achievement of that goal. For example, if the company has a three-year business plan that it wants to achieve, it may be appropriate to have a three-year **vesting period** on the **option**s.

3.7.3.8. Treatment of Departing Employees

The Rules should set out whether an employee should be allowed to **exercise** an **option** following termination of employment. It is normal to make a distinction between "good leavers" and "bad leavers". "Good leavers" are allowed to **exercise** their **option** for a period of, say, six months following termination of employment. A "bad leaver" forfeits his **option** unless the Board of Directors determines otherwise. The Board must **exercise** this power reasonably; it cannot **exercise** it in a "perverse or irrational" way, because to do so would potentially give the employee a right to compensation for loss of **option** rights [*Mallone v BPB Industries plc* [2002] IRLR 452] (see section 3.7.3.22).

Note that there are special rules on the way departing employees can be treated for **CSOP** and **SAYE**. See section 3.7.8.8.1.11 for **CSOP** and sections 4.3.1.8.1.10 to 4.3.1.8.1.13 for **SAYE**.

Examples of "good leaver" reasons for termination are:

- death;
- injury, ill health or disability;
- **redundancy**;
- **retirement** - although it may not be appropriate to **grant** an **option** to someone who is likely to retire before the end of the **vesting period**, and defining "retirement" by reference to a particular age may constitute unlawful age discrimination;
- wrongful or unfair dismissal – it is common to find that **optionholder**s who are unfairly dismissed following a change of control are allowed to **exercise** their **options**. This enables an **optionholder** who believes he has been unfairly dismissed to purport to **exercise** his **option**, and bring this into account in an action against the new owners;
- sale of the business in which the **optionholder** works;
- sale of the **subsidiary** that employs the **optionholder**.

Examples of "bad leaver" reasons for termination are:

- resignation
- dismissal for cause

Note however that, if a good leaver is allowed to **exercise** his **option** while the shares remain unlisted, it may be desirable for the Articles to include a provision compelling him to offer the shares for sale.

The Rules should set out the rights of an **optionholder** who takes parental leave; this provision needs careful drafting to avoid any breach of employment law. It is important that time spent on parental leave should count towards the **vesting period**. Secondly, if the **optionholder** fails to return from parental leave, it is important to be able to determine exactly when the employment ceased.

The Rules also need to provide for continuity of employment for **optionholder**s transferred within the group. In other words, the transfer of an **optionholder** from one group company to another should not cause the **option** to lapse.

3.7.3.9. Accelerated Vesting on Flotation

If the company is aiming for a flotation, it may be desirable to allow some or all of the **option**s to become **exercisable** immediately following the flotation. This acts as an incentive to the management to achieve the necessary conditions for flotation and a reward for the efforts made in securing a successful flotation.

However, there are two difficulties with this approach. The first is that if all the **option**s are allowed to **vest**, it will be necessary to install new incentive arrangements to retain the **optionholder**s after the flotation.

The second is that the sponsors of the flotation may not be willing to allow senior employees to sell their shares for a period of time; in which case it would be pointless for them to **exercise** their **option**s.

A compromise would be to allow, say, one third of **option**s to **vest** on flotation, another third after 12 months, and the remaining third after 24 months.

3.7.3.10. Change of Control

A change of control of the company could happen for two reasons.

First, it could happen because a new **holding company** is imposed as part of a group reorganisation, perhaps in preparation for a flotation; in these circumstances it is unlikely to be appropriate for **option**s to become **exercisable**.

Second, it could happen because an unconnected third party acquires the company, perhaps through a trade sale. In these circumstances **optionholder**s may feel uncertain about their future employment prospects and care has to be taken to decide whether it is appropriate for them to be allowed to **exercise** their **option**s prematurely.

Another consideration is that, if the company's shares are currently **corporation tax deductible shares**, but the acquirer is an unlisted company, then the relief will not be available for **option**s that are **exercise**d after the change of control has occurred (see section 17.4).

Consider including the following provisions in the Rules of the Plan:

- The Rules should distinguish between a change of control arising from a group reorganisation and one arising from an acquisition of the company by a third party. In the case of a group reorganisation, **option**s should not become **exercisable**. Instead they should be automatically exchanged for **option**s in the new **holding company**. Note however that it will not be possible to include an automatic exchange provision in the Rules of a **CSOP** or **SAYE** Plan (see section 21.4, box 3).

- The Rules should allow the Directors to declare all or some **options** to be **exercisable** if they believe that a change of control is about to occur, and that relief under FA 2003, Sch23 will not be available for **options exercised** after the change of control. The Directors would not exercise this power unless they were certain that the change of control would occur.
- The Rules may allow **optionholders** to **exercise** their **options** in the event of a change of control. If there are performance conditions attached to the **options**, then it may be appropriate that only a proportion of the **options** should be **exercisable**, depending on the extent to which the performance conditions have been achieved.
- The Rules may contain a provision for **optionholders** to release their **options** in exchange for **options** over shares in the acquirer. This is necessary in the Rules of a **CSOP** or **SAYE** Plan to allow the **options** to retain their approved status (see section 3.7.8.8.1.13). It is not necessary in **EMI** or unapproved plans.
- The Rules of an EMI or unapproved plan may provide that the **optionholders** cannot **exercise** any unvested **options** if the acquirer offers an exchange of **options**. This enables the acquirer to lock in the **optionholders** by **granting** **options** to them over its own shares in exchange for their existing **options**.
- The Rules should provide that **options** lapse after a reasonable time if they are not either **exercised** or exchanged for **options** over the acquirer's shares. Normally this is six months. However, if the provisions for the compulsory buying-in of minorities are invoked under CA 1985, s429 to s430F, then the **options** should lapse when the acquirer ceases to be bound or entitled to purchase the resulting shares.

3.7.3.11. Exercise Process and Delivery of Shares

The Rules must set out the process for exercising an **option**. Normally, the **optionholder** has to provide the Company Secretary with the **option** certificate, a notice of exercise, and a cheque for the **exercise price**. In addition, the **optionholder** should provide the company with a cheque for any PAYE or NIC he has to pay (see section 3.7.3.13), unless he has made alternative arrangements for paying these. If the **optionholder** fails to make good the PAYE within 90 days there will be an additional charge under ITEPA 2003, s222 (see section 3.7.3.14).

The company should then issue, or procure the transfer of, the shares to the **optionholder** within a fixed period of time – usually 30 days. It is usual to provide that newly issued shares rank *pari passu* in all respects with the shares already in issue, except that they do not rank for any rights attaching to shares by reference to a record date preceding the **exercise date**.

3.7.3.12. Non-Transferability

EMI, **CSOP** and **SAYE options** must not be transferable except on death (see sections 3.7.6.5.2.3 and 3.7.8.8.1.10).

Unapproved options can be transferable, but they rarely are since the purpose of the **option** is to motivate the **optionholder**, and this motivation could be lost or diluted if the **optionholder** no longer personally benefited from the **option**. There may, however, be inheritance tax planning opportunities available through transferring an **option** to a family trust. Note, however, that there may not be any income tax saving through a transfer of an **option** (see section 8.5).

3.7.3.13. PAYE and NIC Indemnity or Transfer

The Rules should include a provision entitling the company to recover from the **optionholder** any PAYE or primary NIC arising from the **exercise**. There is no statutory right to recover PAYE except from the salary for the month of **exercise**. Primary NIC can be deducted from the sale proceeds of the shares, but only with the written consent of the **optionholder** (see section 9.1).

In addition, the Rules should contain power for the company to require the **optionholder** to enter into an indemnity or transfer agreement in respect of secondary NIC (see section 9.2). The Directors may not intend to use this power for every **option**, but should nevertheless have the power.

Each of these provisions should include the right to sell the shares on the **optionholder**'s behalf and recover the income tax or NIC from the sale proceeds. Otherwise the **optionholder** may be subject to a further tax charge under ITEPA 2003, s222 (see section 3.7.3.14).

3.7.3.14. Section 222 Liability

ITEPA 2003, s222 applies where an employer makes a "notional payment" to an employee, for which it is required to account for PAYE, but there is insufficient cash remuneration from which the employer can deduct PAYE, and the employee fails to "make good" the tax to the employer within 90 days of the chargeable event.

Examples of "notional payments" are the **exercise** of **options** or the **vesting** of shares, which can give rise to PAYE withholding obligations, but where there is no cash from which to withhold PAYE.

Where ITEPA 2003, s222 applies, the employee is treated as having received additional earnings equal to the amount of tax that is not made good. This amount is also subject to NIC [SSCR 2001, reg 22(4)].

"Making good" is not a fully defined concept, but it means that the employee must bear the economic cost. For example, the employee will "make good" by allowing the employer to sell some of the shares and withhold the PAYE from the proceeds.

3.7.3.15. Section 431(1) election

The Rules should contain power for the company to require the **optionholder** to enter into a **Section 431(1) election** on the **exercise date**, as a condition for being allowed to **exercise** the **option**. The Directors would only use this power if the shares were **restricted securities** on the **exercise date**. By making the election, the Directors would protect the company against a future uncapped exposure to NIC, at the expense of a possibly larger immediate income tax liability for the employee and a possibly larger immediate NIC liability (see section 22.2.2).

Note that an **optionholder** who **exercises** a **CSOP option**, an **SAYE option** or an **EMI option** in circumstances where income tax relief is available on the full gain, is deemed to make a Section 431 election [ITEPA 2003, s431A].

3.7.3.16. Variation of share capital

The Rules should provide for the **options** to be adjusted to reflect a **variation of share capital**, such as a capitalisation or rights issue. The procedures for making the adjustments are described in section 13.3.1.

A problem can arise if the **options** are to be satisfied by issuing new shares, and the adjustment would cause the **exercise price** to be less than the nominal value of the shares. In these circumstances, the adjustment cannot be made unless the company is able to capitalise sufficient reserves to pay up the difference between the nominal value of the shares and the **exercise price** (see section 18.4).

Note that there are special rules for adjusting **approved options** and **qualifying options** (see section 3.7.8.8.1.8 for **approved options** and sections 3.7.6.8.1 and 3.7.6.7.1.8 for **qualifying options**).

3.7.3.17. Availability of Shares

The Rules will usually impose an obligation on the company either to keep available sufficient authorised but unissued shares to be able to satisfy all outstanding **options**, or to be able to procure the transfer of sufficient existing shares. A failure to comply with this obligation would give the **optionholder** the right to sue the company for damages.

HM Revenue & Customs will not approve a **CSOP** or **SAYE** Plan unless this obligation is included.

3.7.3.18. Interpretation Clause

The Rules should provide that the Directors have power to interpret the Rules, and that their interpretation is final in the case of any dispute.

3.7.3.19. Costs of Establishment and Administration

The Rules should state who is to bear the costs of establishing and administering the Plan. In the case of a group plan, it may be appropriate for the costs to be borne by the employing subsidiaries and there could be transfer pricing issues if the costs are not charged to the subsidiaries (see section 17.9).

3.7.3.20. *Amendments to the Plan*

The Rules should set out the procedure for amending the Plan. Normally, the Directors will have the power to do this. However, certain provisions may be "protected", so that they cannot be amended without the consent of the shareholders. This will only be the case if the shareholders originally had to authorise the establishment of the Plan (see section 3.7.2.1), in which case they may have reserved the right also to approve amendments to particular provisions, such as any limits clauses.

Since the Rules form part of a contract between the company and each **optionholder**, it is usual to provide that **optionholders** have to consent to any amendment that adversely affects **options** that have already been **granted**. Generally the Rules will provide that any such amendment has to be approved either by 75% of **optionholders** voting at a meeting, or by a resolution in writing approved by **optionholders** who together hold at least 75% of the **options** by value.

Note that amendments to a key feature of a **CSOP** or **SAYE** Plan must be approved by HM Revenue & Customs in advance (see section 3.7.8.8.1.16).

3.7.3.21. *Termination Clause*

The Rules will usually contain a provision that no further **options** can be granted after a particular date – generally the tenth anniversary of the establishment of the Plan. This is not a legal requirement, but is often required by shareholders so that they have an opportunity to review the share incentive arrangements and decide whether to authorise a continuation of them.

3.7.3.22. *Loss of Employment*

The Rules should provide that an **optionholder** has no claim to damages for loss of **option** rights if his employment is terminated.

In *Mallone v BPB Industries plc*, the court held that an **optionholder** did have the right to compensation for loss of **option** rights, if the Directors refused to let him **exercise** his **option** through a "perverse or irrational" use of their powers.

3.7.3.23. *Pensionability*

The Rules will usually provide that neither the value of an **option** nor any gain on exercise form part of the **optionholder**'s pensionable income. This is not a legal requirement: an option gain does count as **relevant UK earnings.**

3.7.4. Sources of Shares

There are two main sources of shares to be provided to an employee: the company can issue new shares, or another shareholder can sell existing shares to the employee.

The profit and loss account impact of each of these routes is identical (see section 19.3).

3.7.4.1. *Issue of New Shares*

This has the advantage that it raises new capital for the company. However, all existing shareholders are proportionately diluted. The company cannot issue new shares for less than their nominal value unless it is able to capitalise sufficient reserves to pay up the discount.

3.7.4.2. *Purchase of Existing Shares*

This is only possible if an existing shareholder is willing to sell his shares. Typically this is achieved through an EBT, which purchases shares from people who are willing or obliged to sell them, and then sells them when **award**s are made or **option**s are **exercise**d. The EBT can, for example, purchase shares from a departing employee shareholder if the Articles require him to offer those shares for sale.

The CGT consequences for the EBT are set out in section 10.4.2.6 for onshore trusts and section 10.4.3 for offshore trusts. The CGT treatment of an individual shareholder would be the same as for the EBT depending on whether he was **resident** or not **resident** in the UK for capital gains tax purposes.

The inheritance tax consequences for the EBT are set out in sections 10.4.1.4 and 10.4.1.5. If an individual were to grant an option, this could be a transfer of value, unless the exclusion for commercial transactions in IHTA 1984, s10 applied. It is not clear whether the grant of an option over shares in an unquoted trading company qualifies for business property relief under IHTA 1984, s104.

3.7.5. Unapproved options

3.7.5.1. *Tax Treatment of Employee*

See section 8.1.1

3.7.5.1.1. PAYE

See section 8.1.2.5

3.7.5.1.2. NIC

See section 8.1.3.1.

3.7.5.1.3. Reporting

See section 8.1.5.

3.7.5.1.4. Capital Gains Treatment

See section 8.1.4.1

3.7.5.2. *Tax Treatment of Employer*

3.7.5.2.1. *Corporation Tax Deductibility*

See section 17.4.3.

3.7.5.2.2. *NIC*

See section 8.1.3.1.

3.7.5.2.3. *Reporting*

See section 8.1.5.

3.7.5.3. *Accounting Treatment*

See section 19.3.6.5.

3.7.5.4. *Sources of Shares*

See section 3.7.4.

3.7.5.5. *Matrix Summary of Advantages and Disadvantages of Share Options*

Feature	**Advantage**	**Disadvantage**
Availability	Available to all companies	
Flexibility	Entirely flexible	
Limits	No limits	
Accounting (p/l)		Fair value of **option** charged to p/l and spread over **vesting period**
Accounting (balance sheet)		Issue of new shares dilutes existing shareholders
Corporation Tax	Deduction may be available for **option gain** on **exercise**	
Income Tax and NIC		PAYE and NIC on **exercise** if **readily convertible assets**
Capital Gains Tax		Business Asset Taper Relief period starts from **exercise date**

3.7.5.6. *Frequently Asked Questions on Unapproved Share Options*

3.7.5.6.1. *What happens if the optionholder suffers a loss because the value of the shares falls after the exercise date but before he sells them?*

There will be no adjustment to the amount charged to tax as employment income. However, the individual will realise a capital loss. In some circumstances it is possible to set a capital loss against taxable income [ICTA 1988, s574] (see section 12.12).

3.7.5.6.2. *If the optionholder dies, what is the tax treatment if his personal representatives exercise the option?*

The gain on **exercise** is not chargeable to income tax [ITEPA 2003, s477(2)].

The value of the **option** at the date of death will form part of the **optionholder**'s estate for inheritance tax purposes.

If the personal representatives **exercise** the **option** and sell the shares, their base cost will be the value of the **option** at death plus the **exercise price**. In practice this means that the capital gain will be the growth in value of the shares after death.

3.7.5.6.3. *If an optionholder is unfairly or wrongfully dismissed, can he sue for loss of option rights?*

Possibly, yes, even if the Rules of the Plan specifically seek to exclude this.

3.7.5.6.4. *If an individual grants an option, how is he taxed?*

The **grant** of the **option** is a disposal for CGT purposes. However, CGT will be charged only on the **grant price**, if there is any. This is because there is no **market value** substitution in relation to the **grant** of the **option** [TCGA 1992, s149A].

The **grant** of the **option** may also be a transfer of value for IHT purposes unless the exception in IHTA 1984, s10 for commercial transactions applies. It is unclear whether the grant of an option over business property qualifies for relief under IHTA 1984, s104.

3.7.5.6.5. *If an individual sells shares to the optionholder on the exercise of an option, how is he taxed?*

The sale of the shares is a disposal for CGT purposes. There is no **market value** substitution [TCGA 1992, s144ZA]. Therefore CGT will be calculated by reference to the **exercise price** of the **option**.

Taper relief will run from the **exercise date** of the **option**.

3.7.5.6.6. *Is there an inheritance tax charge if a close company grants a share option?*

In principle, if a **close company grant**s an **option** to an individual where there is a **discount at grant**, this is prima facie a chargeable transfer of value [IHTA 1984, s94].

However, the exclusion in IHTA 1984, s10(1) should apply to a standard option plan being set up to reward and remunerate employees.

3.7.6. EMI Options

3.7.6.1. Description

An Enterprise Management Incentive ("**EMI**") **option** is a highly tax-efficient form of incentive. If all the relevant conditions are met, there is actually a tax subsidy, in the sense that the corporation tax relief given to the employing company can be greater than the amount of tax paid by the **optionholder**.

An EMI **option** has the following potential advantages over other forms of reward:

- no income tax charge on the **exercise** of the **option**, assuming that there is no **discount at grant** and no disqualifying event occurs (see section 8.2.1.2.1);

- taper relief for the shares starts to run from the **grant date** of the **option** rather than the **exercise date** (see section 8.2.4);
- the employer may be able to claim a corporation tax deduction when the **option** is **exercised** (see section 17.4)
- the shares used can be subject to restrictions, such as limited voting or dividend rights, as long as they are **ordinary share capital**.

The conditions are set out in section 3.7.6.2 below.

3.7.6.2. Checklist for Granting an EMI Option

For an **option** to be a "**qualifying option**" for **EMI** purposes, certain conditions must be satisfied. Some of these conditions apply to the **option** itself; some to the company whose shares are used ("the **relevant company**"); others to any employee who is to receive the **option**.

If there is any doubt as to whether the company qualifies for **EMI**, apply to HMRC Small Company Enterprise Support Centre for advance assurance.

Here is a checklist to go through before establishing an **EMI** Plan and granting a **qualifying option**. The checklist

- first - determines whether the company and its shares meet the relevant requirements
- second – determines whether the employee in question is eligible to be granted an **EMI option**
- third – determines whether the terms of the **option** qualify as an **EMI option**.

Requirement	**ITEPA 2003, Sch5**	**Commentary**
Does the **relevant company** satisfy the independence requirement?	Para 9	3.7.6.3
Does the **relevant company** satisfy the qualifying subsidiaries requirement?	Para 10	3.7.6.3.2
Does the **relevant company** satisfy the property managing subsidiaries requirement	Para 11A	3.7.6.3.3
Does the **relevant company** satisfy the gross assets requirement?	Para 12	3.7.6.3.4
Does the **relevant company** satisfy the trading activities requirement?	Paras 13 to 23	3.7.6.3.5
Do the shares in the **relevant company** qualify?	Para 35	3.7.6.3.6
Does the employee meet the employment requirement?	Para 25	3.7.6.4.1
Does the employee meet the working time requirement?	Para 26	3.7.6.4.2
Does the employee meet the "no **material**	Para 28	3.7.6.4.3

Requirement	ITEPA 2003, Sch5	Commentary
interest" requirement?		
Does the **option** meet the purpose test?	Para 4	3.7.6.5.1.1
Is the **option** within the £100,000 limit on unexercised **options**?	Para 5	3.7.6.5.1.2.1
Is the **option** within the £100,000 three year limit?	Para 6	3.7.6.5.1.2.2
Is the **option** within the £3 million limit	Para 7	3.7.6.5.1.2.3
Is the **option** capable of **exercise** within ten years?	Para 36	3.7.6.5.2.1
Is there an appropriately worded written agreement?	Para 37	3.7.6.5.2.2

3.7.6.3. Qualification Requirements for the Relevant Company and its Shares

3.7.6.3.1. Independence Requirement

There are three limbs to the independence requirement, each of which must be satisfied.

First, the **relevant company** must not be a **51% Subsidiary** of any other company [ITEPA 2003, Sch5, para 9(2)(a)].

Second, the **relevant company** must not be under the **Section 840 control** of any other company, or under the joint control of another company and a **connected person** of that other company [ITEPA 2003, Sch5, para 9(2)(b)].

Finally, there must be no arrangements in existence that would cause the **relevant company** to fail either of the first two limbs [ITEPA 2003, Sch5, para 9(3)]. However, the **relevant company** can make arrangements for a group reorganisation that does not cause a change of the underlying control, in other words a "qualifying exchange of shares" [ITEPA 2003, Sch5, para 9(4)].

Sometimes an external investor holds a warrant or convertible instrument which, if exercised or converted, would give that investor control of the **relevant company.** If the investor could exercise or convert the right at any time, then the **relevant company** would fail the independence requirement. However, if the right cannot be exercised unless a future event occurs, and that event may never occur, then HM Revenue & Customs have accepted in certain cases that this is not an arrangement that causes a failure of the independence requirement.

If the **relevant company** is controlled by a partnership that includes a company, then it seems it cannot pass the independence requirement. This is because the corporate partner will be connected to the other partners.

The first and second of these limbs must be satisfied both on the **grant date** of the **option** and throughout the lifetime of the **option**. If either ceases to be satisfied, there will be a disqualifying event [ITEPA 2003, s534(1)(a) and (b)].

3.7.6.3.2. Qualifying Subsidiaries Requirement

The **relevant company** can satisfy the qualifying subsidiaries requirement either by having no subsidiaries at all, or by having "subsidiaries", all of which are "qualifying subsidiaries" [ITEPA 2003, Sch5, para 10(1)].

A "subsidiary", for these purposes, means a company of which the **relevant company** has **Section 416 control**, either alone or jointly with a **connected person** [ITEPA 2003, Sch5, para 10(2)].

A subsidiary is a "qualifying subsidiary" if

- it is a **51% subsidiary** of the **relevant company** [ITEPA 2003, Sch5, para 11(2)(ca)]; and
- it is not under the **Section 840 control** of any person other than the **relevant company** or another one of its subsidiaries [ITEPA 2003, Sch5, para 11(2)(d)]

There must not be any arrangements in existence by virtue of which either of these conditions would cease to be met [ITEPA 2003, Sch5, para 11(2)(e)]. However, a subsidiary does not cease to be a qualifying subsidiary just because it is wound up for commercial reasons [ITEPA 2003, Sch5, para 11(4)], disposed of for commercial reasons [ITEPA 2003, Sch5, para 11(6)] or goes into administration or receivership for commercial reasons [ITEPA 2003, Sch5, para 11(8)]. Note that the winding up, disposal, administration or receivership must not be carried out for tax avoidance purposes.

3.7.6.3.3. Property Managing Subsidiaries Requirement

The **relevant company** will not qualify for EMI if it has a property managing subsidiary that is not its "qualifying 90% subsidiary" [ITEPA 2003, Sch5, para 11A(1)].

The term "qualifying 90% subsidiary" is defined in detail in ITEPA 2003, Sch5, para 11B. Effectively the **relevant company** must own at least 90% of the share capital, voting rights and rights to return of capital, and there must be no arrangements in place whereby this could cease to be true.

3.7.6.3.4. Gross Assets Requirement

The EMI legislation is aimed at smaller companies. The gross assets requirement means that it cannot apply to larger companies or groups.

If the **relevant company** is a "single company", i.e. it does not have any subsidiaries, its gross assets recorded on a balance sheet drawn up immediately prior to the grant of the option must not exceed £30 million [ITEPA 2003, Sch5, para 12(1)].

If the **relevant company** is the **parent company** of a group, the test relates to the gross assets of the group [ITEPA 2003, Sch5, para 12(2)].

HM Revenue & Customs' interpretation of the gross assets test for a group is set out in SP2/00. This says that the consolidated gross assets are not relevant. Instead, what is relevant is the gross assets of the individual companies ignoring inter company indebtedness, investments in subsidiaries, and goodwill arising on consolidation. This is important because it allows the company, in effect, to ignore goodwill arising on the purchase of a subsidiary, which would appear in the consolidated balance sheet, but not in the solus accounts of the **parent company**.

If the company or group grows, so that it no longer satisfies the gross assets requirement, this is not a disqualifying event, so it does not affect the status of **option**s already granted. However, no new **qualifying option**s can be granted by that company.

3.7.6.3.5. Trading Activities Requirement

The EMI legislation was not intended to reward growth in share values that arises from growth in underlying asset values, or from financial trades. To achieve this, it includes the concepts of a "qualifying trade", "non-qualifying activities" and "excluded activities". These are defined below.

Note that the **relevant company** must meet the trading activities requirement both at the **grant date** and throughout the **option period**. If it fails to meet this requirement there will be a disqualifying event [ITEPA 2003, s534(1)(c)].

Furthermore, if the **relevant company** met the trading requirement only because it was preparing to carry on a qualifying trade, there will be a disqualifying event if it ceases to make those preparations or it fails to commence that qualifying trade within two years following the **grant date** [ITEPA 2003, s534(4)].

3.7.6.3.5.1 Application to a Single Company

If the **relevant company** is a "single company" it must exist wholly for the purpose of carrying on one or more qualifying trades, and it must actually be carrying on a qualifying trade, or preparing to do so [ITEPA 2003, Sch5, para 13(1)].

The company is allowed to hold and use property if that property is used for the purposes of the qualifying trade or trades [ITEPA 2003, Sch5, para 13(2)(a)]. It is also allowed to exist for other purposes that are either not significant, or are significant only in relation to incidental matters [ITEPA 2003, Sch5, para 13(2)(b)].

3.7.6.3.5.2 Application to a Group of companies

Where the **relevant company** is the **parent company** of a group, then

- at least one group company must exist wholly for the purpose of carrying on one or more "qualifying trades", and must actually be carrying on a qualifying trade, or preparing to do so [ITEPA 2003, Sch5, para 14(1)(a)]; and
- the business of the group as a whole must not consist, wholly or substantially, in carrying on non-qualifying activities [ITEPA 2003, Sch5, para 14(1)(b)].

The business of the group means all the activities of the group as if they were regarded as one business [ITEPA 2003, Sch5, para 14(2)]. The meaning of the word "substantially" in this context is unclear. Guidance was formerly given in HM Revenue & Customs Manual that it meant more than 20%, but it could be judged on turnover, or capital employed, or other factors. However, this guidance appears to have been withdrawn.

Some transactions that would ordinarily be excluded activities, i.e. holding shares or securities and making loans, are ignored provided they take place between group companies [ITEPA 2003, Sch5, para 14(3)(a)].

Similarly, it is acceptable for a group company to hold and manage property, provided this is used for the purposes of a qualifying trade or trades [ITEPA 2003, Sch5, para 14(3)(b)].

If a group company meets the trading activities requirement for a single company (see section 3.7.6.3.5.1), then any incidental activities it carries out are ignored [ITEPA 2003, Sch5, para 14(3)(c)].

The group may also exist for other purposes that are either not significant, or are significant only in relation to incidental matters [ITEPA 2003, Sch5, para 14(4)(b)].

3.7.6.3.5.3 Qualifying Trade

3.7.6.3.5.3.1 Carried on wholly or mainly in the UK

A qualifying trade is one that is carried on wholly or mainly in the United Kingdom [ITEPA 2003, Sch5, para 15(1)(a)]. It is acceptable for a company to sell its goods and services outside the UK, but if the overseas activities grow to a point where they may become more than half its total business, then it should consider putting the foreign activities into a separate subsidiary. The group as a whole can continue to satisfy the trading requirement provided at least one company is trading wholly or mainly in the United Kingdom [ITEPA 2003, Sch5, para 14(1)(a)(i)].

Conversely, if the **parent company** is foreign, it may still qualify for **EMI** provided it has at least one subsidiary that is trading predominantly in the UK.

3.7.6.3.5.3.2 Conducted on a Commercial Basis and with a view to the Realisation of Profits

A qualifying trade must be conducted on a commercial basis and with a view to realising profits [ITEPA 2003, Sch5, para 15(1)(b)].

Research and development can itself be a qualifying trade but only if it is intended that a separate qualifying trade should derive or benefit from the fruits of the research and development [ITEPA 2003, Sch5, para 15(2)]. "Research and development" in this context means whatever is regarded as such in accordance with generally accepted accounting practice, as modified by the Research and Development (Prescribed Activities) Regulations, SI 2004/712 [ICTA 1988, s837A].

Preparing to carry out research and development on its own does not constitute preparing to carry on a qualifying trade [ITEPA 2003, Sch5, para 15(3)].

3.7.6.3.5.3.3 Not carrying on excluded activities

A qualifying trade cannot consist (either wholly or as to a substantial part) in the carrying on of excluded activities [ITEPA 2003, Sch5, para 15(1)(c)].

3.7.6.3.5.4 Excluded Activities

The excluded activities are set out in full in ITEPA 2003, Sch5, para 16, as supplemented by paras 17 to 23. They fall into four categories:

- financial-based businesses such as banking and leasing;
- property-based businesses, such as nursing homes, farming and hotels;
- accounting and legal businesses;
- providing services or facilities to a closely associated business.

The first two are presumably excluded because the value of such a business can increase because of factors outside the control of management, such as property prices or interest rates. The third is perhaps so that such firms cannot set up service companies and grant EMI options to their employees to deliver tax-free reward.

In any case of doubt as to whether particular activities are excluded, it is best to ask HM Revenue & Customs for their views. The staff at the Small Companies Enterprise Centre ("SCEC") are particularly helpful.

3.7.6.3.5.5 Non-Qualifying Activities

Non-qualifying activities are excluded activities, and activities carried out otherwise than in the course of a trade [ITEPA 2003, Sch5, para 14(5)(c)].

3.7.6.3.6. Tests applying to the Shares

The shares must be **ordinary share capital** of the **relevant company** [ITEPA 2003, Sch5, para 35(1)(a)].

The **optionholder** must acquire shares that are **fully paid up** when he **exercise**s his **option** [ITEPA 2003, Sch5, para 35(1)(b)]. The shares will not be regarded as **fully paid up** if there is any undertaking to pay cash to the **relevant company** at a future date [ITEPA 2003, Sch5, para 35(2)].

The shares must not be **redeemable**, or be subject to conditions that may cause them to become **redeemable** at a future date [ITEPA 2003, Sch5, para 35(1)(c) and (3)].

3.7.6.4. Qualification Requirements for the Optionholder

3.7.6.4.1. Employment Requirement

A **qualifying option** can only be **grant**ed to someone who is an employee of the **relevant company** or of a qualifying subsidiary of the **relevant company** [ITEPA

2003, Sch5, para 25]. If the **optionholder** ceases to meet this requirement, this will be a disqualifying event in relation to him [ITEPA 2003, s535(1)(a)].

3.7.6.4.2. Working Time Requirement

An employee cannot be granted an **EMI option** unless he meets the working time requirement: his "committed time" (expressed as a weekly average) must equal or exceed the "statutory threshold" [ITEPA 2003, Sch5, para 26(1)].

His committed time means the time he spends on the business of the company or the group [ITEPA 2003, Sch5, para 26(2)].

The statutory threshold is the lower of:

- 25 hours per week or
- 75% of the employee's working time [ITEPA 2003, Sch5, para 26(1)].

The employee's working time is the time he spends on "remunerative work", whether as an employee or as a self-employed person, and whether inside or outside the UK [ITEPA 2003, Sch5, para 27(2) and (3)].

In calculating both "committed time" and "working time", it is possible to include any time which the employee would have been required to spend on the business of the group but for injury, ill health or disability, pregnancy, childbirth, or parental leave, reasonable holiday entitlement, or not being required to work during a period of notice of termination of employment [ITEPA 2003, Sch5, para 26(3) and 27(1)(b)].

If the employee ceases to meet the working time requirement, this will be a disqualifying event [ITEPA 2003, s535(1)(b)]. Therefore, if there is any doubt as to whether the employee qualifies, consider amending his working arrangements so that he actually works a minimum 25-hour week.

If the employee does not actually work a minimum 25-hour working week, then the 75% test has to be applied at the end of each tax year by looking at the average hours worked during that year [ITEPA 2003, s535(2)]. For the year in which the **grant date** occurs, the part of the year preceding the **grant date** is ignored [ITEPA 2003, s535(5)].

An **optionholder** could nevertheless fail the working time requirement during the course of the year. For example, if the **optionholder** works 20 hours per week for the **relevant company**, and then enters into a contract with an unrelated company under which he works another 20 hours per week for that company, he must fail the working time requirement at the end of the following month, because his committed time cannot be more than 50% of his working time.

3.7.6.4.3. No Material interest Requirement

The individual is not eligible for an EMI **option** if he or an associate has a **material interest** in the **relevant company** or any member of the group [ITEPA 2003, Sch5, para 28(1)]. "**Material interest**" for EMI purposes means more than 30% of the ordinary share capital [ITEPA 2003, Sch5, para 29(2)].

3.7.6.5. Qualification Requirements for the Option

3.7.6.5.1. General Requirements

The general requirements must be satisfied on the **grant date** of the **EMI option**. They relate to:

- the purpose for which the **option** is granted(see section 3.7.6.5.1.1).
- the maximum entitlement of the **optionholder** (see sections 3.7.6.5.1.2.1 and 3.7.6.5.1.2.2).
- the maximum value of shares under **option** by the **relevant company** (see section 3.7.6.5.1.2.3).

3.7.6.5.1.1 Purpose of Option

The **option** must be granted "for commercial reasons in order to recruit or retain an employee in a company". It must not be granted "as part of a scheme or arrangement the main purpose (or one of the main purposes) of which is the avoidance of tax" [ITEPA 2003, Sch5, para 4].

On a literal reading of these words, it is difficult to see how this test can ever be satisfied, since the main reason for establishing an **EMI** plan rather than an unapproved scheme must be to avoid tax by taking advantage of the **EMI** reliefs.

However, in practice, HM Revenue & Customs appear to take a narrow view, and the author has not known HM Revenue & Customs to challenge an **EMI** plan for failure to comply with this paragraph.

Nevertheless, care has to be taken, particularly in cases where no commercial purpose other than tax avoidance is served by the **EMI option**. For example, a company, which had already granted an unapproved option to an employee, might want to cancel the unapproved option and replace it with an **EMI option** at the same **exercise price**. It is hard to show any reason for doing this other than to avoid tax. The author is aware of cases where this has happened, but usually there has been some significant difference between the terms of the old option and the new **EMI option**, such as a different **option period**, or different performance conditions, which tend to show a new commercial purpose for the **EMI option**.

3.7.6.5.1.2 Maximum Value of Options

There are three separate limits on the value of **options**. Two relate to the total value that can be **grant**ed to any one **optionholder**. The third relates to the total value of shares in a **relevant company** that can be subject to **qualifying options**.

First, it is important to note that each limit applies to the **CGT value** of the shares on the **grant date** of the **option** [ITEPA 2003, Sch5, para 5(6)(a)]. Where the **optionholder** holds different **options** **grant**ed on different dates, each **option** is looked at separately. The limits do not apply to the **exercise price** of the **option**, which is irrelevant for these tests.

It is also important to note that the **unrestricted market value** of the shares should be determined, i.e. the **CGT value** without regard to certain kinds of restrictions to which the shares are subject [ITEPA 2003, Sch5, paras 5(7) and 6(7) and 7(6)]. These are the same kinds of restrictions as those which could make shares "**restricted securities**" for the purposes of ITEPA 2003, Part 7, Chapter 2.

See section 3.7.6.6.1 for further discussion of the valuation criteria.

3.7.6.5.1.2.1 £100,000 Limit on Unexercised Qualifying options

The first limit looks at all unexercised **qualifying option**s that the **optionholder** holds on the **grant date** [ITEPA 2003, Sch5, para 5(1)]. Any **qualifying option**s that the **optionholder** has already **exercise**d, or which he has released, or which have lapsed, do not need to be taken into account.

For the purposes of this limit, unexercised **CSOP option**s are treated as **qualifying option**s [ITEPA 2003, Sch5, para 5(4)].

However, **CSOP option**s that the **optionholder** holds through some non-associated employment do not have to be taken into account. **CSOP option**s are only relevant if they were granted by the employer company or another member of its group [ITEPA 2003, Sch5, para 5(4)].

The total **CGT value** of the shares subject to unexercised **qualifying option**s cannot exceed £100,000 [ITEPA 2003, Sch5, para 5(1)].

If the £100,000 limit has already been reached, any further **option**s granted to the same **optionholder** cannot be **qualifying option**s [ITEPA 2003, Sch5, para 5(2)], although the Rules may instead say that such an **option** is deemed not to have been granted.

If the **grant** of the new **option** itself causes the £100,000 limit to be broken, the excess over the limit will not be a **qualifying option** [ITEPA 2003, Sch5, para 5(3)]. So, for example, imagine an **optionholder** who already holds **EMI option**s over shares which had a **market value** of £75,000 when those **option**s were **grant**ed. If a further **grant** of **option**s is made to him over shares with an **unrestricted market value** of £50,000, only the first £25,000 could qualify as EMI **option**s.

Note that if a further **CSOP option** is granted to the **optionholder** by the employer company or another member of its group, and this causes the £100,000 limit to be broken, this will be a disqualifying event [ITEPA 2003, s536(1)(e)].

3.7.6.5.1.2.2 £100,000 Three-Year Limit on Qualifying options

The second limit relates to all **qualifying option**s granted to the **optionholder** within the previous three years [ITEPA 2003, Sch5, para 6(2)]. It includes **option**s that have already been **exercised**, or which the **optionholder** has released [ITEPA

2003, Sch5, para 6(5)]. It also includes **options granted** by two or more companies in the same group [ITEPA 2003, Sch5, para 6(3)].

However, it does not include **CSOP options**, and it does not include **EMI options** that have lapsed, e.g. for failure to achieve performance conditions.

If the **CGT value** of all such **qualifying options** is exactly £100,000, then any further **options** granted to that same **optionholder** will not qualify as EMI **options** [ITEPA 2003, Sch5, para 6(2)].

This "three year restriction period" lasts until the third anniversary of the most recent grant of **options** to that **optionholder** [ITEPA 2003, Sch5, para 6(6)].

Strangely, this limit only applies where the **optionholder** has been granted **qualifying options** over shares worth exactly £100,000. This is because ITEPA 2003, Sch5, para 6(1) refers to "**qualifying options** in respect of shares with a total value of £100,000". If the **optionholder** had been granted **options** over shares with a total **CGT value** of £95,000, he could release all of them and be granted further **qualifying options** over shares worth up to £100,000 within three years. It is not clear that this interpretation was ever intended by the legislators, but it has been accepted by HM Revenue & Customs officials on many occasions.

3.7.6.5.1.2.3 £3 million Limit

The third limit applies to the total **CGT value** of shares subject to **qualifying options** in a **relevant company**, looking at options granted to all the optionholders. Unexercised **qualifying options** cannot exist over more than £3 million worth of shares in any one company.

If the £3 million limit has already been reached, any further **options** granted over shares in the **relevant company** cannot be **qualifying options** [ITEPA 2003, Sch5, para 7(2)].

If the grant of a new **option** causes the £3 million limit to be broken, the excess over the limit will not be a **qualifying option** [ITEPA 2003, Sch5, para 7(3)].

If two or more **options** are granted at the same time, and this causes the £3 million limit to be broken, then a proportion of each **option** can take effect as a **qualifying option**. The proportion relates to the relative values of the shares over which the **options** were granted. Take the example of a company which had already granted **options** over £2,800,000 worth of shares and imagine it granted five further **options**: three over £100,000 worth of shares and two over £50,000 worth of shares. It would have exceeded the limit by £200,000. The three **options** over £100,000 worth of shares would each take effect as **qualifying options** over £50,000 worth of shares and unapproved options over £50,000 worth of shares. The two **options** over £50,000 worth of shares would each take effect as **qualifying options** over

£25,000 worth of shares and unapproved options over £25,000 worth of shares [ITEPA 2003, Sch5, para 7(5)].

3.7.6.5.2. The Terms of the Option

The terms of the **option** have to satisfy certain conditions.

3.7.6.5.2.1 Ten Year Option period

The **option** must be capable of being **exercise**d within ten years of the **grant date**, although it can have a longer **option period** [ITEPA 2003, Sch5, para 36(1)]. If the **option** is subject to any conditions, those conditions must be capable of being fulfilled within ten years [ITEPA 2003, Sch5, para 36(2)].

3.7.6.5.2.2 Written Agreement

The **option** must take the form of a written agreement between the grantor and the **optionholder** [ITEPA 2003, Sch5, para 37(1)]. Sometime an **EMI option** is granted using an **option** certificate that is executed as a deed by the grantor, but not signed by the **optionholder**. There appear to be different views within HM Revenue & Customs as to whether this is acceptable; the author is aware that some HM Revenue & Customs officials have rejected **option**s granted on this basis. The safer course of action is to require the **optionholder** to sign the agreement.

ITEPA 2003, Sch5, para 37 sets out certain items that must be included in the **option** agreement. They are:

- the **grant date**;
- a statement that the **option** is granted under the provisions of ITEPA 2003, Sch5;
- the number, or maximum number, of shares that may be acquired through the **option** – note that an EMI **option** can be granted over a variable number of shares, where the actual number derives from a formula, but there must be a maximum;
- the **exercise price**, if there is an **exercise price** or, if the **exercise price** is variable and cannot yet be determined, the method by which the **exercise price** is to be determined;
- when and how the **option** may be **exercise**d;
- any performance, **vesting**, or similar conditions;
- if the shares are **restricted securities**, details of the restrictions.

3.7.6.5.2.3 Non-Transferability

The **option** agreement must prohibit the **optionholder** from assigning any of his rights under the **option** [ITEPA 2003, Sch5, para 38(a)].

If the **optionholder** dies, his personal representatives cannot be allowed to **exercise** the **option** more than twelve months after the death [ITEPA 2003, Sch5, para 38(b)].

3.7.6.6. Valuation Issues

Valuations are required for two reasons when **grant**ing an EMI **option**:

First, it is necessary to determine the **unrestricted market value** of the shares for the purposes of the limits on the maximum value of **options** (see section 3.7.6.5.1.2).

Second, there is a potential charge to income tax if there is a **discount at grant** (see section 8.2.1.2.2).

For the purposes of the EMI code, **market value** is the **CGT value** (see section 15.2). For an unlisted company, the valuation must be agreed with HMRC Shares Valuation. HM Revenue & Customs' website sets out the process for doing this at http://www.hmrc.gov.uk/shareschemes/svd2.htm. In particular, note that it is essential to complete Form VAL 231W, which can be downloaded from http://www.hmrc.gov.uk/shareschemes/val231.pdf.

3.7.6.6.1. Valuation for the purposes of the limits on Maximum Value

If the shares are **restricted securities**, the restrictions are to be ignored in determining the value for the purposes of the limits on the maximum value of **options** [ITEPA 2003, Sch5, paras 5(7), 6(7) and 7(6)]. See section 3.5.4.1 for guidance as to whether the shares are **restricted securities**.

The valuation criterion to use is, again, the **unrestricted market value** (see section 15.3). Therefore, the valuation should take account only of information that would be available to any prospective purchaser of the relevant block of shares [TCGA 1992, s273(3)].

3.7.6.6.2. Valuation to determine whether there is a discount at grant

For the purposes of determining whether there was a **discount at grant**, it is necessary to value the shares on the **grant date**. The valuation criterion to use is, again, the **CGT value** (see section 15.2) [ITEPA 2003, Sch5, para 55].

However, there is nothing in the **EMI** code that requires the valuer to ignore all restrictions on the shares for this purpose, as there is for applying the maximum value limits.

In the author's view, restrictions that are inherent in the shares should be taken into account in valuing the shares for these purposes. Such restrictions would be written into the Articles of Association so that they bound any future purchaser of the shares. This means that the **market value** of shares that are restricted in this way will be lower for the purposes of determining whether there is a **discount at grant**, and therefore it is less likely that there will be a **discount at grant**.

However, restrictions that are personal to the **optionholder** should be ignored in determining **market value** for these purposes, because they would not affect any potential purchaser. Such restrictions might be found in, for example, a shareholder's agreement that the **optionholder** is required to sign on exercising the **option**. Therefore, the **market value** of shares that are restricted in this way may be higher than if the restrictions were inherent in the shares. This means it is more likely that there will be a **discount at grant**.

3.7.6.6.3. Dilution Effect

EMI **options** may sometimes be granted over a substantial percentage of the **relevant company**'s share capital and may therefore be very dilutive when they are **exercised**. The valuer should take account of this effect in valuing the shares.

3.7.6.7. Documentation and Registration

3.7.6.7.1. The Plan Rules

A copy of the Plan Rules will usually be appended to the option agreement. Strictly there is no need for EMI **options** to be granted through a Plan – they can be stand-alone agreements between the **relevant company** and the **optionholder**.

See section 3.7.3 for details of the design of the Rules. In addition to what is noted in that section, the Rules would normally contain the following:

3.7.6.7.1.1 Participating Companies

A rule that **qualifying options** can only be granted to employees of qualifying subsidiaries (see section 3.7.6.3.2).

3.7.6.7.1.2 Shares

A rule specifying that the shares used in the Plan must be **ordinary share capital** (see section 3.7.6.3.6).

3.7.6.7.1.3 Eligible Employee

A rule that **qualifying options** may only be granted to people who meet the qualification requirements set out in section 3.7.6.4.

3.7.6.7.1.4 Individual Limits

A "blue pencil" rule that if **options** are accidentally granted which exceed the EMI limits (see sections 3.7.6.5.1.2.1 and 3.7.6.5.1.2.2), then those **options** take effect as non-**qualifying options**. See section 3.7.8.5.3 for HM Revenue & Customs' views on how such a rule should be operated.

3.7.6.7.1.5 Overall Limit

A rule that **options** cannot be granted if they exceed the £3 million limit (see section 3.7.6.5.1.2.3).

3.7.6.7.1.6 Non-Transferability

See section 3.7.8.8.1.10.

3.7.6.7.1.7 Deceased Optionholders

See section 3.7.8.8.1.12.

3.7.6.7.1.8 Variation of share capital

A rule that **options** cannot be varied in such a way as to cause a disqualifying event, either because

- the terms of the **option** are varied in such a way as to increase the value of shares under **option** [ITEPA 2003, s536(1)(a)(i)]; or
- the terms of the **option** are varied in such a way that the **option** no longer meets the requirements of ITEPA 2003, Sch5 [ITEPA 2003, s536(1)(a)(ii)].

3.7.6.7.2. Registration

Whenever a company grants an EMI **option** it must send Form EMI1 to SCEC. A copy of this can be downloaded from the HMRC website at http://www.hmrc.gov.uk/shareschemes/emi/appendix1.htm. It must also send a declaration by the employee that he or she satisfies the working time commitment and a declaration by a director or the company secretary of the employer company that the requirements of Schedule 5 are met and that the information provided is to the best of his or her knowledge correct and complete.

The company does not have to send a copy of the option agreement in with the new form, but the company and employee should keep copies for their own records since HM Revenue & Customs may require them to be produced.

3.7.6.8. Tax Treatment of Optionholder

For details of the tax treatment of the **optionholder** see section 8.2.

3.7.6.8.1. Disqualifying Events

If a disqualifying event occurs, this has two adverse consequences for the **optionholder**.

First, if the **optionholder exercises** the **option** more than 40 days after a disqualifying event, then the **optionholder** is charged to income tax on any growth in value of the shares between the disqualifying event and the **exercise date** (see section 8.2.1.2.4).

Second, if the **optionholder exercises** the **option** more than 40 days after a disqualifying event, taper relief for capital gains tax purposes will run from the **exercise date** rather than the **grant date** (see section 8.2.4).

The following are disqualifying events for an EMI **option**:

- the **relevant company** ceases to meet the independence requirement (see section 3.7.6.3.1) [ITEPA 2003, s534(1)(a) and (b)];
- the **relevant company** ceases to meet the trading activities requirement (see section 3.7.6.3.5 [ITEPA 2003, s534(1)(c)];
- the **relevant company** originally met the trading activities requirement only because it was preparing to carry on a qualifying trade, and it ceases those preparations, or fails to commence the qualifying trade within two years of the first **grant date** [ITEPA 2003, s534(4)];
- the **optionholder** ceases to meet the employment requirement (see section 3.7.6.4.1) [ITEPA 2003, s535(1)(a)];

- the **optionholder** ceases to meet the working time requirement (see section 3.7.6.4.2) [ITEPA 2003, s535(1)(b) and (2)];
- the terms of the **option** are varied in such a way as to increase the value of shares under **option** [ITEPA 2003, s536(1)(a)(i)];
- The terms of the **option** are varied in such a way that the **option** no longer meets the requirements of ITEPA 2003, Sch5 [ITEPA 2003, s536(1)(a)(ii)];
- the shares under **option** no longer meet the requirements of ITEPA 2003, Sch5, because of a variation of the share capital of the **relevant company** which (a) affects the value of the shares under **option** and which (b) alters the rights attaching to any shares in the **relevant company**, whether by creating, varying or removing rights, or imposing, varying or removing a restriction relating to the shares;
- there is a variation of the share capital of the **relevant company** which

  (a) affects the **market value** of the shares under **option** and which

  (b) alters the rights attaching to any shares in the **relevant company**, whether by creating, varying or removing rights, or imposing, varying or removing a restriction relating to the shares; and either

  (1) that variation causes the shares under **option** no longer to meet the requirements of ITEPA 2003, Sch5 [ITEPA 2003, s536(1)(b)] or

  (2) that variation increases the **market value** of the shares under **option** and either

  (i) it was not made by the **relevant company** for commercial reasons; or

  (ii) one of the main purposes for making it was to increase the **market value** of the shares under **option**

  [ITEPA 2003, s536(1)(c)];
- the shares under **option** are converted into shares of a different class, unless all shares of the original class are converted into shares of the same single new class, and, immediately before the conversion took place, either

  (a) the majority of shares of the original class were **open market shares**; or

  (b) the **relevant company** was an **employee-controlled company** by virtue of holdings of shares of the original class

  [ITEPA 2003, s536(1)(d)]
- the **optionholder** is **grant**ed a **CSOP option** and this causes the total value of his un**exercise**d **qualifying options** to break the £100,000 limit (see section 3.7.6.5.1.2.1) [ITEPA 2003, s536(1)(e)].

3.7.6.8.2. PAYE

See section 8.2.2.

3.7.6.8.3. NIC

See section 8.2.2.

3.7.6.8.4. Reporting

See section 8.2.3.

3.7.6.8.5. Capital Gains Treatment

See section 8.2.4.

3.7.6.9. Tax Treatment of Employer

3.7.6.9.1. Corporation Tax Deductibility

See section 17.

3.7.6.9.2. NIC

See section 8.2.2.

3.7.6.9.3. Reporting

See section 8.2.3.

3.7.6.10. Matrix Summary of Advantages and Disadvantages of EMI Options

Feature	**Advantage**	**Disadvantage**
Availability		Not available to all companies
Flexibility	Shares can be subject to restrictions, such as limited voting or dividend rights, as long as they are **ordinary share capital**	
Limits		Subject to £100,000 limits and £3 million limit
Accounting (p/l)	Profit and loss account charge limited to value of **option** on **grant date**	Cannot be "trued up" if subject to market-based performance condition
Accounting (balance sheet)	Issue of new shares increases capital	Dilutes existing shareholders if new shares issued
Corporation Tax	Automatic deduction available in many circumstances	Automatic deduction not available for **exercises** following sale to unlisted company
Income Tax and NIC	Income tax and NIC limited to **discount at grant** (if any) where no disqualifying event	Wide range of disqualifying events can reduce favourable income tax and NIC treatment
Capital Gains Tax	Taper relief starts from **grant date** where no disqualifying event	Wide range of disqualifying events can remove favourable capital gains tax treatment

3.7.7. Frequently Asked Questions on EMI Plans

3.7.7.1. If an optionholder surrenders a CSOP option, does it still count against the £100,000 limit?

No, only existing but unexercised **CSOP options** count against the £100,000 limit [ITEPA 2003, Sch5, para 5(4)].

3.7.7.2. Is there a disqualifying event if the company's overseas operations grow to represent more than half of the overall business?

Yes, this could be a problem if the **relevant company** operates through overseas branches. However, if the **relevant company** incorporates subsidiaries to carry out its overseas activities, then they do not affect the availability of EMI relief as long as they are not carrying on non-qualifying activities [ITEPA 2003, Sch5, para 14(1)(b)]. It is necessary to show that at least one company in the group is carrying on a trade in the UK [ITEPA 2003, Sch5, para 14(1)(a)].

3.7.7.3. Can an EMI option have an option period which lasts more than ten years?

Yes, provided that it is capable of being **exercise**d within ten years [ITEPA 2003, Sch5, para 36(1)]. However, tax relief will not apply if the **option** is **exercise**d more than ten years after the **grant date** [ITEPA 2003, s529(2)].

3.7.7.4. Can an individual grant an EMI option?

Yes.

3.7.8. CSOP Options

3.7.8.1. Description

A Company Share Option Plan ("**CSOP**") **option** is a tax-efficient form of incentive. If all the relevant conditions are met, and the employee holds the shares for at least a year following the **exercise date**, there may actually be a tax subsidy, in the sense that the corporation tax relief given to the employing company is greater than the amount of tax paid by the **optionholder**.

Unlike an **EMI** Plan, a **CSOP** must be approved by HM Revenue & Customs before an **approved option** may be granted under it.

A **CSOP option** has the following potential advantages over other forms of reward:

- no income tax charge on the **exercise** of the **option** (see section 8.3.1.2)
- the employer may be able to claim a corporation tax deduction when the **option** is **exercise**d (see section 17.4).

The conditions are set out in section 3.7.8.2.

HM Revenue & Customs' guidance on **CSOP**s for employers is available at http://www.hmrc.gov.uk/shareschemes/CSOP_employers.htm

3.7.8.2. Checklist for Implementation of a CSOP

For an **option** to be an approved **CSOP option**, certain conditions must be satisfied. Some of these conditions apply to the **option** itself; some to the company whose shares are used ("the **scheme company**"); others to any employee who is to receive the **option**.

If there is any doubt as to whether the company qualifies for **CSOP**, discuss this with HM Revenue & Customs Employee Shares and Securities Unit.

Here is a checklist to go through before establishing a **CSOP** or **granting** an **option** under it.

Requirement	**ITEPA 2003, Sch4**	**Commentary**
Participants who are full-time directors - must work 25 hours per week (excluding meal breaks) or	Para 8(1)	3.7.8.5.1
Participants must be employees	Para 8(2)	3.7.8.5.1
Employee must meet the "no **material interest**" requirement at **grant** and **exercise**	Para 9	3.7.8.5.2
Market value must be defined in the Plan Rules	Para 22(1)	4.3.1.7
Market value of unlisted shares must be agreed with Shares Valuation	Para 22(2)	4.3.1.7
Plan Rules must contain the £30,000 Limit on un**exercise**d **option**s	Para 6	3.7.8.5.3
Plan Rules must not allow **option**s to be **grant**ed with an **exercise price** less than **market value**	Para 22	3.7.8.8.1.7
Option must be **grant**ed for consideration or under seal		3.7.8.8.1.4
Scheme shares must satisfy the legislative requirements	Para 15	3.7.8.3
Shares must be **ordinary share capital**	Para 16	3.7.8.3.1
Shares must satisfy the listing requirement	Para 17	3.7.8.3.3
Shares must be **fully paid up** and not **redeemable**	Para 18	3.7.8.3.2
Shares must be subject only to permitted restrictions	Para 19	3.7.8.3.4
Shares must satisfy the "other shareholdings" test	Para 20	3.7.8.3.5
Options must not be transferable except on	Paras 23 and 25	3.7.8.8.1.10

Requirement	ITEPA 2003, Sch4	Commentary
death		
Performance conditions must be objective		3.7.8.8.1.5
Performance conditions may only be adjusted if events happen		3.7.8.8.1.5
Any adjustment to performance conditions must be fair and reasonable		3.7.8.8.1.5
Following the adjustment, the performance condition must be no more difficult to satisfy than the original **option** was on the **grant date**		3.7.8.8.1.5
Death of **optionholder**		3.7.8.8.1.12
Good leavers– no discretion		3.7.8.8.1.11
Bad Leavers – any discretion must be **exercised** fairly and reasonably		3.7.8.8.1.11
Specified retirement age cannot be less than 55	Para 35A	3.7.8.8.1.11
Optionholder can have accelerated **exercise** on specified events such as change of control		3.7.8.8.1.13
Optionholder's right to **exercise** must be clearly expressed	Para 5	3.7.8.8.1.4
The Plan Rules must not contain non-essential features	Para 5	3.7.8.6.1
Shares must be allotted or transferred within 30 days of the **exercise date**	Para 19	3.7.8.8.1.14
Shares must rank *pari passu* with shares of the same class	Para 19	3.7.8.3.4
Exchange of **options** may be permitted on change of control	Para 26	8.5.6.3
If exchange is permitted, it must take place within statutory period	Para 26	8.5.6.3
Value and total **exercise price** must not be affected	Para 27(4)(c)	21.4, rows 9 and 10
After exchange, original **scheme organiser** remains responsible for Plan	Para 27(4)(b)	21.4, row 8
HM Revenue & Customs must approve adjustments following variation of capital	Para 22(3) and (4)	3.7.8.8.1.8
HM Revenue & Customs must approve amendments to a key feature	Para 30(2)(aa)	3.7.8.8.1.16
Group scheme or single-company scheme	Para 3	3.7.8.4.1

Requirement	ITEPA 2003, Sch4	Commentary
Jointly owned companies	Para 34	3.7.8.4.2
PAYE withholding requirement and NIC transfer		3.7.8.8.1.15

3.7.8.3. *Approval Requirements for the Shares*

The shares must meet the statutory requirements [ITEPA 2003, Sch4, para 15].

3.7.8.3.1. Ordinary share capital

THIS SECTION APPLIES TO **SIP**, **SAYE** AND **CSOP**

The shares to be used in the Plan must be **ordinary share capital** of the **scheme company** [ITEPA 2003, Sch2, para 26, Sch3, para 18 and Sch4, para 16].

The **scheme company** will usually be the same as the **scheme organiser**, but it could be another company that has **Section 840 control** of the **scheme organiser** [ITEPA 2003, Sch2, para 26(b), Sch3, para 18(b) and Sch4, para 16(b)].

The **scheme company** could also be a member of a **consortium** that has **Section 840 control** of the **scheme organiser**, or of another company that itself has **Section 840 control** of the **scheme organiser** [ITEPA 2003, Sch2, para 26(c); Sch3, para 18(c) and Sch4, para 16(c)].

3.7.8.3.2. Fully paid up and not redeemable

THIS SECTION APPLIES TO **SIP**, **SAYE** AND **CSOP**

Under a **CSOP** or **SAYE**, the **optionholder** must acquire shares that are **fully paid up** when he **exercise**s his **option** [ITEPA 2003, Sch3, para 20 and Sch4, para 18].

Shares acquired through a **SIP** must be **fully paid up** on the **acquisition date** or **award** date [ITEPA 2003, Sch2, para 28(1)].

Shares acquired through a **SIP**, **CSOP** or **SAYE** must not be **redeemable** [ITEPA 2003, Sch2, para 28(1), Sch3, para 20 and Sch4, para 18].

3.7.8.3.3. The listing requirement

THIS SECTION APPLIES TO **SIP**, **SAYE** AND **CSOP**

The shares to be used in the Plan must fall into one or more of the following categories:

- shares in a company that is listed on a **recognised stock exchange** [ITEPA 2003, Sch2, para 27(1)(a), Sch3, para 19(1)(a) and Sch4, para 17(1)(a)];
- shares in a company that is not under the **Section 840 control** of any other company [ITEPA 2003, Sch2, para 27(1)(b), Sch3, para 19(1)(b) and Sch4, para 17(1)(b)];
- shares in a company that is under the **Section 840 control** of a company that is both (a) listed on a **recognised stock exchange** and (b) not close, or would not

be close if it were **resident** in the UK [ITEPA 2003, Sch2, para 27(1)(c) and (2), Sch3, para 19(1)(c) and (2), and Sch4, para 17(1)(c) and (2)].

Sometimes the **scheme company** is controlled by a family or other trust with a sole corporate trustee. In these circumstances, it will not be possible to establish an **approved plan**, unless the corporate trustee is itself listed or under the **Section 840 control** of a listed company – for example if the corporate trustee is a subsidiary of a bank. If this is a problem, it can be rectified by appointing a second trustee to act jointly with the corporate trustee [HMRC Manual ESS11009][27]

Sometimes the **scheme company** is controlled by a limited partnership, perhaps in a private equity situation. In these circumstances, the general partner will often be a corporate entity and it may have power under the partnership deed to have **Section 840 control** over the **scheme company**. This would prevent the **scheme company**'s shares from being used in an **approved plan** unless the general partner is itself under the **Section 840 control** of a listed company. This may be the case if it is a subsidiary of a bank [HMRC Manual ESS11010][28].

In determining whether the **scheme company** is under the **Section 840 control** of another company, only the shares then in issue are relevant. It is not relevant if more shares may be issued later, e.g. on conversion of loan stock or the **exercise** of **options**.

3.7.8.3.4. Subject only to permitted restrictions

THIS SECTION APPLIES TO **SAYE** AND **CSOP**

ITEPA 2003, Sch3, para 21 and Sch4, para 19 provide that shares to be used for a **CSOP** or **SAYE** must not be subject to restrictions, unless either those restrictions apply to all shares of the same class, or are permitted restrictions.

This is the requirement that private companies most often have difficulty in complying with, because owners of private companies will often want to impose restrictions that treat other employees differently from themselves or members of their family.

Particular issues relate to pre-emption conditions (see section 3.7.8.3.4.1) and restrictions on transferability (see section 3.7.8.3.4.2).

3.7.8.3.4.1 Pre-Emption Conditions

THIS SECTION APPLIES TO **SAYE** AND **CSOP**

Frequently, the Board of Directors of a private company will want to be able to compel a departing employee to sell any shares he holds, because they will want to control the register tightly.

---

[27] http://www.hmrc.gov.uk/manuals/essumanual/essu10000/essu11009.htm

[28] http://www.hmrc.gov.uk/manuals/essumanual/essu10000/essu11010.htm

A restriction that compels former employees to offer their shares for sale is permitted, provided it is in the Articles of Association, and that it applies to all directors or employees [ITEPA 2003, Sch3, para 21(2)(a) and Sch4, para 19(2)(a)].

Similarly, if a former employee (or his estate) acquires shares by exercising an **option** after terminating employment, he can be required to offer those shares for sale [ITEPA 2003, Sch3, para 21(2)(b) and Sch4, para 19(2)(b)].

The sale of the shares must be for cash, and the terms of the sale must be set out in the Articles of Association [ITEPA 2003, Sch3, para 21(3)(a) and Sch4, para 19(3)(a)]. The same terms must apply to anyone selling shares of the same class [ITEPA 2003, Sch3, para 21(3)(b) and Sch4, para 19(3)(b)].

3.7.8.3.4.2 Restrictions On Transferability

Another restriction that the Board of Directors of a private company will often want to impose on employee shareholders is the power to refuse to register a transfer of shares. This is a permitted restriction, provided that the Board gives an undertaking to HM Revenue & Customs not to use the power in a way that discriminates against people who acquired their shares through a **CSOP** or **SAYE**, and notifies these people accordingly [ITEPA 2003, Sch3, para 21(7) and Sch4, para 19(7)].

Any other restrictions on the participant's freedom to dispose of the shares will generally be unacceptable [ITEPA 2003, Sch3, para 21(4) and Sch4, para 19(4)].

Here are some common examples of restrictions that are found in relation to shares of private companies, with commentary on whether HM Revenue & Customs find them acceptable or unacceptable for **CSOP** and **SAYE**.

3.7.8.3.4.3 Restrictions that HM Revenue & Customs consider unacceptable

- The shares delivered through the **CSOP** or **SAYE** have inferior voting or dividend rights compared to other shares of the same class [HMRC Manual ESS12030][29].
- When new shares are issued, other shareholders are given priority over employees in applying for them [HMRC Manual ESS12030][30].
- When shares are offered for sale, another person has priority in purchasing them – except where that person has the same right whether or not he actually holds any shares, in which case the priority rights attach to the person rather than to the shares. An example of this would be where an EBT has a first right of refusal on shares that are offered for sale [HMRC Manual ESS12032][31].

---

[29] http://www.hmrc.gov.uk/manuals/essumanual/essu12000/essu12030.htm

[30] http://www.hmrc.gov.uk/manuals/essumanual/essu12000/essu12030.htm

[31] http://www.hmrc.gov.uk/manuals/essumanual/essu12000/essu12032.htm

- A shareholder who holds at least a certain percentage of the share capital has a prior right to acquire more shares when they are offered for sale [HMRC Manual ESS12033][32].
- **CSOP** and **SAYE** participants are not allowed to transfer their shares to trusts without going through the compulsory offer for sale procedures, but other shareholders are allowed to do this [HMRC Manual ESS12034][33]
- When a **CSOP** or **SAYE** participant wants to sell his shares, he is obliged to do so on terms which are different from those which apply to other shareholders [HMRC Manual ESS12056][34].
- When a **CSOP** or **SAYE** participant leaves employment, he is required by a shareholders' agreement to offer his shares for sale [HMRC Manual ESS12052][35].
- When a **CSOP** or **SAYE** participant leaves employment, the Articles of Association require him to offer his shares for sale on terms which are not the same as those that apply to other shareholders [HMRC Manual ESS12056][36]
- If a **CSOP** or **SAYE** participant transfers his shares to another person, such as a family member, that person is also obliged to offer his shares for sale if the **CSOP** or **SAYE** participant ceases to be an employee [HMRC Manual ESS12061][37].
- Certain named individuals, who hold shares of the same class as the scheme shares, are excluded from the requirement to offer those shares for sale on termination of employment [HMRC Manual ESS12062][38].
- If an employee or director ceases employment for a specified reason, such as **retirement**, he is not required to offer his shares for sale [HMRC Manual ESS12062][39].
- When an employee or director ceases employment, he is required to offer to sell only part of his holding [HMRC Manual ESS12062][40].

---

32 http://www.hmrc.gov.uk/manuals/essumanual/essu12000/essu12033.htm

33 http://www.hmrc.gov.uk/manuals/essumanual/essu12000/essu12034.htm

34 http://www.hmrc.gov.uk/manuals/essumanual/essu12000/essu12056.htm

35 http://www.hmrc.gov.uk/manuals/essumanual/essu12000/essu12052.htm

36 http://www.hmrc.gov.uk/manuals/essumanual/essu12000/essu12056.htm

37 http://www.hmrc.gov.uk/manuals/essumanual/essu12000/essu12061.htm

38 http://www.hmrc.gov.uk/manuals/essumanual/essu12000/essu12062.htm

39 http://www.hmrc.gov.uk/manuals/essumanual/essu12000/essu12062.htm

40 http://www.hmrc.gov.uk/manuals/essumanual/essu12000/essu12062.htm

- If an employee or director is compelled to offer his shares for sale on termination of employment, but nobody offers to buy *all* his shares, then he does not have to sell any shares [HMRC Manual ESS12062[41] and 12100[42]].
- When an employee or director ceases employment, the directors have the power to decide not to compel him to offer his shares for sale [HMRC Manual ESS12062][43].
- When an employee or director ceases employment, the Articles of Association allow the purchaser to pay for the shares in something which is not cash [HMRC Manual ESS12081][44].
- When an employee or director offers his shares for sale, the pricing mechanism is different from that used when other people sell their shares [HMRC Manual ESS12091][45]
- Another shareholder is allowed to transfer his shares without going through the same procedures as an employee would have to on terminating employment – unless this transfer is approved by *all* the other shareholders [HMRC Manual ESS12105][46].
- There is a shareholders' agreement that limits or removes the voting rights of shares held by employees.
- There is a shareholders' agreement that limits or removes the rights of shares held by employees to receive dividends.
- There is a shareholders' agreement that restricts the ability of employees to transfer their shares.
- There is a shareholders' agreement that says that an employee who offers his shares for sale receives a different price from a non-employee.
- When the employee **exercises** his **option**, he is obliged to **grant** someone else an **option** to purchase the shares from him.

3.7.8.3.4.4 Restrictions that HM Revenue & Customs consider to be acceptable

- The **scheme company** is incorporated under non-UK law, and is subject to restrictions imposed under that law, such as US securities law [HMRC Manual ESS13015][47].

---

41 http://www.hmrc.gov.uk/manuals/essumanual/essu12000/essu12062.htm

42 http://www.hmrc.gov.uk/manuals/essumanual/essu12000/essu12100.htm

43 http://www.hmrc.gov.uk/manuals/essumanual/essu12000/essu12062.htm

44 http://www.hmrc.gov.uk/manuals/essumanual/essu12000/essu12081.htm

45 http://www.hmrc.gov.uk/manuals/essumanual/essu12000/essu12091.htm

46 http://www.hmrc.gov.uk/manuals/essumanual/essu12000/essu12105.htm

47 http://www.hmrc.gov.uk/manuals/essumanual/essu13000/essu13015.htm

- The **optionholder** took out a loan to **exercise** an approved **CSOP option**, and the loan agreement contains provisions as to security and repayment [ITEPA 2003, Sch4, para 19(6)].
- A restriction attaches to all shares of the same class, either because it is contained in the company's Articles of Association or because it was imposed by a special resolution of the company [HMRC Manual ESS12011][48]. An example of this would be drag along provisions and tag along provisions whereby all shareholders can be forced to, or have the right to, sell their shares to someone who offers to purchase all, or more than a certain percentage, of the company's share capital.
- A restriction attaches to shares of other classes [HMRC Manual ESS12012][49].
- A restriction attaches to other shares of the same class, but those shares cannot be scheme shares [HMRC Manual ESS12012][50].
- A **SIP** Trustee is able to transfer shares to **SIP** participants without first having to offer those shares to other shareholders [HMRC Manual ESS12035][51].
- Certain individuals hold shares of the same class as the scheme shares, but their shares are restricted under a shareholders' agreement. That class of shares can be used in a **CSOP**, provided those individuals are excluded from participating in the **CSOP**. However, that class of shares cannot be used in an **SAYE** Plan, because those individuals could not be excluded from participation without breaking the "similar terms" requirements [HMRC Manual ESS12024][52].
- The Articles of Association require all former employees and directors to offer their shares for sale on termination of employment. The terms of the sale are the same as apply to any other shareholder who offers his shares for sale. This requirement also applies to former employees (and their personal representatives) who **exercise option**s after termination of employment [HMRC Manual ESS12060][53].
- An employee who ceases employment and is required to offer his shares for sale, is allowed to keep any shares that nobody wants to purchase [HMRC Manual ESS12065][54].

---

48 http://www.hmrc.gov.uk/manuals/essumanual/essu12000/essu12011.htm

49 http://www.hmrc.gov.uk/manuals/essumanual/essu12000/essu12012.htm

50 http://www.hmrc.gov.uk/manuals/essumanual/essu12000/essu12012.htm

51 http://www.hmrc.gov.uk/manuals/essumanual/essu12000/essu12035.htm

52 http://www.hmrc.gov.uk/manuals/essumanual/essu12000/essu12024.htm

53 http://www.hmrc.gov.uk/manuals/essumanual/essu12000/essu12060.htm

54 http://www.hmrc.gov.uk/manuals/essumanual/essu12000/essu12065.htm

- If another shareholder voluntarily offers his shares for sale, he can withdraw some or all of his shares from sale after the process has started, but an employee who is compelled to sell his shares on termination of employment cannot withdraw any of his shares from sale [HMRC Manual ESS12096][55].
- The Articles allow shareholders to transfer shares to family members without first offering them to the other shareholders, and this Article applies to everyone who holds shares of the class used in the **CSOP** or **SAYE** Plan [HMRC Manual ESS12107][56].

3.7.8.3.5. The "other shareholdings" test

THIS SECTION APPLIES TO **SAYE** AND **CSOP**

ITEPA 2003, Sch3, para 22 and Sch4, para 20 apply if the **scheme company** has more than one class of **ordinary share capital**. In these circumstances, it is important to select carefully the class which will be scheme shares used for the Plan.

The class to be used must be either **employee-control shares** or **open market shares**. The reason for this is to stop the participants in the plan from being unfairly disadvantaged by being given shares with special rights.

If the scheme shares are **employee-control shares**, then the thinking is that employees are unlikely to damage their own interests by using special shares. Similarly, if the scheme shares are **open market shares**, then the external investors are unlikely to accept shares that are disadvantaged.

So, where there is more than one class of share capital, it is necessary to determine who owns the majority of shares of the class that will be used for scheme shares.

3.7.8.3.5.1 Structures that are acceptable

It is acceptable for a majority of the class to be held by employees and directors of the Group, if they jointly control the **scheme company** through their holdings of that particular class of shares.

It is acceptable for a majority to be held by employees and directors of the Group, if they did not acquire their shares **by reason of employment**. The expanded definition of "**employment-related** securities" is not relevant for this paragraph. Therefore, to determine whether the shares were acquired **by reason of employment**, it is necessary to refer to basic principles. HM Revenue & Customs' views on this used to be published in the Manual at SSM4.4.[57] However, this text has been withdrawn from the HMRC website, and is reproduced in Chapter 25 on

---

[55] http://www.hmrc.gov.uk/manuals/essumanual/essu12000/essu12096.htm

[56] http://www.hmrc.gov.uk/manuals/essumanual/essu12000/essu12107.htm

[57] http://www.hmrc.gov.uk/manuals/ssmmanual/HTML/SSM04/04_0004_SSM4.4.htm

page 407. Examples of where there is a strong argument that employees did not acquire their shares **by reason of employment** are where they acquired their shares as entrepreneurs, through a public offer, or through a bonus or rights issue.

It is acceptable for a majority to be held by external investors, if the investors are not themselves employees or directors of the Group and they are not **associated companies** in relation to the **scheme company**.

3.7.8.3.5.2 Structures that are not acceptable

If the **scheme company** is controlled by its directors and employees through holdings of one class of shares, it is not acceptable to use a different class of shares if that class is also held as to a majority by people who acquired their shares **by reason of employment**.

It is not acceptable to use a class of shares of which the majority is held by persons who acquired their shares **by reason of employment**, or trustees for those persons.

It is not acceptable to use a class of shares of which the majority is held by **associated companies**.

3.7.8.4. Approval Requirements for Participating Companies

3.7.8.4.1. Group scheme or a single-company scheme

THIS SECTION APPLIES TO **SIP**, **SAYE** AND **CSOP**

A company that establishes a **CSOP** or **SAYE** is called "the **scheme organiser**" [ITEPA 2003, Sch3, para 2(2), Sch4, para 2(2)]. A company that establishes a **SIP** is called "the company" in the **SIP** code but is referred to as "the **scheme organiser**" in this book [ITEPA 2003, Sch2, para 2(2)].

The **scheme organiser** need not be the same as the company whose shares are used in the Plan ("the **scheme company**").

If the **scheme organiser** has **Section 840 control** of other companies, then it can establish a "group scheme", in other words, a Plan that allows participation by employees of both itself and of the companies that it controls [ITEPA 2003, Sch2, para 4(1), Sch3, para 3(1), Sch4, para 3(1)].

If the plan is intended to apply to a **group of companies**, then it is important to select carefully which of them should be the **scheme organiser**. In most circumstances, it should be the highest company in the group. This is because a group scheme cannot extend to sister subsidiaries of the **scheme organiser**.

Figure 1 shows a typical group structure. P is the ultimate **parent company** of the group; O is under the **Section 840 control** of P and is the **scheme organiser**; S is also under the **Section 840 control** of P; C is under the **Section 840 control** of O. The group scheme can use shares in P, but only employees of O and C can participate in it.

If, instead, P were the **scheme organiser**, then employees of all four companies could participate in the group scheme.

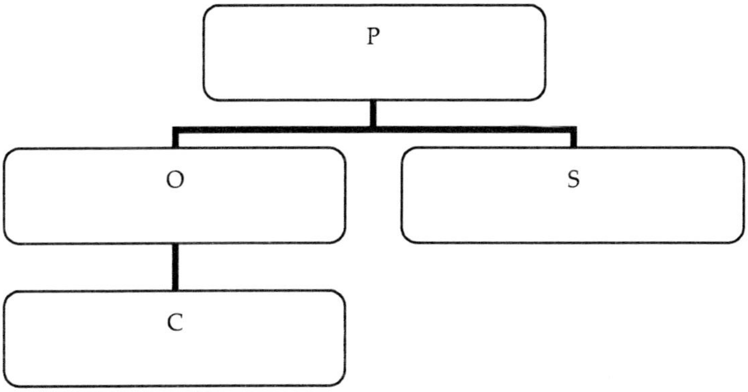

Figure 1

In the **CSOP** and **SAYE** codes, the **scheme organiser** in relation to a group scheme is called the **parent scheme company**, while the companies that participate are called the **constituent companies** [ITEPA 2003, Sch3, para 3 and Sch4, para 3].

In the **SIP** code, the **scheme organiser** in relation to a group scheme is called the **parent company**, while the companies that participate are called the **constituent companies** [ITEPA 2003, Sch2, para 4].

3.7.8.4.2. Jointly owned companies

THIS SECTION APPLIES TO **SIP**, **SAYE** AND **CSOP**

The **scheme organiser** can extend participation in the Plan to employees of a **jointly owned company** [ITEPA 2003, Sch2, para 91, Sch3, para 46, Sch4, para 34]. However, there are two issues with this.

The first is that the Plan will no longer be an **employees' share scheme** for company law purposes, since participation will no longer be limited to employees of subsidiaries. This means that important company law exemptions will no longer apply (see section 18).

Second, the **jointly owned company** can only participate in one group scheme. If the other owner of the company also offers a group scheme, employees of the **jointly owned company** cannot participate in both [ITEPA 2003, Sch2, para 91(4)(a), Sch3, para 46(4)(a), Sch4, para 34(4)(a)]. Furthermore, if the **jointly owned company** is part of a sub-group of companies, then different companies within the sub-group cannot participate in different group schemes [ITEPA 2003, Sch2, para 91(4)(b), Sch3, para 46(4)(b), Sch4, para 34(4)(b)].

3.7.8.5. Approval Requirements for the Optionholder

3.7.8.5.1. Employment Requirement

The Plan Rules must prevent **CSOP options** from being granted to anyone who is not either:

- a full-time director of the **scheme organiser** or a **constituent company**; or
- an employee of the **scheme organiser** or a **constituent company** who is not also a director.

[ITEPA 2003, Sch4, para 8]

The term "full-time director" is not defined in the legislation. In practice, HM Revenue & Customs will not approve the Plan if it allows directors to participate who are contracted to work for less than 25 hours per week, excluding meal breaks [HMRC Manual ESS27015][58].

Often, a director will actually be employed by his own service company, which will supply his services to the Group. Such a person is unlikely to be eligible to participate in a **CSOP** because time spent working for the service company will not count as time spent working directly for the Group [HMRC Manual ESS27030][59].

3.7.8.5.2. No material interest requirement

THIS SECTION APPLIES TO **SIP**, **SAYE** AND **CSOP**

The individual is not eligible to participate in a **SIP** or be **grant**ed or **exercise** a **CSOP** or **SAYE option** if he has a **material interest** in the **scheme company** or any member of the group [ITEPA 2003, Sch2, para 19(1), Sch3, para 11(1) and Sch4, para 9(1)]. "**Material interest**" is defined in the glossary, and for **SIP**, **CSOP** and **SAYE** purposes means 25% [ITEPA 2003, Sch2, para 20(2), Sch3, para 12(2) and Sch4, para 10(2)].

3.7.8.5.3. £30,000 limit on unexercised options

There is a £30,000 limit on the value of unexercised **CSOP options** that any individual can hold [ITEPA 2003, Sch4, para 6].

The value for these purposes means the **market value** of the shares on the **grant date** of the **option** [ITEPA 2003, Sch4, para 6(3)].

The limit applies to all **options** granted under any **CSOP** established by the **scheme organiser** or an **associated company** [ITEPA 2003, Sch4, para 6(1)].

HMRC will not approve the **CSOP** unless this limit is contained in the Plan Rules.

It is sensible to include a "blue pencil" provision in the Plan Rules to prevent an inadvertent breach of this provision. This is a provision which has the automatic effect of limiting the size of an **option** granted in excess of £30,000 limit: for

---

[58] http://www.hmrc.gov.uk/manuals/essumanual/essu26000/essu27015.htm

[59] http://www.hmrc.gov.uk/manuals/essumanual/essu26000/essu27030.htm

example the provision might say that, where an **option** is granted that purportedly breaks the £30,000 limit, it takes effect only up to the £30,000 limit [HMRC Manual ESS28060][60].

3.7.8.6. *Approval Requirements for the Plan*

3.7.8.6.1. Non-essential features

THIS SECTION APPLIES TO **SAYE** AND **CSOP**

There must not be features of a **CSOP** or **SAYE** Plan which are neither essential nor reasonably incidental to the purpose of providing benefits for employees and directors in the nature of share **option**s [ITEPA 2003, Sch3, para 5 and Sch4, para 5].

In HM Revenue & Customs' view the term "scheme" used here refers not only to the Plan Rules themselves, but to the totality of the arrangements put in place by the **scheme organiser**, so including other offers or promises made by the **scheme organiser** or its associates [HMRC Manual ESS2111][61].

Here are some examples of features that HMRC consider to be unacceptable:

- **Optionholder**s are allowed to pay the **exercise price** of their **option**s in instalments [HMRC Manual ESS2102][62].
- **Optionholder**s are allowed to pay the **exercise price** of their **option**s by surrendering other shares that they have in the company [HMRC Manual ESS2102][63].
- The **scheme company** has a right to settle the **option** by paying the **optionholder** a cash amount equal to the growth in value of the shares, i.e. a share appreciation right [HMRC Manual ESS2102][64].
- When the **optionholder exercise**s the **option** he is obliged to enter into an agreement to purchase additional shares [HMRC Manual ESS2102][65].
- An employee cannot be **grant**ed or cannot **exercise** a **CSOP option** unless he agrees to waive his right to participate in a **SIP** or **SAYE** [HMRC Manual ESS2102][66].

Here are some examples of features that HMRC consider to be acceptable:

---

60 http://www.hmrc.gov.uk/manuals/essumanual/essu28000/essu28060.htm

61 http://www.hmrc.gov.uk/manuals/essumanual/essu2100/essu2111.htm

62 http://www.hmrc.gov.uk/manuals/essumanual/essu2100/essu2102.htm

63 http://www.hmrc.gov.uk/manuals/essumanual/essu2100/essu2102.htm

64 http://www.hmrc.gov.uk/manuals/essumanual/essu2100/essu2102.htm

65 http://www.hmrc.gov.uk/manuals/essumanual/essu2100/essu2102.htm

66 http://www.hmrc.gov.uk/manuals/essumanual/essu2100/essu2102.htm

- A participant in a **CSOP** is obliged to make savings with a third party bank towards the **exercise price** [HMRC Manual ESS2104][67].
- On the **grant date** of a **CSOP option**, the employee has to make an advance payment of the **exercise price**, which is refundable if the **option** lapses [HMRC Manual ESS2105][68].
- The employing company makes a cash payment to the **optionholder** to enable him to **exercise** the **option**, and this amount is taxed as general earnings [HMRC Manual ESS2114][69].
- The **optionholder** has a contractual right to receive a cash payment equal to the **exercise price** on the **exercise date** [HMRC Manual ESS2115][70].
- The **CSOP option** is **grant**ed "in parallel" with another **option**, which might be approved or unapproved. This means that the **optionholder** can choose to **exercise** only one but not both of the **option**s – to the extent that he **exercise**s one **option**, the other **option** falls away. But this is only acceptable if the other **option** does not contain a cash alternative [HMRC Manual ESS2120][71].

3.7.8.6.2. Requirements for the Plan Rules

Section 3.7.8.8 sets out provisions that should be included in the Plan Rules.

3.7.8.7. Valuation Issues

See section 4.3.1.7.

3.7.8.8. Documentation and Approval

3.7.8.8.1. The Plan Rules

See section 3.7.3 for details of the design of the Rules. In addition to what is noted in that section, the Rules would normally contain the following:

3.7.8.8.1.1 Participating Companies

The Plan Rules should specify that **option**s can only be granted to employees of **constituent companies** (see section 3.7.8.4).

3.7.8.8.1.2 Share

The Plan Rules should specify that the shares used in the Plan must be **fully paid up** and not **redeemable ordinary share capital** (see sections 3.7.8.3.1 and 3.7.8.3.2).

---

67 http://www.hmrc.gov.uk/manuals/essumanual/essu2100/essu2104.htm

68 http://www.hmrc.gov.uk/manuals/essumanual/essu2100/essu2105.htm

69 http://www.hmrc.gov.uk/manuals/essumanual/essu2100/essu2114.htm

70 http://www.hmrc.gov.uk/manuals/essumanual/essu2100/essu2115.htm

71 http://www.hmrc.gov.uk/manuals/essumanual/essu2100/essu2120.htm

3.7.8.8.1.3 Eligible Employee

The Plan Rules should specify that **option**s may only be granted to people who meet the qualification requirements set out in section 3.7.8.5.1 and 3.7.8.5.2.

3.7.8.8.1.4 Option must be Contractual

An **option** must be a contractual right of the **optionholder**. For a UK company, this means it must either be granted for consideration or by deed. The **option** must clearly state any conditions on the **optionholder**'s right to **exercise**.

3.7.8.8.1.5 Performance Conditions

HM Revenue & Customs' views on performance conditions are set out in the Manual at ESS2030[72] to ESS2057[73].

In particular, note that a performance condition must be objective [HMRC Manual ESS2043[74]]. There can be a power to amend or waive the condition during the **exercise period** if events happen, but such a power must also be **exercise**d using objective machinery [HMRC Manual ESS2052[75]]. Any amendment must be fair and reasonable.

In practice, HM Revenue & Customs will accept a form of wording which makes it clear that the Directors can only amend a performance condition if the effect is neutral, i.e. the condition is no more difficult to satisfy following the amendment [HMRC Manual ESS2052[76]]. Furthermore, the Rules can permit the Directors to waive a condition that is no longer a fair measure of performance.

3.7.8.8.1.6 Individual Limits

The Plan Rules should contain a rule that no individual can have an **option** over shares worth more than £30,000, measured as at the **grant date**. This should be coupled with a "blue pencil" rule; this states that if **option**s are accidentally granted which exceed the £30,000 limit, then those **option**s take effect as unapproved **option**s. See section 3.7.8.5.3 for HM Revenue & Customs' views on how such a rule should be operated.

3.7.8.8.1.7 Determination of Exercise price

The Plan Rules should prevent a **CSOP option** from being granted with an **exercise price** less than the **CGT value** of the shares on the **grant date**, unless HMRC agree that an earlier date can be used [ITEPA 2003, Sch4, para 22(2)]. The

---

72 http://www.hmrc.gov.uk/manuals/essumanual/essu2000/essu2030.htm

73 http://www.hmrc.gov.uk/manuals/essumanual/essu2000/essu2057.htm

74 http://www.hmrc.gov.uk/manuals/essumanual/essu2000/essu2043.htm

75 http://www.hmrc.gov.uk/manuals/essumanual/essu2000/essu2052.htm

76 http://www.hmrc.gov.uk/manuals/essumanual/essu2000/essu2051.htm

exercise price must be stated on the **grant date**, and cannot thereafter be changed unless there is a **variation of share capital** [ITEPA 2003, Sch4, para 22(3)].

The sort of circumstances where HM Revenue & Customs will accept the **CGT value** being determined by reference to an earlier date than the **grant date** are where there is an "invitation and acceptance" procedure for **options**. If there is an invitation and acceptance procedure, the **grant date** must be within 30 days of the first day by reference to which the **exercise price** was established [HMRC Manual ESS28019][77].

HM Revenue & Customs will accept a Plan Rule that contains a formula such as: "The **exercise price** shall be x or such higher price as may be agreed with HMRC Shares Valuation". This allows for any delay in agreeing values with HM Revenue & Customs [HMRC Manual ESS29007][78].

The **exercise price** can also be determined according to a formula, so that, for example, it rises or falls in line with the profitability of the company, provided it can never be less than the **CGT value** on the **grant date** (or earlier date) [HMRC Manual ESS29008][79]. The **exercise price** can also vary over time so that, for example, a higher **exercise price** is paid on **exercise** before three years, but, again, the **exercise price** can never be less than the **CGT value** on the **grant date** or earlier date [HMRC Manual ESS29009][80].

The **exercise price** must be in addition to any **grant price** that is paid for the **option**. Any amount paid for the **option** on the **grant date** must clearly show how much of that is the **grant price**, and how much is an advance payment of the **exercise price** [HMRC Manual ESS29011][81]. Any advance payment of the **exercise price** must be refundable if the **option** lapses [HMRC Manual ESS2105][82].

3.7.8.8.1.8 Variation of share capital

THIS SECTION APPLIES TO **CSOP** AND **SAYE**

The **exercise price** and number of shares subject to an **option** can be adjusted to take account of a variation in share capital [ITEPA 2003, Sch3, para 28(3) and Sch4, para 22(3)]. The formula for the adjustment is set out in section 13.3.1. The adjustment must be approved by HM Revenue & Customs in advance [ITEPA 2003, Sch3, para 28(4) and Sch4, para 22(4)].

---

77 http://www.hmrc.gov.uk/manuals/essumanual/essu28000/essu28019.htm

78 http://www.hmrc.gov.uk/manuals/essumanual/essu29000/essu29007.htm

79 http://www.hmrc.gov.uk/manuals/essumanual/essu29000/essu29008.htm

80 http://www.hmrc.gov.uk/manuals/essumanual/essu29000/essu29009.htm

81 http://www.hmrc.gov.uk/manuals/essumanual/essu29000/essu29011.htm

82 http://www.hmrc.gov.uk/manuals/essumanual/essu2100/essu2105.htm

3.7.8.8.1.9 Maximum Number of Shares

If the **CSOP option** is granted over a variable number of shares, there must be a maximum number of shares that can be acquired through the **option** [HMRC Manual ESS28067][83].

3.7.8.8.1.10 Non-Transferability

THIS SECTION APPLIES TO **EMI**, **SAYE** AND **CSOP**

The Plan Rules should state that **option**s are not transferable, although they can be transmitted on death [ITEPA 2003, Sch3, para 29, Sch4, para 23 and Sch5, para 38].

3.7.8.8.1.11 Departing employees

The Plan Rules should set out the circumstances in which a former employee is permitted to **exercise** his **option**.

The employment requirement for **CSOP** (see section 3.7.8.5.1) only applies on the **grant date**. It is therefore possible for a former director or employee to **exercise** a **CSOP option** and obtain tax relief after termination of employment [ITEPA 2003, Sch4, para 24]. However, companies generally will not want a former employee to continue to hold his **option** for more than a few months after terminating employment.

The Plan Rules can contain "good leaver" provisions, but HMRC's practice is to limit the way in which these can take effect.

If an **optionholder** terminates employment because of injury, disability, **redundancy** or **retirement**, the Directors cannot have any discretion as to whether he is allowed to **exercise** his **option**. The Rules must either allow him to **exercise** or prevent him from exercising [HMRC Manual ESS2082][84]. See also *IR Share Focus 1* (July 2002)[85].

If the Plan Rules specify a **retirement** age, this should be the same for men and women and it should not be less than 55 [ITEPA 2003, Sch4, para 35A]. This is because an **optionholder** who retires at the specified **retirement** age and **exercise**s an **option** within the following six months will not be charged to income tax on the **option gain**, even if the **exercise** is within three years of the **grant date** (see section 8.3.1.2).

Where the **optionholder** terminates for any other reason, the Directors can have discretion as to whether to allow him to **exercise**, but the discretion must be **exercise**d fairly and reasonably. The Rules can also provide that the **option**

---

83 http://www.hmrc.gov.uk/manuals/essumanual/essu28000/essu28067.htm

84 http://www.hmrc.gov.uk/manuals/essumanual/essu2000/essu2082.htm

85 http://www.hmrc.gov.uk/shareschemes/news/share_focus1.pdf

terminates automatically six months following termination of employment unless the Directors permit **exercise** [HMRC Manual ESS2082][86].

Note that it can be discriminatory if people who retire on reaching the specified **retirement** age are allowed to **exercise** their **options**, but people who choose to leave the labour market at a younger age are not. One way around this is for the Directors to operate a policy whereby people who leave the labour market entirely are allowed to **exercise** their **options**, whereas people who leave to join competitors are not.

3.7.8.8.1.12 Deceased Optionholders

THIS SECTION APPLIES TO **EMI** AND **CSOP**

The Plan Rules should specify what is to happen if an **optionholder** dies. There is no obligation to allow the personal representatives of a deceased **optionholder** to **exercise** the **option**. If the personal representatives are allowed to **exercise** the **option**, then this cannot be for a period of more than twelve months after the death [ITEPA 2003, Sch4, para 25 and Sch5, para 38(b)].

3.7.8.8.1.13 Change of Control

THIS SECTION APPLIES TO **SAYE** AND **CSOP**

The Plan Rules may contain "change of control" provisions (see section 3.7.3.10), but these must be objective. They cannot give the Directors discretion to allow some, but not all, **optionholder**s to **exercise** their **option**s.

The Plan Rules should contain "rollover" provisions. If the Plan Rules do not contain "rollover" provisions, then an approved rollover will not be possible in the event of a change of control – in other words, the **option**s will lose their approved status following the rollover [HMRC Manual ESS15012][87] (see section 8.5.6.3).

3.7.8.8.1.14 Allotment of Shares within 30 days

THIS SECTION APPLIES TO **SAYE** AND **CSOP**

The Plan Rules must provide that, when an **optionholder exercise**s a **CSOP option** or an **SAYE option**, the shares are registered and allotted in his name within 30 days [HMRC Manual ESS12023][88].

3.7.8.8.1.15 PAYE Withholding and NIC Transfers

PAYE withholding and NIC can arise on the **exercise** of a **CSOP option** (see section 8.3.2).

---

86 http://www.hmrc.gov.uk/manuals/essumanual/essu2000/essu2082.htm

87 http://www.hmrc.gov.uk/manuals/essumanual/essu13000/essu15012.htm

88 http://www.hmrc.gov.uk/manuals/essumanual/essu12000/essu12023.htm

The Rules can require the **optionholder** to reimburse the employer company for PAYE, and/or accept a transfer of NIC, as a condition of exercising the **option**. See section 3.7.3.13 for more discussion of this.

The **optionholder** must accept any such obligation, which will usually be stated in the ancillary documents.

Note that HM Revenue & Customs will not allow such an obligation to be a condition of the **option** being **grant**ed, or of the shares being allotted.

The **optionholder** must be given the opportunity to pay any liability to PAYE or NIC either from his own funds or through deductions from salary. Failing this, the company can be authorised to sell sufficient of his shares to meet the liability.

If the **optionholder** fails to "make good" the PAYE within 90 days, there will be a further income tax liability under ITEPA 2003, s222 (see section 3.7.3.14).

3.7.8.8.1.16 Amendments to the Rules

THIS SECTION APPLIES TO **CSOP**, **SIP** AND **SAYE**

The Plan Rules should provide that no "key feature" of the Plan can be altered without the prior consent of HM Revenue & Customs. If a "key feature" is altered without HMRC's consent, this will be a "disqualifying event" and HMRC may be allowed to withdraw approval for the Plan [ITEPA 2003, Sch2, para 84(1)(b), Sch3, para 42(2)(aa), Sch4, para 30(2)(aa)].

A key feature is any feature that is necessary for the Plan to be approved [ITEPA 2003, Sch2, para 84(6), Sch3, para 42(2B), Sch4, para 30(4)].

However, even if a key feature of the Plan is altered, this does not automatically mean that HMRC are entitled to withdraw approval; the alteration must be such that the Plan would not be capable of approval if a new application were made [ITEPA 2003, Sch2, para 84(2), Sch3, para 42(2A), Sch4, para 30(3)].

3.7.8.8.2. Approval Process

The process for applying for approval of a CSOP is set out on HM Revenue & Customs' website at
http://www.hmrc.gov.uk/shareschemes/csop_first_steps_app_eer.htm

There is a two-stage process. First, HM Revenue & Customs will review the documents and confirm that they meet the statutory requirements – this is called "informal approval".

Subsequently, the **scheme organiser** can adopt the **CSOP** and send in the final documents, whereupon HM Revenue & Customs will grant formal approval and the Plan can start to be operated. A list of the documents required for formal approval is at
http://www.hmrc.gov.uk/shareschemes/csop_form_app_eer.htm

3.7.8.9. Tax Treatment of Employee

See section 8.3.1.

3.7.8.9.1. PAYE and NIC

See section 8.3.2.

3.7.8.9.2. Reporting

See section 8.3.3.

3.7.8.9.3. Capital Gains Treatment

See section 8.3.4.

3.7.8.10. Tax Treatment of Employer

See section 17.4.3 for deductibility of **option** gains and section 17.6 for deductibility of establishment costs.

3.7.8.11. Accounting Treatment

See section 19.3.6.5.

3.7.8.12. Sources of Shares

See section 3.7.4.

3.7.8.13. Matrix Summary of Advantages and Disadvantages of CSOP options

Feature	**Advantage**	**Disadvantage**
Availability	Available to a wider range of companies than EMI	Not available to all companies
Flexibility		Restrictions required to protect the interests of existing owners may not be permitted (see section 3.7.8.3.4). Possible to use a separate class of shares but only if the "other shareholdings" test is satisfied (see section 3.7.8.3.5)
Limits		Subject to £30,000 limit
Accounting (p/l)	Profit and loss account charge limited to value of **option** on **grant date**	Cannot be "trued up" if subject to market-based performance condition
Accounting (balance sheet)	Issue of new shares increases capital	Dilutes existing shareholders if new shares issued
Corporation Tax	Automatic deduction available in many circumstances	Automatic deduction not available for **exercises** following sale to unlisted company
Income Tax and NIC	No income tax or NIC if **exercise** more than three years after	

Feature	Advantage	Disadvantage
	grant date (or by **good leaver** within six months of termination)	
Capital Gains Tax		Taper relief starts from **exercise date**

3.7.9. Frequently Asked Questions

THE FOLLOWING QUESTIONS APPLY TO BOTH **CSOP** AND **SAYE**

3.7.9.1. ***Will HM Revenue & Customs grant approval for a CSOP or SAYE in relation to options that have already been granted?***

No. Any **option**s **grant**ed before the date of HM Revenue & Customs' formal approval letter must be treated as unapproved.

3.7.9.2. ***Is it possible for a third party shareholder, such as an EBT, to grant approved options over shares it holds?***

Yes. However, the shareholder must either already hold the shares or have a right to acquire them. The **scheme organiser** must be consulted before the **option**s are **grant**ed.

3.7.9.3. ***How does the scheme organiser add new subsidiaries to the list of participating companies?***

The **scheme organiser** must notify HM Revenue & Customs and provide all the relevant details of the new participating companies. This must happen before it can **grant** any **option**s to employees of the new participating companies [HMRC Manual ESS1041[89]].

3.7.9.4. ***Is it acceptable for a group company to make a cash compensation payment to a participant where it is not possible to adjust options to take account of a corporate event?***

No. This would be an unacceptable feature of the Scheme [HMRC Manual ESS2112[90]].

3.7.9.5. ***Is it acceptable for a third party to make a cash compensation payment to a participant where it is not possible to adjust options to take account of a corporate event?***

Yes, because HM Revenue & Customs would not regard this as a feature of the Plan. [HMRC Manual ESS2112[91]].

---

[89] http://www.hmrc.gov.uk/manuals/essumanual/essu1000/essu1041.htm

[90] http://www.hmrc.gov.uk/manuals/essumanual/essu2100/essu2112.htm

[91] http://www.hmrc.gov.uk/manuals/essumanual/essu2100/essu2112.htm

3.7.9.6. After participants have exercised their options, is it possible to pay cash compensation for failure to adjust options?

Yes. HM Revenue & Customs would not regard this as a feature of the Plan [HMRC Manual ESS2112[92]].

3.7.9.7. Can a group company make cash payments to employees so that they can exercise their share options?

Yes, as long as it is explained to the employees that the cash is general earnings chargeable to income tax and to NIC [HMRC Manual ESS2114[93]].

3.7.9.8. Can the scheme organiser grant approved options in parallel with phantom options?

No. The effect of this would be that the participant would have a choice between receiving cash or shares [HMRC Manual ESS2115[94]].

3.7.9.9. Can the scheme organiser grant approved options in parallel with other options, whether approved or unapproved?

Yes, as long as the parallel **option** does not have a cash alternative. [HMRC Manual ESS2120[95]]

3.7.9.10. Can you deduct notional selling costs in calculating the tax on the exercise of an approved option in an unapproved manner?

No. The tax liability would be calculated in accordance with ITEPA 2003, s476, which does not allow a deduction for notional selling costs – see section 8.1.2.4)

THE FOLLOWING QUESTION APPLIES TO **CSOP**, **SAYE** AND **SIP**

3.7.9.11. Will HM Revenue & Customs grant approval for a CSOP, SAYE or SIP before it has been formally established by the Company?

Yes. They will grant provisional approval to take effect from the moment the scheme is established, provided there are no changes to the form of the scheme, the legislation, or the circumstances of the **scheme company** in the interim.

THE FOLLOWING QUESTIONS APPLY ONLY TO **CSOP**

3.7.9.12. Can an option be granted over a variable number of shares?

Yes. This is possible as long as the Rules, or the **option** contract, contain an objective way of calculating the number of shares at the **exercise date**, and there is a maximum number [HMRC Manual ESS2062[96]].

---

[92] http://www.hmrc.gov.uk/manuals/essumanual/essu2100/essu2112.htm

[93] http://www.hmrc.gov.uk/manuals/essumanual/essu2100/essu2114.htm

[94] http://www.hmrc.gov.uk/manuals/essumanual/essu2100/essu2115.htm

[95] http://www.hmrc.gov.uk/manuals/essumanual/essu2100/essu2120.htm

[96] http://www.hmrc.gov.uk/manuals/essumanual/essu2000/essu2062.htm

3.7.9.13. *When an optionholder terminates employment, to what extent can the Directors have a discretion as to whether to allow him to exercise his CSOP option?*

If an **optionholder** terminates employment because of injury, disability, **redundancy** or **retirement**, the Directors cannot have a discretion. The Rules must specify whether the **optionholder** can **exercise** in these circumstances. In any other circumstances, the Directors can have a discretion to decide in individual circumstances.

3.7.9.14. *Can the scheme organiser grant an option with a variable exercise price?*

Yes, as long as the **exercise price** cannot be reduced to less than the **market value** of the shares on the **grant date** [HMRC Manual ESS29009[97]].

3.7.9.15. *Is cashless exercise possible in an approved scheme?*

Yes, it is possible to have arrangements whereby the employee borrows money to **exercise** the **option** and then sells sufficient shares to cover the **exercise price**. See *IR Share Focus 1*[98].

3.7.9.16. *Is it possible to pay the exercise price in instalments?*

No – see HMRC Manual ESS2102[99].

3.7.9.17. *Is it possible for the optionholder to pay the exercise price by surrendering shares he already owns?*

No – see HMRC Manual ESS2102[100].

3.7.9.18. *Is it possible for the Plan to have a "cash alternative", i.e. where the optionholder can be paid the option gain in cash rather than receiving shares?*

No – see HMRC Manual ESS2102[101].

3.7.9.19. *Can the optionholder be required to enter into an agreement before exercising the option to sell the shares after exercising the option?*

No – see HMRC Manual ESS2102[102].

3.7.9.20. *Can a CSOP option be conditional on the optionholder refraining from participating in an SAYE or SIP?*

No – see HMRC Manual ESS2102[103].

---

[97] http://www.hmrc.gov.uk/manuals/essumanual/essu29000/essu29009.htm

[98] http://www.hmrc.gov.uk/shareschemes/news/share_focus1.pdf

[99] http://www.hmrc.gov.uk/manuals/essumanual/essu2100/essu2102.htm

[100] http://www.hmrc.gov.uk/manuals/essumanual/essu2100/essu2102.htm

[101] http://www.hmrc.gov.uk/manuals/essumanual/essu2100/essu2102.htm

[102] http://www.hmrc.gov.uk/manuals/essumanual/essu2100/essu2102.htm

3.7.9.21. *Can a CSOP option be conditional on the optionholder saving towards the exercise price?*

Yes, provided that the only reason for imposing the condition is to ensure that the **optionholder** has sufficient funds to **exercise** the **option** [HMRC Manual ESS2104[104]].

3.7.9.22. *Can a CSOP option be conditional on the optionholder making an advance payment towards the exercise price?*

Yes, but the advance payment must be refundable in full in the event of the **option** lapsing [HMRC Manual ESS2105[105]]. It is important to distinguish this from requiring the **optionholder** to pay a **grant price** for the **option**, which would not be refundable.

3.7.9.23. *Can a CSOP option have an exercise price expressed in a foreign currency?*

Yes, but there must be a formula in the Rules for determining the sterling equivalent on the **grant date**, to ensure the £30,000 limit is not broken [HMRC Manual ESS29010[106]].

---

103 http://www.hmrc.gov.uk/manuals/essumanual/essu2100/essu2102.htm

104 http://www.hmrc.gov.uk/manuals/essumanual/essu2100/essu2104.htm

105 http://www.hmrc.gov.uk/manuals/essumanual/essu2100/essu2105.htm

106 http://www.hmrc.gov.uk/manuals/essumanual/essu29000/essu29010.htm

4. Designing and Implementing New Employee Reward Plan

4.1. Stakeholder Plans

4.1.1. Description

A stakeholder plan is the simplest and least onerous type of pension plan for a small employer to offer to its employees.

A stakeholder plan must be a money purchase arrangement, so the employer's costs are easily controllable. There is no open-ended funding commitment in the same way as there is with a **defined benefits plan**.

Management charges in relation to a stakeholder plan are strictly limited – they may not exceed more than 1% of the value of the fund in any year, and they are taken from the fund rather than from contributions.

The provider can set a minimum contribution amount, but this cannot be greater than £20, which makes the stakeholder plan accessible to low-paid employees with limited savings capacity.

Small employers will usually use an insurance company to act as the stakeholder manager, but it is possible to establish a stakeholder plan under trust, provided at least one third of the trustees are independent. Using a trust-based scheme is unlikely to be a cost-effective approach for a small employer, because of the additional time commitment of organising trustee meetings, and the cost of paying an independent trustee.

4.1.2. Regulatory Treatment

4.1.2.1. Compulsory Offer of Stakeholder Plans

It is compulsory for certain employers to offer a stakeholder plan to their staff. The Pensions Regulator has published a decision tree that employers can use to determine whether they have to offer a stakeholder plan. This is at

http://www.thepensionsregulator.gov.uk/stakeholderPensions/DecisionTree/index.asp.

In particular, there are exemptions for:

- employers with fewer than five employees, and
- employers who offer personal pension schemes to their staff, where the employer contributes at least 3% of basic salary, employees can contribute additional sums by payroll deduction, and there are no penalties for employees who cease contributing or transfer out.

4.1.2.2. *Actions Required of Employer*

The responsibilities required of the employer in relation to a stakeholder plan are limited.

The employer must:

- consult employees about the choice of stakeholder provider and then designate one or more providers;
- inform employees and representative organisations (such as trade unions) about the plan;
- allow employees to contribute to the plan by salary deduction, and ensure that the appropriate amounts are deducted and paid to the provider;
- keep accurate records of the amounts contributed by employees.

4.1.2.3. *Selecting a Stakeholder Provider*

A complete list of stakeholder providers is available on the Pension Regulator's website at

http://www.thepensionsregulator.gov.uk/stakeholderPensions/theRegister/RegisterSearch/SchemeList.aspx. However, some stakeholder providers only accept business from certain kinds of employer, and others are closed to new business.

An independent financial adviser should be able to help an employer to select an appropriate stakeholder provider.

4.1.3. Tax Treatment of Employee

See section 3.3.4.

4.1.4. Tax Treatment of Employer

See section 3.3.7.

4.1.5. Matrix Summary of Advantages and Disadvantages of Stakeholder Plans

See section 3.3.8.

4.2. Offers of Shares to Employees

4.2.1. Overview

This section deals with two common ways in which shares can be offered or awarded to employees generally. The methods discussed are:

- Discounted Share Offers (see section 4.2.3)
- Share Incentive Plan (see section 4.2.4).

See section 3.5.1 for descriptions of other plans that may be more appropriate for senior executive plans.

4.2.2. Company Law Issues

Company law issues regarding offers of shares are described in more detail in section 18.

4.2.2.1. *Financial Assistance*

See section 18.7.

4.2.2.2. *Loans to Directors*

See section 18.11.

4.2.2.3. *Disclosure*

See section 18.9.

4.2.3. Discounted Share Offers

4.2.3.1. *Description*

Sometimes a company offers its shares to its employees at a **discount** to the market price. The purpose of the **discount** is to encourage employees to invest in the shares. Since private company shares are usually illiquid, employees may need the **discount** as an additional incentive to invest in the shares.

Sometimes the shares will be "blocked", i.e. not saleable for a defined period.

4.2.3.2. *Tax Treatment of Employee*

Income tax charges can arise on the acquisition of shares and, in some circumstances, in relation to the subsequent growth in value. Capital gains tax may also apply to all or a proportion of the subsequent growth in value.

4.2.3.2.1. *Income Tax On Acquisition*

See section 11.1.2 if the shares are not restricted.

See section 11.1.3 if the shares are blocked.

4.2.3.2.2. *Post-Acquisition Income Tax*

See section 12.3.

4.2.3.2.3. *Capital Gains Treatment*

See section 12.11.3 if the shares were restricted.

See section 12.11.5 if the shares were not restricted.

4.2.3.3. *Tax Treatment of Employer*

See section 17.4.2.

4.2.3.4. *Accounting Treatment*

See section 19.3.6.1.

4.2.3.5. *Sources of Shares*

See section 3.7.4.

4.2.3.6. *Matrix Summary of Advantages and Disadvantages*

See section 3.5.3.6.

4.2.4. Share Incentive Plan (SIP)

4.2.4.1. Description

A Share Incentive Plan ("**SIP**") is a tax-advantaged plan for enabling employees to invest in shares. There are substantial tax and NIC savings for both the employer and employee.

A **SIP** must be operated on a "similar terms" basis and open to all employees who meet a minimum service requirement (see section 4.2.4.12.1).

The shares in a **SIP** are initially held by the **SIP** Trustee [ITEPA 2003, Sch2, para 71].

There are four different methods in which employees can acquire shares under a **SIP**:

- Free Shares (see section 4.2.4.2)
- Partnership Shares (see section 4.2.4.3)
- Matching Shares (see section 4.2.4.4)
- Dividend Shares (see section 4.2.4.5)

The company does not have to make all four methods available at once. A company can offer only Free Shares, or only Partnership Shares, or both. A company that offers Partnership Shares may also offer Matching Shares, but does not have to. Matching Shares and Dividend Shares cannot be offered on their own.

Shares acquired through a **SIP** can be transferred directly into an Individual Savings Account ("ISA"). Ordinarily, an ISA cannot hold unquoted securities, but there is an exclusion for unquoted shares acquired through a SIP [Individual Savings Account Regulations 1998, reg 7(2)(h)(iii)]. The transfer must take place within 90 days of the shares ceasing to be subject to the **SIP** [Individual Savings Account Regulations 1998, reg 7(10)(ba)]. The CGT value of the shares, measured as at the date of transfer into the ISA, counts against the individual's annual £7,000 limit on ISA contributions [Individual Savings Account Regulations 1998, reg 7(2)(h)].

The employee is also able to transfer the shares acquired through the **SIP** directly into a **registered pension scheme** (see section 3.3.4.1.5). In effect, this means that the employee gets two lots of tax relief – no income tax on the acquisition of the shares and further tax relief on the transfer into the **registered pension scheme**.

HM Revenue & Customs' guidance for employers on **SIP** is available at http://www.hmrc.gov.uk/shareschemes/sip_employers.htm.

4.2.4.2. *Free Shares*

4.2.4.2.1. Description

An employer can **award** up to £3,000 worth of Free Shares per employee each year through a **SIP** (see section 4.2.4.2.2). The **award** is free of income tax and NIC (see section 4.2.4.2.5).

The **award**s can be made conditional on performance (see section 4.2.4.2.3). The employee must not sell the shares or withdraw them from the **SIP** for at least three years (see section 4.2.4.2.4) and to secure the full tax advantages, the employee must leave them in the **SIP** for five years (see section 4.2.4.2.5.3). The shares can be forfeitable if the employee leaves or tries to sell the shares within three years (see section 4.2.4.2.6).

4.2.4.2.2. Limit

A company can **award** up to £3,000 worth of Free Shares to each employee in each tax year [ITEPA 2003, Sch2, para 35(1)]. If the shares are **restricted securities**, their **unrestricted market value** must be assessed [ITEPA 2003, Sch2, para 35(3)]. This limit must be contained in the **SIP** Rules.

4.2.4.2.3. Performance Conditions

Free Shares can be **award**ed to all employees on similar terms.

However, in order to increase the **SIP**'s incentive effect, the **award**s can be subject to performance conditions. The performance conditions must be objective and can be linked to the business performance of the company as a whole, or a business unit, or even an individual employee [ITEPA 2003, Sch2, para 39]. The unit whose performance is being measured is a "performance unit".

The performance conditions must be disclosed to employees as soon as possible, although the employer need not disclose matters that are commercially confidential [ITEPA 2003, Sch2, para 40].

Two types of performance measures are allowed: Method 1 and Method 2.

4.2.4.2.3.1 Method 1

Under a Method 1 **SIP**, no more than 80% of the shares can be **award**ed by reference to performance [ITEPA 2003, Sch2, para 41(2)(b)]. The remainder must be **award**ed on a similar terms basis without reference to performance [ITEPA 2003, Sch2, para 41(2)(a)].

No individual can receive a performance-related **award** of shares that is more than four times the number of non-performance-related shares **award**ed to any other individual [ITEPA 2003, Sch2, para 41(2)(c)].

A worked example of this can be found on HM Revenue & Customs' website at http://www.hmrc.gov.uk/shareschemes/share_incentive/free.htm#1

4.2.4.2.3.2 Method 2

Under Method 2, there is no limit on the percentage of the shares that can be **award**ed by reference to performance. However, every employee in the performance unit must participate on similar terms [ITEPA 2003, Sch2, para 42(2)].

Different performance targets can be set for different performance units, but they must be consistent with each other [ITEPA 2003, Sch2, para 42(3)].

Performance targets are consistent if, at the time when they are set, they can reasonably be viewed as being comparable in terms of the likelihood of their being met by the performance units to which they apply [ITEPA 2003, Sch2, para 42(6)].

4.2.4.2.4. Holding Period

Any employee who receives Free Shares or Matching Shares must sign an agreement, which imposes a holding period on the Free or Matching Shares [ITEPA 2003, Sch2, para 36(1)].

This must be at least three years, but no more than five years. [ITEPA 2003, Sch2, para 36(2)].

During the holding period, the employee may not sell the shares, and must leave them registered in the name of the **SIP** Trustee [ITEPA 2003, Sch2, para 36(1)].

However, the holding period ends when the employee terminates employment [ITEPA 2003, Sch2, para 36(5)].

ITEPA 2003, Sch2, para 61 applies the same rules to Matching Shares as to Free Shares.

4.2.4.2.5. Tax Treatment

4.2.4.2.5.1 Acquisition of Shares

There is no income tax charge in relation to an **award** of Free or Matching Shares [ITEPA 2003, s490(2)]. The value of Free Shares or Matching Shares is disregarded in calculating the employee's earnings for NIC purposes [SSCR 2001, Sch3, Part IX, para 7].

4.2.4.2.5.2 Termination of Employment as a Good leaver

When an employee ceases to be in **relevant employment**, his **SIP** shares lose their favourable tax treatment from that time onwards. This may give rise to an income tax charge. However, there will be no income tax charge if he is a **good leaver** [ITEPA 2003, s498].

4.2.4.2.5.3 Free or Matching Shares Ceasing to be Subject to the Plan

There will be an income tax charge if an employee either

- withdraws his Free or Matching Shares from the **SIP**; or
- terminates employment with the group (except as a **good leaver**) and retains his Free or Matching Shares

within five years following the **award date** of the Free or Matching Shares [ITEPA 2003, s505(1)]. The date this occurs is called the exit date [ITEPA 2003, s505(1)(b)].

There is no income tax charge if the employee is a **good leaver** [ITEPA 2003, s505(6)(b)] or if he forfeits his Free or Matching Shares [ITEPA 2003, s505(6)(a)] (see section 4.2.4.2.6).

If the exit date is within three years after the **award date**, the taxable amount is the **CGT value** of the shares on the exit date [ITEPA 2003, s505(2)].

If the exit date is three years or more, but less than five years, after the **award date**, the taxable amount is the lower of (a) the **CGT value** of the shares on the **award date** and (b) the **CGT value** of the shares on the exit date [ITEPA 2003, s505(3)]. However, note that the calculation will be adjusted if there has been a capital receipt in relation to the shares (see section 4.2.4.7).

See section 4.2.4.6 for PAYE and NIC.

4.2.4.2.6. Forfeitability

Free and Matching Shares can be forfeitable during a **forfeiture period** of up to three years [ITEPA 2003, Sch2, para 32(5)].

The shares can only be forfeitable in the following circumstances:

- the employee ceases to be in **relevant employment**
- the employee attempts to withdraw his shares from the **SIP** Trustee
- the employee withdraws the corresponding Partnership Shares from the Plan (does not apply to Free Shares).

[ITEPA 2003, Sch2, para 32(1)].

However, Free Shares and Matching Shares cannot be forfeited if an employee terminates employment as a **good leaver** (see section 4.2.4.2.5.2) [ITEPA 2003, Sch2, para 32(2)].

4.2.4.3. *Partnership Shares*

4.2.4.3.1. Description

An employer can allow employees to sacrifice up to £1,500 worth of salary each year to acquire Partnership Shares through a **SIP** (see section 4.2.4.3.2). The salary used to acquire the shares is free of income tax and NIC (see section 4.2.4.3.8.1).

The offer of shares cannot be conditional on performance; Partnership Shares must be offered to all employees on similar terms [ITEPA 2003, Sch2, para 9]. The employee must not sell the shares or withdraw them from the **SIP** for at least three years (see section 4.2.4.3.7) and to secure the full tax advantages, the employee must leave them in the **SIP** for five years (see section 4.2.4.3.8.5). The shares cannot be forfeitable.

4.2.4.3.2. Limit

An employee can sacrifice up to £1,500 worth of salary each year to acquire Partnership Shares [ITEPA 2003, Sch2, para 46(1)]. This can be specified as a monthly limit of £125 or an annual limit of £1,500 or either.

However, if the employee's salary is less than £15,000, then the effective limit is 10% of his salary [ITEPA 2003, Sch2, para 46(2)].

The **scheme organiser** can specify lower limits [ITEPA 2003, Sch2, para 46(3)], and it can specify different limits in respect of different **award**s of shares [ITEPA 2003, Sch2, para 46(4)]. The limits can be expressed to exclude certain parts of the employee's earnings, such as overtime or bonus payments [ITEPA 2003, Sch2, para 46(4)(b)]. However, HM Revenue & Customs believe that any item that is excluded must be one that applies to all participants. In *IR Share Focus 2* they give the example that bonuses cannot be excluded if only some participants receive bonuses[107].

For the purposes of testing the 10% limit, the Rules must contain a definition of "salary". This means cash earnings after deducting allowable pension contributions and charitable payroll giving [ITEPA 2003, Sch2, para 43(4)].

4.2.4.3.3. Minimum Contribution

The **SIP** Rules can impose a minimum contribution limit, but this cannot be greater than £10 per month [ITEPA 2003, Sch2, para 47].

4.2.4.3.4. Partnership Share Agreement

In order to acquire Partnership Shares, the employee must enter into a partnership share agreement [ITEPA 2003, Sch2, para 44(1)]. The partnership share agreement contains the following terms:

- the employee authorises his employing company to make deductions from his salary for the purchase of Partnership Shares [ITEPA 2003, Sch2, para 44(1)(a)];
- the other party to the agreement undertakes to ensure that partnership shares are **award**ed to the employee in accordance with the **SIP** [ITEPA 2003, Sch2, para 44(1)(b)];
- it specifies what amounts are to be deducted from the employee's salary, and at what intervals [ITEPA 2003, Sch2, para 45(3)]. The employee and the company can vary this;
- the deductions can be stated as fixed amounts or as a percentage of salary [ITEPA 2003, Sch2, para 45(4)];
- if there is an accumulation period (see section 4.2.4.3.6), when it begins and ends [ITEPA 2003, Sch2, para 51(3)];

---

107 http://www.hmrc.gov.uk/shareschemes/news/share-focus2.pdf

- if the **SIP** Trustee cannot acquire an exact whole number of shares with the partnership share money, the partnership share agreement should provide for the surplus cash to be carried forward and used to acquire shares at the next opportunity; otherwise the surplus cash must be repaid to the participant [ITEPA 2003, Sch2, para 52(6)].

4.2.4.3.5. Effect on Benefits

If an employee elects to acquire Partnership Shares, this reduces his salary for the purposes of calculating his entitlement to certain statutory benefits (see section 4.2.4.20). The partnership share agreement must include a prescribed form of wording notifying the employee of this [ITEPA 2003, Sch2, para 48].

4.2.4.3.6. Accumulation Period

4.2.4.3.6.1 What is an Accumulation Period?

A **SIP** can have an accumulation period for Partnership Shares. This means that the employees' salary deductions are accumulated for a period of up to twelve months and used to acquire shares at the end of the accumulation period.

4.2.4.3.6.2 Acquisition of Shares where no Accumulation Period

If there is no accumulation period, then the salary deductions must be used to acquire shares within at most 30 days after they have been collected from the employees [ITEPA 2003, Sch2, para 50(4)]. The shares are acquired at the market price on the **acquisition date** [ITEPA 2003, Sch2, para 50(2)]. Any remaining cash is either returned immediately to the employee or carried forward and added to the next salary deduction [ITEPA 2003, Sch2, para 50(5)].

4.2.4.3.6.3 Acquisition of Shares where Accumulation Period

If there is an accumulation period, then the accumulated savings are used to acquire shares within at most 30 days after the end of the period [ITEPA 2003, Sch2, para 52(5)]. The shares are acquired at the lower of their **CGT value** at the beginning and at the end of the accumulation period [ITEPA 2003, Sch2, para 52(3)].

4.2.4.3.6.4 Advantages and Disadvantages of an Accumulation Period

A company that intends to buy shares from other shareholders to deliver to employees as Partnership Shares should not use an accumulation period. There is a risk that the **CGT value** of the shares will rise during the accumulation period, with the result that the accumulated savings are not sufficient funds to purchase the shares to which employees are entitled.

However, a company that intends to issue new shares through the **SIP** should use an accumulation period because this will involve less administration than issuing more shares each month.

Another advantage of an accumulation period is that the Rules can prevent participants from stopping and re-starting savings more than once during the period [ITEPA 2003, Sch2, para 54(4)]. If there is no accumulation period, the Rules must allow participants to stop and re-start savings as often as they wish, which can lead to administrative difficulties [ITEPA 2003, Sch2, para 54(1)].

4.2.4.3.7. Holding Period

The **scheme organiser** cannot impose a holding period on the Partnership Shares; employees must be able to withdraw the shares at any time [ITEPA 2003, Sch2, para 57(1)].

The employee must also be free to withdraw from a partnership share agreement at any time, whereupon his savings must be returned to him [ITEPA 2003, Sch2, para 55(1)].

4.2.4.3.8. Tax Treatment

4.2.4.3.8.1 Salary Deductions

There is no income tax charge on the salary deducted under a partnership share agreement [ITEPA 2003, s492(1)]. The salary deducted is disregarded in calculating the employee's earnings for NIC purposes [SSCR 2001, Sch3, Part IX, para 6].

However, any salary deducted before 6 April 2006 will not be pensionable earnings for the purposes of calculating HM Revenue & Customs' limits on pension schemes [ITEPA 2003, s492(2)].

4.2.4.3.8.2 Stamp Duty

There is no stamp duty or stamp duty reserve tax on the transfer of Partnership or Dividend Shares to a participant [FA 2001, s95].

4.2.4.3.8.3 Termination of Employment as a Good Leaver

See section 4.2.4.2.5.2.

4.2.4.3.8.4 Cash Payments from the Plan

There will be an employment income tax charge if the **SIP** Trustee pays cash over to the employee [ITEPA 2003, s503]. This can arise for several reasons, but is most likely to happen where an employee leaves during an accumulation period.

4.2.4.3.8.5 Partnership Shares Ceasing to be Subject to the Plan

There will be an income tax charge if an employee either

- withdraws his Partnership Shares from the **SIP**; or
- terminates employment with the group (except as a **good leaver**) and

within five years following the **acquisition date** of the Partnership Shares [ITEPA 2003, s506(1)]. The date this occurs is called the exit date [ITEPA 2003, s505(1)(b)].

There is no income tax charge if the employee is a **good leaver** [ITEPA 2003, s506(6)].

If the exit date is within three years after the **acquisition date**, the taxable amount is the **CGT value** of the shares on the exit date [ITEPA 2003, s506(2)].

If the exit date is three years or more, but less than five years, after the **acquisition date**, the taxable amount is the lower of (a) the amount of salary deducted to acquire the shares and (b) the **CGT value** of the shares on the exit date [ITEPA 2003, s506(3)]. However, note that the calculation will be adjusted if there has been a capital receipt in relation to the shares (see section 4.2.4.7).

See section 4.2.4.6 for PAYE and NIC.

4.2.4.3.9. Forfeitability

Partnership Shares cannot be forfeitable.

4.2.4.4. *Matching Shares*

4.2.4.4.1. Description

When an employee acquires Partnership Shares through a **SIP**, the employer can **award** Matching Shares, in a ratio that can be as generous as two Matching Shares for every Partnership Share (see section 4.2.4.4.2). The **award** is free of income tax and NIC (see section 4.2.4.2.5.1).

The Matching Shares must be the same class and have the same rights as the Partnership Shares to which they relate [ITEPA 2003, Sch2, para 59(1)(a)]. They must be **award**ed on the same day as the Partnership Shares to which they relate [ITEPA 2003, Sch2, para 59(1)(b)].

The **award**s cannot be made conditional on individual performance, although since the **scheme organiser** is under no obligation to **award** Matching Shares, it could choose to do so only to reward a period of good overall performance. The terms on which Matching Shares are **award**ed must be the same for every participant [ITEPA 2003, Sch2, para 59(1)(c)].

The employee must not sell the shares or withdraw them from the **SIP** for at least three years (see section 4.2.4.2.5.3) and to secure the full tax advantages, the employee must leave them in the **SIP** for five years (see section 4.2.4.2.5.3). The shares can be forfeitable if the employee leaves or tries to sell the shares within three years (see section 4.2.4.2.6).

4.2.4.4.2. Limit

The **scheme organiser** can **award** up to two Matching Shares to each employee for each Partnership Share acquired in each tax year [ITEPA 2003, Sch2, para 60].

The ratio of Matching Shares to Partnership Shares cannot be more generous than two for one, and must be determined by number, not, for example, by value [ITEPA 2003, Sch2, para 60(2)].

4.2.4.4.3. Performance Conditions

Matching Shares cannot be subject to performance conditions.

4.2.4.4.4. Holding Period

See section 4.2.4.2.4.

4.2.4.4.5. Tax Treatment

4.2.4.4.5.1 Acquisition of Shares

See section 4.2.4.2.5.1.

4.2.4.4.5.2 Termination of Employment as a Good leaver

See section 4.2.4.2.5.2.

4.2.4.4.5.3 Matching Shares Ceasing to be Subject to the Plan

See section 4.2.4.2.5.3.

See section 4.2.4.6 for PAYE and NIC.

4.2.4.4.6. Forfeitability

See section 4.2.4.2.6.

4.2.4.5. Dividend Shares

4.2.4.5.1. Description

When the SIP Trustee receives dividends in respect of Free Shares, Partnership Shares or Matching Shares, it must usually pay them immediately to the employees who own the underlying shares [ITEPA 2003, Sch2, para 69].

However, if the **scheme organiser** so directs, the SIP Trustee must reinvest all the dividends in acquiring further shares [ITEPA 2003, Sch2, para 62(1)(a)]. These are called Dividend Shares and must be the same class, and have the same rights, as the shares on which the dividends were paid [ITEPA 2003, Sch2, para 65].

Alternatively, the SIP Trustee can ask employees to elect as to whether they want to receive the dividends in cash, or to have their dividends reinvested in Dividend Shares [ITEPA 2003, Sch2, para 62(1)(b)].

The SIP Trustee must actually invest the dividend in Dividend Shares within 30 days of the dividend payment date [ITEPA 2003, Sch2, para 66(2)].

Dividends that are reinvested in Dividend Shares are initially exempt from dividend income tax (see section 4.2.4.5.4.1).

Awards of Dividend Shares cannot be made conditional on performance. The SIP Trustee must treat all participants fairly and equally in exercising its powers to acquire Dividend Shares [ITEPA 2003, Sch2, para 66(1)].

The employee must not sell the shares or withdraw them from the SIP for at least three years (see section 4.2.4.5.3). The shares cannot be forfeitable (see section 4.2.4.5.7).

4.2.4.5.2. Limit

The **SIP** Trustee can reinvest up to £1,500 of cash dividends in acquiring Dividend Shares for each employee in each tax year [ITEPA 2003, Sch2, para 64(1)]. The Dividend Shares must be the same class of shares as the Free, Partnership or Matching Shares to which they relate [ITEPA 2003, Sch2, para 65].

4.2.4.5.3. Holding Period

Dividend Shares are subject to a three-year holding period [ITEPA 2003, Sch2, para 67].

During the holding period, the employee may not sell the shares, and must leave them registered in the name of the **SIP** Trustee [ITEPA 2003, Sch2, para 36(1)].

However, the holding period ends when the employee terminates employment [ITEPA 2003, Sch2, para 36(5)].

4.2.4.5.4. Tax Treatment

4.2.4.5.4.1 Acquisition of Shares

There is no income tax charge in relation to a cash dividend reinvested in Dividend Shares [ITTOIA 2005, s770(2)]. However, the participant is not entitled to a tax credit in relation to the amount reinvested [ITTOIA 2005, s397(6)]. Dividend Shares are not earnings for NIC purposes.

4.2.4.5.4.2 Stamp Duty

See section 4.2.4.3.8.2.

4.2.4.5.5. Cash Dividends Not Paid Out

Often the cash dividend will not divide equally into a round number of shares. Where this happens, the balance of the dividend can be kept by the **SIP** Trustee and added to the next dividend [ITEPA 2003, Sch2, para 68(2)].

There is no income tax charge in relation to a cash dividend held back by the **SIP** Trustee for later reinvestment in Dividend Shares [ITTOIA 2005, s770(2)]. However, the participant is not entitled to a tax credit in relation to the cash dividend [ITTOIA 2005, s397(6)].

4.2.4.5.5.1 Termination of Employment as a Good leaver

See section 4.2.4.2.5.2.

4.2.4.5.5.2 Dividend Shares Ceasing to be Subject to the Plan

There will be a dividend income tax charge if an employee terminates employment with the group (except as a **good leaver**) within three years following the **acquisition date** of the Dividend Shares [ITTOIA 2005, s394].

There is no income tax charge if the employee is a good leaver [ITEPA 2003, s498].

The taxable amount is the amount of the original cash dividend that was reinvested [ITTOIA 2005, s394(3)]. The tax credit, however, is based on the tax credit fraction in force on the date the Dividend Shares cease to be subject to the SIP [ITTOIA 2005, s394(5)].

However, note that the calculation will be adjusted if there has been a capital receipt in relation to the shares (see section 4.2.4.7).

4.2.4.5.6. Cash that Cannot be Reinvested

If the cash cannot be reinvested within three years, or the employee leaves before the cash is reinvested, then the cash must be paid out to the employee immediately [ITEPA 2003, Sch2, para 68(4)]. The employee will then be taxed on the cash paid out as a distribution [ITTOIA 2005, s393(3)]. The tax credit is based on the tax credit fraction in force on the date the cash dividend is paid out [ITTOIA 2005, s393(5)].

4.2.4.5.7. Forfeitability

Dividend Shares cannot be forfeitable [ITEPA 2003, Sch2, para 65(b)].

4.2.4.6. *PAYE and NIC*

4.2.4.6.1. PAYE on Shares Ceasing to be Subject to the Plan

An employment income tax charge can arise if Free, Partnership, or Matching Shares cease to be subject to the **SIP** prematurely. See section 4.2.4.2.5.3 in relation to Free and Matching Shares and section 4.2.4.3.8.5 in relation to Partnership Shares

If the shares are **readily convertible asset**s at the time they cease to be subject to the **SIP**, the tax is withheld through PAYE [ITEPA 2003, s509(2)]. The amount subject to PAYE is the amount of employment income [ITEPA 2003, s509(3)].

In deciding whether the shares are **readily convertible asset**s, the fact that the **SIP** Trustee may be willing to make a market in the shares is ignored [ITEPA 2003, s509(5)].

The **SIP** Rules can oblige the participant to reimburse the employer company for the tax. But if this obligation is not in the Rules, the **SIP** Trustee is instead obliged to pay the amount of the tax to the employer company [ITEPA 2003, s510(2)].

If the employer company no longer exists, or for some other reason it is impracticable for the employer company to deduct PAYE, then the withholding obligation falls on the **SIP** Trustee [ITEPA 2003, s511].

4.2.4.6.2. PAYE on Capital Receipts

A capital receipt on **SIP** shares can be taxable employment income (see section 4.2.4.7). The **SIP** Trustee must pay to the employer company an amount equal to the employment income [ITEPA 2003, s513(2)]. The employer company must then deduct PAYE and pay the balance to the participant [ITEPA 2003, s513(3)].

If the employer company no longer exists, or for some other reason it is impracticable for the employer company to deduct PAYE, then the withholding obligation falls on the **SIP** Trustee [ITEPA 2003, s514].

4.2.4.6.3. NIC

Any amount that is taxable under the **SIP** code and is subject to PAYE is also subject to NIC [SSCR 2001, reg 22(8)].

4.2.4.7. *Capital Receipts*

If a participant receives any money or money's worth in respect of shares held in a **SIP**, this will be a capital receipt unless it falls within a limited range of exceptions [ITEPA 2003, s502(2) and (3)]. An example would be if the **scheme company** had a rights issue, and the **SIP** Trustee sold the rights for cash. Any capital receipt is taxable as employment income [ITEPA 2003, s501(4)] unless it relates to Free, Partnership or Matching Shares that have been held for five years or more, or Dividend Shares that have been held for three years or more [ITEPA 2003, s501(3)]. See section 4.2.4.6.2 for the PAYE consequences and section 4.2.4.6.3 for NIC.

A receipt will not be a capital receipt if it is already taxable under a different part of the **SIP** code or it constitutes the proceeds of disposal of the shares, or if it takes the form of new shares received in a company reconstruction [ITEPA 2003, Sch2, para 87].

Also, if there is a rights issue and the participant directs the **SIP** Trustee to sell enough of the rights to be able to take up the balance, this will not be a capital payment [ITEPA 2003, s502(5)].

When there has been a capital payment in relation to any shares, the amount of the capital payment is deducted in calculating any subsequent tax charge on those shares [ITEPA 2003, s505(4) for Free and Matching Shares, ITEPA 2003, s506(4) in relation to Partnership Shares, and ITTOIA 2005, s395(2) in relation to Dividend Shares].

4.2.4.8. *Capital Gains Tax*

4.2.4.8.1. *Exemption for the SIP Trustee*

A **SIP** Trustee can acquire shares before it actually needs to transfer them to employees. During the period when it holds the shares, the value of the shares may rise, so that the **SIP** Trustee would realise a gain on the eventual transfer to the participants.

In these circumstances, the **SIP** Trustee may be exempt from capital gains tax depending on the amount of time that passes between the acquisition and the disposal:

- if any of the shares were **readily convertible asset**s on the **acquisition date**, the period is two years [TCGA 1992, Sch7D, para 2(2)];
- if none of the shares were **readily convertible asset**s on the **acquisition date**, but they subsequently become **readily convertible asset**s, the period is the longer of five years from the **acquisition date** or two years from the date on which the shares became **readily convertible assets** [TCGA 1992, Sch7D, para 2(3)(b)];

- if none of the shares were **readily convertible asset**s on the **acquisition date** and they do not subsequently become **readily convertible asset**s, the period is five years [TCGA 1992, Sch7D, para 2(3)(a)];
- notwithstanding this, if the shares were acquired with an employer contribution that was made at (or within twelve months before) a time when the **SIP** held 10% or more of the **ordinary share capital**, and dividend and capital rights in the company, then the period is ten years from the **acquisition date** [TCGA 1992, Sch7D, para 2(4)].

4.2.4.8.2. Exemption for the Participant

When the shares cease to be subject to the **SIP**, the Trustee is deemed to dispose of them, and the participant to acquire them, at **market value** [TCGA 1992, Sch7D, para 5(1)]. This means that the growth in value of the shares during the period in which they are subject to the **SIP** is free from capital gains tax.

4.2.4.9. Checklist for Implementation of a SIP

In order to establish and operate a **SIP**, certain conditions must be satisfied. Some of these conditions apply to the Trust Deed and Plan Rules; some to the **scheme company**; others to any employee who participates.

If there is any doubt as to whether the **scheme company** qualifies for **SIP**, discuss this with HM Revenue & Customs Employee Shares and Securities Unit.

Here is a checklist to go through before establishing a **SIP** or **award**ing shares under it.

Requirement	**ITEPA 2003, Sch2**	**Commentary**
Purpose of the Trust	Para 71	4.2.4.13.1
Shares Transferred from a **QUEST** can only be Free or Matching Shares	Para 78	4.2.4.13.2
Partnership share money to be paid to **SIP** Trustee as soon as practicable	Para 49(1)	4.2.4.13.3
Partnership share money to be held in a bank or building society	Para 49(3)	4.2.4.13.4
Partnership share money: any interest arising must be passed to participant by **SIP** Trustee	Para 49(4)	4.2.4.13.5
SIP Trustee to give notice of foreign tax deducted from foreign cash dividend	Para 75(5)	4.2.4.13.7
SIP Trustee to give notice showing number, description, **market value** and holding period for Free Shares and Matching Shares	Para 75(2)	4.2.4.13.8

Requirement	ITEPA 2003, Sch2	Commentary
SIP Trustee to give notice showing number, description & amount used for Partnership Shares	Para 75(3)	4.2.4.13.9
SIP Trustee to give notice showing number, description, **market value**, holding period and amount carried forward for Dividend Shares	Para 75(4)	4.2.4.13.10
SIP Trustee not to dispose of Free, Matching or Dividend Shares during holding period	Para 73	4.2.4.13.11
SIP Trustee must deal with disposals & rights as directed by participants	Para 72(1)	4.2.4.13.12
SIP Trustee must maintain PAYE records	Para 80(1)	4.2.4.13.13
SIP Trustee must maintain records to monitor participants in connected plans	Para 71A	4.2.4.13.14
SIP Trustee must inform participants of facts relating to their income tax liability	Para 80(3)	4.2.4.13.15
SIP Trustee must pay out any money or money's worth	Para 74(1)	4.2.4.13.16
SIP Trustee may dispose of shares or accept money to meet any PAYE obligations	Para 79(1)	4.2.4.13.17
The **SIP** must have at least two trustees unless the trustee is a limited company	Para 71(1)	4.2.4.13.18
Every **SIP** Trustee must be **resident** in the UK	Para 71(1)	4.2.4.13.19
The Trust Deed must comply with the rule against perpetuities (unless governed by Scots law)	Para 71(1)	4.2.4.13.20
Early termination of **SIP**	Para 89	4.2.4.13.21
The **SIP** must not contain any discouraging features	Para 8(3)	4.3.4.4.1.3
The **SIP** must not contain non-essential features	Paras 7(2) and 71(4)	4.2.4.13.24
There must be no preferential treatment for directors or senior employees	Para 10	4.2.4.12.3
No other conditions	Para 11	4.2.4.12.4
No loan arrangements	Para 12	4.2.4.12.5
Every UK **resident** and **ordinarily resident** employee must be eligible	Para 8(1)(b)	4.2.4.12.1.3

Requirement	**ITEPA 2003, Sch2**	**Commentary**
Every employee with qualifying service must be eligible	Para 15(2)(b)	4.2.4.12.1.1
Any other non-**resident/ordinarily resident** employees can be eligible at company's discretion	Para 14(7)	4.2.4.12.1.3
No Free Shares, Partnership Shares or Matching Shares if shares **award**ed in the same tax year under a connected plan	Para 18	4.2.4.12.1.4
Plan must contain limits for Free, Partnership and Dividend shares where participation is in more than one connected plan in a tax year	Para 18A	4.2.4.12.1.4
Participant must not have a **material interest**	Para 19	3.7.8.5.2
Participant must be employed by a **constituent company** on **award** date	Para 15(1)	4.2.4.12.1.1
Participation must be available on the same terms	Para 9	4.2.4.12.2
No **award** unless individual was eligible at 'appropriate time'	Para 14	4.2.4.12.7
Free shares: Rules must require a free share agreement	Para 36(1)	4.2.4.2.4
Free shares: Rules must impose holding period of three to five years	Para 36(2)	4.2.4.2.4
Free shares: Rules must impose limit of £3,000 per year	Para 35(1)	4.2.4.2.2
Free shares: Rules must set out terms on which there can be performance allowances	Para 38	4.2.4.2.3
Partnership shares: Rules must require a partnership share agreement	Para 44	4.2.4.3.4
Partnership share money: limits of £125 per month or £1500 per tax year and 10% of salary for partnership shares	Para 46	4.2.4.3.2
Partnership shares: any specified minimum not to be more than £10	Para 47	4.2.4.3.3
Partnership Shares: scaling down must be proportionate	Para 53(5)	4.2.4.13.25
Partnership share money: participant must be able to stop and re-start deductions	Para 54(1)	4.2.4.3.6.4

Requirement	ITEPA 2003, Sch2	Commentary
Partnership share money: **SIP** Trustee must apply this to acquire partnership shares on **acquisition date**	Para 50(1) and 52(2)	4.2.4.3.6.2 and 4.2.4.3.6.3
Partnership share money: surplus after acquisition of shares to be carried forward or repaid	Para 52(6)	4.2.4.3.4
Participant must be able to withdraw from the partnership share agreement and be repaid any partnership share money	Para 55(1) and (3)	4.2.4.3.7
Participant must be able to withdraw Partnership Shares from the **SIP**	Para 57(1)	4.2.4.3.7
Partnership share money must be repaid on withdrawal of approval/plan termination	Para 56	4.2.4.13.6
Matching Shares: must be the same class and rights as matched Partnership Shares	Para 59(1)(a)	4.2.4.4.1
Matching Shares: **award** must be on the same day as matched Partnership Shares	Para 59(1)(b)	4.2.4.4.1
Matching Shares: **award**s must be on exactly the same basis	Para 59(1)(c)	4.2.4.4.1
Matching Shares: **award** ratio not more than two for one	Para 60(2)	4.2.4.4.2
Matching Shares: Rules must impose holding period of three to five years	Para 61	4.2.4.2.4
Dividend Shares: Rules must impose holding period of three years	Para 67	4.2.4.5.3
Dividend Shares: Rules must impose limit of £1500 per year	Para 64(1)	4.2.4.5.2
Dividend Shares: must be the same class and have the same rights as shares generating the dividend	Para 65	4.2.4.5.1
Dividend Shares: participants must be treated fairly and equally	Para 66(1)	4.2.4.5.1
Dividend Shares: cash to be applied in acquiring shares on an **acquisition date** within 30 days after its receipt	Para 66(2)	4.2.4.5.1
Dividend Shares: amounts not reinvested must be paid to the participant	Para 68(4)	4.2.4.5.6
Retirement age must be not less than 50 and the same for men and women	Para 98	4.2.4.13.26

Requirement	ITEPA 2003, Sch2	Commentary
Definition of Salary	Para 43(4)	4.2.4.3.2
Group Plan or Single-Company Plan	Para 4	3.7.8.4.1
Jointly owned companies	Para 91	3.7.8.4.2
Shares must be **ordinary share capital**	Para 26	3.7.8.3.1
Shares must satisfy the listing requirement	Para 27	3.7.8.3.3
Shares must be **fully paid up** and not **redeemable**	Para 28(1)	3.7.8.3.2
Shares must not be prohibited	Para 29	4.2.4.11.3
Shares must be subject only to permitted restrictions	Para 30	4.2.4.10.4
Definition of **market value** – Rules must contain provision for Shares Valuation agreement where appropriate	Para 92	4.2.4.15
HM Revenue & Customs must approve amendments to a key feature	Para 84(1(b)	3.7.8.8.1.16

4.2.4.10. *Approval requirements for the Shares*

4.2.4.10.1. Ordinary share capital

See section 3.7.8.3.1.

4.2.4.10.2. Fully paid up and not redeemable

See section 3.7.8.3.2.

4.2.4.10.3. The listing requirement

See section 3.7.8.3.3.

4.2.4.10.4. Subject only to permitted restrictions

Shares to be used for a **SIP** must not be subject to restrictions, unless either those restrictions apply to all shares of the same class, or are permitted restrictions [ITEPA 2003, Sch2, para 30(1)].

The permitted restrictions are:

- the **SIP** shares can have no or limited voting rights [ITEPA 2003, Sch2, para 31]
- Free and Matching Shares can be forfeitable on termination of employment within three years (except for **good leavers**) [ITEPA 2003, Sch2, para 32] (see section 4.2.4.2.6)
- the **SIP** Shares can be subject to permitted pre-emption conditions.

This is the requirement that private companies most often have difficulty in complying with, because owners of private companies will often want to impose restrictions that treat other employees differently from themselves or members of their family.

Particular issues relate to pre-emption conditions (see section 4.2.4.10.4.1) and restrictions on transferability (see section 4.2.4.10.4.2).

4.2.4.10.4.1 Pre-Emption Conditions

Frequently, the Board of Directors of a private company will want to be able to compel a departing employee to sell any shares he holds, because the Board will want to control the register tightly.

A restriction that compels former employees to offer their shares for sale is permitted, provided it is in the Articles of Association, and that it applies to all directors or employees of the **scheme company** and any other company of which it has **Section 840 control** [ITEPA 2003, Sch2, para 33(1)]. The restriction can also apply to "permitted transferees", i.e. persons to whom the employee is authorised by the Articles to transfer his shares [ITEPA 2003, Sch2, para 33(2)].

The sale of the shares must be for a consideration specified in the Articles of Association [ITEPA 2003, Sch2, para 33(3)]. Anyone else selling shares of the same class must not be able to sell their shares on better terms [ITEPA 2003, Sch2, para 33(3)(c)].

4.2.4.10.4.2 Restrictions on Transferability

Another restriction that the Board of Directors of a private company will often want to impose on employee shareholders is the power to refuse to register a transfer of shares. This is a permitted restriction, provided that the Board gives an undertaking to HM Revenue & Customs not to use the power in a way that discriminates against people who acquired their shares through a **SIP**, and notifies these people accordingly [ITEPA 2003, Sch2, para 30(4)].

Any other restrictions on the participant's freedom to dispose of the shares will generally be unacceptable [ITEPA 2003, Sch2, para 30(2)].

Here are some common examples of restrictions that are found in relation to shares of private companies, with commentary on whether HM Revenue & Customs find them acceptable or unacceptable for **SIP**.

4.2.4.10.4.3 Restrictions that HMRC consider unacceptable

- The shares delivered through the **SIP** have inferior dividend rights compared to other shares of the same class [HMRC Manual ESS12030][108].
- When new shares are issued, other shareholders are given priority over employees in applying for them [HMRC Manual ESS12030][109].
- When shares are offered for sale, another person has priority in purchasing them – except where that person has the same right whether or not he actually

[108] http://www.hmrc.gov.uk/manuals/essumanual/essu12000/essu12030.htm

[109] http://www.hmrc.gov.uk/manuals/essumanual/essu12000/essu12030.htm

holds the shares, in which case the priority rights attach to the person rather than to the shares. An example of this would be where an EBT has a first right of refusal on shares that are offered for sale [HMRC Manual ESS12032][110].

- A shareholder who holds at least a certain percentage of the share capital has a prior right to acquire more shares when they are offered for sale [HMRC Manual ESS12033][111].
- **SIP** participants are not allowed to transfer their shares to trusts without going through the compulsory offer for sale procedures, but other shareholders are allowed to do this [HMRC Manual ESS12034][112].
- When a **SIP** participant wants to sell his shares, he is obliged to do so on terms which are worse than those which apply to other shareholders [ITEPA 2003, Sch2, para 33(3)(c)].
- When a **SIP** participant leaves employment, he is required by a shareholders' agreement to offer his shares for sale [HMRC Manual ESS12052][113].
- Certain named individuals, who hold shares of the same class as the **SIP** shares, are excluded from the requirement to offer those shares for sale on termination of employment [HMRC Manual ESS12062][114].
- If an employee or director ceases employment for a specified reason, such as **retirement**, he is not required to offer his shares for sale [HMRC Manual ESS12062][115].
- When an employee or director ceases employment, he is required to sell only part of his holding [HMRC Manual ESS12062][116].
- If an employee or director is compelled to offer his shares for sale on termination of employment, but nobody offers to buy *all* his shares, then he does not have to sell any shares [HMRC Manuals ESS12062[117]. and 12100[118]].
- When an employee or director ceases employment, the directors have power to decide not to compel him to offer his shares for sale [HMRC Manual ESS12062][119].

---

110 http://www.hmrc.gov.uk/manuals/essumanual/essu12000/essu12032.htm

111 http://www.hmrc.gov.uk/manuals/essumanual/essu12000/essu12033.htm

112 http://www.hmrc.gov.uk/manuals/essumanual/essu12000/essu12034.htm

113 http://www.hmrc.gov.uk/manuals/essumanual/essu12000/essu12052.htm

114 http://www.hmrc.gov.uk/manuals/essumanual/essu12000/essu12062.htm

115 http://www.hmrc.gov.uk/manuals/essumanual/essu12000/essu12062.htm

116 http://www.hmrc.gov.uk/manuals/essumanual/essu12000/essu12062.htm

117 http://www.hmrc.gov.uk/manuals/essumanual/essu12000/essu12062.htm

118 http://www.hmrc.gov.uk/manuals/essumanual/essu12000/essu12100.htm

119 http://www.hmrc.gov.uk/manuals/essumanual/essu12000/essu12062.htm

- When an employee or director ceases employment, the Articles of Association allow the purchaser to pay for the shares in something which is not cash [HMRC Manual ESS12081][120].
- When an employee or director offers his shares for sale, the pricing mechanism is different from that used when other people sell their shares [HMRC Manual ESS12091][121].
- Another shareholder is allowed to transfer his shares without going through the same procedures as an employee would have to on terminating employment – unless this transfer is approved by *all* the other shareholders [HMRC Manual ESS12105][122].
- There is a shareholders' agreement which limits or removes the rights of shares held by employees to receive dividends.
- There is a shareholders' agreement which restricts the ability of employees to transfer their shares.
- There is a shareholders' agreement that says that a **SIP** participant who offers his shares for sale receives a lower price than a non-employee.

4.2.4.10.4.4 Restrictions that HMRC consider to be acceptable

- The **scheme company** is incorporated under non-UK law, and is subject to restrictions imposed under that law, such as US securities law [HMRC Manual ESS13015][123].
- A restriction attaches to all shares of the same class, either because it is contained in the company's Articles of Association or because it was imposed by a special resolution of the company [HMRC Manual ESS12011][124]. An example of this would be drag along provisions and tag along provisions whereby all shareholders can be forced to, or have the right to, sell their shares to someone who offers to purchase all, or more than a certain percentage, of the company's share capital.
- A restriction attaches to shares of other classes [HMRC Manual ESS12012][125].
- A restriction attaches to other shares of the same class, but those shares cannot be scheme shares [HMRC Manual ESS12012][126].

---

120 http://www.hmrc.gov.uk/manuals/essumanual/essu12000/essu12081.htm

121 http://www.hmrc.gov.uk/manuals/essumanual/essu12000/essu12091.htm

122 http://www.hmrc.gov.uk/manuals/essumanual/essu12000/essu12105.htm

123 http://www.hmrc.gov.uk/manuals/essumanual/essu13000/essu13015.htm

124 http://www.hmrc.gov.uk/manuals/essumanual/essu12000/essu12011.htm

125 http://www.hmrc.gov.uk/manuals/essumanual/essu12000/essu12012.htm

126 http://www.hmrc.gov.uk/manuals/essumanual/essu12000/essu12012.htm

- A **SIP** Trustee is able to transfer shares to **SIP** participants without first having to offer those shares to other shareholders [HMRC Manual ESS12035][127].
- Certain individuals hold shares of the same class as the scheme shares, but their shares are restricted under a shareholders' agreement. [HMRC Manual ESS12024][128].
- The Articles of Association require all former employees and directors to offer their shares for sale on termination of employment. The terms of the sale are the same as apply to any other shareholder who offers his shares for sale. [HMRC Manual ESS12060][129].
- An employee who ceases employment and is required to offer his shares for sale, is allowed to keep any shares that nobody wants to purchase [HMRC Manual ESS12065][130].
- If another shareholder voluntarily offers his shares for sale, he can withdraw some or all of his shares from sale after the process has started, but an employee who is compelled to sell his shares on termination of employment cannot withdraw any of his shares from sale [HMRC Manual ESS12096][131].
- The Articles allow shareholders to transfer shares to family members without first offering them to the other shareholders, and this Article applies to everyone who holds shares of the class used in the **SIP** [HMRC Manual ESS12107][132].

4.2.4.11. *Approval Requirements for Participating Companies*

4.2.4.11.1. Group scheme or a single-company scheme

See section 3.7.8.4.1.

4.2.4.11.2. Jointly owned companies

See section 3.7.8.4.2.

4.2.4.11.3. Prohibited Companies

A **SIP** cannot use shares in a "service company" or a company that controls a service company and is itself controlled by the persons to whom the service company provides services [ITEPA 2003, Sch2, para 29(1)].

The mischief that this paragraph is seeking to prevent is where an organisation transfers employees into a service company, which then provides their services to the rest of the group. The service company would operate on a cost plus basis, so

---

[127] http://www.hmrc.gov.uk/manuals/essumanual/essu12000/essu12035.htm

[128] http://www.hmrc.gov.uk/manuals/essumanual/essu12000/essu12024.htm

[129] http://www.hmrc.gov.uk/manuals/essumanual/essu12000/essu12060.htm

[130] http://www.hmrc.gov.uk/manuals/essumanual/essu12000/essu12065.htm

[131] http://www.hmrc.gov.uk/manuals/essumanual/essu12000/essu12096.htm

[132] http://www.hmrc.gov.uk/manuals/essumanual/essu12000/essu12107.htm

its revenue and profits would be controlled by the rest of the group. Although the **SIP** shares would have value, their value would be capable of manipulation. Therefore, in the absence of this paragraph, it would be possible for an organisation to provide tax-free remuneration to its employees in the form of **SIP** shares without actually giving up any real equity.

4.2.4.12. Approval Requirements relating to Participants

4.2.4.12.1. Is the Plan open to all employees?

A **SIP** must be open to any employee who meets the criteria laid down in ITEPA 2003, Sch2, paras 13 to 24. In practice, this means that they must be invited to participate in an **award**. The criteria are:

4.2.4.12.1.1 Director or employee

He must be an employee of the **scheme organiser** or a **constituent company**, and have been so throughout any qualifying period (see section 4.2.4.12.1.2) [ITEPA 2003, Sch2, para 15(2)].

4.2.4.12.1.2 Qualifying Period

The Plan Rules can stipulate a qualifying period. The qualifying period may be different for different **award**s of shares, but for each **award** it must be the same for all employees, whether of the **scheme organiser** or any **constituent company** [ITEPA 2003, Sch2, para 16(7)].

The qualifying period relates to continuous employment with a qualifying company. The term "qualifying company" includes not only the **scheme organiser** and any **constituent company** but also any other company that was a **constituent company** when the individual was employed by it, or which was an **associated company** of the **scheme organiser** or any current or former **constituent company** [ITEPA 2003, Sch2, para 17].

The maximum qualifying periods are:

4.2.4.12.1.2.1 Free Shares

Eighteen months ending with the **award** date [ITEPA 2003, Sch2, para 16(2)].

4.2.4.12.1.2.2 Partnership and Matching Shares

If there is no accumulation period, the maximum qualifying period for partnership and matching shares is eighteen months ending with the deduction of partnership share money from salary [ITEPA 2003, Sch2, para 16(3) and (5)].

If there is an accumulation period, the maximum qualifying period for partnership and matching shares is six months ending with the start of the accumulation period [ITEPA 2003, Sch2, para 16(4) and (6)].

4.2.4.12.1.3 Resident and Ordinarily resident in the UK

An employee who meets the other criteria and is both **resident** and **ordinarily resident** in the UK must be invited to participate [ITEPA 2003, Sch2, para 8(1)(b)].

An employee who is not both **resident** and **ordinarily resident** in the UK, but otherwise meets the criteria, can be invited to participate [ITEPA 2003, Sch2, para 14(7)]. However, the Rules can impose additional conditions on such people [ITEPA 2003, Sch2, para 14(8)].

4.2.4.12.1.4 Participation in Connected SIPs

The Rules must prevent an employee from participating simultaneously in more than one **SIP** established by the **scheme company** or any **connected company** [ITEPA 2003, Sch2, para 18].

If an employee participates in the same tax year in more than one **SIP** established by the **scheme company**, or any **connected company**, then the limits on participation apply on a consolidated basis to both or all the SIPs [ITEPA 2003, Sch2, para 18A].

4.2.4.12.1.5 No Material interest

See section 3.7.8.5.2.

4.2.4.12.2. Participation must be available on the same terms

Every person who is invited to participate in the **SIP** must be allowed to do so on the same terms, and those who accept must actually participate on the same terms [ITEPA 2003, Sch2, para 9].

In practice, this is not usually a problem, since the identical terms are offered to every employee who meets the criteria. However, it would be possible, although unusual, to vary the terms to reflect different levels of remuneration, different length of service or hours worked [ITEPA 2003, Sch2, para 9(3)].

It is possible to use more than one factor as long as there is a straight line progression from the lowest paid to highest paid employees. It is not acceptable to "multiply" the factors since the effect could be to benefit higher paid employees disproportionately [ITEPA 2003, Sch2, para 9(4) and (7)].

4.2.4.12.3. There must not be preferential treatment for directors or senior employees

There are two limbs to this test. The first applies to every **SIP**: there must not be any feature of the **SIP** that is likely to have the effect of conferring benefits wholly or mainly on directors or the most highly paid employees [ITEPA 2003, Sch2, para 10(1)].

The second limb of the test only applies where the **scheme organiser** is a member of a group of companies. This does not necessarily mean that the **SIP** has to be a group plan; it could also apply to a single-company scheme.

In these circumstances, it is necessary to show that the identity of the **scheme organiser** and the **constituent companies** is not such as to confer benefits wholly or mainly on directors or the most highly paid employees in the group [ITEPA 2003, Sch2, para 10(3)].

An example of the mischief that this is meant to prevent would be where there were two employing companies in the group: one which employed the directors and higher earners; the other which employed the lower earning employees. If a **SIP** were set up for the first company only, then the second limb of the test would be failed. However, a **SIP** could be set up for both companies or the second company without failing this test.

To ensure compliance with this test, HM Revenue & Customs require a list of all the **constituent companies** to be supplied with the application for approval. The **scheme organiser** must declare that the **SIP** applies to all companies in the group or, if it does not, explain why some companies have been excluded. There may, of course, be sound commercial reasons for excluding some companies, and HM Revenue & Customs will accept these.

Similarly, if a **constituent company** ceases to participate, HM Revenue & Customs may query the removal.

4.2.4.12.4. No Other Conditions

There can be no conditions on an employee participating in a **SIP** beyond those required or authorised by the **SIP** code [ITEPA 2003, Sch2, para 11].

4.2.4.12.5. No Loan Arrangements

There can be no loans made in connection with the arrangements for the **SIP** or the operation of the **SIP** [ITEPA 2003, Sch2, para 12].

This is to stop companies operating arrangements whereby, for example, all employees are issued with Free Shares in lieu of salary, but receive loans from the employing company to maintain their net cash income.

4.2.4.12.6. Employee must meet the employment requirement

A participant in a **SIP** must be either a director or an employee of the **scheme organiser** or another **constituent company** of a group scheme [ITEPA 2003, Sch2, para 15]. Employees who are not **resident** or not **ordinarily resident** in the UK may be allowed to participate.

4.2.4.12.7. Participant must be eligible at the appropriate time

An individual is not eligible to participate in a **SIP** unless he meets the employment requirement at the appropriate time, which differs depending on the nature of the shares [ITEPA 2003, Sch2, para 14(1)]:

- Free Shares: the appropriate time is the **award** date [ITEPA 2003, Sch2, para 14(2)];
- Partnership Shares with no accumulation period: the appropriate time is whenever partnership share money is deducted from his salary [ITEPA 2003, Sch2, para 14(3)];

- Partnership Shares with accumulation period: the appropriate time is when the first deduction of partnership salary is made [ITEPA 2003, Sch2, para 14(4)]
- Matching Shares: the appropriate time is the same as for the Partnership Shares to which the Matching Shares relate [ITEPA 2003, Sch2, para 14(5) and (6)].

4.2.4.12.8. No material interest requirement

See section 3.7.8.5.2.

4.2.4.13. *Approval Requirements for the Plan*

4.2.4.13.1. Purpose of the Trust

The Trust Deed should recite that the purpose of the Trust is to acquire shares and appropriate them to employees in accordance with the Plan [ITEPA 2003, Sch2, para 71(2)].

4.2.4.13.2. Acquisition of Shares from ***QUEST***

Until 2003, there were certain tax advantages to holding shares in a qualifying employee share ownership trust ("**QUEST**"). Those advantages no longer exist, so the **QUEST** Trustee may consider transferring its shares to a **SIP** to benefit employees more effectively.

It is possible for the **QUEST** Trustee to make a "qualifying transfer" to a **SIP** of shares that it either held on 26 November 2002 or purchased using cash it held on that date [FA 1989, s69(3AA) to (3AD) as amended by FA 2003, s142(2)]. The fact that the transfer is "qualifying" means that the **QUEST** Trustee does not trigger an income tax liability.

The **SIP** Trust Deed must provide that, if the **SIP** Trustee does acquire shares through such a qualifying transfer, it can only use them by distributing them to participants as Free or Matching Shares [ITEPA 2003, Sch2, para 78(1)(a)]. The **SIP** Trustee must distribute those shares before it distributes any other shares it holds [ITEPA 2003, Sch2, para 78(1)(b)].

4.2.4.13.3. Partnership share money to be paid to SIP Trustee as soon as practicable

The Trust Deed must provide that, once the employing company has withheld the partnership share money from salary, it must pay it to the **SIP** Trustee as soon as practicable. The **SIP** Trustee must hold the money until it invests it in shares [ITEPA 2003, Sch2, para 49(1)].

4.2.4.13.4. Partnership share money to be held in a bank or building society

The Trust Deed must provide that, while the **SIP** Trustee holds any partnership share money, it must deposit it with a building society or an entity that is permitted to accept deposits within either ICTA 1988, s840A(1)(b) or (c) [ITEPA 2003, Sch2, para 49(3)]. The deposit does not have to bear interest.

4.2.4.13.5. Interest on Partnership share money must be passed to participant

The Trust Deed must provide that, if the **SIP** Trustee puts partnership share money into an interest-bearing account, it must pay the interest over to the participants [ITEPA 2003, Sch2, para 49(4)].

4.2.4.13.6. Partnership share money must be repaid on withdrawal of approval/plan termination

The Rules must provide that, if the **SIP** is terminated, or HM Revenue & Customs withdraw approval, any partnership share money must be returned to the participants as soon as practicable [ITEPA 2003, Sch2, para 56].

4.2.4.13.7. SIP Trustee to give notice of foreign tax deducted from foreign cash dividend

The Trust Deed must provide that, if the **SIP** Trustee holds shares in a foreign company and receives dividends on those shares, it must inform the participant of the amount of any foreign tax deducted from the dividend [ITEPA 2003, Sch2, para 75(5)].

4.2.4.13.8. SIP Trustee to give notice of Free and Matching Shares

The Trust Deed must provide that, if the **SIP** Trustee makes an **award** of Free or Matching Shares to a participant, it must as soon as practicable, give the participant notice of:

- the number and description of the shares;
- their **market value** on the **award** date; and
- the holding period applicable to them.

[ITEPA 2003, Sch2, para 75(2)].

4.2.4.13.9. SIP Trustee to give notice of Partnership Shares

The Trust Deed must provide that, if the **SIP** Trustee makes an **award** of Partnership Shares to a participant, it must as soon as practicable, give the participant notice of:

- the number and description of the shares;
- the amount of partnership share money used to acquire them; and
- their **market value** on the **acquisition date.**

[ITEPA 2003, Sch2, para 75(3)].

4.2.4.13.10. SIP Trustee to give notice of Dividend Shares

The Trust Deed must provide that, if the **SIP** Trustee acquires Dividend Shares on behalf of a participant, it must as soon as practicable, give the participant notice of:

- the number and description of the shares;
- Their **market value** on the **acquisition date;**
- the holding period applicable to them; and
- any amount carried forward for subsequent investment.

[ITEPA 2003, Sch2, para 75(4)].

4.2.4.13.11. SIP Trustee not to dispose of Free, Matching or Dividend Shares during holding period

The Trust Deed must contain a rule preventing the **SIP** Trustee from disposing of any Free, Matching or Dividend Shares during the holding period applicable to them [ITEPA 2003, Sch2, para 73]. However, the **SIP** Trustee can dispose of the shares in certain circumstances:

- if there is a general offer for the shares [ITEPA 2003, Sch2, para 37]
- if the **SIP** Trustee sells rights in order to raise cash to subscribe for other rights [ITEPA 2003, Sch2, para 77]
- if the **SIP** Trustee has to sell a participant's shares to meet PAYE obligations in relation to that participant [ITEPA 2003, Sch2, para 79]
- if the **SIP** is terminated [ITEPA 2003, Sch2, para 90(5)]

4.2.4.13.12. SIP Trustee must deal with disposals & rights as directed by participants

The Trust Deed must require the **SIP** Trustee to deal with the shares and any rights attached to them only in accordance with directions given by the participant whose shares they are [ITEPA 2003, Sch2, para 72(1)]. However, the Trust Deed can provide for participants to be able to give general directions to the Trustee [ITEPA 2003, Sch2, para 72(3)].

4.2.4.13.13. SIP Trustee must maintain PAYE records

The Trust Deed must require the **SIP** Trustee to maintain adequate records of the PAYE liabilities of both itself and the employing company [ITEPA 2003, Sch2, para 80(1)].

4.2.4.13.14. SIP Trustee must maintain records to monitor participants in connected plans

As mentioned in section 4.2.4.12.1.4, it is possible for a participant to participate in more than one **SIP** established by **connected companies** in the same tax year. The **SIP** Trustee must maintain records of any SIPs established by **connected companies** to monitor the application of the overall limits [ITEPA 2003, Sch2, para 71A].

4.2.4.13.15. SIP Trustee must inform participants of facts relating to their income tax liability

The Trust Deed must require the **SIP** Trustee to inform participants of any facts relevant to determining their income tax liability, whether that is employment income or dividend income [ITEPA 2003, Sch2, para 80(3)].

4.2.4.13.16. SIP Trustee must pay out any money or money's worth

If the **SIP** Trustee receives any money or money's worth in relation to the **SIP** shares, it must pay this out to the participants [ITEPA 2003, Sch2, para 74(1)]. This does not however apply to any new shares received in a company reconstruction, or to cash dividends that are reinvested, or to money that has to be retained to meet PAYE liabilities.

4.2.4.13.17. SIP Trustee may dispose of shares or accept money to meet any PAYE obligations

The Trust Deed must allow the **SIP** Trustee to dispose of the participant's shares if it incurs a liability to account for PAYE in relation to that participant. Alternatively, the Trustee can receive cash from the participant to cover the PAYE [ITEPA 2003, Sch2, para 79(1)].

This also includes any liability imposed on the employing company, since the **SIP** Trustee is required to pay enough money to the employing company to allow it to meet the obligation [ITEPA 2003, s510(2)].

4.2.4.13.18. The SIP must have at least two trustees unless the trustee is a limited company

The **SIP** must have "a body of trustees" [ITEPA 2003, Sch2, para 71(1)]. HM Revenue & Customs interpret this to mean that the **SIP** must either have at least two individual trustees, or a limited company as trustee.

4.2.4.13.19. Every SIP Trustee must be resident in the UK

Every trustee of a **SIP** must be **resident** in the UK [ITEPA 2003, Sch2, para 71(1)].

4.2.4.13.20. Rule Against Perpetuities

In order for the Trust Deed to be valid, it must comply with the rule against perpetuities if it is governed by English or Northern Irish law. This is normally achieved by providing that the Trust must expire after 80 years. The rule against perpetuities does not apply if the Trust is governed by Scots law.

4.2.4.13.21. Early termination of SIP

The Trust Deed must provide that, if the **scheme organiser** terminates the **SIP** prematurely, it must serve a plan termination notice on: the **SIP** Trustee; HM Revenue & Customs; and every individual who either holds shares through the **SIP** or has entered into a partnership share agreement [ITEPA 2003, Sch2, para 89].

4.2.4.13.22. HM Revenue & Customs must approve amendments to key features of the ***SIP***

The Trust Deed must provide that HM Revenue & Customs have to give prior approval to any amendment to a key feature of the **SIP** [ITEPA 2003, Sch2, para 84(1)(b)].

4.2.4.13.23. SIP must not contain any discouraging features

See section 4.3.1.4.1.3.

4.2.4.13.24. The SIP must not contain non-essential features

There must not be features of a **SIP** which are neither essential nor reasonably incidental to the purpose of providing benefits for employees and directors in the nature of shares which give them a continuing stake in the **scheme company** and/or complying with the **SIP** code [ITEPA 2003, Sch2, para 7(2) and 71(4)].

If the **scheme organiser** offers employees a choice between Free Shares and cash, HM Revenue & Customs will regard this as a non-essential and unacceptable feature. This was the position they historically took in relation to approved profit sharing schemes [HMRC Manual ESS2521[133]] and it is believed that they take the same view in relation to **SIPs**. However, it is possible for a company to pay a discretionary bonus to employees who choose not to take up Free Shares, if the promotional material for the **SIP** does not refer to this [HMRC Manual ESS2523[134]].

There is not much learning in the public domain about what else HM Revenue & Customs will consider a non-essential feature.

4.2.4.13.25. Scaling Down

Scaling down is the process that must happen if participants apply for more Partnership Shares than are available. In these circumstances, the **SIP** Trustee must scale down all the applications proportionately. [ITEPA 2003, Sch2, para 53(5)].

4.2.4.13.26. Specified Retirement Age

The **SIP** Rules must contain a specified **retirement** age. This must be the same for men and women and must not be less than 50. Clearly, whatever age is selected, it discriminates against employees who have not attained that age. It is therefore prudent to set the age at 50 because this usually discriminates against a smaller proportion of the workforce.

There is no income tax charge where shares cease to be subject to the **SIP** because an employee retires on reaching the specified **retirement** age [ITEPA 2003, s498(2)(e)] because he is a **good leaver** (see section 4.2.4.2.5.2).

4.2.4.14. *Selecting a Trustee/Administrator*

In practice, most companies choose to select an external professional trust company to act as the **SIP** Trustee. This is because the compliance obligations imposed on the **SIP** Trustee are onerous, and it is generally better to use an organisation that has developed and fully tested systems.

Some administrators are more willing to deal with smaller companies than others. Before making a final selection, the **scheme organiser** should contact several potential administrators, informing them of employee numbers, likely take-up, whether there is more than one payroll and how payroll is maintained, and discussing what additional services they can offer, such as preparing presentations to employees.

4.2.4.15. *Valuation Issues*

The **SIP** Rules must set out how **market value** is to be determined. The valuation criterion is the same as for capital gains tax [ITEPA 2003, Sch2, para 92(2)]. For an

---

[133] http://www.hmrc.gov.uk/manuals/essumanual/essu2100/essu2521.htm

[134] http://www.hmrc.gov.uk/manuals/essumanual/essu2100/essu2523.htm

unlisted company, the valuation must be agreed with HMRC Shares Valuation. HM Revenue & Customs' website sets out the process for doing this at http://www.hmrc.gov.uk/shareschemes/svd2.htm. In particular, note that it is essential to complete Form VAL 230W, which can be downloaded from http://www.hmrc.gov.uk/shareschemes/val230.pdf

4.2.4.16. Documentation and Approval

4.2.4.16.1. The Trust Deed and SIP Rules

Section 4.2.4.9 sets out a checklist of items that must be contained in the **SIP** Trust Deed and Rules in order for HM Revenue & Customs to be able to approve the **SIP**.

Model documents, including a specimen Trust Deed and Rules, a Free Share Agreement and a Partnership Share Agreement, are available for download from HM Revenue & Customs' website at
http://www.hmrc.gov.uk/shareschemes/model_doc.htm

In addition to these items, that must be included, there are other powers that can be given to the **SIP** Trustee if the **scheme organiser** wishes.

The two most important of these are:

4.2.4.16.1.1 Power to Borrow

The Trust Deed can give the **SIP** Trustee power to borrow to acquire shares or for other purposes [ITEPA 2003, Sch2, para 76]. This enables the **SIP** Trustee to acquire a block of shares for future distribution to participants.

4.2.4.16.1.2 Power to Sell Rights to take up Other Rights

The Trust Deed can give the **SIP** Trustee power to sell rights in order to raise funds to take up other rights. However, the participant can instruct the **SIP** Trustee not to do this [ITEPA 2003, Sch2, para 77].

4.2.4.16.2. Approval Process

The process for applying for approval of a **SIP** is set out on HM Revenue & Customs' website at
http://www.hmrc.gov.uk/shareschemes/share_incentive/apply.htm#5

There is a two-stage process. First, HM Revenue & Customs will review the documents and confirm that they meet the statutory requirements – this is called "informal approval".

Subsequently, the **scheme organiser** can adopt the **SIP** and send in the final documents, whereupon HM Revenue & Customs will grant formal approval and the **SIP** can start to be operated. A list of the documents required for formal approval is at the same URL as above.

4.2.4.17. *Corporation Tax Deductibility*

4.2.4.17.1. Free and Matching Shares

The employing company can claim a deduction for the **CGT value** of Free or Matching Shares **award**ed to its employees [ICTA 1988, Sch4AA, para 2(1)]. The deduction is taken in the year in which the Free or Matching Shares are **award**ed [ICTA 1988, Sch4AA, para 2(2)(b)]. This is subject to the cases where no deduction is allowed, mentioned in section 4.2.4.17.3.

If the **SIP** is a group plan, the deduction is apportioned between the **constituent companies** in proportion to the number of their employees who participate [ICTA 1988, Sch4AA, para 2(4)].

No other deductions are permitted in relation to the Free or Matching Shares, whether by the employing company or any other company [ICTA 1988, Sch4AA, paras 2(3) and 2(7)].

4.2.4.17.2. Partnership Shares

The employing company is allowed on general principles to claim a deduction for the partnership share money, i.e. the salary sacrificed by the employee to invest in shares.

In addition, if the **CGT value** of the shares on the **award** date exceeds the partnership share money, the employing company can claim a corporate tax deduction for the excess [ICTA 1988, Sch4AA, para 3(2)]. The deduction is taken in the year in which the Free or Matching Shares are **award**ed [ICTA 1988, Sch4AA, para 3(2)(b)]. This is subject to the cases where no deduction is allowed, mentioned in section 4.2.4.17.3.

No other deductions are permitted in relation to the Free or Matching Shares, whether by the employing company or any other company [ICTA 1988, Sch4AA, paras 3(3) and 3(4)].

4.2.4.17.3. Cases where no Deduction is Allowed

No corporate tax deduction is allowed in the following cases:

- where the participant's earnings are not subject to UK taxation [ICTA 1988, Sch4AA, para 4(2)]
- where the shares are liable to depreciate rapidly in value – this prevents a company from securing a deduction for shares where there is no intention of actually conferring real value on employees [ICTA 1988, Sch4AA, para 4(5)]
- where a deduction has previously been given to the employing company or an **associated company** in respect of the same shares for the **SIP** or any other trust [ICTA 1988, Sch4AA, para 4(6)]
- where a special deduction has previously been given in relation to the shares [ICTA 1988, Sch4AA, para 4(9)] (see section 4.2.4.17.5).

- where shares that have previously been forfeited are **award**ed again [ICTA 1988, Sch4AA, para 6(3)].

4.2.4.17.4. Establishment Costs and Operating Expenses

The **scheme organiser** can claim a deduction for the costs of establishing a **SIP** [ICTA 1988, Sch4AA, para 9(1)] and for the operating expenses under general principles.

4.2.4.17.5. Special Deduction for SIP holding 10% of Share Capital

ICTA 1988, Sch4AA, paras 9 and 10 set out the terms of a special deduction, that was introduced to encourage smaller companies to establish SIPs to acquire shares from exiting shareholders.

The special deduction is available for a contribution to a **SIP** that, either at that time or within the following twelve months, holds 10% or more of the **scheme company**'s **ordinary share capital**, carrying rights to at least 10% of profits and assets on a winding up [ICTA 1988, Sch4AA, para 9(2)].

The **SIP** Trustee must use the money to acquire shares, but cannot acquire them from a company [ICTA 1988, Sch4AA, para 9(1)].

The deduction can be clawed back if the **SIP** fails to **award** at least 30% of the shares within five years, and all the shares within ten years [ICTA 1988, Sch4AA, para 10(1)]. However, the deduction will be reinstated if the **SIP** later **award**s all the shares [ICTA 1988, Sch4AA, para 10(4)].

If the **SIP award**s shares to someone who is not subject to UK taxation, the corresponding proportion of the deduction will be withdrawn [ICTA 1988, Sch4AA, para 10(8)].

4.2.4.18. NIC

See section 4.2.4.6.3.

4.2.4.19. Reporting

An annual return is needed for each **SIP**. A copy can be downloaded from HMRC's website at http://www.hmrc.gov.uk/forms/form39.pdf. In addition, the **SIP** Trustee must complete a self-assessment trust return.

4.2.4.20. Effect on Social Security Benefits

An employee who acquires Partnership Shares through a **SIP** may be adversely affected in terms of his entitlement to statutory sick pay, statutory maternity pay, the state pension and other means-tested benefits or tax credits. This is explained in HM Revenue & Customs' booklet IR177, which can be downloaded from http://www.hmrc.gov.uk/shareschemes/ir177.pdf

4.2.4.21. *Accounting Treatment*

See section 19.3.6.7.

4.2.4.22. *Sources of Shares*

See section 3.7.4.

4.2.4.23. *Matrix Summary of Advantages and Disadvantages of SIPs*

Feature	Advantage	Disadvantage
Availability		Only available to certain companies
Flexibility	Flexible choice between different forms of reward	
Limits	Up to £9,000 worth of tax-free shares can be delivered each year	
Accounting (p/l)		Value of shares charged to profit and loss account (except dividend shares)
Accounting (balance sheet)		Issue of new shares dilutes existing shareholders
Corporation Tax	Deductions available by statute	
Income Tax and NIC	Free of income tax and NIC if conditions fulfilled	
Capital Gains Tax	No CGT on shares while held in **SIP**	
Inheritance Tax	Business Property Relief may be available	

4.2.4.24. *Frequently Asked Questions on SIPs*

4.2.4.24.1. Is it possible for a SIP to deliver shares that have no dividend rights?

No, shares used in a **SIP** must not have worse dividend rights than other ordinary shares.

4.2.4.24.2. Does the scheme organiser have to offer participation in a SIP to an employee who is on notice?

It is possible to include a rule in a **SIP** that excludes employees who are on notice, since this is a criterion that applies fairly to all employees.

4.2.4.24.3. Can a SIP Trustee be resident outside the UK?

No, the **SIP** Trustee must be "a body of trustees consisting of persons **resident** in the UK" [ITEPA 2003, Sch2, para 71].

4.2.4.24.4. *If there is a performance period, can it begin before the SIP has been approved by HM Revenue & Customs?*

Yes, HM Revenue & Customs will be reasonable about this. As long as the performance period did not start too long before the **SIP** was approved, there should be no difficulty. In unpublished correspondence, HMRC have indicated that six months would be acceptable, but twelve months would be too long.

4.2.4.24.5. *How is the SIP Trustee taxed on income?*

The taxation of income received by a **SIP** Trustee is the same as for any other UK **resident** trustee (see section 10.4.4).

The exception is that the Trustee is not subject to tax on dividends at the dividend trust rate, except in relation to dividends on shares that are either disposed of without being **award**ed to employees, or are still held by the Trustee without having been **award**ed to participants within the relevant period [ICTA 1988, s686B(2)].

If the shares are **readily convertible asset**s, the relevant period is two years following the acquisition by the Trustee [ICTA 1988, s686B(3)].

If the shares are not **readily convertible asset**s, the relevant period is five years [ICTA 1988, s686B(4)].

If the shares are not **readily convertible asset**s when they are acquired, but become **readily convertible asset**s within five years, the period of exemption will end on the earlier of (a) five years after acquisition or (b) two years after they became **readily convertible asset**s [ICTA 1988, s686B(4)].

If the shares are acquired through a contribution which benefited from a special deduction (see section 4.2.4.17.5) then the period is ten years [ICTA 1988, s686B(5)].

4.2.4.24.6. *What happens to the shares of an employee who leaves?*

There is no statutory obligation on the **SIP** Trustee to transfer the shares to the departed employee, but the special exemptions will cease to apply.

4.2.4.24.7. *Should the SIP Trustee show appropriations of shares to employees on the Trust tax return?*

Only if a CGT liability can arise, e.g. where the shares were not appropriated to employees within two years (or five years if the shares are not **readily convertible assets**).

4.2.5. Loan Interest Relief

See section 16.5 for loans to acquire shares in **close companies** and section 16.6 for loans to acquire shares in **employee-controlled companies**.

4.3. SAYE Options

4.3.1. Description

A Savings-Related Share Option Plan ("**SAYE**") **option** is a tax-efficient form of incentive. If the Plan meets all the relevant conditions, there may actually be a tax subsidy. This arises because the corporation tax relief given to the employing company is greater than the amount of tax paid by the **optionholder**.

Shares acquired through an **SAYE** Plan can be transferred directly into an ISA. Ordinarily, an ISA cannot hold unquoted securities, but there is an exclusion for unquoted shares acquired through an **SAYE** Plan [Individual Savings Account Regulations 1998, reg 7(2)(h)(i)]. The transfer must take place within 90 days of the **exercise date** [Individual Savings Account Regulations 1998, reg 7(10)(a)]. The CGT value of the shares, measured as at the date of transfer into the ISA, counts against the individual's annual £7,000 limit on ISA contributions [Individual Savings Account Regulations 1998, reg 7(2)(h)]

The employee is also able to transfer the shares acquired through an **SAYE Plan** directly into a **registered pension scheme** (see section 3.3.4.1.5).

Unlike an EMI Plan, HM Revenue & Customs must approve an **SAYE** Plan before an **approved option** may be **grant**ed under it.

An **SAYE** Plan must be offered to all employees with a minimum service requirement (see section 4.3.1.4.1.2).

Unlike a **CSOP**, an **SAYE option** can be **grant**ed with a **discount at grant** of up to 20%.

The employee must agree to save an amount of between £10 and £250 per month with a savings carrier for a period of three or five years. The contract with the savings carrier allows for payment of a tax-free bonus after three, five or seven years. The amount of the bonus is fixed when the **option** is **grant**ed and is effectively interest.

The number of shares under **option** is calculated by dividing the expected proceeds of the savings contract by the **exercise price** of the **option**.

When the savings contract matures, the **optionholder** can use the proceeds to **exercise** the **option**, wholly or partially, or simply take the cash with the tax-free bonus.

An **SAYE option** has the following potential advantages over other forms of reward:

- Normally no income tax charge on the **exercise** of the **option** (see section 8.4.1.2).
- The employer should be able to claim a corporation tax deduction when the **option** is **exercise**d (see section 17.4).

The conditions are set out in section 4.3.1.1.

HM Revenue & Customs' guidance on **SAYE** Plans for employers is available at http://www.hmrc.gov.uk/shareschemes/saye_employers.htm

4.3.1.1. Checklist for Implementation of an SAYE

For an **option** to be an approved **SAYE option**, certain conditions must be satisfied. Some of these conditions apply to the **option** itself; some to the **scheme company**; others to any employee who is to receive the **option**.

If there is any doubt as to whether the company qualifies for **SAYE**, discuss this with HM Revenue & Customs Employee Shares and Securities Unit.

Here is a checklist to go through before establishing an **SAYE** or **grant**ing an **option** under it.

Requirement	**ITEPA 2003, Sch3**	**Commentary**
Group scheme or single-company scheme	Para 3	3.7.8.4.1
Jointly owned companies	Para 46	3.7.8.4.2
Participants who are full-time directors must work 25 hours per week (excluding meal breaks) or	Para 6(2)(a)	4.3.1.4.1.1
Participants must be employees	Para 6(2)(a)	4.3.1.4.1.1
Any qualifying period must not be more than five years at **grant date**	Para 6(2)(b)	4.3.1.4.1.2
Any employee who is **resident** and **ordinarily resident** in the UK must be invited to participate	Para 6(2)(c)	4.3.1.4.1.1
The Plan Rules may allow participation by any other employee or director of a **constituent company**.		4.3.1.4.4
Participation must be available on similar terms	Para 7	4.3.1.4.2
The Plan Rules must not contain non-essential features	Para 5	3.7.8.6.1
There must be no preferential treatment for directors or senior employees	Para 8	4.2.4.12.3
Employee must meet the "no **material interest**" requirement at **grant** and **exercise**	Para 11	3.7.8.5.2
Market value must be defined in the Plan Rules	Para 28(2)	4.3.1.7
Options cannot be **grant**ed with an **exercise price** less than 80% of **market value**	Para 28(1)(b)	4.3.1.8.1.5

Requirement	ITEPA 2003, Sch3	Commentary
Market value of unlisted shares should be agreed with Shares Valuation in advance of the invitation date	Para 28(2)	4.3.1.7
The invitation letter must specify a minimum 14 day application period	IR Practice	4.3.1.8.1.4
Options must be **grant**ed within 30 days of earliest date used to determine **market value** (42 days if scaling down required)	Para 28(1)(a)	4.3.1.8.1.4
Optionholder must take out a savings contract under a **certified SAYE savings arrangement**	Para 24(1)	4.3.1.5.3
Rules must provide for the maximum number of shares to be derived from the proceeds of the savings contract	Paras 25 and 26	4.3.1.5.6
Bonus to be included must be stated at the **grant date**	Para 30	4.3.1.5.6
Scaling down must be carried out in an objective manner	IR Practice	4.3.1.5.7
Rules must prohibit the **optionholder** from using other funds to **exercise** the **option**	Para 24	4.3.1.5.5
Maximum savings contribution must not be more than £250 per month	Para 25(3)(a)	4.3.1.5.4
Minimum savings contribution must not be less than £5 or more than £10	Para 25(3)(b)	4.3.1.5.4
Scheme shares must satisfy the legislative requirements at both the **grant date** and the **exercise date**	Para 17	4.3.1.2
Shares must be **ordinary share capital**	Para 18	3.7.8.3.1
Shares must satisfy the listing requirement	Para 19	3.7.8.3.3
Shares must be **fully paid up** and not **redeemable**	Para 20	3.7.8.3.2
Shares must be subject only to permitted restrictions	Para 21	3.7.8.3.4
Shares must rank *pari passu* with shares of the same class	Paras 20 and 21	3.7.8.3.4
Shares must be allotted within 30 days of the **exercise date**	Para 21	3.7.8.8.1.14
Shares must satisfy the "other shareholdings"	Para 22	3.7.8.3.5

Requirement	ITEPA 2003, Sch3	Commentary
test		
Options must not be transferable	Para 29	3.7.8.8.1.10
Options must not be capable of being **exercise**d before the **bonus date** or more than six months after the **bonus date**	Para 30	4.3.1.8.1.7
Death of **Optionholder**	Para 32	4.3.1.5.8
Good leaver Provisions	Para 34(2)	4.3.1.8.1.10
Accelerated **Exercise** on reaching the specified retirement age	Para 31	4.3.1.8.1.8
Termination due to sale of business or employing company	Para 34(5)	4.3.1.8.1.11
Termination where **option**s held for more than three years	Para 34(3)	4.3.1.8.1.13
Optionholder employed by another group company on **bonus date**	Paras 35(3) and 36	4.3.1.8.1.12
Rules must state when employment terminates	Para 35	4.3.1.4.4
Rules must prevent former employee from exercising **option** except in permitted circumstances	Para 10	4.3.1.4.4
Exchange of **option**s may be permitted on change of control	Para 38	8.5.6.3
If exchange is permitted, it must take place within statutory period	Para 38	8.5.6.3
Value and total **exercise price** must not be affected	Para 39(4)(c) and (d)	21.4, rows 9 and 10
After exchange, original **scheme organiser** remains responsible for scheme	Para 39(4)(b)	21.4, row 8
HM Revenue & Customs must approve adjustments following variation of capital	Para 28(3) and (4)	3.7.8.8.1.8
HM Revenue & Customs must approve amendments to a key feature	Para 42(2)(aa)	3.7.8.8.1.16

4.3.1.2. *Approval requirements for the Shares*

The shares must satisfy the legislative requirements both at the **grant date** and the **exercise date** [ITEPA 2003, Sch3, para 17].

4.3.1.2.1. Ordinary share capital

See section 3.7.8.3.1.

4.3.1.2.2. Fully paid up and not redeemable

See section 3.7.8.3.2.

4.3.1.2.3. The listing requirement

See section 3.7.8.3.3.

4.3.1.2.4. Subject only to permitted restrictions

See section 3.7.8.3.4.

4.3.1.2.5. The "other shareholdings" test

See section 3.7.8.3.5.

4.3.1.3. *Approval Requirements for Participating Companies*

4.3.1.3.1. Group scheme or a single-company scheme

See section 3.7.8.4.1.

4.3.1.3.2. Jointly owned companies

See section 3.7.8.4.2.

4.3.1.4. *Approval Requirements relating to Optionholders*

4.3.1.4.1. Plan must be open to all employees

An **SAYE** Plan must be open to anyone who meets the criteria laid down in ITEPA 2003, Sch3, para 6. The criteria are:

4.3.1.4.1.1 Full-time director or employee

Any person who meets the following conditions must be invited to participate:

- he is a full-time director or employee of the **scheme organiser** or a **constituent company** [ITEPA 2003, Sch3, para 6(2)(a)] (see section 3.7.8.5.1 for commentary on the term "full-time director")
- he has been such a full-time director or employee throughout any qualifying period [ITEPA 2003, Sch3, para 6(2)(b)] (see section 4.3.1.4.1.2)
- he is **resident** and **ordinarily resident** in the UK [ITEPA 2003, Sch3, para 6(2)(c)] and
- he does not have a **material interest** (see section 3.7.8.5.2) in the **scheme company** [ITEPA 2003, Sch3, para 6(2)(d)].

4.3.1.4.1.2 Qualifying Period

The Plan Rules can stipulate a qualifying period, but this cannot be more than five years [ITEPA 2003, Sch3, para 6(2)(b)].

4.3.1.4.1.3 Discouraging Features

THIS SECTION APPLIES TO SAYE AND SIP

An **SAYE** Plan or a **SIP** must not contain any feature which has, or is likely to have, the effect of discouraging employees from participating [ITEPA 2003, Sch2, para 8(3) and Sch3, para 6(3)].

4.3.1.4.2. Participation must be available on similar terms

Every person who meets the criteria laid down in ITEPA 2003, Sch3, para 6 (see section 4.2.4.10) must be offered participation in the **SAYE** Plan on similar terms, and those who accept must actually participate on similar terms [ITEPA 2003, Sch3, para 7].

"Similar terms" is not defined in the legislation. In practice, usually, the identical terms are offered to every employee who meets the criteria. However, it would be possible, although unusual, to vary the terms to reflect different levels of remuneration, different length of service or other "similar factors" [ITEPA 2003, Sch3, para 7(2)].

Other "similar factors" include hours worked [HMRC Manual ESS36045[135]]. However, age and grade are not similar factors [HMRC Manual ESS36046[136]].

It is possible to use more than one factor as long as there is a straight line progression from the lowest paid to highest paid employees. It is not acceptable to "multiply" the factors if the effect would be to benefit higher paid employees disproportionately[HMRC Manual ESS36038[137]].

4.3.1.4.3. There must not be preferential treatment for directors or senior employees

This test only applies where the **scheme organiser** is a member of a group of companies [ITEPA 2003, Sch3, para 8(1)]. This does not necessarily mean that the Plan has to be a group scheme; it could also apply to a single-company scheme.

In these circumstances, it is necessary to show that the **SAYE** Plan "does not and is not likely to have the effect of" disproportionately benefiting directors or the most highly paid employees [ITEPA 2003, Sch3, para 8(1)].

An example of the mischief that this is meant to prevent would be where there were two employing companies in the group: one which employed the directors and higher earners; the other which employed the lower earning employees. If an **SAYE** Plan were set up for the first company only, then this test would be failed. However, an **SAYE** Plan could be set up for both companies or the second company without failing this test.

To ensure compliance with this test, HM Revenue & Customs require a list of all the constituent companies to be supplied with the application for approval. The **scheme organiser** must declare that the Plan applies to all companies in the group or, if it does not, explain why some companies have been excluded [HMRC

135 http://www.hmrc.gov.uk/manuals/essumanual/essu33000/essu36045.htm

136 http://www.hmrc.gov.uk/manuals/essumanual/essu33000/essu36046.htm

137 http://www.hmrc.gov.uk/manuals/essumanual/essu33000/essu36038.htm

Manual ESS2302[138]]. There may, of course, be sound commercial reasons for excluding some companies, and HM Revenue & Customs will accept these.

Similarly, if a **constituent company** ceases to participate, HM Revenue & Customs may query the removal [HMRC Manual ESSU2303].

4.3.1.4.4. Employee must meet the employment requirement

A participant in an **SAYE** Plan must be either a director or an employee of the **scheme organiser** or another **constituent company** of a group scheme [ITEPA 2003, Sch3, para 10]. Employees who are not **resident** or not **ordinarily resident** in the UK may be allowed to participate.

Note that this is tested both at the **grant date** and the **exercise date** of the **option**. The Rules must provide that an **optionholder** who terminates employment with the group will forfeit his **option** [ITEPA 2003, Sch3, para 35]. A former employee or director may however be able to **exercise** his **option** for a short period after termination depending on the circumstances of the termination (see sections 4.3.1.8.1.10 to 4.3.1.8.1.13).

Note also that there is no requirement for directors to be full-time.

4.3.1.4.5. No material interest requirement

See section 3.7.8.5.2.

4.3.1.5. *Approval Requirements for the Plan*

4.3.1.5.1. Non-essential features

See section 3.7.8.6.1.

4.3.1.5.2. Requirements for the Plan Rules

Section 4.3.1.8 sets out provisions that should be included in the Plan Rules.

4.3.1.5.3. Requirement to take out Savings Contract

When an **SAYE option** is **grant**ed, the **optionholder** must take out a savings contract (**certified SAYE savings arrangement**) with a savings carrier [ITEPA 2003, Sch3, para 24]. See section 4.3.1.6 for guidance on selecting a savings carrier.

The savings contract will be for a period of three or five years. If the savings period is three years, then a "bonus", representing tax-free interest, will be payable at the end of the three year savings period. If the savings period is five years, then the bonus can be payable at the end of five years, or a larger bonus can be payable after seven years. There is a link to the most recent bonus rates at http://www.hmrc.gov.uk/shareschemes/saye_savings_contract_eer.htm

The bonus must be selected at the start of the savings period. The date on which the bonus is paid is called the **bonus date** [ITEPA 2003, Sch3, para 30(3)].

---

[138] http://www.hmrc.gov.uk/manuals/essumanual/essu2100/essu2302.htm

The employer can specify only one savings period, e.g. the savings carrier might offer only a three-year savings contract. Similarly, the employer could specify that the seven-year bonus is not available for a five-year savings contract. If the employer allows the savings carrier to offer more than one choice, then the employee must be free to choose between them.

4.3.1.5.4. Savings Contribution Limits

The Rules must impose a maximum savings limit of £250 per month. This should include all the savings that the participant is making under all current **certified SAYE savings arrangement**s [ITEPA 2003, Sch3, para 25(3)(a)].

The Rules can also set a minimum savings amount, but this cannot be less than £5 or more than £10 per month [ITEPA 2003, Sch3, para 25(3)(b)].

4.3.1.5.5. Prohibition on using other funds to exercise option

The **optionholder** can **exercise** the **option** using only the repayments and interest under the **certified SAYE savings arrangement**. It is not possible to use other funds to **exercise** an **SAYE option** [ITEPA 2003, Sch3, para 24].

4.3.1.5.6. Determination of Number of Shares under Option

The number of shares under **option** must be determined by dividing the anticipated proceeds of the savings contract by the **exercise price** [ITEPA 2003, Sch3, para 25]. It is possible to exclude a bonus in determining how much of the proceeds of the savings contract can be used to **exercise** the **option**, although this must be decided at the **grant date** [ITEPA 2003, Sch3, para 26].

If the aggregate of all applications for **option**s is greater than the number of shares available, then it is possible to "scale down" (see section 4.3.1.5.7).

4.3.1.5.7. Scaling Down

Scaling down is the process that must happen if employees apply for **options** over more shares than are available. Most frequently, the **scheme organiser** will scale down using HM Revenue & Customs' suggested method [HMRC Manual ESS26050[139]]. However, this is not obligatory, and in practice, HM Revenue & Customs will allow the **scheme organiser** to use any other objective and fair method [HMRC Manual ESS26052][140].

4.3.1.5.8. Deceased Optionholders

The personal representatives of a deceased **optionholder** must be allowed to **exercise** the **option**. If the **optionholder** dies before the **bonus date**, the personal representatives are allowed to **exercise** the **option** within a period of twelve months after the death. If the **option** holder dies on, or within six months after, the

---

139 http://www.hmrc.gov.uk/manuals/essumanual/essu26000/essu26050.htm

140 http://www.hmrc.gov.uk/manuals/essumanual/essu26000/essu26052.htm

bonus date, the personal representatives are allowed to **exercise** the **option** within a period of twelve months after the **bonus date** [ITEPA 2003, Sch3, para 32].

4.3.1.6. Selecting a Savings Carrier

The savings contract must be a **certified SAYE savings arrangement**. Although in theory any bank, building society or authorised European institution can offer a **certified SAYE savings arrangement**, in practice there is only a small number of savings carriers who are willing to offer them for **SAYE** Plans. ProShare maintains an up-to-date list, with details of contacts and services offered[141]. Some institutions are more willing to deal with smaller companies than others. Before making a final selection, the **scheme organiser** should contact several potential carriers, informing them of employee numbers, likely take-up, whether there is more than one payroll and how payroll is maintained, and discussing what additional services they can offer, such as preparing presentations to employees.

4.3.1.7. Valuation Issues

THIS SECTION APPLIES TO **CSOP** AND **SAYE**

The Plan Rules must set out how **market value** is to be determined. The valuation criterion is the same as for capital gains tax [ITEPA 2003, Sch3, para 48(1) and Sch4, para 36(1)]. For an unlisted company, the valuation must be agreed with HMRC Shares Valuation. HMRC's website sets out the process for doing this at http://www.hmrc.gov.uk/shareschemes/svd3.htm

4.3.1.8. Documentation and Approval

4.3.1.8.1. The Plan Rules

See section 3.7.3 for details of the design of the Rules. In addition to what is noted in that section, the Rules would normally contain the following:

4.3.1.8.1.1 Participating Companies

See section 3.7.8.8.1.1.

4.3.1.8.1.2 Share

See section 3.7.8.8.1.2.

4.3.1.8.1.3 Eligible Employee

See section 3.7.8.8.1.3.

4.3.1.8.1.4 Invitation Procedure

The Plan Rules should set out an invitation and acceptance procedure, whereby invitations are sent to all eligible employees. The employees must then have a period to consider the invitation and decide whether to accept. The **scheme organiser** must **grant** the **option**s within 30 days of the earliest date by reference to

---

141 http://www.proshare.org/

which the **market value** was established, although this can be increased to 42 days if there has to be scaling down [HMRC Manual ESS25043].[142]

4.3.1.8.1.5 Determination of Exercise price

The Plan Rules should prevent an **SAYE option** from being **grant**ed with an **exercise price** less than the 80% of **market value** of the shares. The **market value** is measured on the invitation date, unless HM Revenue & Customs agree that an earlier date can be used [ITEPA 2003, Sch3, para 28(2)]. The **exercise price** must be stated on the **grant date**, and cannot thereafter be changed unless there is a **variation of share capital** [ITEPA 2003, Sch3, para 28(3)] (see section 3.7.8.8.1.8).

4.3.1.8.1.6 Non-Transferability

See section 3.7.8.8.1.10.

4.3.1.8.1.7 Timing of Exercise of Options

The Plan Rules must provide that an **optionholder** can **exercise** an **SAYE option** only on or within six months after the **bonus date** [ITEPA 2003, Sch3, para 30(1)]. Accelerated **exercise** must, however, be allowed in certain events (see sections 4.3.1.8.1.9 and 4.3.1.8.1.10) and may be permitted in other events (see sections 4.3.1.8.1.11, 4.3.1.8.1.13, and 3.7.8.8.1.13).

4.3.1.8.1.8 The Specified Age

The Rules must state the specified age for the Plan [ITEPA 2003, Sch3, para 31(1)]. This must be the same for both men and women. It cannot be less than 60 or more than 75 [ITEPA 2003, Sch3, para 31(2)]. It is necessary to determine certain rights of accelerated **exercise** (see section 4.3.1.8.1.9).

Although the specified age is required by statute, it is potentially discriminatory under the Employment Equality (Age) Regulations 2006. The most prudent course is to set the specified age at 60, since in most circumstances this is likely to discriminate against the smallest number of employees.

4.3.1.8.1.9 Accelerated Exercise – Reaching the Specified Age

An **optionholder** who reaches the specified age must be allowed to **exercise** his **option** within the following six months, even if he continues in employment [ITEPA 2003, Sch3, para 33(1)]. However, he cannot **exercise** the **option** more than six months after the **bonus date** [ITEPA 2003, Sch3, para 33(2)].

4.3.1.8.1.10 Termination of Employment – Injury, Disability, Redundancy and Retirement

An **optionholder** who terminates employment because of injury, disability, or **redundancy** must be allowed to **exercise** his **option** within the following six months [ITEPA 2003, Sch3, para 34(2)(a)].

---

142 http://www.hmrc.gov.uk/manuals/essumanual/essu25000/essu25043.htm

An **optionholder** who retires, either on reaching the specified age or (if different) his contractual **retirement** age, must be allowed to **exercise** his **option** within the following six months [ITEPA 2003, Sch3, para 34(2)(b)].

However, he cannot **exercise** the **option** more than six months after the **bonus date** [ITEPA 2003, Sch3, para 34(6)].

4.3.1.8.1.11 Termination of Employment – Sale of Subsidiary or Business

The Rules of the Scheme may contain provisions allowing **optionholder**s to **exercise** prematurely, if their employment is terminated because the business or subsidiary that employs them is sold outside the group [ITEPA 2003, Sch3, para 34(5)].

Either of two possible provisions can be included in the Rules.

The first possibility is to allow any **optionholder** who terminates employment in those circumstances to **exercise** his **option** within six months after the termination date [ITEPA 2003, Sch3, para 34(5A)(a)].

The second possibility is to allow an **optionholder** to **exercise** his **option** only if he both terminates employment with the group in these circumstances, and subsequently terminates employment with the company or business that has been sold because of injury, disability, **redundancy** or **retirement** on reaching the specified age or his contractual **retirement** age. The Rules can provide that the **optionholder** can **exercise** his **option** within six months of the second termination [ITEPA 2003, Sch3, para 34(5A)(b)].

However, in no circumstances can the **optionholder exercise** the **option** more than six months after the **bonus date** [ITEPA 2003, Sch3, para 34(6)].

4.3.1.8.1.12 Termination of Employment – Transfer to Another Group Company

If an **optionholder** terminates employment with the **scheme organiser**, or a **constituent company**, but continues to be employed by an **associated company**, he is not treated as having terminated employment with the group and therefore has no right of accelerated **exercise** [ITEPA 2003, Sch3, para 35(3)].

The Plan Rules may provide that, if he continues to hold the **option** and be employed by an **associated company** on the **bonus date**, he may **exercise** his **option** within six months after the **bonus date** [ITEPA 2003, Sch3, para 36]. If the Rules do not make this provision, the **optionholder** will not be able to **exercise** the **option** because he will not satisfy the employment requirement (see section 4.3.1.4.4).

4.3.1.8.1.13 Termination of Employment – Any Other Circumstances

The following rules relate to an **optionholder** who terminates employment and who is not a **good leaver**.

The Rules must state that, if the employment terminates within three years of the **grant date**, the **optionholder** may not **exercise** the **option** under any circumstances [ITEPA 2003, Sch3, para 34(4)].

The Rules may include a provision allowing any **optionholder** who terminates employment for any reason more than three years after the **grant date** to **exercise** his **option** within six months after the termination date [ITEPA 2003, Sch3, para 34(3)(b)]. Alternatively, the Rules may provide that an **optionholder** who terminates more than three years after the **grant date** cannot **exercise** his **option** at all [ITEPA 2003, Sch3, para 34(3)(a)].

4.3.1.8.1.14 Change of Control

See section 3.7.8.8.1.13.

4.3.1.8.1.15 Allotment of Shares within 30 days

See section 3.7.8.8.1.14.

4.3.1.8.2. Approval Process

The process for applying for approval of an **SAYE** Plan is set out on HM Revenue & Customs' website at
http://www.hmrc.gov.uk/shareschemes/saye_first_step_eer.htm

There is a two-stage process. First, HM Revenue & Customs will review the documents and confirm that they meet the statutory requirements – this is called "informal approval".

Subsequently, the **scheme organiser** can adopt the **SAYE** Plan and send in the final documents, whereupon HMRC will grant formal approval and the Plan can start to be operated. A list of the documents required for formal approval is at
http://www.hmrc.gov.uk/shareschemes/saye_formal_app_eer.htm

4.3.2. Tax Treatment of Employee

See section 8.4.1.

4.3.2.1. PAYE

See section 8.4.2.

4.3.2.2. NIC

See section 8.4.2.

4.3.2.3. Reporting

See section 8.4.3.

4.3.2.4. Capital Gains Treatment

See section 8.4.4.

4.3.3. Tax Treatment of Employer

4.3.3.1. Corporation Tax Deductibility

See section 17.4.3 for deductibility of **option gains** and section 17.6 for deductibility of establishment costs.

4.3.4. Accounting Treatment

See section 19.3.6.6.

4.3.5. Sources of Shares

See section 3.7.4.

4.3.6. Matrix Summary of Advantages and Disadvantages of SAYE Options

Feature	Advantage	Disadvantage
Availability	Available to a wider range of companies than EMI	Not available to all companies
Flexibility		Restrictions required to protect the interests of existing owners may not be permitted (see section 3.7.8.3.4). Possible to use a separate class of shares but only if the "other shareholdings" test is satisfied (see section 3.7.8.3.5)
Limits		Subject to £250 monthly savings limit
Accounting (p/l)	Profit and loss account charge limited to value of **option** on **grant date**	
Accounting (balance sheet)	Issue of new shares increases capital	Dilutes existing shareholders if new shares issued
Corporation Tax	Automatic deduction available in many circumstances	Automatic deduction not available for **exercises** following sale to unlisted company
Income Tax and NIC	No income tax or NIC if **exercise** more than three years after **grant date** (or by **good leaver** at any time)	
Capital Gains Tax		Taper relief starts from **exercise date**

4.3.7. Frequently Asked Questions for SAYE

See the Frequently Asked Questions for **approved plans** in section 3.7.9.

4.3.7.1. *Can the approval of an SAYE plan cover options already granted?*

No. Only **options granted** on or after the date of the approval letter have approved status [HMRC Manual ESS608[143]].

4.3.7.2. *What happens when an SAYE Plan loses its approved status?*

An **SAYE** Plan can lose its approved status when a disqualifying event occurs [ITEPA 2003, Sch3, para 42(1)]l.

Any existing **options** will retain their approved status, although no new **approved options** can be **granted** [ITEPA 2003, Sch3, para 42(3)].

4.3.7.3. *Can some UK group companies be excluded from being participating companies?*

It is not necessary to allow all the group companies to participate, but if the effect is to limit participation by lower-paid employees, HM Revenue & Customs will not approve the Plan unless the **scheme organiser** has a valid commercial reason for excluding those subsidiaries [HMRC Manual ESS2300-2302[144]].

4.3.7.4. *If the scheme company goes through an initial public offering (" IPO"), can the IPO price be taken as market value?*

Yes, but if the IPO is not an offer to the public at a fixed price, then the **options** must be **granted** unconditionally before the IPO takes place [HMRC Manual ESS25050[145]]. This may not be commercially acceptable.

If the IPO is an offer for sale to the public at a fixed price, HM Revenue & Customs will allow the **exercise price** to be defined as the offer price if all the following conditions are satisfied, assuming that the IPO does not have any unusual features:

- the company must unconditionally **grant** the **options** within 30 days after the opening of the IPO;
- prospective participants must complete all the necessary formalities for participation in the Plan before the closing date for the IPO; and
- the company must unconditionally **grant** the **options** no later than the day before the shares are actually admitted to trading on the relevant exchange.

[HMRC Manual ESS25051[146]].

---

143 http://www.hmrc.gov.uk/manuals/essumanual/essu600/essu608.htm

144 http://www.hmrc.gov.uk/manuals/essumanual/essu2100/essu2300.htm

145 http://www.hmrc.gov.uk/manuals/essumanual/essu25000/essu25050.htm

146 http://www.hmrc.gov.uk/manuals/essumanual/essu25000/essu25051.htm

4.3.7.5. *Is it possible for the scheme organiser to grant SAYE options that are conditional on an IPO taking place?*

This is possible if the IPO will take place within four weeks of the **grant date** and before the participants make their first savings contributions [HMRC Manual ESS25056[147]].

4.3.7.6. *Does the participant have to give consideration for the grant of an SAYE option?*

The participant does not have to give monetary consideration. The participant gives consideration by entering into the savings contract and complying with his obligations under it [HMRC Manual ESS2022[148]].

4.3.7.7. *Is it possible to have an SAYE option over a variable number of shares?*

No.

4.3.7.8. *When an optionholder terminates employment, to what extent can the Directors have a discretion as to whether to allow him to exercise his SAYE option?*

If an **optionholder** terminates employment because of injury, disability, **redundancy** or **retirement**, the Directors cannot have a discretion. The Rules must specify whether the **optionholder** can **exercise** in these circumstances.

If the **optionholder** terminates employment for any other reason within three years of the **grant date** of the **option**, he cannot be allowed to **exercise** his **option**.

If the **optionholder** terminates employment for any other reason more than three years after the **grant date**, then the Directors can have a discretion to decide in individual circumstances.

4.3.7.9. *Can an SAYE option have a variable exercise price?*

No.

4.4. Other Benefits

Many employers provide non-cash benefits to their employees. There can be several reasons for this:

- Employees appreciate the removal of the "hassle factor", i.e. they do not have to negotiate and pay for the benefits themselves
- In some cases, the benefit may be free of income tax or NIC. This generates savings that can be shared between the employer and the employee
- The employer may be able to negotiate a lower cost with the provider of the benefit, perhaps because of greater bargaining power. These savings can be shared between the employer and employee.

---

[147] http://www.hmrc.gov.uk/manuals/essumanual/essu25000/essu25056.htm

[148] http://www.hmrc.gov.uk/manuals/essumanual/essu2000/essu2022.htm

It is becoming common for employers to operate a "flexible benefits" plan, whereby employees have the opportunity to select from a menu of benefits. This enables the employee to fine-tune his benefits package to suit his lifestyle.

A single childless employee may, for example, not attach any value to life assurance, and might choose no cover, or a minimum amount of cover, in return for higher salary or a bigger car.

An employee with a family might want the maximum amount of life cover, particularly if the employer is able to negotiate better rates than the employee could personally.

Section 4.4.2 discusses how salary sacrifice works and HM Revenue & Customs' approach to it.

In some areas, particularly the taxation of company cars, the legislation and practice has become very complex. This chapter will direct the reader towards useful sources of data and advice.

4.4.1. Taxation of Benefits: General Rules

The general rule is that the employee is taxed on the cost to the employer of providing the benefit, less any amount contributed by the employee. This is the "cash equivalent" of the benefit [ITEPA 2003, s203(2)].

The cost is the marginal cost to the employer of providing the benefit [*Pepper v Hart* [1992] STC 898]. For example, if a bus company provides free staff travel on its own buses, the marginal cost is likely to be minimal because the cost of running the bus service is the same, regardless of the number of passengers.

There are special rules for "lower-paid employees", basically those employees (other than directors) who earn less than £8,500 [ITEPA 2003, s217(1)]. They are taxable only on second-hand value of the benefits, which may be nil in many cases [ITEPA 2002, s216(1)]. Directors are never treated in this way, even if they earn less than £8,500.

Class 1 NIC applies to loan write-offs, certain vouchers and certain other assets, but most benefits are subject to Class 1A NIC, which is payable only by the employer.

4.4.2. Flexible Benefits

A flexible benefits plan allows employees to choose their benefits based on their individual needs and lifestyle. It works by giving the employees a total reward budget and allowing them to determine how much of that budget is paid in cash, and how much in the form of other benefits. An employee might be allowed to choose between, say, £97 of cash or £100 of vouchers – each would use up the same amount of his or her budget. In this way, the employer can share any savings with the employee, whether those savings derive from the employer's greater bargaining power or from tax or NIC advantages.

One way of describing this is as a "salary sacrifice" plan; in other words, the employee sacrifices salary and is provided with a different benefit of equal value.

The starting point in the tax analysis of a flexible benefits plan is that the employer and employee are free to negotiate whatever reward package they choose, and the taxation has to be based on the agreed contractual rights.

However, if employees have a contractual right to give up the benefit whenever they choose and take cash instead, HM Revenue & Customs will argue that the salary sacrifice is ineffective [*Heaton v Bell* 48 TC 211]. If the salary sacrifice is ineffective, the employee continues to be taxed on the original salary under ITEPA 2003, s62, rather than on the benefit.

For a flexible benefits plan to be effective for tax purposes, it is necessary for the employer and employee to agree that the employee's contractual remuneration consists of a salary of £x plus certain benefits, with the employee having no right to change the way in which the remuneration is provided. This does not prevent the employer and employee from renegotiating the remuneration later, but that must arise through agreement rather than through the employee having a right to require a change. HM Revenue & Customs will accept a plan that allows the employee to convert the benefits back into cash at annual intervals, or on the happening of certain agreed "work or lifestyle events", such as promotion, change between full-time and part-time working, marriage, divorce, birth of a child, or similar events.

The new contract must be entered into before the remuneration is received for tax purposes and earned for employment law purposes; it cannot take effect retroactively. See section 3.1.3.1 for details of when remuneration is deemed to be received for tax purposes.

It is imperative that the terms of the new contract must be enforceable under employment law. The new contract must genuinely reduce the employee's salary in return for the provision of a benefit.

HMRC Manual EIM42769[149] sets out what HM Revenue & Customs see as the requirements for a successful salary sacrifice arrangement.

4.4.3. Incentive Award Schemes

Employers often operate incentive award schemes. Under these schemes, employees receive awards for achieving particular targets or to mark exceptional achievement.

---

149 http://www.hmrc.gov.uk/manuals/eimanual/EIM42769.htm

The award is taxable employment income of the employee, even if it is provided by a third party, such as a supplier of the employer.

- If the award is made in cash, it will be taxable through PAYE, and NIC will be applied.
- If the award is a voucher, the taxable amount is the cost to the provider of making the award [ITEPA 2003, s87].
- Similarly, if the award is provided to a director or higher-paid employee, whether or not as a voucher, the taxable amount is the full cost to the provider of making the award [ITEPA 2003, s203] SP6/85 sets out how HM Revenue & Customs calculate the benefit..
- If the award is provided to a lower-paid employee, and it is not a voucher, the taxable amount is the second hand value of the item provided [*Wilkins v Rogerson* 39 TC 344].

However, the employer will usually settle the tax through a PSA, so that the employee does not have to declare the award or pay tax on it.

It is possible instead for the employer to operate a Taxed Award Scheme, but in practice this is less widely used because, unlike a PAYE Settlement Agreement, it requires the employee to declare the award on his tax return. Further details of Taxed Award Schemes are in the HMRC Manual EIM11235[150].

4.4.4. Cars

Employees are often provided with the use of company cars. The tax treatment of these benefits is very complex and it is beyond the scope of this book to explain the system in detail.

The rules on taxation of company car benefits apply whenever a car is made available to an employee (or a member of the employee's family or household), by reason of employment, and it is available for private use [ITEPA 2003, s114]. In these circumstances, the employee will be taxed on the cash equivalent of the benefit [ITEPA 2003, s120].

The calculation of the cash equivalent of the benefit is set out in ITEPA 2003, s121. It is a percentage of an amount calculated by taking the list price of the car when new, adding any accessories, and deducting any capital contribution made by the employee towards the provision of the car. If this amount is more than £80,000, then the taxable benefit is a percentage of £80,000.

The percentage depends on the carbon dioxide emission rating of the car. This is expressed in grams per kilometre (g/km). The relevant percentage is 15% plus 1% for every 5g/km by which the car's emissions exceed the lower threshold for the

---

150 http://www.hmrc.gov.uk/manuals/eimanual/EIM11235.htm

year, up to a maximum of 35%. The lower threshold for 2005/6 and subsequent tax years is 140 g/km [ITEPA 2003, s139].

There are other discounts available for cars that run on "green" power, such as bi-fuel cars, electric cars, and LPG cars.

If the employer provides the employee with fuel to be used for private purposes, then the employee is taxed on the same percentage as calculated above, but applied to £14,400 [ITEPA 2003, s150].

There are exemptions and reductions in particular circumstances, such as where the employee makes good some or all of the costs, or the car is shared, or the car is not available throughout the year.

HM Revenue & Customs' interpretation of the tax treatment of employees is set out in the HMRC Manual starting at EIM22700[151].

Potential advantages to employees should be set against the cost to the employer company and, in particular, the availability and timing of capital allowances.

4.4.5. Healthcare and Medical Benefits

Healthcare can be an attractive part of the reward package for many employees.

Generally, for a smaller employer, the best way to provide healthcare and medical benefits is to arrange for the employees to be insured under a group policy issued by a provider such as BUPA or Standard Life. This enables the employees to take advantage of any reduced premium rates that the employer can negotiate.

Where this happens, higher paid employees and directors will be taxed on the premiums, less any amount that they make good [ITEPA 2003, s203]. Lower-paid employees will not be taxed.

It is possible instead for the employer to pay the actual cost of medical treatment as and when it is needed. The employee will usually be taxed on the cost as general earnings. However, a lower-paid employee will not be taxed if the employer directly contracts with and pays the hospital or other medical practitioner, since the benefit is incapable of being turned into cash.

Larger employers will sometimes operate "healthcare trusts" whereby they effectively self-insure the liability to pay for medical benefits. The advantage of this arrangement is that it saves insurance premium tax. If the trust is appropriately structured, HM Revenue & Customs accept that employees are taxed on their share of the employer's contributions into the trust [HMRC Manual EIM21772[152]]. This arrangement is unlikely to be cost-effective for a smaller employer.

---

151 http://www.hmrc.gov.uk/manuals/eimanual/EIM22700.htm

152 http://www.hmrc.gov.uk/manuals/eimanual/eim21772.htm

4.4.6. Life Assurance

Employers will often take out life cover for employees under a group policy. They may also take out "key person" policies to protect the business itself from financial loss in the event that a key individual dies or becomes incapacitated.

If the benefit of the cover belongs to the employees, then higher paid employees and directors will be taxed on the premiums, less any amount that they make good [ITEPA 2003, s203]. Lower-paid employees will be taxed on the cash equivalent of the benefit, which may be low unless the policy can be cashed in.

The benefit of key person cover usually belongs to the employer so the employee is not taxed on the premiums.

If the employer pays a premium on a life policy belonging to the employee, this is also taxable income, and tax is withheld through the PAYE system [ITEPA 2003, s697 and HMRC Manual EIM11861[153]].

4.4.7. Childcare Vouchers

Childcare vouchers are exempt from income tax for up to £55 per week per employee [ITEPA 2003, s270A] and are therefore becoming commonly made available through flexible benefits plans.

In order to be exempt, the childcare voucher must be used in respect of a child who falls into one or both of two categories:

- he or she is a child or stepchild of the employee, whom the employee maintains, either wholly or partially [ITEPA 2003, s270A(3)(a)]. This includes a child who does not actually live with the employee, but for whom the employee has to pay maintenance.
- he or she resides with the employee, and the employee has parental responsibility for the child [ITEPA 2003, s270A(3)(b)]. This includes, for example, a child who is living with and being brought up by a grandparent.

The childcare voucher must be used to purchase qualifying childcare [ITEPA 2003, s270A(4)]. The definition of this varies depending on the part of the United Kingdom where the childcare is provided [ITEPA 2003, s318C].

The voucher must be provided under a scheme that is open to all employees of the employer, or to all employees at a particular location [ITEPA 2003, s270A(5)].

The limit is £55 per employee, rather than £55 per child. However, more than one person can claim the £50 for the same child [ITEPA 2003, s270A(8)].

Additionally, the voucher administration costs are exempt from tax [ITEPA 2003, s270A(6)(b)]. These are defined as the difference between the cost of providing the vouchers and their face value [ITEPA 2003, s270A(6A)].

---

[153] http://www.hmrc.gov.uk/manuals/eimanual/EIM11861.htm

The exemption is an alternative to the exemption for nurseries outside the workplace (see section 4.4.9). An employee can claim one of the exemptions but not both in respect of the same tax week [ITEPA 2003, s270A(9)].

4.4.8. Workplace Nurseries

Employees are not taxed on the benefit of their children being able to use workplace nurseries. Workplace nurseries can form part of a flexible benefits arrangement and be paid for from salary sacrifice (see section 4.4.2).

This exemption was designed to encourage employers to provide nursery places for their employees, either on their own premises or by joining with other employers. It is not available where the employer simply buys in a place at a commercially-run nursery, although in these circumstances the provision may be exempt up to £55 per week (see section 4.4.9).

In order to qualify for the exemption, the child involved must fall into one or more of three categories:

- he or she is a child or stepchild of the employee, whom the employee maintains, either wholly or partially [ITEPA 2003, s318(3)(a)]. This includes a child who does not actually live with the employee, but for whom the employee has to pay maintenance;
- the child resides with the employee [ITEPA 2003, s318(3)(b)]; or
- the employee has parental responsibility for the child [ITEPA 2003, s318(3)(c)]. This includes, for example, a child who is being brought up by a grandparent.

The place where the care is provided cannot be part of a private dwelling and must meet any relevant registration requirements [ITEPA 2003, s318(4)]. This means that the exemption will not be available, for example, where the employer pays for a nanny in the employee's home.

The employer who operates the scheme must make available the premises on which the care is provided, unless the scheme is being operated in partnership with other employers [ITEPA 2003, s318(6)(a)]. If the employer alone provides the premises, it does not have to have any involvement in providing the childcare, which can be subcontracted to a third party provider.

However, often small employers cannot afford the investment necessary to provide care on their own premises. The legislation caters for this by allowing employers to provide care in partnership with each other. The requirements for this are:

- the employer must provide the care under arrangements made jointly with other people [ITEPA 2003, s318(7)(a)];
- the premises must be provided by one or more of the people who are jointly responsible for the care [ITEPA 2003, s318(7)(b)];
- the employer must be wholly or partly responsible for financing the provision of the care [ITEPA 2003, s318(7)(c)]. In HM Revenue & Customs' view, this

means that the employer must make a "real and substantial commitment to funding the facility or providing it with capital" [HMRC Manual EIM21925[154]]; and

- the employer must be wholly or partly responsible for managing the provision of care [ITEPA 2003, s318(7)(c)]. HM Revenue & Customs apply a strict test to this: the employer must do more than be occasionally consulted on policy matters; instead, the employer must take real responsibility for managing the care [HMRC Manual EIM21930[155]].

Finally, the care must be provided under a scheme that is open to all employees of the employer, or to all employees at a particular location [ITEPA 2003, s318(8)].

4.4.9. Nurseries outside the Workplace

Often it will not be practical for an employer to provide care itself or in partnership with other employers, so the complete tax exemption for workplace nurseries will not be available (see section 4.4.8).

The employer can pay a third party to provide childcare, and the employee will be exempt from income tax for up to £55 per week per employee [ITEPA 2003, s318A(1)]. Childcare is commonly made available in this way through flexible benefits plans.

In order to be exempt, the care must be provided to a child who falls into one or both of two categories:

- he or she is a child or stepchild of the employee, whom the employee maintains, either wholly or partially [ITEPA 2003, s318A(3)(a)]. This includes a child who does not actually live with the employee, but for whom the employee has to pay maintenance;
- he or she resides with the employee, and the employee has parental responsibility for the child [ITEPA 2003, s318A(3)(b)]. This includes, for example, a child who is living with and being brought up by a grandparent.

The care must be qualifying childcare [ITEPA 2003, s318A(4)]. The definition of this varies depending on the part of the United Kingdom where the childcare is provided [ITEPA 2003, s318C].

The care must be provided under a scheme that is open to all employees of the employer, or to all employees at a particular location [ITEPA 2003, s318A(5)].

The limit is £55 per employee, rather than £55 per child. However, more than one person can claim the £50 for the same child [ITEPA 2003, s318A(8)].

---

154 http://www.hmrc.gov.uk/manuals/eimanual/EIM21925.htm

155 http://www.hmrc.gov.uk/manuals/eimanual/EIM21930.htm

The exemption is an alternative to the exemption for childcare vouchers (see section 4.4.7). An employee can claim one of the exemptions but not both in respect of the same tax week [ITEPA 2003, s318A(9)].

4.4.10. Workplace Meals

Employees are not taxed in relation to free or subsidised meals provided by their employer. The tax exemption is subject to the following conditions:

- the meals must be provided in a canteen or on the employer's business premises [ITEPA 2003, s317(1)];
- the meals must be provided on a reasonable scale [ITEPA 2003, s317(2)]. HM Revenue & Customs believe that a glass of wine with a meal is reasonable but an elaborate menu with fine wines and cigars is unreasonable [HMRC Manual EIM21671[156]];
- the same facility must be open to all employees of the employer at the same location, although they do not all have to take advantage of it [ITEPA 2003, s317(3)];
- if the meals are provided in the restaurant or dining room of a catering or similar business, then they must be provided and eaten in a part that has been set aside for employees only [ITEPA 2003, s317(4)].

4.4.11. Mobile Telephones

An employee is not taxed if the employer provides the employee with the use of a mobile phone [ITEPA 2003, s319]. This includes the provision of the telephone itself, the line rental, and the cost of private calls.

However, it does not cover the situation where the employer reimburses the employee for calls made on the employee's mobile phone, or where the phone is provided through an ineffective salary sacrifice arrangement, or where the employer provides the employee with vouchers [HMRC Manual EIM21780[157]].

4.4.12. Vouchers

There are generally no tax benefits in providing employees with vouchers, since the employees will generally be taxed either on the cash equivalent of the benefit or the cost of providing it. HMRC Manual EIM16140[158] sets out the scheme of taxation of different kinds of voucher.

Non-cash vouchers, or credit tokens, that are used to obtain specified exempt benefits, are themselves not taxable [ITEPA 2003, s96A].

---

[156] http://www.hmrc.gov.uk/manuals/eimanual/EIM21671.htm

[157] http://www.hmrc.gov.uk/manuals/eimanual/eim21780.htm

[158] http://www.hmrc.gov.uk/manuals/eimanual/EIM16140.htm

Nevertheless, vouchers can still be an attractive benefit to employees, particularly where the employer is able to make use of its greater bargaining power to secure a discount from the provider. For example, a flexible benefits plan might offer the employee the opportunity to sacrifice, say £95 of salary for £100 of vouchers.

4.4.13. Pensions

As mentioned in section 3.3.4.1.4, there are considerable NIC savings to providing pensions through a salary sacrifice arrangement.

4.4.14. Job-related Accommodation

An employee is not taxed in respect of job-related accommodation provided by the employer [ITEPA 2003, s99].

Similarly, if the employer pays the council tax and water or sewerage charges on the property, that is exempt from tax and NIC [ITEPA 2003, s314, SSCR 2001, Sch3, Part VIII, para 10].

4.4.14.1. Necessary for the Performance of Duties

Accommodation is job-related if it is necessary for the employee to live in it in order to be able to perform the duties [ITEPA 2003, s99(1)]. In HM Revenue & Customs' view, the exemption only applies where it is essential that the employee must live in that particular accommodation and no other [HMRC Manual EIM11341[159]]. Accommodation falls within the exemption if it lies within an acceptable perimeter: for example a school caretaker can live on any property in the school grounds.

4.4.14.2. Customary and for the Better Performance of Duties

Accommodation is also job-related if it is provided for the better performance of the employee's duties, and it is customary for employers to provide living accommodation to such employees [ITEPA 2003, s99(2)]. HM Revenue & Customs will not accept that the provision of accommodation is customary unless it is provided to more than half of employees in a particular kind of employment [HMRC Manual EIM11348[160]].

HM Revenue & Customs will accept that accommodation is provided for the better performance of duties if:

- the employee is required to be on call outside normal hours; and
- the employee is in fact frequently called out; and

---

[159] http://www.hmrc.gov.uk/manuals/eimanual/EIM11341.htm

[160] http://www.hmrc.gov.uk/manuals/eimanual/EIM11348.htm

- the accommodation is provided so that the employee may have quick access to the place of employment or other place to which the employee is called.

[HMRC Manual EIM11350[161]].

The case law, however, is not as demanding as HM Revenue & Customs suggest. For example, in *Vertigan v Brady* [1988] STC 91, the taxpayer was a nursery foreman, who was found to pass the "better performance" test notwithstanding that the accommodation was provided more "for Mr Vertigan's convenience and to ensure his recruitment rather than for the better performance of his duties".

4.4.14.3. *Security Threat*

No taxable benefit arises on accommodation provided if there is a special threat to the security of the employee, special security arrangements are in force, and he or she resides in the accommodation as part of those arrangements [ITEPA 2003, s100].

4.4.14.4. *Payment of Additional Accommodation Costs*

If the employer pays additional accommodation costs, such as heating, lighting, cleaning or maintenance costs, this is an additional taxable benefit to the employee.

However, where the accommodation is job-related, the tax charge is limited to 10% of the employee's net earnings [ITEPA 2003, s315].

4.4.15. Accommodation that is Not Job-Related

If the employer provides the employee with accommodation that is not job-related, the value of the benefit is made up of two elements:

4.4.15.1. *First £75,000*

The first part of the taxable benefit is the rental value of the property, less any amount reimbursed by the employee [ITEPA 2003, s105]. If the property costs £75,000 or less, then this is the total value of the taxable benefit.

The rental value is defined as the rent that a landlord might reasonably expect to receive on an annual letting with a landlord repairing obligation [ITEPA 2003, s110]. However, in practice, HM Revenue & Customs use the gross rating value [HMRC Manual EIM11433[162]]. In Scotland, special rules apply since its last rating valuation was carried out more recently than the rest of the UK [ESC A56].

If the employer actually rents the property then the employee is taxed on the higher of the annual value and the rent that the employer pays, less any amount reimbursed by the employee [ITEPA 2003, s105(4)].

---

161 http://www.hmrc.gov.uk/manuals/eimanual/EIM11350.htm

162 http://www.hmrc.gov.uk/manuals/eimanual/EIM11433.htm

4.4.15.2. *Properties costing more than £75,000*

If the property costs more than £75,000 then there is an additional taxable benefit. The cost is the original acquisition cost of the property, and any expenditure on improvements incurred before the start of the current tax year [ITEPA 2003, s104].

The additional taxable benefit is: ORI x (C - £75,000) where

ORI is the official rate of interest measured at the start of the tax year and

C is the cost of the property
[ITEPA 2003, s106(2)].

4.4.15.3. *Properties Acquired More than Six Years Ago*

If the property was acquired more than six years before the employee first occupied it, it would not be appropriate to base the taxable benefit on the original purchase price. Therefore, the cost of the property is taken to be the market value on the date the employee first occupied it, plus any subsequent improvements. This only applies where the cost of the property, using the basic rule, exceeds £75,000 [ITEPA 2003, s106].

4.4.15.4. *Payment of Additional Accommodation Costs*

If the employer pays additional accommodation costs, such as heating, lighting, cleaning or maintenance costs, this is an additional taxable benefit to the employee.

4.4.16. Recreational Facilities

If the employer provides the employee with sporting or other recreational facilities, no liability to income tax or NIC arises [ITEPA 2003, s261 and SSCR 2001, Sch3, Part V, para 5B(b)]. This exemption does not apply where the facilities are available to the public generally [ITEPA 2003, s261(4)]

5. Terminating a Senior Executive

5.1. Income Tax Issues

5.1.1. Overview

This chapter sets out ways in which termination payments can be made to a former employee with a complete or partial exemption from income tax.

Whether a termination payment is taxable depends on how and why it is made.

If it derives from the employment, it will usually be general earnings, taxable in full under ITEPA 2003, s62.

If the payment derives from the termination, then the first £30,000 may be exempt from income tax under ITEPA 2003, s403. Alternatively, it may be completely exempt under other provisions in ITEPA 2003, Part 6, Chapter 3.

If the employee is required to agree to some new post-termination restriction, then any payment made for that will be taxable under ITEPA 2003, s225.

If a payment is made to an employee on **retirement**, from an approved or **registered pension scheme**, this will be tax free within limits (see section 3.3.4.4.1.3).

5.1.2. Diagnostic Tool

In order to determine the correct treatment of a termination payment, it is essential to review all the relevant documentation. This will include: the employment contract, with any supplemental letter to the employee; the staff handbook, if one exists and contains anything about termination entitlements; and the employer's termination policy, if this is documented.

	Note	See section
(1)	If the employee has a contractual right to a severance payment, it will be taxable in full as general earnings. If the employer makes an additional payment to which the employee is not contractually entitled, this may be wholly or partially exempt from tax under ITEPA 2003, s413. Go to note (4).	5.1.3
(2)	A payment in lieu of notice (PILON) will be taxable if HM Revenue & Customs are able to establish that the employee had a right to the payment based on an expectation arising from employment.	5.1.4
(3)	A payment for accepting post-termination restrictions will be taxable under ITEPA 2003, s225 and subject to NIC	5.1.5
(4)	A non-contractual termination payment is exempt up to the first £30,000 under ITEPA 2003, s403.	5.1.6
(5)	If the employee was made redundant, special rules apply. If yes, go to note (6). If no, go to note (10).	Glossary

(6)	The employee may be entitled to a statutory **redundancy** payment. If so, it is exempt from tax under ITEPA 2003, s309. Nevertheless, it is offset against the £30,000 exemption under ITEPA 2003, s403.	5.1.7
(7)	If the employee receives a **redundancy** payment that exceeds his statutory entitlement, HM Revenue & Customs may grant clearance to pay this without deduction of PAYE, to the extent that if falls within the £30,000 exemption.	5.1.8
(8)	NIC does not apply to genuine **redundancy** payments.	5.2.3
(9)	The employer should be able to claim a corporation tax deduction for a genuine **redundancy** payment, although the size of the deduction may be limited following a discontinuance of the trade.	5.3.2
(10)	Has the employee retired? If yes, go to note (11). If not, go to note (17).	Glossary
(11)	A lump sum payment from an approved/**registered pension scheme** is wholly or partially exempt from tax.	5.1.9
(12)	An approved *ex gratia* lump sum **retirement** payment is wholly or partially exempt from tax.	5.1.10
(13)	A payment from an overseas pension scheme may be wholly or partially exempt from UK taxation.	5.1.11
(14)	A payment from a Funded Unapproved Retirement Benefits Scheme (FURBS) may be wholly or partially exempt from tax.	5.1.12
(15)	The employer should be able to claim a corporation tax deduction for a lump sum payment on **retirement**.	5.3.3
(16)	No NIC is charged on pension payments.	5.2.2
(17)	Will the employee agree to the payment being used to fund his **retirement** benefits? If so, go to note (18). If not, go to (21).	
(18)	Making additional payments into a **registered pension scheme** will not give rise to immediate income tax or NIC liabilities, provided the limits are adhered to.	5.1.13
(19)	There is no immediate income tax or NIC charge in relation to contributions to, or accruals of benefit within, an **employer-financed retirement benefits scheme**.	5.1.14
(20)	A payment into a Family Benefit Trust is not chargeable to income tax or NIC if properly structured	3.6.2.1
(21)	A payment or other benefit provided in connection with the termination of employment because of the death, injury or disability of the employee may be exempt under ITEPA 2003, s406.	5.1.15
(22)	If the employee has been **resident** abroad for part of his career he may be able to claim foreign service relief.	5.1.16
(23)	If the employee has worked for the employer for at least 20 years	5.1.17

	then it may be possible to treat all or part of the payment in shares or tangible assets as a tax-free long service award.	
(24)	A payment for outplacement counselling may be exempt from income tax.	5.1.18
(25)	A payment towards the employee's legal costs may be exempt from income tax.	5.1.19
(26)	If the employee receives any benefits in kind as part of the termination settlement, the value of these will be offset against the £30,000 exemption.	5.1.20.1
(27)	If an employment-related loan is written off, or allowed to continue after the termination, the value will be offset against the £30,000 exemption	5.1.20.2
(28)	If the employee is allowed continued health insurance following the termination (other than on retirement), the value will be offset against the £30,000 exemption.	5.1.20.3
(29)	If the employee is a director then special reporting requirements arise in relation to the termination.	5.1.21
(30)	If the termination follows a change of control of the employing company, the corporation tax deductibility of the payment may be challenged for not having a trading purpose.	5.3.1
(31)	If the employee has more than one employment within the group, then each employing company should make a separate payment. If not, the corporation tax deductibility may be challenged.	17.10.1

5.1.3. Employment Rights

If the termination payment derives from the employment, it will be chargeable to tax as general earnings. It will not fall within ITEPA 2003, s403 and will therefore not qualify for the £30,000 exemption (see section 5.1.6). It will also be subject to NIC.

Great care must be taken in analysing the tax treatment of payments in lieu of notice (PILONs) – see section 5.1.4.

Here are some examples of payments deriving from the employment:

Dale v De Soissons (1950) 2 ER 460

In this case the employee had a contractual right to a fixed compensation payment if his employment contract was terminated on a specific date. The payment was held to be general earnings.

Hoffman v Wadman 27 TC 192

Here the employer continued to pay the employee's salary for a year after his employment had been terminated by mutual consent.

Richardson v Delaney 74 TC 167

In this case the employee was sent on garden leave. In other words he continued to be paid his salary but was not required to attend work. This continued while he negotiated a lump sum payment in settlement of his claim for what he alleged was breach of contract. The court decided that the lump sum was fully taxable since the employer had not in fact broken its contract and therefore the payment was a PILON, taxable in full as general earnings.

Abrahams v Performing Rights Society Ltd [1995] IRLR 486

The employer had a right to terminate the contract by paying a PILON. The court held that the payment could not be compensation for breach of contract since it was actually provided for under the contract.

Nigel Skilton v T&K Home Improvements Ltd [2000] IRLR 595

The employment contract provided that if the employee were summarily dismissed on certain grounds, no PILON was payable. The employee was dismissed for a different reason. The court held that the compensation payment was a PILON.

Allum v Marsh SPC 446

The employing company made payments to two former directors "in appreciation of [their] services to the company over many years". The Special Commissioners held that although these payments were voluntary and non-contractual, they were made in recognition of services rendered, and accordingly taxable as general earnings.

Here are some examples of payments that did not derive from the employment:

Hunter v Dewhurst 16 TC 605

The Articles of Association of the employing company provided that a director was entitled to compensation for loss of office if he ceased to be a director in certain circumstances. Commander Dewhurst was the Chairman; he wanted to retire, but the company wanted him to stay on in a part-time capacity in order to consult him on certain matters.

It was agreed that he would resign as Chairman but would be paid a lump sum in return for giving up his rights under the Articles.

The court held that this was not earnings from his office as Chairman but instead was compensation for the loss of his rights under the Articles.

Henley v Murray 31 TC 351

The employee was also the owner of two property companies. The two companies were both in financial difficulties and needed to borrow money from an external source. The lender was not willing to make the loan unless Mr Henley resigned from the two companies. Mr Henley was paid compensation for the loss of his contractual remuneration. The court held that this was not general earnings but instead related to the loss of his contractual rights.

Clayton v Lavender 42 TC 607

The taxpayer was employed on a fixed term contract. Several years before it was due to expire, he notified the employer that he would not want to renew the contract when it expired. The employer offered to release the taxpayer from the remaining term of the contract in return for a lump sum payment to settle any claims the employee might have against the employer. It was decided that this was compensation for the surrender of contractual rights, not earnings.

5.1.4. PILONs

It is not always clear whether a PILON represents damages for breach of contract or a contractual payment. Even if the written employment contract does not give the employee the right to the payment, the PILON may still be earnings if it derives from the employment relationship. HM Revenue & Customs are likely to argue that the payment is earnings, since damages would be taxable under ITEPA 2003, s403, with the benefit of the £30,000 exemption.

HM Revenue & Customs' views on this are set out in *IR Tax Bulletin 63* of 17 February 2003[163]; and the Employment Income Manual. In summary, their views are as follows:

- A "gardening leave" payment is contractual. In other words, the employee continues to be paid for part or all of his notice period but does not actually provide services to the employer.
- A PILON can be taxed as general earnings even if it is not contractual. For example, where the employer "automatically" makes a PILON instead of giving notice, the payment derives from the employment relationship, rather than being damages for breach of contract (see section 5.1.4.1).
- If the employer has a choice between making a PILON under the contract, or paying damages for breach of contract, HM Revenue & Customs will examine all the facts closely before deciding whether the actual payment is earnings or damages An example would be where the contract specifies that the employer "may" make a PILON. It is therefore essential to document carefully the reasons for making the payment (see section 5.1.4.1).
- A PILON may be contractual even if the notice period is shorter than the statutory minimum notice provided by ERA 1996, s86.

In *Wilson v Clayton* [2004] STC 1022 and [2004] All ER (D) 94, Patten J had to consider the taxability of a payment ordered by an employment tribunal. The

---

163 http://www.hmrc.gov.uk/bulletins/tb63.pdf

payment purported to be a statutory compensation payment under ERA 1996, s119. However, the tribunal had no power to order such a payment, and therefore the employer was under no legal obligation to pay it. It therefore had to be a voluntary payment. Nevertheless, the Inland Revenue argued that it derived from the employment and was effectively a bonus. Patten J rejected this argument, saying: "The mere fact that the payment was made between an employer and its employee is not sufficient in itself to make the payment taxable [as general earnings]. On that basis, any payment, of whatever nature, would be caught." Patten J's judgment was confirmed by the Court of Appeal.

This case does cast considerable doubt on HM Revenue & Customs' approach to ITEPA 2003, s403 as set out in *IR Tax Bulletin 63*.

5.1.4.1. Reserved Right to make PILON

The contract may give the employer the right, but not an obligation, to make a PILON. If the employer exercises this right, the PILON will be made in accordance with the contract and will be taxable. As authority for this HM Revenue & Customs cite *EMI Group Electronics v Coldicott* 71 TC 455.

The employer may not exercise the right to pay the PILON; instead the employer may breach the contract and pay damages. The employer may particularly want to do this if the damages are mitigated where the employee finds alternative employment. This was the case in *Cerberus Software Ltd v Rowley* [2001] IRLR 160. Such a payment would not be contractual but would be taxable under ITEPA 2003, s403.

In practice, an employer who wants the payment to be treated as damages rather than earnings should take the following steps:

- Ensure that the Board Minutes or other relevant documentation, such as a letter to the employee, states that the payment is made by way of damages for an identified breach of contract;
- Demonstrate that the amount of the payment is calculated in the same way that damages would be calculated by a court. For example the payment should be mitigated where the former employee has secured alternative employment before the end of the contractual notice period;
- The amount of the payment should also be adjusted to reflect the fact that, as damages, the first £30,000 will be tax-free and the whole payment will be free of NIC.

5.1.4.2. Expectation from Employment

HM Revenue & Customs believe that a PILON which is not contractual as a matter of employment law, may nevertheless derive from the employment relationship and therefore be taxable as earnings. In HM Revenue & Customs' view, if there is a custom or practice of making PILONs in particular circumstances, that can be sufficient to create an expectation in the minds of employees, so that the source becomes the employment relationship. The authorities HMRC cite to support this argument are far from compelling. They are *Laidler v Perry* 42 TC 351 and *Corbett v Duff* 23 TC 763, neither of which relate to PILONs.

HMRC Manual EIM12977[164] refers to a PILON which "is made as an automatic response", and says "it is arguable that the PILON is earnings."

The best defence to this is to make sure that PILONs are not paid automatically, but that the employer makes a genuine critical assessment as to whether to pay compensation and, if so, the amount to pay. This should be conducted using a written internal procedure. In these circumstances, HMRC should accept that the payment represents damages for breach of contract [HMRC Manual EIM12977].

If the employer cannot show that they did in fact go through such a procedure, it may still be possible to argue that the payment did not derive from custom and practice. Various principles can be derived from case law as follows:

- A custom must be "reasonable, certain and notorious" *Bond v CAV Limited* [1983] IRLR 360;
- A policy adopted by management unilaterally cannot become established by way of custom and practice unless as a minimum it has been drawn to the attention of employees or followed without exception for a very substantial period (Browne-Wilkinson J in *Duke v Reliance Systems Limited* [1982] IRLR 347)
- Peter Gibson LJ in *Albion Automotive v Walker and others* [2002] All ER (D) 170, considering whether employees had a right to enhanced **redundancy** payments, said that there are many factors that need to be taken into account to determine whether a right has arisen through custom and practice, including:
  - whether the policy had been drawn to the attention of employees;
  - whether the policy had been followed without exception for a substantial period;
  - the number of occasions on which the policy had been followed;
  - whether payments under the policy had been made automatically;
  - whether the nature of the communication of the policy supported the inference that the employer intended to be contractually bound by it;
  - whether the policy had been adopted by agreement;
  - whether the employees had a reasonable expectation that enhanced payments would be made;
  - whether the terms of the policy had been incorporated in a written agreement; and

---

164 http://www.hmrc.gov.uk/manuals/eimanual/EIM12977.htm

- whether the terms of the policy had been consistently applied.

These were all employment law cases, but the same principles apply in tax law, as is confirmed by Knox J's judgment in *Vertigan v Brady* [1988] STC 91.

The most recent case on this subject is *SCA Packaging v HMRC* SPC 541. In this case, the Special Commissioner dismissed the argument of HM Revenue & Customs that where a payment in lieu is made as a matter of course by an employer over a period of time to employees on their being made redundant, such a payment amounts to an emolument from employment even if it falls short of a contractual entitlement. The Special Commissioner accepted that an emolument can be taxable even if it is not contractual, but said that the fact that a payment is made habitually does not determine where it comes from.

Despite the case law, HM Revenue & Customs take an aggressive approach in arguing that PILONs derive from employment rights in a situation where the employer regularly makes PILONs over a period of time. In particular, HMRC Manual EIM12977[165] makes two assertions that are not supported by the case law.

First, it says that a custom can arise even if an individual employee does not know about it, whereas the case law suggests that a custom must be drawn to employees' attention.

Secondly, it says that a custom can come into being very quickly, although Knox J says that: "a custom can hardly come into force overnight".

5.1.5. Payments for Post-termination Restrictions

When an employee leaves, the former employer may wish to impose restrictions on his future activities- for example to prevent him setting up a competing business in the same location.

The employer may therefore pay the former employee to give a "restrictive undertaking". If this happens, the payment is earnings of the former employee for the tax year in which it is paid [ITEPA 2003, s225(2)]. It will also be earnings for NIC purposes [SSCBA 1992, s4(4)(b)].

A restrictive undertaking is one which "restricts the individual's conduct or activities" [ITEPA 2003, s225(8)]. The charge applies where the individual gives that undertaking in connection with the current, future or past employment [ITEPA 2003, s225(1)(a)].

The charge arises whether the payment is made in relation to the giving of the undertaking, or in respect of the fulfilment of the undertaking [ITEPA 2003, s225(1)(b)].

---

165 http://www.hmrc.gov.uk/manuals/eimanual/EIM12977.htm

It does not matter whether the payment is made to the individual or to any other person [ITEPA 2003, s225(2)], and it does not matter whether or not the undertaking is legally enforceable or qualified in any way [ITEPA 2003, s225(8)].

From a tax perspective, therefore, it is unwise to include a restrictive undertaking in an agreement to terminate someone's employment, because HM Revenue & Customs may argue that all, or at least part, of any termination payment relates to the undertaking and is therefore taxable. HMRC are likely to take this point if the total payment appears "excessive in relation to the claims being settled" [HMRC Manual EIM03605[166]].

If it is commercially necessary to include a restrictive undertaking, it may be prudent for the termination agreement to attribute an amount to the giving of the undertaking.

However, if all that is happening is that an existing obligation is being restated, HMRC accept that no value can be attributed to the restatement [SP3/96].

Similarly, HM Revenue & Customs will not attribute any value to an undertaking not to commence, or to discontinue, legal proceedings [SP3/96]. But if the parties themselves attribute any value to this undertaking, then that amount will be taxable under ITEPA 2003, s225 [HMRC Manual EIM03606[167]].

5.1.6. £30,000 Exemption

A termination payment that is not chargeable to tax under any other provision may be taxable under ITEPA 2003, s403. This section applies to any payment or other benefit received in connection with the termination of the holding of the office or employment, or any change in its duties or emoluments. It does not matter whether the termination payment is made by the employer or by another person.

The tax charge cannot be avoided by making the payment to the employee's dependants, spouse or personal representatives. Any such payments are deemed to have been made to the employee [ITEPA 2003, s401(1)].

The tax charge arises in the year in which the payment or benefit is received by the employee [ITEPA 2003, s403(2)]. In relation to a cash payment, this means the year in which it is made, or a payment on account is made, or the employee becomes entitled to require payment of, or on account of, the benefit [ITEPA 2003, s403(3)(a)]. In relation to a non-cash benefit, this means the year in which is it first used or enjoyed [ITEPA 2003, s403(3)(b)].

---

166 http://www.hmrc.gov.uk/manuals/eimanual/EIM03605.htm

167 http://www.hmrc.gov.uk/manuals/eimanual/EIM03606.htm

If the payment falls within ITEPA 2003, s403, it may be eligible for one or more of several exemptions under ITEPA 2003, Part 6, Chapter 3. These are:

- the first £30,000 of the payment will be exempt from tax [ITEPA 2003, s403(1)];
- there is an exemption for a payment made on the death, or on account of injury to or disability of the holder of an office or employment [ITEPA 2003, s406] (see section 5.1.15);
- there is no tax on termination benefits paid from an approved pension scheme [ITEPA 2003, s407] (see section 5.1.10); and
- part or all of the payment may be exempt insofar as the employee has spent part of his or her career working abroad [ITEPA 2003, s413] (see section 5.1.16).

The £30,000 exemption is set against payments made in earlier years before later years [ITEPA 2003, s404(4)] and against cash payments before non-cash benefits [ITEPA 2003, s404(5)]. Payments made by one or more associated employers are aggregated and set against the exemption [ITEPA 2003, s404].

A payment that is taxable under ITEPA 2003, s403 can be taken into account as relevant earnings for the purposes of retirement annuity contracts [ICTA 1988, s623], but not for personal pension plans [ICTA 1988, s644(4)(b))]. Since it is employment income, it will be taken into account as **relevant UK earnings** in determining the annual limit on contributions to a **registered pension scheme** [FA 2004, s189(2)].

5.1.7. Statutory Redundancy Payments

An employee who has two years' qualifying service has a statutory right to a **redundancy** payment if he is genuinely made redundant. The amount of the payment is calculated using a formula – a ready reckoner is available on the Department for Trade and Industry's website at
http://www.dti.gov.uk/er/redundancy/payments-pl808a.htm#What%20payments?

A statutory **redundancy** payment is exempt from income tax [ITEPA 2003, s309]. However, it reduces the £30,000 annual exemption under ITEPA 2003, s403.

5.1.8. Enhanced Redundancy Payments

The statutory **redundancy** entitlement is relatively low and many employers will wish to pay a greater, or "enhanced", **redundancy** payment.

Assuming the employee does not have any contractual entitlement to an enhanced payment, it will be taxable under ITEPA 2003, s403, so that the £30,000 exemption will be available. Even if the employee does have a contractual entitlement, e.g. because there is a **redundancy** scheme incorporated into the terms of employment, the payment may still fall within ITEPA 2003, s403, if it is genuine compensation for loss of employment.

This analysis was confirmed by the case of *Mairs v Haughey* [1993] STC 569. This case held that a payment under an enhanced **redundancy** scheme was made to relieve the redundant employee for the fact that he was obliged to seek alternative employment; it was not itself earnings from the employment.

A second point was that a **redundancy** payment was usually paid after the employment had terminated and was therefore not earnings from that employment unless it had the character of deferred compensation payable under a contractual right.

HM Revenue & Customs draw a distinction between payments that are genuinely made to compensate the employee for the consequences of **redundancy**, and terminal bonuses. It accepts that the former fall within ITEPA 2003, s403, but not the latter. An employer who wishes to pay enhanced **redundancy** payments should submit the scheme to the PAYE Inspector for a ruling as to whether the payments can be treated as falling within ITEPA 2003, s403 [SP 1/94].

5.1.9. Payments from Registered Pension Schemes

A lump sum payment from a **registered pension scheme** will generally be exempt from tax, as long as it is authorised and it falls within the lifetime allowance limits [ITEPA 2003, s636A]. See section 3.3.4.4.1.3 for details of the limits.

There is no specific statutory exemption from NIC in respect of lump sums, although there is an exemption for pensions [SSCR 2001, Sch3, Part VI, para 1]. HM Revenue & Customs' view is that this exemption also applies where a pension is commuted to a lump sum [HMRC Manual NIM02285[168]].

5.1.10. Approved Lump Sum Payments

An arrangement to make a payment to an employee on **retirement** or death, or in anticipation of **retirement**, is a retirement benefits scheme. In principle, the payment is taxable as employment income [ITEPA 2003, s394].

However, an *ex gratia* payment made on account of death, or injury or disability may be exempt [ITEPA 2003, s406] (see section 5.1.15).

5.1.11. Overseas Pension Schemes

A lump sum payment from an overseas pension scheme may be exempt from tax. This is unlikely to be relevant to smaller employers and is outside the scope of this book. Further information is available in the HMRC Manual at EIM15062[169].

---

168 http://www.hmrc.gov.uk/manuals/nimmanual/nim02285.htm

169 http://www.hmrc.gov.uk/manuals/eimanual/EIM15062.htm

5.1.12. Payments from Employer-Financed Retirement Benefits Schemes

5.1.12.1. Benefits Provided from an Onshore FURBS; no funding after 5 April 2006

See section 3.4.4.2.2.3.

5.1.12.2. Benefits Provided from an Offshore FURBS; no funding after 5 April 2006

See section 3.4.4.2.2.4.

5.1.13. Payments into Registered Pension Schemes

If an employer makes a special contribution into a **registered pension scheme**, this is not taxable [ITEPA 2003, s408]. The payments must comply with the limits and the rules of the pension scheme.

As an alternative, the employer could simply purchase an annuity for the employer from a life insurance company. The annuity should be provided from a **registered pension scheme**, in which case the employee will not be taxed on the purchase, although there could be an annual allowance charge (see section 3.3.4.2).

5.1.14. Payments into Employer-Financed Retirement Benefits Schemes

See section 3.4.4.1.2.2.

5.1.15. Payments on Death, Injury or Disability

If an employee dies, or the employment terminates by reason of injury or disability, the employer may make an *ex gratia* payment. Such a payment will be exempt from income tax [ITEPA 2003, s406].

HM Revenue & Customs accept that "disability" includes not only a sudden affliction but also incapacity arising from chronic illness [SP 10/81]. It does, however, have to be clear from medical evidence that the employee is unable to continue carrying out the functions of the employment [*Horner v Hasted* 67 TC 439].

Since such a payment is not earnings from the employment, it is also outside the scope of NIC.

HM Revenue & Customs are likely to challenge the availability of this exemption unless it is clear that the payment is made on account of disability and for no other reason [HMRC Manual EIM13630[170]].

5.1.16. Foreign Service Relief

Employees who spend all or part of their careers working abroad may be able to claim foreign service relief under ITEPA 2003, s413. This will apply to payments that would otherwise be taxable under ITEPA 2003, s403, but not to amounts that are taxable as general earnings, such as contractual payments.

---

170 http://www.hmrc.gov.uk/manuals/eimanual/EIM13630.htm

Foreign service generally means periods spent **resident** abroad. However, it can also include a period spent working in the UK while **resident** but not **ordinarily resident** here [ITEPA 2003, s413(3)]. Furthermore, it includes a period during which the individual is **resident** here but qualifies for the chargeable overseas earnings deduction in ITEPA 2003, s21(1), is within ITEPA 2003, Part 5, Chapter 6 (seafarers).

There is a complete exemption from tax if the foreign service is at least:

- 75% of the employee's entire period of service ending with the termination date; or
- if the employee has more than ten years' service, the whole of the last ten years; or
- if the employee has more than twenty years' service, half of the period including any ten of the last twenty years [ITEPA 2003, s413(2)].

If the employee has not spent enough time abroad to qualify for the complete exemption, there is still a *pro rata* relief available. After deducting the first £30,000 of the payment, which is exempt under ITEPA 2003, s403, a further proportion of the remainder is exempt, representing the proportion of the employee's total service with the employer which was foreign service.

5.1.17. Long Service Awards

If an employee has at least 20 years' service, the employer can make a tax-free long service award to him [ITEPA 2003, s323]. This can take the form of a tangible asset, or shares in a group company, or certain other kinds of benefit. The value must be "reasonable", which is interpreted to mean not exceeding £50 per year of service. The employee can only receive one such award every ten years.

5.1.18. Outplacement Counselling

The employer may pay for a departing employee to have counselling to cope with losing his employment. The cost of providing counselling will generally not give rise to an employment income charge for the departing employee [ITEPA 2003, s310].

In order to qualify for the exemption, the costs must be incurred in:

- actually providing the services; or
- paying or reimbursing fees for a third party to provide the services to the employee, or
- paying or reimbursing travel expenses incurred in connection with the provision of the services.

Services qualify for the relief if:

- their purpose is to enable the employee to adjust to the cessation of employment, or to enable them to find other gainful employment [ITEPA 2003, s310(2)];

- they consist of giving advice and guidance, imparting or improving skills, and providing or making available the use of office equipment or similar facilities [ITEPA 2003, s310(3)];
- the employee has been employed by the employer for at least two years before the services were provided or if earlier, on the date employment ceases [ITEPA 2003, s310(4)];
- the opportunity to receive the services is generally available to all employees, or to a particular class of employees [ITEPA 2003, s310(5)].

Travel expenses are allowable if mileage allowance relief would have been available to a current employee under ITEPA 2003, s231.

5.1.19. Legal Expenses

The employer should consider settling the legal expenses of a departing employee since this can be done free of tax [ESC A81].

This concession applies where the former employee's claim is settled out of court. The payment should be made directly to the employee's solicitor and should relate only to fees incurred in connection with the termination of employment. There must be a specific term in the settlement agreement that provides for the payment of legal fees.

If the dispute goes to court, the employer may be ordered to pay the employee's legal costs, including expert witness fees. In these circumstances, any payment of costs made under the court order will be excluded from tax under ITEPA 2003, s403.

5.1.20. Benefits in Kind

5.1.20.1. General

Benefits in kind provided to an employee as part of a termination package fall into ITEPA 2003, s403, so the £30,000 exemption is available to set off against the taxable value. They are taxable in the year in which the benefit is used or enjoyed [ITEPA 2003, s403(3)].

The taxable value is the cash equivalent of the benefit calculated under the benefits code or if higher, the amount that would be chargeable as general earnings [ITEPA 2003, s415].

If the employee is allowed to continue to use the former employer's facilities following the termination, then HM Revenue & Customs may either (a) challenge the recovery of the related input tax or (b) argue that the employer is deemed to have made a supply to the former employee by virtue of either VATA 1994, Sch4, para 5(4) or the VAT (Supply of Services) Order 1993. The value of the supply would be the cost to the employer of making the supply [VATA 1994, Sch6, para 7].

5.1.20.2. Loan
If a loan is written off as part of a termination agreement, the employee will be taxed on the amount written off. This is the case even if the write-off occurs in the following tax year [ITEPA 2003, s188(2)].

If the employee is retiring, however, the tax charge arises under ITEPA 2003, s393.

5.1.20.3. Health Insurance
Sometimes the employer will continue to provide health insurance to the employee following termination. The cost of this should be deducted from the £30,000 exemption.

If the employee is insured on an individual basis, the cost to the employer will already be known. If the employee is in a group scheme, the taxable benefit will be the cost that the employee would have incurred if he had insured himself.

However, if the employee is retiring, the cost is taxable under ITEPA 2003, s393.

5.1.21. Special Rules for Directors

5.1.21.1. Shareholder Approval
Shareholders must approve any payment made to a director by way of compensation for loss of office [CA 1985, s312]. However, this does not include a payment of damages for breach of contract or a pension payment [CA 1985, s316(3)].

If the director's service agreement gives him a contractual right to a payment, then shareholder approval is not required for the payment to be made [*Taupo Totara Timber Co Ltd v Rowe* [1978] AC 537].

5.1.21.2. Reporting requirements
Any compensation paid to a former director for loss of office must be disclosed in the annual accounts [CA 1985, Sch6, para 8(1)]. This includes compensation for breach of contract [CA 1985, Sch6, para 8(4)].

5.1.21.3. Duty of disclosure on change of control
If a director receives a payment by way of compensation for loss of office, and this arises in connection with a change of control, then the director must take all reasonable steps to secure that particulars of the proposed payment including the amount, are included in or sent with any notice of the offer made for their shares and which is given to any shareholders [CA 1985, s314].

If he fails to do so the director is deemed to hold any payment which he has received in trust for those persons who have sold their shares as a result of the offer made and the director is required to bear the costs of distributing that sum [CA 1985, s315].

Note that this liability arises not only in relation to a change of control but also to an offer made by or on behalf of an individual with a view to obtaining the right to exercise or control the exercise of not less than one third of the voting power at any general meeting of the company; or any other offer which is conditional to a given extent.

However, it does not apply to a payment of *bona fide* damages for breach of contract or a pension [CA 1985, s316(3)].

5.1.21.4. Resignation of Directors

Directors must resign from office in writing. The company should file Form 228b with the Registrar of Companies. This form can be downloaded from the Companies House website at

http://www.companies-house.gov.uk/forms/generalForms/288B.pdf.

5.1.22. Compensation for Loss of Option Rights

If the employee receives compensation for loss of option rights, this is the receipt of a benefit in connection with the option, which is a chargeable event under ITEPA 2003, s477(3)(c) [HMRC Booklet CWG2, para 158].

5.2. NIC Issues

5.2.1. Overview

NIC is due on payments arising from the contract of employment, but not on payments that fall within ITEPA 2003, s403, since, although such payments may be taxable, they are not earnings from employment.

5.2.2. Retirement Benefits

There is no NIC on pension payments [SSCR 2001, Sch3, Part VI, para 1].

There is no definition of a pension in the legislation but in practice HM Revenue & Customs take a broad interpretation. HMRC will look for some legal obligation to pay the pension. Although usually the payment will come from a pension scheme, a payment made from the employer's own resources may also qualify.

5.2.3. Redundancy Payments

There is no NIC on a genuine **redundancy** payment [SSCR 2001, Sch3, Part X, para 6]. A genuine **redundancy** payment is one that satisfies the tests in ERA 1996, s139.

This applies also to enhanced **redundancy** payments – that is, payments that exceed the statutory minimum [HMRC Manual NIM02600[171]].

5.3. Corporation Tax Issues

5.3.1. Payments relating to sale of shares

Great care must be taken where a termination payment is made to a substantial shareholder who is also selling his shares at the same time. The difficulty is that the

---

171 http://www.hmrc.gov.uk/manuals/nimmanual/nim02600.htm

employing company may have mixed motives for making the payment, so that the "wholly and exclusively" test is failed.

An example of this is *Bassett Enterprises v Pethy* 21 TC 734, where the terms of a share sale agreement provided that certain employee shareholders should receive lump sum compensation payments for the termination of their service contracts. The court held that the payments were not being made for trading purposes, but rather as part of the sale of the shares.

Another important case is *James Snook & Co v Blasdale* 33 TC 244. In this case, the share sale agreement was conditional on certain directors resigning and being paid compensation by the employing company. Donovan J said it was "essential in such cases that the company should prove ... that it considered the question of payment wholly untrammelled by the terms of the bargain its shareholders had struck with those who were to buy their shares and came to a decision to pay solely in the interests of its trade."

However, in *CIR v Patrick Thomson Ltd* (37 TC 145), following the sale of a group of companies, certain subsidiary companies were wound up, and the managing directors of those companies were terminated. The Court of Session could see no connection to the sale agreement, and allowed the deductions.

A recent case is *Allum v Marsh*, where the Special Commissioners held that a payment made to a departing shareholder for the sale of his shares was not made for the purposes of the trade. However, this case concerned the income tax consequences for the shareholder rather than the deductibility for the company.

5.3.2. Redundancy Payments

5.3.2.1. *Statutory Redundancy Payments*

A statutory **redundancy** payment is deductible as a trading expense for a **trading company** [ICTA 1988, s579(2)] and as expenses of management for an investment company [ICTA 1988, s579(3)]. If the payment is made after the discontinuance of the business, it is treated as having been made on the last day before discontinuance [ICTA 1988, s579(2)(b) and (3)(b)]. See section 5.1.7 for details of the income tax treatment.

5.3.2.2. *Enhanced Redundancy Payments*

An enhanced **redundancy** payment will usually be deductible under general principles as a trading expense or, in the case of an investment company, expenses of management.

However, there are some circumstances where HM Revenue & Customs may challenge deductibility either on the grounds that the payment fails the "wholly and exclusively" test or that it is capital. These are identified in HMRC Manual BIM46601[172]. Examples are:

- where the payment is made for the purpose of closing down a trade, and exceeds the employee's statutory or contractual rights;
- where the payment is really consideration for the transfer of shares;
- where the real motive is to benefit a family member; or
- where the payment is made in return for a restrictive undertaking from the employee, unless the employee is taxed on the payment under ITEPA 2003, s225, in which case there is a statutory right to a deduction under FA 1988, s73(2) (see section 5.1.5).

5.3.2.3. *Payments made following discontinuance of the trade*

If the trade or business is discontinued, statutory **redundancy** payments are deductible under ICTA 1988, s579 (see section 5.3.2.1).

Enhanced **redundancy** payments may also be deductible under ICTA 1988, s90, but only if they would have been deductible under general principles, if made before the trade ceased. No deduction is available to the extent that the enhanced payment is greater than three times the statutory payment. A statutory payment must also be made.

The enhanced payment is treated as having been made on the date the business ceased.

HM Revenue & Customs also allow a deduction where there is a partial cessation of the business [SP11/81].

Furthermore, HMRC may allow a provision for future **redundancy** payments, but only where the provision is accurately calculated and properly accrued for in the accounts. The actual payment must be made within nine months of the end of the accounting period [*IR Tax Bulletin* 15 – February 1995[173], p194].

If the payment does not fall within ICTA 1988, s90, it is unlikely that HM Revenue & Customs will allow a deduction. Their view is that **redundancy** payments made in the discontinuance of a business are disallowed on general principles [*CIR v Anglo-Brewing Co Ltd* 12 TC 803].

5.3.3. Retirement Payments

A payment made to an employee or director on **retirement** will generally be deductible for corporation tax purposes.

However, difficulties can arise if the recipient is a controlling shareholder, either solely or jointly with connected parties. In these circumstances, HM Revenue &

---

172 http://www.hmrc.gov.uk/manuals/bimmanual/BIM46601.htm

173 http://www.hmrc.gov.uk/bulletins/tb15.htm

Customs may challenge deductibility on the basis that there was no trading purpose for making the payment, relying on the authority of *Samuel Dracup & Sons Limited v Dakin* 37 TC 377.

HM Revenue & Customs are unlikely to challenge the deduction if the employee is fully taxable on the receipt [HMRC Manual IM8412[174]].

5.3.4. Payments for Post-termination Restrictions

If a payment is earnings of the employee under ITEPA 2003, s225 (see section 5.1.5), it will be deductible for the employer as a trading expense or an expense of management [FA 1988, s73].

This overrides the general rule that a payment made by a **trading company** to protect itself from competition is a disallowable capital payment [*Associated Portland Cement Manufacturers Ltd v Kerr* 27 TC 103].

---

174 http://www.hmrc.gov.uk/manuals/immanual/im8412.htm

6. Pension Schemes

6.1. Registered Pension Schemes

See section 3.3.

6.2. Employer-Financed Retirement Benefits Schemes

See section 3.4.

7. Employee Investment in Employer Securities

7.1. Restricted Shares

See section 3.5.4.

7.2. Convertible Shares

See section 3.5.5.

7.3. Partly-paid Shares

See section 3.5.6.

7.4. Ratchet Arrangements

See section 3.5.7.

7.5. Value Freezing

See section 3.5.8.

7.6. Flowering Shares

See section 3.5.9.

7.7. Loan Interest Relief

Loan interest relief may be available where an employee acquires shares in a **close company** (see section 16.5) or an **employee-controlled company** (see section 16.6).

7.8. Discounted Share Offers

See section 4.2.3.

7.9. Share Incentive Plan (SIP)

See section 4.2.4.

8. Taxation of Securities options

8.1. Acquisition of Shares through Securities option

8.1.1. General Position

The term "**securities option**" is not widely used outside UK tax legislation. The more common terms are "share option" or, in American English, "stock option".

A "**securities option**" in UK tax legislation is not exactly the same as a "share **option**". There are two major differences:

- first: the **securities option** rules apply not just to shares but to everything that falls within the definition of "securities" in ITEPA 2003, s420;
- second, the holder of a "share option" can choose when and whether to "**exercise**" the **option** and acquire the securities. Indeed, the definition of a "**securities option**" is a "right to acquire securities" [ITEPA 2003, s420(8)], which implies the existence of a right not to acquire the securities. However, HM Revenue & Customs believe that the legislation also applies where securities are delivered to the **optionholder** pursuant to a legal entitlement, with or without the **optionholder**'s consent [HMRC Manual ERSM110030][175].

The tax treatment of **securities options** for most employees is set out in ITEPA 2003, Part 7, Chapter 5. However, note that Chapter 5 only applies where the employee concerned was both **resident** and **ordinarily resident** in the UK on the **grant date** of the **option** [ITEPA 2003, s474(1)]. Special rules apply if the employee was not both **resident** and **ordinarily resident** in the UK on the **grant date** (see section 8.4.6) or if the employee is not domiciled in the UK (see section 8.4.7).

There is no tax charge on the **grant** of a **securities option** to a **resident** and **ordinarily resident** employee [ITEPA 2003, s475(1)] except in the unlikely event of there being a **discount at grant** in relation to a **CSOP option** [ITEPA 2003, s475(2)].

The **exercise** of a **securities option**, or more precisely the acquisition of shares or other securities pursuant to an **employment-related securities option**, is generally a chargeable event, giving rise to an employment income tax liability for the employee. This also applies if an **associated person** of the employee acquires the securities. The taxable amount is effectively the "**option gain**". There may be a corporation tax deduction for the employer (see section 17).

Similarly, if the employee realises value from the **option** in some other way, e.g. by assigning it to a non-**associated person**, then this may be a chargeable event [ITEPA 2003, s477(3)(b) or (c)] (see section 8.5).

---

[175] http://www.hmrc.gov.uk/manuals/ersmmanual/ERSM110030.htm

There are exemptions for **EMI Options** (see section 8.2), **CSOP Options** (see section 8.3) and **SAYE Options** (see section 8.4).

For details of the calculation of the employment income tax liability and to determine whether PAYE applies see section 8.1.2.

See section 8.1.5 for details of the reporting obligations.

See section 8.4.5 for guidance as to whether a corporation tax deduction is available.

8.1.2. Income Tax and PAYE

8.1.2.1. The Chargeable Event

The acquisition of securities by the **optionholder** is generally a chargeable event [ITEPA 2003, s477(3)(a)].

The relevant time is the date the **optionholder** unconditionally **exercise**s the **option** so that the beneficial interest in the securities passes to the **optionholder**. The actual date of issue or transfer of the securities is not relevant [ITEPA 2003, s477(4)].

8.1.2.2. The Taxable Amount

The taxable amount is the amount of the gain (AG) (see section 8.1.2.3) less the total of any deductible amounts (DA) (see section 8.1.2.4) [ITEPA 2003, s478(1)].

8.1.2.3. The Amount of the Gain

The amount of the gain (AG) is the **CGT value** of the securities on the **exercise date**, less the **exercise price** (if any) [ITEPA 2003, s479(3)].

Note that if the securities are **restricted securities**, the calculation uses the restricted **CGT value**, unless a **Section 431(1) election** has been made to use the **unrestricted market value** [ITEPA 2003, s431(3)(d)].

Note also that if the securities are **convertible securities**, the value attributed to the conversion entitlement is usually ignored in calculating AG [ITEPA 2003, s437(1)(a)]. However, if the arrangement under which the securities are offered was entered into for tax or NIC avoidance purposes, it is necessary to carry out a hypothetical calculation of what the securities would be worth if the conversion entitlement were immediate and unconditional [ITEPA 2003, s437(3)(a)]. This value must be used if it is higher than the value ignoring the conversion entitlement [ITEPA 2003, s437(2)].

Note further that it is not possible to deduct selling costs (real or notional) in determining the **CGT value** of the securities. This used to be possible for **options exercise**d before 1 September 2003, because the old formulation of ITEPA 2003, s479(1) defined "**market value**" by reference to the sale proceeds of the shares. However, the change to using the **CGT value** precludes a deduction for selling costs.

8.1.2.4. The Deductible Amounts

The deductible amounts (DA) are:

- Any consideration that was given for the acquisition of the **option**, for example if the employee had to pay a **grant price** at the **grant date** [ITEPA 2003, s480(2)(a)].
- Any expenses incurred in connection with the **exercise** of the **option**, for example if the employee has to pay some sort of administration fee [ITEPA 2003, s480(2)(b)].
- If the **option** is a **CSOP option** and there was a **discount at grant**, then the amount of the **discount** should have been taxed as employment income on the **grant date** under ITEPA 2003, s526 (see section 8.3.1.1). If so, this is a deductible amount [ITEPA 2003, s480(4)].
- If the **option** was **grant**ed at a **discount** before 1 September 2003, there may have been a tax charge on the **discount** either as general earnings or under the residual benefits rules. If there was a taxable **discount at grant**, then it is a deductible amount [ITEPA 2003, s480(5)(a)]. Such a tax charge can no longer arise where the employee was **resident** and **ordinarily resident** in the UK on the **grant date** [ITEPA 2003, s475(1)].
- Any amount brought into charge to tax under the legislation that applied before 1 September 2003 in relation to an assignment of the **option** where the following conditions are met:
    - a person who was not the employee assigned the **option** and realised a gain; and
    - either that person had originally acquired the **option** otherwise than by or under an assignment made by way of a bargain at arm's length; or
    - that person and the employee were **connected persons** at the time of the assignment [ITEPA 2003, s480(5)(c) applying ITEPA 2003, old s479(2)(c)].

In addition, it is necessary to deduct:

- Any secondary NIC paid by or recovered from the employee under SSCBA 1992, Sch1, para 3A or 3B [ITEPA 2003, s481] (see section 9.2).
- Any special contribution which was actually paid in relation to the **option** under SSCSOA 2001 before 11 August 2001 [ITEPA 2003, s482] (see section 8.1.3.5).

Note that if there has been a previous chargeable event in relation to the same **option**, then any deductible amount that was deducted in calculating the tax in relation to that chargeable event cannot be deducted again [ITEPA 2003, s480(6)].

8.1.2.5. PAYE

When there is a chargeable event under ITEPA 2003, s477, the employer should withhold income tax through the PAYE system [ITEPA 2003, s700]. There are two exceptions to this:

- PAYE does not apply where **shares** are acquired on the **exercise** of a **securities option grant**ed before 27 November 1996 [ITEPA 2003, s701(2)(c)(iii)]. Note that this does not apply to securities that are not shares, and it does not apply where shares are delivered to the **optionholder** without an **exercise** taking place. Further, it does not apply if the option has been rolled over (see section 8.5.6.1).
- PAYE does not apply where the securities are not **readily convertible asset**s on the date of the chargeable event [ITEPA 2003, s696(1)].

The employee must "make good" the PAYE within 90 days to avoid a further tax charge under ITEPA 2003, s222 (see section 3.7.3.14).

8.1.3. NIC

8.1.3.1. Securities options: General Rule on NIC

Generally, when there is an acquisition of securities pursuant to a **securities option**, this will be a chargeable event under ITEPA 2003, s477. If the securities are **readily convertible asset**s, there will be a corresponding charge to NIC. This is subject to the exceptions described in the rest of this section 8.1.3.1.

The remuneration subject to NIC will be the same as the amount of the gain calculated under ITEPA 2003, s478 reduced by the deductible amounts set out in ITEPA 2003, s480(1) to (6) [SSCBA 1992, s4(4)(a)].

Primary NIC can be recovered from the employee's salary or, by agreement, from a sale of the securities (see section 9.1).

The liability to pay secondary NIC can be passed to the employee either by agreement or transfer (see section 9.2). Note that if the employee pays secondary NIC, he cannot deduct these in calculating the earnings subject to NIC; otherwise the calculation would be circular.

Note also that there is no charge to NIC if the securities are not **readily convertible asset**s when they are acquired [SSCR 2001, Sch3, Part IX, paragraph 7A].

8.1.3.2. Grant date before 6 April 1999

NIC does not generally apply to the **exercise** of **option**s where the **grant date** was before 6 April 1999 [SSCR 2001, Sch3, Part IX, para 16]. However, this exemption only applies to the extent that the **option** is settled with shares; it would not apply for example if the **option** were settled in cash or with other securities.

The exemption does not apply where the value of the shares has been artificially enhanced by more than 10% by things done, on or after 6 April 1999, otherwise than for genuine commercial purposes [SSCR 2001, Sch3, Part IX, para 17] (see section 8.1.3.4). It is believed that this paragraph is intended to catch "adjustable option" arrangements that were widely used in the City between 1999 and 2003.

8.1.3.3. *Options granted before 6 April 1999 and subsequently replaced*

Given that an **option grant**ed before 6 April 1999 is generally outside the scope of NIC (see section 8.1.3.2), it would be unfair if that exemption were lost because of a corporate reorganisation, such as a change of control. Where this happens, often the original **option** will be exchanged for a new **option** over a different class of shares, or shares in a different company.

If an **option** is replaced in this way, the general rule is that the replacement **option** is exempt from NIC in the same way that the original **option** was. However, to prevent avoidance of NIC, the exemption only applies where the exchange of **option**s did not confer any significant new value on the employee.

The exemption is contained in SSCR 2001, Sch3, Part IX, para 16A. It applies where a right to acquire shares was **grant**ed before 6 April 1999 and subsequently replaced. The value of the shares received on **exercise** of the replacement **option** is exempt from NIC. This is subject to two conditions:

- at the time of the exchange of rights, the value of the shares subject to the replacement **option** must not be substantially higher than the value of the shares under the **option** that is being replaced. In other words, the exchange itself must not confer any new value on the employee [SSCR 2001, Sch3, Part IX, para 16A(4)]; and
- the value of the shares under **option** must not have been artificially enhanced by more than 10% by things done, on or after 6 April 1999, otherwise than for genuine commercial purposes [SSCR 2001, Sch3, Part IX, para 17].

If the exemption is not available because the value of shares under the replacement **option was** substantially higher than the value of the shares under the old **option**, then the relevant legislation is SSCR 2001, Sch2, para 11. This sets out a four-step procedure for calculating the amount, if any, which is charged to NIC on the **exercise** of the replacement **option**. Basically, it is the amount by which the value of the replacement **option** exceeded the value of the old **option**, measured on the date of exchange, less any amounts previously brought into charge to NIC.

8.1.3.4. *Option Granted before 6 April 1999 - Value of Shares Artificially Increased*

If an **option** was **grant**ed before 6 April 1999, and the value of the shares under **option** was increased by more than 10% by virtue of things done on or after 6 April 1999, otherwise than for genuine commercial purposes, then the exemptions from NIC in SSCR 2001, Sch3, Part IX, para 16 and para 16A will not apply [SSCR 2001, Sch3, Part IX, para 17].

In these circumstances, SSCR 2001, Sch2, para 11A requires that the **option** is treated in the same way as an **option grant**ed after 6 April 1999. In other words, NIC applies to the taxable amount calculated under ITEPA 2003, s478.

SSCR 2001, Sch3, Part IX, para 11A(3) prevents a double charge to NIC, which could otherwise apply if the original **option** was

- **grant**ed between 10 December 1996 and 6 April 1999
- with a **discount at grant**.

8.1.3.5. Grant date between 6 April 1999 and 19 May 2000

There are special rules for **options granted** between 6 April 1999 and 19 May 2000. If any of the following three circumstances applies, then SSCSOA 2001 exempts the charge to NIC:

- the **option** was "underwater" on 7 November 2000 (in other words, the **exercise price** was higher than the **CGT value** of the shares);
- the shares under **option** were not **readily convertible assets** on 7 November 2000;
- a valid capping election was made and a special contribution was paid to HM Revenue & Customs.

If none of these circumstances applies, there may be a charge to NIC as set out in section 8.1.3.1.

8.1.4. Capital Gains Tax

Where an **optionholder** acquires securities pursuant to a **securities option**, and later sells them, this will be a disposal for capital gains tax purposes. The calculation is different depending on whether the shares were acquired before, or on or after 10 April 2003.

8.1.4.1. Acquisition of Securities through unapproved option on or after 10 April 2003

The capital gain is calculated by taking the sales proceeds of the securities and deducting the following amounts:

- the **exercise price** – [TCGA 1992, s38(1)(a)]. Note that there is no **market value** substitution because TCGA 1992, s17 is disapplied by TCGA 1992, s144ZA;
- any amount which was a taxable amount under ITEPA 2003, s476 in relation to the acquisition of the securities [TCGA 1992, s119A(3)(d)];
- if the **optionholder** was taxed in relation to the **grant** of the **option**, any amount that was taxed as earnings at that time [TCGA 1992, s119A(5)];
- any secondary NIC or special contributions that the employee paid in respect of the **securities option** [TCGA 1992, s119A(5)];
- any amount that is taxed as employment income under ITEPA 2003, s446X (disposals at more than **market value**) [TCGA 1992, s37];
- any amount that constituted employment income in relation to an earlier or simultaneous chargeable event under ITEPA 2003, s426 (**restricted securities**), s439(3)(a) (conversion of **convertible securities**), or s446U (discharge of notional loan) [TCGA 1992, s119A(3)];

- the **grant price** of the **option** (if any);
- taper relief (if any).

8.1.4.2. Acquisition of Securities through unapproved option before 10 April 2003

If the securities were acquired before 10 April 2003, the calculation is the same as above, except that instead of deducting the **exercise price**, the shareholder can deduct the **CGT value** of the shares on the **exercise date**. This is the effect of *Mansworth v Jelley* [2003] STC 53, which has been overruled by legislation in relation to **options exercised** on or after 10 April 2003 [TCGA 1992, s144ZA]. Effectively this means that the shareholder gets double relief for the taxable amount on the **exercise date**.

8.1.5. Reporting Obligations

The **grant** of a **securities option** and the acquisition of securities through a **securities option** are both reportable events. See section 23.

8.2. EMI Options

8.2.1. Income Tax

8.2.1.1. Grant

There is never any income tax on the **grant** of a **qualifying option** [ITEPA 2003, s528].

8.2.1.2. Exercise

The tax liability of an **optionholder** who **exercise**s a **qualifying option** depends on whether there was originally a **discount at grant**, and whether there has been a disqualifying event since the **grant date**.

8.2.1.2.1. No discount at grant; no disqualifying event

If there was no **discount at grant** (i.e. the **exercise price** was not less than the **CGT value** of the shares at the **grant date**), and there has not been a disqualifying event since the **grant date**, then there will be no chargeable event for income tax purposes [ITEPA 2003, s530].

8.2.1.2.2. Discount at grant, no disqualifying event

If there was a **discount at grant**, then that **discount** will be taxed at the **exercise date**. The taxable amount will be: CMV – (ACO + ACS) [ITEPA 2003, s531(2)].

CMV is the lower of the **market value** of the shares on the **grant date** and on the **exercise date** [ITEPA 2003, s531(3)]. This protects the **optionholder** if the **market value** falls between the **grant date** and the **exercise date**.

ACO is the **grant price**, if any.

ACS is the **exercise price**, if any.

The tax and NIC will be calculated and collected in the same way as for an un**approved option** (see sections 8.1.2.5 and 8.1.3).

David Heaton has argued convincingly that there is a gap in the legislation which means that there is no NIC on the **discount at grant**[176]. In summary, the argument is that the charge to NIC on **securities option**s is imposed by SSCBA 1992, s4(4)(a), which says that NIC applies to a gain "calculated under ITEPA 2003, s479". The taxable amount for the **discount at grant** of an EMI **option** is calculated under ITEPA 2003, s531, rather than s479, and is therefore not within the scope of SSCBA 1992, s4(4)(a).

The counter-argument is that ITEPA 2003, s479(4) effectively imports the value generated by s531 into the s479 calculation, so that although it is s531 that says how the calculation is carried out, the calculation is, in fact, being done under s479.

8.2.1.2.3. Replacement Option

If the **option** being **exercise**d replaced another **option**, then the date to look at to determine whether there is a **discount at grant** is the **grant date** of the original **option** [ITEPA 2003, s531(3)].

8.2.1.2.4. Disqualifying Event

If the **optionholder exercise**s an **EMI option** within 40 days following a disqualifying event, the taxable amount will be calculated as described in sections 8.2.1.2.1 and 8.2.1.2.2.

If the **optionholder exercise**s an **EMI option** more than 40 days after a disqualifying event, then the **optionholder** is charged to income tax on any growth in value of the shares between the disqualifying event and the **exercise date**, plus any **discount at grant**. The way this works is as follows:

If the **option** was originally **grant**ed with an **exercise price** not less than the **CGT value**, the taxable amount is PEG – ACO [ITEPA 2003, s531(2)].

PEG is the post-event gain, i.e. the amount by which the **CGT value** of the shares has grown since the disqualifying event [ITEPA 2003, s532(4)].

ACO is the **grant price**, if any.

If the **option** was originally **grant**ed at a **discount**, the taxable amount is (CMV + PEG) – (ACO + ACS) [ITEPA 2003, s532(3)].

CMV is the lower of the **CGT value** on the **exercise date** and the **grant date** [ITEPA 2003, s531(3)].

ACS is the **exercise price**, if any.

---

[176] Tax Journal, 1 November 2004

Therefore the effect of this is to charge income tax on the growth in value following the disqualifying event plus any **discount at grant**.

8.2.1.2.5. Shares are Restricted securities

If the shares are **restricted securities** when the **optionholder exercises** the **option**, and full income tax relief is available, the **optionholder** is deemed to make a **Section 431(1) election** in relation to the shares [ITEPA 2003, s431A(2)(d)]. If there was a **discount at grant**, or if there has been a disqualifying event, the **optionholder** should consider making a **Section 431(1) election**.

The deemed election does not increase the actual amount of tax payable by the **optionholder** in relation to the **exercise** since, although the taxable amount calculated under ITEPA 2003, s478, is increased, this is wholly exempt from tax anyway under ITEPA 2003, s530. The benefit of the deemed election is that no further tax will arise on a post-acquisition chargeable event under ITEPA 2003, s426.

If there was a **discount at grant**, or there has been a disqualifying event, then making the election may, depending on the circumstances, create a higher immediate tax liability.

8.2.1.3. Assignment or Release of EMI Option

If the **optionholder** does not **exercise** the **EMI option** but instead derives a benefit in some other way, for example by assigning it or releasing it, then this will be treated in the same way as if the **option** did not qualify for relief (see section 8.5).

8.2.2. PAYE and NIC

If any income tax arises on the **exercise** of a **qualifying option** it will be collected through PAYE if the shares are **readily convertible assets** (see section 8.1.2.5).

The employee must "make good" the PAYE within 90 days to avoid a further tax charge under ITEPA 2003, s222 (see section 3.7.3.14).

There is never any NIC on the **grant** of a **qualifying option** [SSCR 2001, Sch3, Part IX, para 3].

However, on the **exercise** of a **qualifying option**, if the shares are **readily convertible assets**, NIC will apply to any amount that is taxed as income [SSCBA 1992, s4(4)(a)].

8.2.3. Reporting Obligations

HM Revenue & Customs' website sets out the reporting requirements for EMI at http://www.hmrc.gov.uk/shareschemes/emi/notify.htm#notify

The employing company must report the **grant** of a qualifying EMI **option** to HM Revenue & Customs within 92 days of the **grant date** [ITEPA 2003, Sch5, para 44(1)].

In addition, the **scheme organiser** must report the **grant** and **exercise** of the **option** by 6 July of the following tax year [ITEPA 2003, Sch5, para 52]. HMRC will supply the relevant form (Form 40). A copy is available on HMRC's website at http://www.hmrc.gov.uk/forms/emi40.pdf.

The **optionholder** must also report the **exercise** on his tax return. If the **optionholder** receives a tax return, it must be submitted to HM Revenue & Customs by 31 October of the tax year immediately following the exercise if the optionholder submits his tax return in paper form, or by 31 January if he submits the return electronically. If a tax liability arises, but the **optionholder** does not receive a tax return for the tax year, he or she must notify HM Revenue & Customs of his or her chargeability to tax [TMA 1970, s7].

8.2.4. Capital Gains Tax

When an **optionholder** sells shares that were acquired through an **EMI option**, the capital gains tax position depends on whether or not there was a disqualifying event in relation to the **option**.

In either case, the capital gains tax will be calculated in the same way as for a non-**qualifying option** (see section 8.1.4). However, if there was no disqualifying event, or the **exercise** took place within 40 days after the disqualifying event, taper relief runs from the **grant date** of the **EMI option** [TCGA 1992, Sch7D, para 15].

Note that if the optionholder acquires shares on the same day, some on the exercise of a **qualifying option**, a **CSOP option**, or an **SAYE** option, with tax relief, and others without tax relief, then the optionholder can elect to treat them as two separate acquisitions of shares for the purposes of the share identification rules [TCGA 1992, s105A]. This enables the optionholder to manage his capital gains tax exposure.

8.3. CSOP Options

8.3.1. Income Tax

8.3.1.1. Grant

The **grant** of an approved **CSOP option** does not normally give rise to a charge to tax [ITEPA 2003, s523].

Nevertheless, it is possible, although very unlikely, that there could be a **discount at grant**. If there is, it will be taxable on the grant date [ITEPA 2003, s526].

8.3.1.2. Exercise

The **optionholder** may be exempt from income tax if he **exercise**s the **option** at a time when the **CSOP** remains approved by HM Revenue & Customs [ITEPA 2003, s519].

In order to benefit from the exemption, the **optionholder** must **exercise** the **option** either

(a) more than three years after the **grant date, or**
(b) within six months following termination of employment because of injury, disability, **redundancy** or **retirement** on reaching the age specified in the Plan Rules [ITEPA 2003, s524].

If the exemption is not available, the **exercise** of the **option** will be treated in the same way as an unapproved **option** (see section 8.1.2).

8.3.1.3. Assignment or Release of CSOP Option

If the **optionholder** does not **exercise** the **CSOP option** but instead derives a benefit in some other way, for example by assigning it or releasing it, then this will be treated in the same way as if the **option** were not approved (see section 8.5).

8.3.2. PAYE and NIC

On the **exercise** of a **CSOP option**, if the exemption from income tax does not apply and the shares are **readily convertible assets**, then the employer must withhold tax through the PAYE system. The definition of a **readily convertible asset** is extended by ITEPA 2003, s701(2)(c)(ia) to include shares acquired on an **exercise** of an approved **CSOP option** within three years of the **grant date**.

The employee must "make good" the PAYE within 90 days to avoid a further tax charge under ITEPA 2003, s222 (see section 3.7.3.14).

NIC will also apply in these circumstances. This is because SSCR 2001, reg 1(2) imports the definition of **readily convertible asset** from ITEPA 2003, s702, which in turn uses the definition of asset in ITEPA 2003, s701(2)(c).

8.3.3. Reporting Obligations

HMRC's website sets out the reporting requirements for a **CSOP** at
http://www.hmrc.gov.uk/shareschemes/CSOP_report_req_eer.htm

The **scheme organiser** must report the **grant** and **exercise** of the **option** by 6 July of the following tax year. HM Revenue & Customs will supply the relevant form (Form 35). A copy is available on HM Revenue & Customs' website at http://www.hmrc.gov.uk/forms/csop35-06.pdf.

Note that if the Plan Rules include "blue pencil" provisions, these cannot be used to mitigate the effects of poor housekeeping. If an **option** is included in the Form 35 return to HM Revenue & Customs as being a **CSOP option**, but it cannot actually have been a **CSOP option** because it exceeded the £30,000 limit, HM Revenue & Customs will deny relief to the whole **option**, not just the part that exceeds the limit [*IR Share Focus 2* (December 2003)[177]].

If the **optionholder** receives a tax return for the year of exercise he or she must declare the **exercise** of the **option** and include the taxable amount (if any). If the

---

177 http://www.hmrc.gov.uk/shareschemes/news/share-focus2.pdf

optionholder receives a tax return, it must be submitted to HM Revenue & Customs by 31 October of the tax year immediately following the exercise if the optionholder submits his tax return in paper form, or by 31 January if he submits the return electronically. If there is a taxable amount, and the optionholder does not receive a tax return, he or she must notify HM Revenue & Customs of his or her chargeability to tax [TMA 1970, s7].

8.3.4. Capital Gains Tax

The capital gains tax treatment of shares acquired on the **exercise** of an approved **CSOP option** depends on whether income tax relief was available on the **exercise**.

If income tax relief was not available, then the calculation of the capital gains tax liability will be the same as for an unapproved **option** (see section 8.1.4).

If income tax relief was available on the **exercise**, then the capital gain is calculated by taking the sales proceeds of the securities and deducting the following amounts:

- **Exercise price** – note that there is no **market value** substitution [TCGA 1992, Sch7D, para 13(2)]
- **Grant price** (if any)
- Any **discount at grant** taxed under ITEPA 2003, s526 [TCGA 1992, Sch7D, para 12(2)]
- Any other amount already taxed in relation to the **option** under prior legislation that has now been repealed [TCGA 1992, Sch7D, para 12(3)]
- Taper Relief (if any)

Note that if the optionholder acquires shares on the same day, some on the exercise of a **CSOP** option, or a **qualifying option** or an **SAYE** option, with tax relief, and others without tax relief, then the optionholder can elect to treat them as two separate acquisitions of shares for the purposes of the share identification rules [TCGA 1992, s105A]. This enables the optionholder to manage his capital gains tax exposure.

8.4. SAYE Options

8.4.1. Income Tax

8.4.1.1. Grant

There is never any income tax on the **grant** of an approved **SAYE option** [ITEPA 2003, s518].

8.4.1.2. Exercise

If an **optionholder exercise**s an **SAYE option** three years or more after the **grant date**, no tax liability arises [ITEPA 2003, s519(2)].

If an **optionholder exercise**s an approved **SAYE option** less than three years after the **grant date**, there may be a tax liability depending on the reasons for the **exercise**. If the **exercise** occurs following a change of control of the company whose shares are used, or a sale of the company or business which employs the **optionholder**, then the exemption from tax does not apply [ITEPA 2003, s519(3)]. The calculation of the taxable amount is the same as for an unapproved **option** (see section 8.1.2.2).

Even if HM Revenue & Customs withdraw approval from the **SAYE** Plan because of a "disqualifying event" under ITEPA 2003, Sch3, para 42, the exemption from income tax remains available [ITEPA 2003, Sch3, para 42(3)].

8.4.1.3. Assignment or Release of SAYE Option

If the **optionholder** does not **exercise** the **SAYE option** but instead derives a benefit in some other way, for example by assigning it or releasing it, then this will be treated in the same way as if the **option** were not approved (see section 8.5).

8.4.2. PAYE and NIC

There is no requirement to account for PAYE on the **grant** or **exercise** of an **SAYE option**. This is because ITEPA 2003, s701(2)(c)(i) says that shares acquired through an **SAYE** Plan are not "assets" for the purposes of PAYE. Similarly, ITEPA 2003, s701(2)(c)(ii) says that an **SAYE option** is not an "asset". Since they are not "assets", they cannot be **readily convertible asset**s within ITEPA 2003, s702.

The same logic applies to take **SAYE option**s outside the scope of NIC, since SSCR 2001, reg 1(2) imports the definition of **readily convertible asset** from ITEPA 2003, s702.

8.4.3. Reporting Obligations

The reporting requirements for **SAYE** are explained on HMRC's website at
http://www.hmrc.gov.uk/shareschemes/saye_rep_req_eer.htm

The **scheme organiser** must report the **grant** and **exercise** of the **option** to HM Revenue & Customs by 6 July of the tax year following the year in which the **grant** or **exercise** takes place. The report should be made using Form 34 which HM Revenue & Customs will supply. A copy can be downloaded from http://www.hmrc.gov.uk/shareschemes/form34.pdf .

The **optionholder** must declare the **exercise** of the **option** and include the taxable amount (if any) in his tax return for the year of **exercise**. If the **optionholder** receives a tax return, it must be submitted to HM Revenue & Customs by 31 October of the tax year immediately following the exercise if the optionholder submits his tax return in paper form, or by 31 January if he submits the return electronically. If there is a taxable amount, and the optionholder does not receive a tax return, he or she must notify HM Revenue & Customs of his or her chargeability to tax [TMA 1970, s7].

8.4.4. Capital Gains Tax

The capital gains tax treatment of shares acquired on the **exercise** of an approved **SAYE option** depends on whether income tax relief was available on the **exercise**.

If income tax relief was not available, then the calculation of the capital gains tax liability will be the same as for an unapproved **option** (see section 8.1.4).

If income tax relief was available on the **exercise**, then the capital gain is calculated by taking the sales proceeds of the securities and deducting the following amounts:

- **Exercise price** – note that there is no **market value** substitution [TCGA 1992, Sch7D, para 10(4)]
- Taper Relief (if any)
- Annual Exemption (if any)

Note that if the optionholder acquires shares on the same day, some on the exercise of an SAYE option with tax relief, and others without tax relief, then the optionholder can elect to treat them as two separate acquisitions of shares for the purposes of the share identification rules [TCGA 1992, s105A]. This enables the optionholder to manage his capital gains tax exposure.

8.4.5. Share Options and Corporation Tax Deductibility

The employing company may be able to claim corporation tax relief in relation to the **option**.

Relief may either be available for the **option gain** when the employee **exercise**s the **option** under FA 2003, Sch23 (see section 17.4).

If that relief is not available, the employing company may be able to claim relief under general principles for the costs of providing the shares (see section 17.1).

8.4.6. Optionholder Not Ordinarily resident on Grant date

8.4.6.1. Tax at Grant

ITEPA 2003, Part 7, Chapter 5 does not apply where the **optionholder** is not **ordinarily resident** in the UK [ITEPA 2003, s474(1)]. Therefore there can be a tax charge at the **grant date** of an **option** to a **resident**, but not **ordinarily resident**, employee. This is because the exemption in ITEPA 2003, s475(1) does not apply [*Abbott v Philbin* 39 TC 82]. The **option** is treated as general earnings, and the taxable value is the money's worth value [ITEPA 2003, s62(3)].

In practice, HM Revenue & Customs accept that the money's worth value is nil if the **exercise price** is equal to or greater than the **market value** of the securities on the **grant date** [HMRC Manual ERSM110200][178].

---

178 http://www.hmrc.gov.uk/manuals/ersmmanual/ERSM110200.htm

If the **option** itself is a **readily convertible asset** on the **grant date**, then the tax should be collected through PAYE [ITEPA 2003, s696(1)] and NIC will apply [SSCR 2001, Sch2, para 5(1)(b)].

The employee must "make good" the PAYE within 90 days to avoid a further tax charge under ITEPA 2003, s222 (see section 3.7.3.14).

8.4.6.2. Tax at Exercise

If the **optionholder** was not **resident** in the UK on the **grant date**, but is **resident** on the **exercise date**, HM Revenue & Customs will regard the source of the **option** as being the overseas employment and, accordingly, will not seek to tax the **optionholder** in relation to the **exercise** [HMRC FAQ 3C(c)][179].

If the **optionholder** was **resident**, but not **ordinarily resident**, in the UK on the **grant date**, and is still **resident** in the United Kingdom on the **exercise date**, the **exercise** itself is not a chargeable event.

However, ITEPA 2003, Part 7, Chapter 3C will apply because the securities have been acquired for less than their **CGT value**. Therefore the employee will be treated as having received an interest-free loan from the employer [ITEPA 2003, s446S(1)]. The general rules on employment-related loans in ITEPA 2003, Part 3, Chapter 7 apply, with the exception of those rules that are only applicable to real loans rather than notional loans [ITEPA 2003, s446S(2)]. For example, the £5,000 *de minimis* exemption for small loans applies also to a liability under Chapter 3C (see chapter 16).

8.4.6.3. The Notional Loan

The notional loan is deemed to have been made on the **exercise date** of the **option** [ITEPA 2003, s446S(1)]. It remains outstanding until the securities are disposed of to someone who is not an **associated person** [ITEPA 2003, s446U(1)(a)]. The employee is then taxed on the amount of the notional loan.

The amount of the notional loan is MV - DA [ITEPA 2003, s446T(1)].

8.4.6.4. Market value in the Notional Loan Calculation

MV is the **CGT value** of the securities on the **exercise date**.

In determining MV, the securities should be treated as if they were **fully paid up**, even if they are not [ITEPA 2003, s446T(2)].

Note that if the securities are **restricted securities**, the calculation uses the restricted **CGT value**, unless the **optionholder** has become **ordinarily resident** by the **exercise date** and makes a **Section 431(1) election** to use the **unrestricted market value** [ITEPA 2003, s431(3)(c)].

---

179 http://www.hmrc.gov.uk/shareschemes/faq_emprelatedsecurity-ch3c.htm#c

Note that if the securities are **convertible securities**, the value attributed to the conversion entitlement is usually ignored in calculating MV [ITEPA 2003, s437(1)(b)]. However, if the arrangements under which the securities are offered were entered into for tax or NIC avoidance purposes, it is necessary to carry out a hypothetical calculation of what the securities would be worth if the conversion entitlement were immediate [ITEPA 2003, s437(3)(b))]. This value must be used if it is higher than the value ignoring the conversion entitlement [ITEPA 2003, s437(2)].

Note further that it is not possible to deduct selling costs (real or notional) in determining MV.

8.4.6.5. *The Deductible Amounts in the Notional Loan Calculation*

DA are the deductible amounts. These include the following:

- the **grant price** of the **option** (if any) [ITEPA 2003, s446T(3)(a)]
- the **exercise price** of the **option** [ITEPA 2003, s446T(3)(a)]
- any amount charged to tax in relation to the acquisition of the securities [ITEPA 2003, s446T(3)(b)]. By concession, this includes any amount charged to income tax on the **grant** of the **option** [HMRC FAQ 3C(b)][180]
- if an election under ITEPA 2003, s425(2) was made on the acquisition of the securities, the amount charged to tax on the first subsequent chargeable event [ITEPA 2003, s446T(3)(c)]
- if the securities were acquired on the conversion of **convertible securities**, the amount taxed on the conversion [ITEPA 2003, s446T(3)(d)].

8.4.6.6. *Overseas Workday Relief*

If the **optionholder** performs part of his duties outside the UK, HM Revenue & Customs will treat part of the gain as being outside the scope of UK tax. Usually, HMRC will agree to apportion the gain on a pure time basis, i.e. by looking at the total period between **grant** and **exercise**, and determining what proportion of this is represented by overseas workdays. The balance of the gain, representing UK workdays, will be the notional loan as calculated under section 8.4.6.3 above [HMRC FAQ 3C(c)][181].

8.4.6.7. *Interaction between Notional Loan and Restricted securities Rules*

The interaction between the notional loan rules in Chapter 3C and the **restricted securities** rules in Chapter 2 gives scope for double taxation. HM Revenue & Customs have stated that they will apply Chapter 2 instead of Chapter 3C in cases where both could apply, so as to avoid double taxation [HMRC FAQ 3C(a)].[182].

---

[180] http://www.hmrc.gov.uk/shareschemes/faq_emprelatedsecurity-ch3c.htm#b

[181] http://www.hmrc.gov.uk/shareschemes/faq_emprelatedsecurity-ch3c.htm#c

[182] http://www.hmrc.gov.uk/shareschemes/faq_emprelatedsecurity-ch3c.htm#a

8.4.6.8. PAYE on the Discharge of the Notional Loan

See section 12.8.4.7.

8.4.6.9. NIC on Discharge of Notional Loan

See section 12.8.4.8.

8.4.6.10. Reporting the Notional Loan

See section 12.8.4.6.

8.4.7. Optionholder domiciled outside the UK

If the **optionholder** is (a) **resident** and **ordinarily resident** in the UK, but (b) domiciled outside the UK, (c) employed by a foreign employer, and (d) the duties of the foreign employment are performed wholly outside the UK, then general earnings from that foreign employment are "overseas earnings" as defined in ITEPA 2003, s23(2).

HM Revenue & Customs accept that an **option granted** in respect of such an employment is outside the scope of UK taxation, unless and to the extent that the gain is remitted to the UK [HMRC FAQ 3C(c)][183].

However, if the **optionholder** also has an associated UK employment, ITEPA 2003, s24 limits the amount of overseas earnings that are exempt from UK tax. If this applies, then the exemption for the **option gain** will be similarly limited.

8.5. Assignment or Release of Securities option

If an **optionholder** assigns or releases an **option**, he is taxable on any consideration he receives for the assignment [ITEPA 2003, s477(3)(b)]. Similarly, if the **optionholder** receives any benefit in connection with the **option**, this will be taxable [ITEPA 2003, s477(3)(c)]. Different rules apply where the **optionholder** was not **resident**, or not **ordinarily resident**, on the **grant date** of the **option** (see section 8.5.5).

Note, however, that there may not be any income tax saving through a transfer of an **option** since

- if the transferee is an **associated person**, the employee will be charged to income tax on a subsequent chargeable event in relation to the **option** (see section 8.1.2.1);
- if the transferee is not an **associated person**, then the consideration will be taxable (see section 8.5).

Since there is no **market value** substitution under ITEPA 2003, s477(3)(b), there might be a planning opportunity in assigning the **option** to a non-**associated person** for no, or a low, consideration.

---

183 http://www.hmrc.gov.uk/shareschemes/faq_emprelatedsecurity-ch3c.htm#c

If there is an **option** rollover, in other words the **option** is exchanged, wholly or partly, for the **grant** of another right to acquire securities in that or any other body corporate, then that part of the consideration is excluded from the calculation of the tax liability [ITEPA 2003, s483]. For further details of **option** rollovers, see section 8.5.6.

8.5.1. Income Tax and PAYE

Any income tax arising in relation to the assignment or release of the **option** should be withheld through the PAYE system [ITEPA 2003, s700(3)]. This is the case even if the **option** was **grant**ed before 27 November 1996, because the exclusion for pre-1996 **option**s only applies where shares are actually acquired [ITEPA 2003, s701(2)(c)(iii)].

The employee must "make good" the PAYE within 90 days to avoid a further tax charge under ITEPA 2003, s222 (see section 3.7.3.14).

8.5.2. NIC

When an income tax liability arises on the assignment or release of a right to acquire securities, there will also be an NIC liability [SSCBA 1992, s4(4)(a)]. This applies to **option**s **grant**ed before 6 April 1999 because the exclusion for older **option**s only applies where shares are acquired [SSCR 2001, Sch3, Part IX, para 16].

Often, in a takeover situation, the **option**s will be released to the acquiring company in return for a "cash cancellation payment". In these circumstances, the liability to pay secondary NIC remains with whoever is the secondary contributor under SSCBA 1992, s7. Usually this is the employer. However, SSCR 2001, Sch4, para 4 allows the person who pays the cash cancellation payment to undertake the payroll reporting and accounting as agent for the secondary contributor.

If the **option** was **grant**ed between 6 April 1999 and 19 May 2000 then the assignment or release may be exempt from NIC under SSCSOA 2001 (see section 8.1.3.5).

8.5.3. Capital Gains Tax

The **option** is an asset for capital gains tax purposes, so the assignment or release may also be a disposal of an asset for those purposes. TCGA 1992, s22 says that there can be a disposal of the **option** even if it ceases to exist after it has been released. However, there is no double charge to tax because TCGA 1992, s37 says that any amount which is taxable as income in relation to the assignment or release is excluded from the sale proceeds in the CGT calculation.

Note also that if the **option** is abandoned for no consideration, rather than being released for consideration, this is not a disposal for CGT purposes [TCGA 1992, s144(4)].

Note also that the **option** may be a non-UK situs asset, e.g. where it is a contractual right against a foreign parent company or an offshore trust. In these circumstances, if the **optionholder** is not domiciled within the UK, there will not be any CGT liability if the gains are not remitted to the UK [TCGA 1992, s12].

8.5.4. Corporation Tax Deductibility

The maker of a cash cancellation payment has no statutory right to a corporation tax deduction under FA 2003, Sch23 because that schedule only applies where shares are acquired.

It may be difficult to obtain a deduction under general principles. If the maker of the payment is an acquiring company, HM Revenue & Customs are likely to argue that the payment is part of the acquisition costs rather than a revenue payment. If the maker of the payment is the employing company, it may be seen as a payment to remove a capital obligation of the employing company or its parent.

For further discussion of this point, see section 17.8.

8.5.5. Optionholder Not Resident or Not Ordinarily resident on Grant date

ITEPA 2003, s476 does not apply to the assignment or release of an **option** where the **optionholder** was not both **resident** and **ordinarily resident** in the UK on the **grant date** [ITEPA 2003, s421E]. There is no other provision to charge income tax in these circumstances.

There may, however, be a capital gains tax liability in relation to the disposal of the **option** (see section 8.5.3).

The assignment or release of the **option** is a disposal of an asset for CGT purposes, even if the **option** ceases to exist after it has been released [TCGA 1992, s22].

8.5.6. Option Rollovers

Very often, when one company acquires another company, the **optionholder**s in relation to the target company are given the opportunity to exchange their **option**s for new **option**s over shares in the acquiring company. This is referred to as an "**option** rollover". Usually, that can be structured in a way that is entirely free from any tax consequences, as explained in this section.

8.5.6.1. Income Tax Rollover Relief for Unapproved options

ITEPA 2003, s483 removes any possible charge to income tax on the roll-over of an unapproved **option**. However, if the old **option**s were outside the scope of PAYE, because they were **grant**ed before 27 November 1996, that benefit will not flow through to the new **option**s, because they will be treated having been **grant**ed on the date of the rollover.

8.5.6.2. NIC on Exchange of Unapproved option

For NIC purposes, the exchange of one **option** for another is the **grant** of a new **securities option**. There is no NIC on the exchange of one **option** for another, because this constitutes the **grant** of a new **securities option**, which is exempt from NIC under SSCR 2001, Sch3, Part IX, para 3. The treatment of the new option is generally the same as the old option, but see section 8.1.3.3 in relation to options granted before 6 April 1999 which are rolled over.

However, insofar as the **option** is released for cash, this will be subject to NIC (see section 8.5.2).

8.5.6.3. Income Tax Rollover Relief for Approved options (CSOP and SAYE)

Where there is a **company reorganisation** of a company that operates a **CSOP** or **SAYE**, it is possible for the **optionholder**s to release their existing **CSOP** or **SAYE option**s in exchange for new **option**s.

If HM Revenue & Customs approve the rollover, the new **option**s will retain the approved status of the old **option**s and will be treated as having been **grant**ed when the old **option**s were **grant**ed [ITEPA 2003, Sch3, para 39(5) and Sch4, para 27(5)]. If the rollover is not approved, the new **option**s will be treated as unapproved **option**s **grant**ed on the date the new **option** was **grant**ed.

It is important to ensure that the rollover complies with ITEPA 2003, Sch3, para 38 and 39 (for **SAYE option**s) or Sch4, para 26 and 27 (for **CSOP option**s) and to obtain HM Revenue & Customs' approval for the exchange of **option**s before it takes place.

ITEPA 2003, Sch3, para 38 and Sch4, para 26 are virtually identical. They each set out the provisions that must be in the Plan Rules in order for an approved rollover to take place. If these provisions are not in the Plan Rules, there cannot be an approved rollover [HMRC Manual ESS15012][184].

To determine whether an approved rollover can occur, use the checklist in section 21.4.

8.5.6.4. Income Tax Rollover Relief for EMI Options

Where there is a **company reorganisation** of a company that operates an **EMI** plan, it is possible for the **optionholder**s to release their existing **EMI option**s in exchange for new **option**s.

If the rollover complies with the legislation, the new **option**s will retain the qualifying status of the old **option**s and will be treated as having been **grant**ed when the old **option**s were **grant**ed [ITEPA 2003, Sch5, para 41(5)].

It is important to ensure that the rollover complies with ITEPA 2003, Sch5, paras 39 to 43. To determine whether a qualifying rollover can occur, use the checklist in section 21.5.

---

184 http://www.hmrc.gov.uk/manuals/essumanual/essu13000/essu15012.htm

The grantor must notify HM Revenue & Customs within 92 days of the **grant** of a replacement **option**. The grantor should write a covering letter explaining that the new **option**s are indeed replacement **option**s.

When an **EMI option** is replaced by a new **option**, the author understands HM Revenue & Customs' view to be that the ten year maximum life of an **option** starts again from the **grant date** of the replacement **option**.

8.5.6.5. Capital Gains Tax Issues on Rollover

There is no capital gains tax on the assignment or release of a right to acquire shares in exchange for the grant of another right to acquire shares [TCGA 1992, s237A]. Note however that this exclusion is limited to rights over shares as opposed to other securities.

8.5.7. Reporting Obligations in relation to the Assignment or Release of Options

The assignment or release of or obtaining a benefit from a **securities option** is a reportable event [ITEPA 2003, s421K(3)(h)]. See section 23.

The **grant** of a replacement **EMI option** must be reported to HM Revenue & Customs within 92 days.

9. NIC Recovery and Transfers

9.1. Recovering Primary NIC from an Employee

It can sometimes be difficult for an employer to recover primary NIC from an employee, particularly where this relates to non-monetary earnings such as shares or **options**. Difficulties can arise, for example, where the earnings are paid after the employee has terminated employment, so that there are no cash earnings from which the primary NIC can be deducted.

It is possible for the employer and the employee to agree that the employer has the right to sell sufficient of the securities to cover the primary NIC. Such an agreement can only be made in relation to securities in respect of which the employee is charged to tax as employment income [SSCR 2001, Sch4, para 7(11A)].

The agreement can relate both to current and former employees, and to securities provided both in the current tax year and in the next tax year following termination of employment [SSCR 2001, Sch4, para 7(9)].

The agreement must be in writing and made in advance [SSCR 2001, Sch4, para 7(12)]. Therefore it may be difficult to get an employee to agree to this in relation to **option**s or securities that have already been awarded. There is no particular form that the agreement has to take[185].

Further information is available on the HM Revenue & Customs website at
http://www.hmrc.gov.uk/shareschemes/recouping-employees-nics.htm

9.2. Secondary NIC Transfers

Generally it is illegal for an employer to seek to recover secondary NIC from an earner [SSCBA 1992, Sch1, para 3A]. However, there are exceptions for liabilities that arise in relation to:

- a post-acquisition chargeable event on **restricted securities** [SSCBA 1992, Sch1, para 3A(2B)(a)] (see section 12.3.2);
- a post-acquisition chargeable event on **convertible securities** [SSCBA 1992, Sch1, para 3A(2B)(b)] (see section 12.4.2);
- a post-acquisition chargeable event in relation to a **securities option** [SSCBA 1992, Sch1, para 3A(2B)(c)] (see section 8.1.2.1).

It is not possible for the employee to take on liability for NIC that arises in relation to the acquisition of securities with an artificially depressed **market value** [SSCBA 1992, Sch1, para 3A(2A)(a)] (see section 12.5). Similarly, NIC that becomes due as a

---

185 http://www.hmrc.gov.uk/shareschemes/recouping-employees-nics.htm#g

result of retrospective tax legislation cannot be passed on to the employee [SSCBA 1992, Sch1, para 3A(2A)(b)].

The Government was persuaded to introduce these exceptions because the employer has no control over the amount of the liability nor, in cases where the employee triggers the chargeable event by converting securities or exercising an **option**, the timing of the liability.

There are two ways in which the employee can take on the liability. Method 1 is by an agreement under SSCBA 1992, Sch1, para 3A. Such an agreement can take any form and does not need to be reviewed or approved by HMRC. The employer is still responsible for actually paying the NIC to HMRC, but has a right to be reimbursed by the earner.

Method 2 is by an election under SSCBA 1992, Sch1, para 3B. The key difference here is that the liability is actually transferred to the employee, who becomes directly liable to HM Revenue & Customs. Since HM Revenue & Customs are taking on the risk of non-payment, the election has to be approved by HM Revenue & Customs before it takes effect.

In either case it is possible for the liability to be shared between the employer and earner. For example, the employer might agree to pay the first £10,000 and the earner might agree to pay any excess.

The earner gets income tax relief for any secondary NIC that he has paid. This is achieved by making the amount a "deductible amount" in the calculation of the income tax liability (see sections 8.1.2.4 and 12.3.4.4).

HM Revenue & Customs have published two draft forms of election, and employers can use whichever they prefer. There is a one-part election[186], a single document which both employer and employee have to sign, and a two-part election[187], where the employer signs one copy, and the employee signs a different copy. The choice between these depends on the administrative convenience of the employer. HMRC have published guidance on the completion of the elections at http://www.hmrc.gov.uk/shareschemes/elections.htm#modjoint

The employer does not have to use either of HM Revenue & Customs' drafts. It is possible for employers to prepare their own bespoke transfer elections. HM Revenue & Customs must approve these elections, which must contain the specific information set out below:

a details of the shares or **option**s to which it relates, or of the period within which the shares or **option**s to which it relates are intended to be **grant**ed;

---

186 http://www.hmrc.gov.uk/shareschemes/joint_election_1.rtf

187 http://www.hmrc.gov.uk/shareschemes/joint_election_2.rtf

b a statement that the election relates to any amount on which the earner is liable to pay contributions and an explanation of the effect of the legislation imposing the NIC charge;

c the amount or proportion (as the case may be) of the liability for secondary contributions to be transferred;

d a statement that its purpose is to transfer the liability for the secondary contributions referred to in paragraph (c) from the secondary contributor to the earner;

e a statement as to the method by which the secondary contributor will secure that the liability for amounts of contributions, transferred under the election, is met;

f a statement as to the circumstances in which it shall cease to have effect;

g a declaration by the earner that he agrees to be bound by its terms; and

h evidence sufficient to show that the secondary contributor agrees to be bound by its terms [HMRC FAQ e4].[188]

HM Revenue & Customs do not need to see a copy of the signed election [HMRC FAQ e8].[189]

The employer continues to be responsible for the payroll records and the NIC should be noted on the end of year term sheets as if the employer had paid it [HMRC FAQ e9].[190]

---

188 http://www.hmrc.gov.uk/shareschemes/non_app_nics_elections.htm#e4

189 http://www.hmrc.gov.uk/shareschemes/non_app_nics_elections.htm#e8

190 http://www.hmrc.gov.uk/shareschemes/non_app_nics_elections.htm#e9

10. Employee Benefit Trusts: Uses and Tax Treatment

10.1. Uses

Employee Benefit Trusts (EBTs) are used for many different purposes, but the principal uses are: making a market in shares of an unquoted company; "warehousing" shares pending distribution to employees; and providing benefits.

10.1.1. Market-making Trusts

An EBT can make a market in shares of a private company by purchasing shares from willing sellers, or from former employees who are required to offer their shares for sale. It can sell the shares on to continuing employees, possibly through the **exercise** of share **option**s or the **vesting** of incentive plan awards.

This may be more administratively convenient than allowing shareholders to deal directly with employees. Often the company's Articles of Association will permit transfers to and from the EBT to be made without requiring the consent of other shareholders.

Using an EBT as a market-maker in this way can have the disadvantage that the shares become **readily convertible asset**s (see section 21.1). It also needs to be carefully planned to ensure that the costs to the business are manageable; costs arise if shares are purchased at market value but sold on at a discount; ultimately those costs will have to be borne by the business.

10.1.2. Warehouse Trusts

An EBT can be used to "warehouse" shares when a substantial shareholder wishes to sell. The company can make a gift or loan to the EBT, which can use this to purchase the shares from the shareholder and distribute them to employees over a period of years.

This requires careful planning in that the company is tying up cash in the loan to the EBT. Depending on how and when the EBT distributes the shares, this loan may not be repaid in full, or at all.

Although the selling shareholder should be subject to capital gains tax on the sale of the shares, HM Revenue & Customs may argue that ICTA 1988, s703 applies, with the effect that the gain is taxed as income (see section 10.3.3).

10.1.3. Provision of Benefits

An EBT can be used to provide benefits to employees, either cash or non-cash benefits. The employee is taxed on receipt of the benefits in exactly the same way as if the employer had paid them directly to the employee.

See section 3.6 for commentary on the use of EBTs to reward senior employees.

10.2. Taxation of a Company that Contributes or Transfers Assets to an EBT

10.2.1. Corporation Tax Deductibility

See section 17.1 for a summary of the general principles and section 17.3 for the possibility of deferral under FA 2003, Sch24.

10.2.2. Inheritance Tax

If the employer is a **close company**, and the payment into the EBT constitutes a transfer of value, the value of the payment may be apportioned among the **participators** in the **close company**, and IHT will be charged accordingly.

10.2.2.1. IHTA 1984, s12

A voluntary contribution into an EBT will not constitute a transfer of value if it is deductible for corporation tax purposes [IHTA 1984, s12]. See section 17 for a commentary on the corporation tax deductibility of payments.

It is not clear how IHTA 1984, s12 interacts with FA 2003, Sch24. HM Revenue & Customs have stated in unpublished correspondence that their view is that IHTA 1984, s12 does not apply if the corporation tax deduction is deferred by FA 2003, Sch24. This is on the basis that, although the payment may be deductible in principle, it is not actually deducted against the profits of the year in which it is paid. The author does not believe that this is correct; IHTA 1984 s12 applies to payments that are deductible in principle, whether or not they are actually deducted.

10.2.2.2. IHTA 1984, s13

A contribution to an EBT will not be a transfer of value if it is made to a trust which qualifies under IHTA 1984, s86 (see section 10.4.1.1) and the beneficiaries include either:

(a) all or most of the directors and employees of the company concerned; or
(b) all or most of the directors and employees of the company concerned and any one or more of its subsidiaries.

[IHTA 1984, s13]

For this exemption to apply, the EBT must exclude not only all the present **participators** in the **close company** which makes the contribution for which the relief is claimed [IHTA 1984, s13(2)(a)], but also: any person who is a **participator** in any other **close company** which has made a voluntary contribution to the same EBT and obtained the relief [IHTA 1984, s13(2)(b)]; any person who has, within the previous ten years, been such a **participator** [IHTA 1984, s13(2)(c)]; and anyone connected with such a person.

There is a *de minimis* exclusion if the **participator**'s interest in the **close company** is less than five per cent of the issued share capital, or of any class of the issued share capital, or of the assets of the company on a winding-up [IHTA 1984, s13(3)]. Such a **participator**, and any person connected with him, can be a beneficiary of the EBT without losing the IHTA 1984, s13 exemption.

Furthermore, if the only way in which the EBT permits such a person to benefit is by the making of payments which are chargeable to income tax (or would be if the recipient were **resident** in the UK), then payments to the EBT may still qualify for relief.

10.2.3. Capital Gains Tax

TCGA 1992, s239 applies to a disposal by an individual which is also an exempt transfer for IHT purposes by virtue of IHTA 1984, s28 (employee trusts - see section 10.3.1).

It also applies to the transfer of an asset by a **close company** to an EBT, if IHTA 1984, s13 also applies to that disposal (see section 10.2.2.2).

Furthermore, it applies to a transfer by a company which is not close, if IHTA 1984, s13 would have applied if the company had been close [TCGA 1992, s239(4)].

The effect of TCGA 1992, s239 is to provide for an automatic "hold over" relief for the disposal, provided it is made either as a gift or as a sale at less than the CGT base cost. If this is the case, then the transferor is treated as having made neither a gain nor a loss for CGT purposes, and the EBT Trustee is treated as having acquired the asset at the same time and for the same consideration as the original acquisition by the transferor [TCGA 1992, s239(2)].

Furthermore, TCGA 1992, s17 is disapplied in relation to disposals relieved under IHTA 1984, s28. This means that, if the disposal is by way of sale at an undervalue, but at a price greater than the CGT base cost, it is only the surplus of the actual sale price over the base cost that is taxable, rather than the surplus of the **CGT value** over the base cost [TCGA 1992, s239].

Another aspect of TCGA 1992, s239 is that the application of TCGA 1992, s125 to a disposal by a **close company** is modified. TCGA 1992, s125 applies where a **close company** disposes of an asset for less than its **market value**, otherwise than under a bargain at arm's length. The effect of TCGA 1992, s125 is to require the difference between the actual consideration (if any) and the **CGT value** of the asset, to be apportioned between the issued shares of the company. The amount so apportioned is then deducted from the base cost of the shares when the owner of the shares eventually disposes of them.

TCGA 1992, s125 does still apply to disposals to which TCGA 1992, s239 applies, but, instead of apportioning the difference between the **CGT value** of the asset and the actual consideration, it is necessary to apportion the difference between the base cost of the asset and the actual consideration [TCGA 1992, s239(3)].

10.3. Taxation of an Individual who Contributes or Transfers Assets to an EBT

10.3.1. Inheritance Tax

Sometimes a shareholder in a company will want to make a personal contribution to an EBT.

Any disposition made by an individual to an EBT which reduces the value of his estate is, *prima facie*, a transfer of value. However, an exemption is available under IHTA 1984, s28, if the conditions are satisfied.

IHTA 1984, s28(1) restricts the exemption to transfers by an individual who is beneficially entitled to shares in a company, to an EBT that qualifies under IHTA 1984, s86 (see section 10.4.1.1).

Note that there need not actually be a transfer of shares in the company by the individual to the EBT; what is essential is that the value transferred should be attributable to shares in or securities of the company, which become comprised in the Trust Fund.

The relief is therefore available for an individual who allows his shareholding to be reduced in value by the issue of new shares to the EBT. But the relief is not available for an individual who sells part or all of his shareholding back to the company for cancellation, even if the effect is to pass control to the EBT. The reason for this, according to the Financial Secretary to the Treasury during debates on the 1975 Finance Bill, is that a sale back to the company at less than market value could be used to transfer value to other shareholders apart from the EBT.

The EBT must not only comply with IHTA 1984, s86, but must also include as beneficiaries "all or most of the persons employed by or holding office with the company" [IHTA 1984, s28(1)(b)]. Note that this only relates to employees and office-holders of the company itself, and not its subsidiaries. In practice, employees and office-holders of subsidiaries are usually included.

IHTA 1984, s28(2) imposes further conditions on the availability of the exemption. In brief, the EBT must have a majority of the ordinary shares of the company and effective control of the voting rights, either at the time of the transfer or within twelve months thereafter. There must be no agreement enabling anyone other than the EBT Trustee to divest the EBT of those ordinary shares and voting rights.

IHTA 1984, s28(4) prevents the individual from reducing the value of his estate by making exempt transfers to an EBT but, in practice, using the EBT exclusively for the benefit of himself and his family. IHTA 1984, s28(4) says that the EBT must exclude certain categories of persons, i.e.

- any person who is now, or has been within the last ten years, a **participator** either in the company whose shares are involved, whether or not that company is close, or in any **close company** which has made a disposition

whereby property has become comprised in the same settlement (i.e. the EBT), and which was relieved under IHTA 1984, s13 (see section 10.2.2.2); and
- anyone connected with such a person.

However, IHTA 1985, s28(5) limits the exclusion to those **participators** who have a significant interest in the company, i.e. being beneficially entitled to, or to rights to acquire, five per cent of any class of the share capital, or to five per cent or more of the assets on a winding up.

A more important exception to the exclusion is in IHTA 1984, s28(6). It permits the Trust Fund to be used for the benefit of people who would otherwise be excluded, but only by making payments to them that are taxable as income, or would be taxable as income if the recipient were UK **resident**. Most payments to UK **residents** will be subject to employment income tax anyway (see section 10.4.1.3). However, other forms of benefit, such as soft loans, are not permitted.

10.3.2. Capital Gains Tax

See section 10.2.3.

10.3.3. ICTA 1988, s703

If an individual sells shares in a company to its EBT, this would normally be treated as a disposal for capital gains purposes. However, HM Revenue & Customs believe that, in some circumstances, it may be a transaction in securities from which the individual obtains a tax advantage, which is therefore taxable as income [ICTA 1988, s703].

HM Revenue & Customs have raised this argument where the company has funded the EBT in order to make the purchase from a shareholder who was making a partial disposal of his shareholding. The author does not have experience of HM Revenue & Customs actually giving a notice under ICTA 1988, s703(9), but he is aware that HMRC have refused clearance under ICTA 1988, s707.

HM Revenue & Customs' argument appears to be that the company could have paid a dividend to the shareholder and issued new shares to the EBT. This would have given the shareholder the same amount of pre-tax cash and the EBT would hold the same number of shares. The issue of new shares would affect all other shareholders who might not agree to the reduction in their percentage shareholding and this would appear to be a *bona fide* commercial reason. However, HM Revenue & Customs have been known to refuse clearance in these circumstances, perhaps because they believe that enabling a tax advantage to be obtained was a main object.

10.4. Taxation of the EBT Trustee

10.4.1. Inheritance Tax

10.4.1.1. Complying with IHTA 1984, s86

If an EBT complies with IHTA 1984, s86, then it will benefit from a tax-advantaged IHT treatment; also individuals and close companies making gifts to the EBT may be able to take advantage of exemptions in the IHT and CGT legislation.

To comply with IHTA 1984, s86, there must be restrictions on the persons for whose benefit the property in the EBT can be applied. Those restrictions must last either indefinitely or for a defined period of time. The fact that, for example, at the end of the EBT's life, any undistributed capital or income would belong to a person who was outside the class of beneficiaries does not, of itself, cause the EBT to fail to comply with IHTA 1984, s86. Similarly, a power to amend the Trust Deed, for example in order to include new beneficiaries, would not cause IHTA 1984, s86, to cease to apply [IHTA 1984, s86(1)].

The class of persons for whose benefit the trust property can be applied must be defined by reference to their trade or employment. This would normally be (but need not be) employment with or office with a particular company or group of companies. The employment need not be current; former employees can be included [IHTA 1984, s86(1)(a)].

Although the inclusion of the words "or office with" means that, for example, non-executive directors of the company can be included in the class of beneficiaries, it would cause the EBT to cease to be an **employees' share scheme** for company law purposes (see section 18.8).

Spouses, relations, and **dependants** of employees and former employees may also be included as potential beneficiaries [IHTA 1984, s86(1)(b)]. However, if it is necessary or desirable for the EBT to constitute an **employees' share scheme**, the class of beneficiaries should be restricted to the classes specified in CA 1985, s743 (see section 18.8).

If the class of beneficiaries is defined by reference to employment with a particular company or group of companies, then "all or most" of the employees and office-holders of that company or group must be included as potential beneficiaries. "All or most" means more than half. In practice, however, unless the EBT Deed includes all employees except, perhaps, for named individuals, HMRC Capital Taxes will not give a clearance that IHTA 1984, s86 applies. The question of whether or not more than half of the employees were beneficiaries would need to be reviewed in relation to each possible occasion of charge.

10.4.1.2. Ten-Yearly Charge

An EBT will generally be a "settlement without an interest in possession". If the EBT does not comply with IHTA 1984, s86, then it will be subject to the ten-yearly charge under IHTA 1984, s64.

However, if the EBT does comply with IHTA 1984, s86, it is not subject to the ten-yearly charge, because property held in a trust that complies with this section is not "relevant property" [IHTA 1984, s58(1)(b)].

10.4.1.3. Making a payment to a beneficiary

Usually, if an EBT makes a payment of cash to a beneficiary, or transfers an asset to a beneficiary, this will give rise to an employment income tax liability. Therefore, the payment is not a chargeable transfer for IHT purposes [IHTA 1984, s70(3)(b)].

This exemption applies even to non-resident beneficiaries, as long as it can be shown that the payment would have been taxable as income, if the beneficiary had been UK **resident**.

It is hard to conceive of circumstances in which a payment to a beneficiary from an EBT would not be chargeable to income tax. However, even if such circumstances occurred, the payment would still not be a chargeable transfer if the beneficiary concerned were not (and were not connected to) someone within the class described in IHTA 1984, s72(3) [IHTA 1984, s72(2)(b)].

10.4.1.4. Granting an option to a beneficiary

If an EBT Trustee **grant**s an **option** to a beneficiary to purchase an asset from them, it is arguable that this is a "disposition that reduces the value of settled property" [IHTA 1984, s72(2)(c)]. It is not a "payment" and (if the **option** is a right to purchase securities) it does not give rise to a UK income tax liability (see section 8.1.1).

There may nevertheless not be a charge to IHT since, if the **option** is **grant**ed under an employees' share **option** plan, it will fall within the exclusion for commercial transactions in IHTA 1984, s70(4).

10.4.1.5. Selling an asset on the exercise of an option

When an **option** is **exercise**d and the EBT Trustee transfers an asset to a beneficiary, this is "a payment out of the settled property". This means that there is no charge to tax unless the beneficiary is (or is connected to) a person within IHTA 1984, s72(3) [IHTA 1984, s72(2)(a)].

10.4.1.6. Transfer of assets from one EBT to another EBT

Sometimes when EBTs are wound up or merged, it will be necessary to transfer settled property from one EBT to another EBT. This can be effected without any charge to inheritance tax, if the transfer is immediate or takes effect within one month [IHTA 1984, s86(5)].

10.4.1.7. Loan to a Beneficiary

If an EBT lends money to a beneficiary, this will not normally reduce the value of the settled property, and therefore will not be chargeable to inheritance tax.

10.4.1.8. Payments of Costs and Expenses

The EBT Trustee will usually have to pay the costs and expenses of running the EBT. This will reduce the value of the settled property, but there will not be a charge to inheritance tax [IHTA 1984, s70(3)(a)].

10.4.1.9. Transaction that reduces value of Trust Fund

If an EBT Trustee carries out a transaction that reduces the value of the Trust Fund, without actually being a payment or transfer of assets, this will give rise to a charge to inheritance tax [IHTA 1984, s72(2)(c)]. An example of this would be voting in favour of a shareholders' resolution that alters the rights of the shares that the Trustee holds.

10.4.1.10. Calculation of Tax Liability

If an inheritance tax liability arises under IHTA 1984, s72, the applicable tax rate is determined by IHTA 1984, s70(6). The longer the assets have been held in the trust, the higher the rate of tax, as set out in **Table 5**.

Period Assets held in Trust	Applicable Rate of Tax per Quarter	Tax Rate for Period	Cumulative Effective Tax Rate at End of Period
Years 1-10	0.25%	10%	10%
Years 11-20	0.20%	8%	18%
Years 21-30	0.15%	6%	24%
Years 31-40	0.10%	4%	28%
Years 41-50	0.05%	2%	30%

Table 5: IHT rates for IHTA 1984, section 86 Trusts

10.4.1.11. Treatment of Trusts outside Section 86

If the EBT does not satisfy IHTA 1984, s86, the normal IHT regime for settlements without interests in possession applies [IHTA 1984, s58 to s69].

In principle, there is a charge to IHT whenever the EBT Trustee makes a distribution to a beneficiary [IHTA 1984, s65(1)(a)]. However, there is an exclusion where the distribution takes the form of a payment, which is income in the hands of the beneficiary (or would be if he were **resident** in the UK) [IHTA 1984, s65(5)(b)]. The term "payment" includes a transfer of assets other than money [IHTA 1984, s63].

The second possible occasion of charge is a depreciatory transaction by the Trustee [IHTA 1984, s65(1)(b)]. For example, the **grant** of an **option** to an employee could, in principle, be an occasion of charge if the value of the trust property is reduced by the **grant** of the **option**.

Each tenth anniversary of the creation of the EBT is a further occasion of charge to IHT [IHTA 1984, s64].

10.4.2. Capital Gains Tax: Disposals by Onshore EBTs

10.4.2.1. General Rule

For capital gains tax purposes, there is no difference in treatment between an onshore discretionary EBT and any other UK **resident** discretionary trust.

10.4.2.2. Rate of Tax

An EBT Trustee pays capital gains tax on its chargeable gains at the rate applicable to trusts [TCGA 1992, s4(1AA)].

10.4.2.3. Annual Exemption

An EBT Trustee does not have the same annual exemption as an individual. The amount of the exemption depends on the number of other trusts established by the same company [TCGA 1992, Sch1, para 2].

10.4.2.4. Business Asset Taper Relief

Usually, there will not be any beneficiary of the EBT with an interest in possession. Therefore no employee will be an "eligible beneficiary" as defined in TCGA 1992, SchA1, para 7. This in turn means that even if the Trustee holds shares in a listed company that employs the beneficiaries, it will not usually be eligible for business asset taper relief, since that company will not be a "qualifying company" in relation to the Trustee.

10.4.2.5. Transfer of Assets to Beneficiary

The transfer of assets to a beneficiary is a CGT disposal [TCGA 1992, s71]. The Trustee is deemed to have disposed of the shares at their **CGT value** since this is not an arm's length transaction [TCGA 1992, s17]. This can lead to a double charge to tax, unless ESC D35 is available (see section 10.4.2.7).

10.4.2.6. Grant and Exercise of Options

If an EBT Trustee **grant**s an **option** to a beneficiary, there is no **market value** substitution [TCGA 1992, s149A]. If the beneficiary actually has to pay a **grant price** for the **option**, this will be a part disposal by the Trustee.

When the beneficiary **exercise**s the **option** and acquires the asset from the Trustee, then again there is no **market value** substitution [TCGA 1992, s144ZA]. The Trustee will be chargeable to tax on any actual gain it makes.

10.4.2.7. Extra-Statutory Concession D35

There can be a double charge to tax when an EBT Trustee transfers an asset to a beneficiary. This is because the Trustee will be deemed to have disposed of the asset for its **market value**, even though it may not actually receive any consideration. The beneficiary however must treat the money's worth value of the asset as general earnings for income tax purposes.

The purpose of ESC D35 is to remove the double charge. It applies only where the EBT qualifies under IHTA 1984, s86 (see section 10.4.1.1) and the Trustee transfers the asset to the employee for no payment. It does not apply if the Trustee sells the asset to the employee for less than its **market value**.

If the terms of ESC D35 are satisfied, HM Revenue & Customs will not charge the Trustee to capital gains tax on the disposal.

Another potential occasion of double taxation is where a **restricted securities** charge arises for the employee in relation to shares held in an EBT. When the employee becomes fully entitled to the shares, this can be a deemed disposal by the Trustee for CGT purposes [TCGA 1992, s71(1)]. HM Revenue & Customs have confirmed that ESC D35 applies in relation to an income tax charge under the conditional shares legislation on shares acquired before 16 April 2003. It is believed that HM Revenue & Customs take the same view where there is a chargeable event under ITEPA 2003, s427(3)(a).

If ESC D35 is not available, for example where the EBT Trustee sells an asset to a beneficiary for less than its **market value**, then the Trustee should consider structuring the disposal through the **grant** of an **option** that is immediately **exercisable**. This prevents the **market value** substitution (see section 10.4.2.6).

Note also that ESC D35 does not apply where the beneficiary is **resident** outside the UK, and does not apply where the beneficiary would be excluded from benefiting under the EBT under IHTA 1984, s28(4) (see section 10.3.1).

10.4.2.8. Holdover Relief

The Trustee may be able to claim holdover relief if it disposes of shares to a beneficiary [TCGA 1992, s165 (as extended by TCGA 1992, Sch7, para 2(1)].

This only applies if the shares are:

- shares in a **trading company**, or the **holding company** of a **trading group**, and
- the shares are not listed on a **recognised stock exchange**, and
- the trustees hold at least 25% of the voting rights.

If holdover relief is available, the Trustee is are taxed only on any actual gain it makes, and the beneficiary acquires the shares for the actual price he pays, if any.

However, there is a major disadvantage to doing this. The beneficiary will be subject to a general earnings charge to income tax on any **discount** (see section 3.5.3.2). The amount charged to income tax is added to the beneficiary's base cost for CGT purposes (either because there is **market value** substitution under TCGA 1992, s17 if the shares are not restricted or convertible, or because this is required by TCGA 1992, s149AA if the shares are either restricted or convertible). But the same amount, i.e. the held over gain, will be deducted from the base cost under TCGA 1992, s165(4)].

The net effect of this is that the beneficiary is deemed to acquire the shares for the price he actually paid, if any. Therefore the same amount will be taxed both as income on receipt and as a capital gain on disposal.

Holdover relief is in principle also available where the disposal is a chargeable transfer for inheritance tax purposes [TCGA 1992, s260]. Generally, though, a transfer of an asset to an employee beneficiary will not be a chargeable transfer, so this relief is rarely available in practice (see section 10.4.1.3).

10.4.3. Capital Gains Tax: Disposals by Offshore EBTs

If the EBT Trustee is **resident** outside the UK, it will not be subject to UK capital gains tax.

HM Revenue & Customs accept that an EBT that is a genuine commercial arrangement by a company to attract, retain and motivate good quality staff does not have the necessary "element of bounty" to be a settlement [*IR Tax Bulletin 16*[191]].

An offshore EBT is therefore outside the scope of the rules that can attribute gains made by offshore settlements to their settlors or beneficiaries.

10.4.4. Income Tax: Onshore EBTs

If an EBT Trustee is **resident** in the UK, it will be chargeable to income tax on the same basis as other discretionary trusts, subject to some minor differences.

10.4.4.1. UK Dividend Income

Where a Trustee **resident** in the UK receives a distribution from a UK company, it is entitled to an attaching tax credit of one-ninth of the dividend [ITTOIA 2005, s397(1)].

After deducting any allowable expenses, the Trustee then has to pay tax on the grossed-up amount at the dividend trust rate [ICTA 1988, s686(1AA)].

Example:

UK Company pays a dividend of £900.

ITTOIA 2005, s397(1) grants the Trustee a tax credit of £100.

The Trustee pays tax on £1,000 at 32.5%, which is £325. Since it is deemed to have already paid tax of £100, the net tax payable is £225, making an effective tax rate of 25% (22.5/90).

---

[191] http://www.hmrc.gov.uk/bulletins/tb16.htm#capital gains

10.4.4.2. *UK Scrip Dividends with Cash Alternative*

The Trustee may be offered the choice between a cash dividend and a scrip dividend (i.e. a dividend in the form of additional shares). If it chooses the scrip dividend, the position is as follows.

The first step is to determine what the cash equivalent of the share capital is in relation to the dividend. In most circumstances this will be the cash dividend alternative, i.e., the cash that it could otherwise have received; but in some circumstances it may not be [ITTOIA 2005, s412].

The Trustee is deemed to have received the cash equivalent as income, grossed up at the dividend ordinary rate [ITTOIA 2005, s411].

The Trustee has the benefit of a notional tax credit, which it can set off against its actual tax liability, although it cannot claim repayment of it [ITTOIA 2005, s414].

The grossed up cash equivalent is "distribution type income" [ICTA 1988, s686(5A)(c)]. After deducting any allowable expenses, it is charged to tax at the dividend trust rate [ICTA 1988, s686(1AA)(a)].

Example:

UK Company offers the Trustee a choice between a dividend of £900 or additional shares. The Trustee chooses the shares.

ITTOIA 2005, s411 deems the Trustee to receive income of £900.

ITTOIA 2005, s414 deems the Trustee to have paid tax of £100 on the deemed income of £900.

The Trustee pays tax on £1,000 at 32.5%, which is £325. Since it is deemed to have already paid tax of £100, the net tax payable is £225, making an effective tax rate of 25% (22.5/90).

10.4.4.3. *UK Scrip Dividends without Cash Alternative*

If a UK company issues new shares to a trustee shareholder as a scrip dividend , and the shares are treated as capital rather than revenue in the hands of the Trustee, there is no UK income tax liability on the shares [ITTOIA 2005, s410(3)].

10.4.4.4. *Foreign Dividend Income*

Where a UK **resident** EBT Trustee receives dividends from a foreign company, this is taxable as a distribution [ICTA 1988, s686(5A)(b)]. The gross amount, including any foreign tax withheld from the dividend (or imputed to the dividend), but net of expenses, is taxable at the dividend trust rate. The Trustee can set a credit for any foreign tax against its UK tax liability, up to the tax which would have been paid at the dividend trust rate.

Example: An EBT holds stock in a US company, which pays a dividend worth £1,000 after conversion from dollars into sterling. The Trustee has filed the necessary forms to allow the US company to withhold US tax at the reduced rate of 15%. The amount actually received by the Trustee is £850, and the company pays £150 to the US Internal Revenue Service.

The Trustee's UK taxable income is £1,000, on which it is taxed at the dividend trust rate, so its total tax liability is £325. It can deduct the US withholding tax of £150, so the net UK tax liability is £175.

10.4.4.5. Interest Income

If an EBT Trustee receives UK source interest income, it will be taxed on this (after deducting allowable costs) at the rate applicable to trusts [ICTA 1988, s686(1)].

There is an exemption from tax for the Trustee if it borrows money from a company and then lends it on to employees to acquire shares through an **employees' share scheme**. Any interest that the Trustee receives from the participants in the scheme is offset against equivalent interest it has to pay to the lender [ITTOIA 2005, s752].

10.4.4.6. Rental Income

If an EBT Trustee receives UK source rental income, it will be taxed on this (after deducting allowable costs) at the rate applicable to trusts [ICTA 1988, s686(1)].

10.4.4.7. Deductibility of Expenses

ICTA 1988, s686 charges tax on an EBT Trustee at "the rate applicable to trusts" or, in the case of distribution type income, the dividend trust rate. However, this tax is charged only on the amount which is available for distribution to the beneficiaries, so the Trustee is allowed to deduct its expenses in calculating the taxable amount.

Any income that is used to pay expenses remains taxable at whatever rate it would otherwise be taxable at [ICTA 1988, s686(2AA)]. So distribution type income is taxed at the dividend ordinary rate, interest income at the lower rate, and rental income at the basic rate.

Example:
The Trustee's income consists of a UK dividend of £900, with an attaching tax credit of £100. It incurs expenses of £400. The tax calculation is as follows:

Gross income = £1,000 of which

£600 is taxed at the dividend trust rate (32.5%) = £195

£400 is taxed at the dividend ordinary rate (10%) = £40

making a total tax liability of £235, of which £100 is covered by the tax credit, leaving tax of £135 tax due through self-assessment.

ICTA 1988, s689B sets out the order in which expenses are offset against income of more than one type.

10.4.4.8. Extra-Statutory Concession A68

ESC A68 mitigates a double charge to tax that would otherwise arise where an employee receives a distribution from an EBT.

The double tax charge arises because the Trustee is subject to tax under ICTA 1988, s686 at the rate applicable to trusts and/or the dividend trust rate. However, ICTA 1988, s687 does not apply to distributions since they are employment income. This means that the beneficiary has to treat the income as gross, rather than as net of tax paid by the Trustee.

ESC A68 applies only where the Trustee has properly filed UK tax returns for every year in which it has UK source taxable income, and has actually paid the tax due (or has tax credits covering it).

The Trustee must also have a full history of the "tax pool". The tax pool is the total amount of tax it has paid, after deducting any amounts that have been credited against the liability of a beneficiary who is not an employee, or which have already been repaid under ESC A68.

Whenever a distribution is made to an employee and taxed as employment income, the Trustee is allowed to make a repayment claim for the lesser of (a) the amount paid to the employee multiplied by tax at the rate applicable to trusts and (b) whatever is in the tax pool.

Example:

The Trustee received interest income of £1,000. Tax is charged on this at the rate applicable to trusts, so the Trustee pays tax of £400 (40%), leaving £600 available for distribution. The tax pool is £400.

The Trustee makes a payment of £600 to an employee, and withholds PAYE of £240.

The Trustee can then make a claim under ESC A68 to be repaid £240, being 40% of the amount distributed (£600), since this is less than the tax

After HMRC have repaid the £240 to the Trustee, the remaining tax pool is £160.

10.4.5. Income Tax: Offshore EBTs

If an EBT Trustee is not **resident** in the UK, it will be subject to UK income tax only on income which has a UK source. It may in practice be very difficult for HM Revenue & Customs to collect tax from the Trustee; however, if the Trustee does not account for UK tax properly, its beneficiaries will not be able to make use of ESC B18 (see section 10.4.5.7).

10.4.5.1. UK Dividend Income

An offshore EBT will generally waive dividends on any shares it holds in the employing company. This is because it would otherwise pay tax on those dividends, and would have to bear the cost of preparing tax returns.

Although dividend income is normally excluded from taxation in the hands of a non-resident [FA 1995, s128], this exclusion does not apply to an EBT with a UK resident beneficiary [FA 1995, s128(5)].

Where an EBT Trustee **resident** outside the UK receives a distribution from a UK company, it is not entitled to the attaching tax credit. Generally only UK **resident** taxpayers are allowed the tax credit [ITTOIA 2005, s397(1)]. Some non-**resident** individuals are also allowed the tax credit [ITTOIA 2005, s397(4)].

However, the Trustee is deemed to have paid tax on the dividend at the dividend ordinary rate [ITTOIA 2005, s399(2)].

For the purposes of calculating liability to tax, the Trustee is then deemed to have received a distribution of the grossed up amount of the actual dividend [ITTOIA 2005, s399(4)].

After deducting any allowable expenses, the Trustee then has to pay tax on that grossed-up amount at the dividend trust rate [ICTA 1988, s686(1AA)].

Example:

UK Company pays a dividend of £900.

ITTOIA 2005, s399(4) deems the Trustee to receive a dividend of £1,000.

ITTOIA 2005, s399(2) deems the Trustee to have paid tax of £100 on the deemed dividend of £1,000.

The Trustee pays tax on £1,000 at 32.5%, which is £325. Since it is deemed to have already paid tax of £100, the net tax payable is £225, making an effective tax rate of 25% (22.5/90).

10.4.5.2. *UK Scrip Dividends with Cash Alternative*

See section 10.4.4.2.

10.4.5.3. *UK Scrip Dividends without Cash Alternative*

See section 10.4.4.3.

10.4.5.4. *Interest Income*

See section 10.4.4.5, but note that the borrower must usually withhold tax from the interest at source [ICTA 1988, s349(2)] unless the borrower is, for example, a bank.

10.4.5.5. *Rental Income*

See section 10.4.4.6, but note that the borrower must usually withhold tax from the rent at source [ICTA 1988, s42A].

10.4.5.6. *Deductibility of Expenses*

See section 10.4.4.7.

10.4.5.7. *Extra-Statutory Concession B18*

ESC B18 mitigates a double charge to tax that would otherwise arise where a UK **resident** beneficiary receives a distribution from an overseas EBT.

The double tax charge arises because the overseas EBT is subject to tax under ICTA 1988, s686 at the rate applicable to trusts and/or the dividend trust rate. However, ICTA 1988, s687 does not apply to distributions since they are foreign source income. This means that the beneficiary has to treat the income as gross, rather than as net of tax paid by the Trustee.

ESC B18 applies only where the EBT Trustee has properly filed UK tax returns for every year in which it has UK source taxable income, and has actually paid the tax due.

If this has happened, the employee can make a claim to HM Revenue & Customs to reclaim the UK tax paid by the Trustee on the amount distributed to him. He cannot, however, recover tax which the Trustee is treated as having paid, such as the tax credit attaching to UK dividends.

11. Employment-related Securities: Tax Charges on Acquisition

11.1. Award of Securities

If an employee is **award**ed free shares, or given the opportunity to acquire shares for less than their **market value**, the benefit of this may be taxable as employment income. The calculation and timing of any tax charge depend on the exact circumstances, as follows:

- If the shares have been released from a **SIP**, go to section 11.1.1
- If the employee is **resident**, but not **ordinarily resident**, in the UK on the **acquisition date**, go to section 11.1.2.
- If the employee is **resident** and **ordinarily resident** in the UK on the **acquisition date**, and the securities are not restricted, go to section 11.1.2.
- If the employee is **resident** and **ordinarily resident** in the UK on the **acquisition date**, and the securities are restricted, but not forfeitable, go to section 11.1.3.
- If the employee is **resident** and **ordinarily resident** in the UK on the **acquisition date**, and the securities are forfeitable for a period which is capable of exceeding five years, go to section 11.1.3.
- If the employee is **resident** and **ordinarily resident** in the UK on the **acquisition date**, and the securities are forfeitable for a period which cannot exceed five years, go to section 11.1.4.
- If the employee acquires securities that have been artificially reduced in value, go to section 11.1.5.
- If the employee acquires securities for less than **market value** through arrangements for the avoidance of tax or NIC, go to section 11.1.6.

11.1.1. Release of Shares from SIP

There is no tax charge when shares are released to an employee from a **SIP**, unless they are released to him before the end of the **blocking period**s specified in the legislation [ITEPA 2003, s490] (see sections 4.2.4.2.5.3and 4.2.4.3.8.5).

11.1.2. Employee Resident but Not Ordinarily resident; Employee Resident and Ordinarily resident – Securities Not Restricted

There is a potential general earnings charge if an employee who is **resident**, but not **ordinarily resident**, in the UK, acquires securities **by reason of employment**. This applies whether or not the securities are restricted.

Similarly, there is a potential general earnings charge if an employee who is **resident** and **ordinarily resident** in the UK acquires unrestricted securities **by reason of employment** [*McLoughlin v HMRC* SPC 542].

The taxable amount is the amount by which the money's worth value of the securities exceeds the **acquisition price** (if any). The money's worth value allows for any restrictions. In either case, the value of any conversion entitlement should be ignored, unless the securities are acquired as part of an arrangement to avoid tax or NIC [ITEPA 2003, s437].

PAYE is due if the shares are **readily convertible assets** on the **acquisition date** [ITEPA 2003, s696(1)]. NIC is also due [SSCR 2001, Sch3, Part III, para 1].

The employee must "make good" the PAYE within 90 days to avoid a further tax charge under ITEPA 2003, s222 (see section 3.7.3.14).

The acquisition of the shares is a reportable event [ITEPA 2003, s421K] (see section 23 for reporting obligations).

If the shares are issued to the employee partly-paid, then the rules on acquisitions at an undervalue in ITEPA 2003, Part 7, Chapter 3C may apply. Ordinarily, this will result in a notional loan tax charge during the period the employee holds the shares, and on disposal (see section 12.8); however if the arrangements were structured to avoid tax or NIC, a tax charge may arise on acquisition (see section 11.1.6).

11.1.3. Restricted securities (forfeitable for five years or more or non-forfeitable)

If an employee acquires **restricted securities** that are either:

- not forfeitable or
- subject to **forfeiture** restrictions which are capable of lasting for five years or more,

then the default position is that there will be a general earnings charge calculated in the same way as set out in section 11.1.2.

If the employee is **ordinarily resident** in the UK, he and the employer may make a **Section 431** election, and choose either:

- that FMV (see section 11.1.5) should be determined as if there were no restrictions on the securities [ITEPA 2003, s431(1)] or
- that FMV should be determined as if any specified restriction did not apply [ITEPA 2003, s431(2)].

See section 22.2 for guidance on when it is appropriate to make an election.

If the employee acquired the securities on or after 2 December 2004, and one of the main purposes of the arrangements under which the right or opportunity to acquire the securities was made available is the avoidance of tax or NIC, then the employer and employee are deemed to have made a **Section 431(1) election** [ITEPA 2003, s431B].

PAYE is due if the shares are **readily convertible assets** on the **acquisition date** [ITEPA 2003, s696(1)]. NIC is also due [SSCR 2001, Sch2, para 7].

The employee must "make good" the PAYE within 90 days to avoid a further tax charge under ITEPA 2003, s222 (see section 3.7.3.14).

The acquisition of the securities is a reportable event (see section 23).

If no election is made, or a **Section 431(2) election** is made so that certain restrictions continue to be taken into account in determining the initial tax charge, then there may be a further chargeable event when the securities cease to be restricted (see section 12.3.2).

It is also possible that a further income tax charge can arise under the rules on acquisitions of securities at an undervalue in ITEPA 2003, Part 7, Chapter 3C. This would be the case if, for example, the holder has to pay a further amount in order for the securities to be fully paid. Ordinarily, this will result in a notional loan tax charge on disposal (see section 12.8); however if the arrangements were structured to avoid tax or NIC, a tax charge may arise on acquisition (see section 11.1.6).

11.1.4. Restricted securities (forfeitable for less than five years)

Generally, there is no income tax charge when a **resident** and **ordinarily resident** employee acquires **restricted securities**, which are subject to forfeiture restrictions which must lapse within five years [ITEPA 2003, s425(2)]. There are five exceptions to this, which are:

- where the securities are acquired on conversion [ITEPA 2003, s425(2)(a)];
- where there is a notional loan charge under ITEPA 2003, s446U [ITEPA 2003, s425(2)(b)];
- where the securities are acquired pursuant to a **securities option** [ITEPA 2003, s425(2)(c)]; or
- where the employer and employee make an election for immediate taxation, either a **Section 425 election** under ITEPA 2003, s425(3), or a **Section 431 election** under ITEPA 2003, s431;
- where the securities are acquired on or after 2 December 2004, and one of the main purposes of the arrangements under which the securities are issued is the avoidance of tax or NIC either on the acquisition date or subsequently – because in these circumstances the employer and employee will be deemed to have made a **Section 431(1) election** [ITEPA 2003, s431B].

Where the employer and employee make a **Section 425 election**, there will be a general earnings charge calculated in the same way as in section 11.1.2.

Where the employer and employee make a **Section 431 election**, then they can choose either:

- that FMV should be determined as if there were no restrictions on the securities [ITEPA 2003, s431(1)] or

- that FMV should be determined as if any specified restriction did not apply [ITEPA 2003, s431(2)].

PAYE is due if the shares are **readily convertible assets** on the **acquisition date** [ITEPA 2003, s696(1)]. NIC is also due [SSCR 2001, Sch2, para 7].

The employee must "make good" the PAYE within 90 days to avoid a further tax charge under ITEPA 2003, s222 (see section 3.7.3.14).

The acquisition of the securities is a reportable event (see section 23).

If:

- no election is made; or
- a **Section 425 election** is made; or
- a **Section 431(2) election** is made so that certain restrictions continue to be taken into account in determining the initial tax charge,

then there may be a further chargeable event when the securities cease to be subject to one or more of the restrictions (see section 12.3.2).

It is also possible that a further income tax charge can arise under the rules on acquisitions of securities at less than their **CGT value**. This would be the case if, for example, the holder has to pay a further amount in order for the securities to be fully paid. Ordinarily, this will result in a notional loan tax charge on disposal (see section 12.8); however if the arrangements were structured to avoid tax or NIC, a tax charge may arise on acquisition (see section 11.1.6).

11.1.5. Shares that have been Artificially Depressed in Value

If the **CGT value** of the securities has been artificially depressed by at least 10% as a result of things done otherwise than for genuine commercial purposes in the period of seven years ending with the acquisition, then the employee is subject to an employment income tax charge [ITEPA 2003, s446B].

The taxable amount is

FMV - MV

FMV = what the **CGT value** of the securities would have been if the artificial depression had not taken place, disregarding any restrictions on the securities [ITEPA 2003, s446D(1)], and disregarding any conversion entitlement attached to the securities [ITEPA 2003, s446D(2)].

MV = the higher of:

(a) the consideration given for the securities

(b) the **CGT value** of the securities allowing for the depression in value but taking account of any restrictions on the securities and disregarding any conversion entitlement attached to the securities [ITEPA 2003, s446D].

PAYE is due if the shares are **readily convertible assets** on the **acquisition date** [ITEPA 2003, s696(1)]. NIC is also due [SSCR 2001, Sch2, para 7].

The employee must "make good" the PAYE within 90 days to avoid a further tax charge under ITEPA 2003, s222 (see section 3.7.3.14).

The acquisition of the securities is a reportable event (see section 23).

In addition, there may be a general earnings charge if the **money's worth value** of the securities, calculated as above, is higher than the consideration given for them by the employee and there may be further tax charges in relation to the securities under ITEPA 2003, s446E (see section 12.5).

11.1.6. Pre-acquisition Avoidance Cases

There is usually a general earnings charge when an employee acquires securities for less than their **money's worth value** (see section 11.1).

However, there can be circumstances where there is nothing that can be taxed as general earnings. For examples, see section 12.8.

Ordinarily, this will result in a notional loan tax charge, as explained in section 12.8. However, if the arrangements under which the securities were offered were entered into to avoid tax or NIC, then the amount of the notional loan counts as income for the tax year in which the acquisition takes place [ITEPA 2003, s446UA].

The tax should be withheld through the PAYE system [ITEPA 2003, s698(1)(ea)]. The PAYE charge arises on the acquisition date of the securities [ITEPA 2003, s698(6)(da)].

For details of the calculation of the notional loan see section 12.8.4.3.

11.2. Exercise of Securities option

See section 8.1.

11.3. Acquisition through Conversion

There can be an employment income tax liability where securities are acquired on conversion. See section 12.4.2.

11.4. Acquisition through Public Offer

There is no income tax charge when an employee acquires securities through a public offer [ITEPA 2003, s544].

11.5. Corporation Tax Relief

See section 17.

12. Employment-related Securities: Post-Acquisition Tax Charges

12.1. Forfeitable Shares Acquired before 17 March 1998

If an employee acquired forfeitable shares before 17 March 1998, he should have paid tax on the **acquisition date** on the **market value** of the shares at that time, discounted to reflect the risk of **forfeiture**. There should be no further tax charge when the risk of **forfeiture** is lifted.

However, the Inland Revenue did not interpret the law in that way at that time. The Inland Revenue received legal advice that their interpretation of the law was incorrect, and legislation was introduced in FA 1998 to align the law to the Inland Revenue's previous interpretation.

A concessionary treatment was given to employees who should have been taxed on the **acquisition date** but were not. This is set out in *IR Tax Bulletin 35*[192]. In effect, the employee will be taxed on the value of the shares on the **acquisition date**, but the tax will not be payable until the restrictions on the shares are lifted.

12.2. Conditional Securities Acquired before 16 April 2003

12.2.1. When the tax charge applies

This section only applies to securities acquired on or after 17 March 1998 and before 16 April 2003 where the employee was **resident** and **ordinarily resident** in the UK on the **acquisition date**.

The old "conditional share" rules can only apply where someone acquired securities **by reason of employment** on or after 17 March 1998 and before 16 April 2003, and the employee in question was **resident** and **ordinarily resident** in the UK on the **acquisition date**.

They will apply if the holder can be compelled to forfeit the securities or to offer them for sale at less than their **CGT value**, unless the only circumstances in which this can happen are those set out below:

- where the securities were issued partly paid, or nil paid, and the employee will forfeit them if he fails to pay for them in full;
- where an employee who terminates employment with the group is compelled by the Articles of Association of the company to offer the securities for sale or transfer them;
- where an employee whose employment with the group is terminated because of misconduct is forced to offer the securities for sale or forfeit them

---

192 http://www.hmrc.gov.uk/bulletins/tb35.htm#anchor515295

- where the securities are **redeemable**.

If there are any other circumstances in which the holder can be forced to offer the securities for sale at less than **CGT value**, or forfeit them, then they are "only conditional" [ITEPA 2003, old s424].

12.2.2. The effect of the conditional share rules

This means that the employee will be chargeable to income tax on the whole of any growth in value of the securities during his period of ownership. Unlike the **restricted securities** rules that apply to securities acquired on or after 16 April 2003, there is no apportionment of the chargeable gain between capital gains tax and income tax.

12.2.3. The Chargeable Event

The chargeable event is the earliest of the following three events [ITEPA 2003, s427]:

- when the securities cease to be "only conditional" – in other words when the employee can no longer be forced to forfeit them or sell them for less than **CGT value**;
- when the employee can be no longer be forced to forfeit the securities or sell them for less than **CGT value** except for the exempt circumstances listed in section 12.2.1 above;
- when the employee disposes of the securities (including exchanging them for other **securities** (see section 13.1.6)).

12.2.4. The taxable amount

The taxable amount is:

- the **CGT value** of the holder's interest in the securities immediately after they cease to be conditional less
- the deductible amounts (see below) [ITEPA 2003, old s428(1)]

This means that if the securities are forfeited for no payment, then there is no tax charge, because the value of the holder's interest in the securities immediately after the event is zero.

12.2.5. Deductible Amounts

The following are the deductible amounts:

- the consideration the holder originally gave for his interest in the securities [ITEPA 2003, old s428(2)(a)];
- if the holder acquired the securities by exercising an **option**, the **grant price** (if any) [ITEPA 2003, old s429(3)(a)];
- if the employee has already been subject to employment income tax in respect of his acquisition of his interest in the securities, the taxable amount [ITEPA 2003, old s428(2)(b)];

- if the securities are shares, and the employee has already been subject to employment income tax due to a variation in their rights, or due to the shares being in a subsidiary company, the taxable amount [ITEPA 2003, old s428(3)].

12.2.6. PAYE and NIC

PAYE applies if the securities are **readily convertible assets** when the chargeable event occurs [ITEPA 2003, old s698].

The employee must "make good" the PAYE within 90 days to avoid a further tax charge under ITEPA 2003, s222 (see section 3.7.3.14).

NIC also applies [SSCR 2001, reg 22(5)].

12.2.7. Reporting

The employing company (and the company that issued the shares, if this is different) must notify HM Revenue & Customs when a taxable event occurs [ITEPA 2003, old s432 and old s433]. The report must be filed before 7 July of the following tax year. See section 23.

12.2.8. Corporation Tax Relief

Corporation tax relief may be available under FA 2003, Sch23 (see section 17.4.4.1).

12.3. Restricted Securities

12.3.1. Application of the Restricted Securities Rules

The **restricted securities** rules are contained in ITEPA 2003, Part 7, Chapter 2. This chapter only applies to securities acquired on or after 16 April 2003 where the employee was **resident** and **ordinarily resident** in the UK on the **acquisition date** [ITEPA 2003, s421E(1)].

12.3.2. The Chargeable Event

The chargeable event is the earliest of the following events:

- the securities cease to be restricted in circumstances where an **associated person** is beneficially entitled to them both before and after the event [ITEPA 2003, s427(3)(a)];
- there is a removal or variation of any restriction relating to the securities, without their ceasing to be **restricted securities** [ITEPA 2003, s427(3)(b)];
- the securities are disposed of for consideration to someone who is not an **associated person** [ITEPA 2003, s427(3)(c)].

12.3.3. Exclusions from Chapter 2

12.3.3.1. Section 431 Election

If the employer and employee made a **Section 431(1) election** to disapply the **restricted securities** rules in full within 14 days after the acquisition, no tax charge arises under the **restricted securities** rules.

If a **Section 431(2) election** was made in relation to a specified restriction, and the chargeable event relates to that restriction, no tax charge arises under the **restricted securities** rules.

12.3.3.2. Acquisition through SIP, CSOP, SAYE or EMI

If the employee acquires the shares through a **SIP**, or through the tax-exempt **exercise** of a **CSOP**, **SAYE** or **EMI option**, there is a deemed **Section 431(1) election** so that no subsequent tax liability can arise under Chapter 2 [ITEPA 2003, s431A].

12.3.3.3. Artificial Depression Rules

If a tax charge arose on the acquisition of the securities under the "artificial depression" rules (see section 11.1.5) then no further charge can arise under Chapter 2 [ITEPA 2003, s446B].

12.3.3.4. Employee-controlled company

If

- the company whose shares are used is employee-controlled by virtue of shares of the same class as the **restricted securities** and
- all the other shares of the same class are affected by an event similar to the chargeable event

then there is no charge to income tax in relation to this chargeable event [ITEPA 2003, s429(1)].

However, this exclusion does not apply in three circumstances:

- if the **CGT value** of the shares was artificially increased by at least 10% during the period of seven years ending with the **acquisition date** [ITEPA 2003, s446NA(1)]; or
- if a charge has ever arisen in relation to those securities under Chapter 3B [ITEPA 2003, s446NA(3)] (see section 12.6.1); or
- if something has been done which affects the securities (at or before the date when there would have been a chargeable event) as part of a scheme or arrangement of which one of the main purposes is the avoidance of tax or NIC [ITEPA 2003, s429(1A)].

12.3.3.5. Open market shares

If

- the majority of shares of the same class as the **restricted securities** are "**open market shares**" and
- all the other shares of the same class are affected by an event similar to the chargeable event

then there is no charge to income tax in relation to this chargeable event [ITEPA 2003, s429(1)].

However, this exclusion does not apply in three circumstances:

- if the **CGT value** of the shares was artificially increased by at least 10% during the period of seven years ending with the **acquisition date** [ITEPA 2003, s446NA(1)]; or
- if a charge has ever arisen in relation to those securities under Chapter 3B [ITEPA 2003, s446NA(3)] (see section 12.6.1); or
- if something has been done which affects the securities (at or before the date when there would have been a chargeable event) as part of a scheme or arrangement of which one of the main purposes is the avoidance of tax or NIC [ITEPA 2003, s429(1A)].

12.3.4. Calculation of the Taxable Amount

The taxable amount is a proportion of the **market value** of the securities at the time of the chargeable event. It is that proportion of the increase in value that relates to the release of restrictions.

HM Revenue & Customs can provide a Restricted Securities Calculator (based on an Excel 97 spreadsheet) to help compute the taxable gain. All the user needs to do is insert the basic information and the spreadsheet will apply the formulae automatically. For further information see HMRC FAQ 2(c)[193].

In order to calculate the taxable amount, it is necessary to understand various terms:

12.3.4.1. UMV – the Unrestricted Market Value

UMV is the **unrestricted market value** of the securities. In other words, it is the value of the securities at the time of the chargeable event ignoring any restrictions [ITEPA 2003, s428(2)]. However, it is also necessary to ignore any conversion rights attached to the securities [ITEPA 2003, s428(8)].

12.3.4.2. IUMV – the Initial Unrestricted Market Value

IUMV is the initial **unrestricted market value** of the securities. In other words, it is the value of the securities on the **acquisition date** ignoring any restrictions [ITEPA 2003, s428(3)]. It is also necessary to ignore any conversion rights attached to the securities [ITEPA 2003, s428(8)].

12.3.4.3. AMV – the Actual Market Value

AMV is the actual **CGT value** of the securities immediately after the chargeable event, including any restrictions that still apply to which the securities [ITEPA 2003, s428(5)] but ignoring any conversion rights [ITEPA 2003, s428(8)].

12.3.4.4. DA – the Deductible Amounts

DA is the total of the deductible amounts. These are:

- the **acquisition price** (if any) of the securities,

---

[193] http://www.hmrc.gov.uk/shareschemes/faq_emprelatedsecurity-ch2.htm#c

- any amount that was taxed as general earnings in respect of the acquisition of the securities,
- any amount that counted as employment income in relation to the securities under the old conditional share rules (see section 12.2) or the old post-acquisition benefits rules,
- if the securities were acquired on a conversion of other **employment-related** securities, any taxable amount under the **convertible securities** rules (see section 12.4) (including the original version of those rules) arising from the conversion,
- if the acquisition of the **employment-related** securities was pursuant to a **securities option**, any taxable amount under the **securities option**s rules (see section 8) (including the original version of those rules) arising from the acquisition [ITEPA 2003, s428(7)].

In addition, it is possible to deduct any secondary NIC paid by or recovered from the employee under SSCBA 1992, Sch1, para 3A or 3B [ITEPA 2003, s428A] (see section 9.2).

12.3.4.5. *IUP – the Initial Untaxed Proportion*

IUP is the initially untaxed proportion, i.e. the proportion of the initial **unrestricted market value** (IUMV) that is not either paid for by the employee, or taxed in the employee's hands. It is measured only once, on the **acquisition date** of the securities.

It is calculated as (IUMV–DA)/IUMV [ITEPA 2003, s428(3)].

Example:
*The securities have an initial **unrestricted market value** (IUMV) of £500*
*The actual **CGT value** (AMV) on the **acquisition date** is £300*
*The employee paid £200 for the shares and made a **Section 425 election** to be taxed on a further £100*

IUP is 0.4 [(£500-£300)/£500]

12.3.4.6. *OP – the Outstanding Proportion*

OP is the outstanding proportion, i.e. the proportion of the UMV of the securities that is represented by the restrictions immediately after the chargeable event. It is only measured when a chargeable event occurs, but the securities remain restricted after the chargeable event.

It is calculated as (UMV-AMV)/UMV [ITEPA 2003, s428(5)].

Example
*The securities have an **unrestricted market value** (UMV) of £1,000 immediately following the chargeable event*
*The actual **CGT value** (AMV) immediately following the chargeable event is only £900 because of the remaining restrictions*

OP is 0.1 [(£1,000-£900)/£1,000].

12.3.4.7. PCP – the Previously Charged Proportion

PCP is the previously charged proportion, i.e. the proportion of the UMV of the securities that has already been charged in relation to a previous chargeable event. Therefore, in relation to the first (or only) chargeable event, PCP is zero [ITEPA 2003, s428(4)].

It is calculated by taking the aggregate of IUP-PCP-OP in relation to each previous chargeable event.

12.3.4.8. CE – the Consideration and Expenses

CE is the consideration and expenses, in other words any amount that has to be paid, or expenses that must be incurred, in relation to the chargeable event. So for example, if the chargeable event is the disposal of the securities, CE will be the costs of sale.

12.3.4.9. CD – the Consideration for Disposal

CD is only relevant if the chargeable event is the disposal of the securities, and the consideration received by the holder is less than the AMV of the securities. This could happen, for example, if the holder is a "bad leaver" who is forced to sell the securities for their nominal value although AMV is higher.

CD is the actual consideration received by the holder of the shares [ITEPA 2003, s428(9)].

However, it is not possible to make the adjustment contemplated in ITEPA 2003, s428(9) if something has been done on or after 2 December 2004, and at or before the disposal, as part of a scheme or arrangement to avoid tax or NIC [ITEPA 2003, s428(10)], or if the value of the securities has been artificially depressed [ITEPA 2003, s446E(10)].

12.3.4.10. Example Calculation 1: One Single Chargeable Event

Here is an example of a calculation where there is one single chargeable event:

Shares are offered to an employee at a **discount**, but the shares are forfeitable if the employee leaves within five years.

IUMV is £100, the **unrestricted market value** of the shares on the **acquisition date.**

DA is £30, the amount the employee actually pays for the shares.

Therefore IUP is 0.7 [(£100-£30)/£100]

Five years later the restrictions fall away, causing a chargeable event.

UMV is £500 – the **CGT value** of the shares on the chargeable event.

PCP is zero because there has been no previous chargeable event.

OP is also zero because there are no further restrictions on the shares.

CE is also zero because, in this example, the holder does not have any expenses to pay in relation to the falling away of the restrictions.

The taxable amount is UMV × (IUP – PCP – OP) – CE [ITEPA 2003, s428(1)].

This resolves to: £500 x 0.7 = £350.

12.3.4.11. Example Calculation 2: Shares awarded free to employee

This is the same example as above, except that the shares are **award**ed to the employee for no payment.

Unless the employee makes a **Section 425 election**, DA will be zero. This means that IUP will be 1, which in turn means that the whole of UMV will be the taxable amount.

12.3.4.12. Example Calculation 3: Shares Forfeited by Employee

This is the same example as in section 12.3.4.10, except that the employee leaves within the five-year period and is forced to sell the shares for £30. Following the sale, the shares are no longer restricted in the hands of the purchaser, so AMV and UMV are the same, say £300. Therefore OP is 0.

CD is less than AMV, so ITEPA 2003, s428(9) becomes relevant, as long as nothing which affects the securities has been done on or after 2 December 2004 for tax or NIC avoidance reasons [ITEPA 2003, s428(10)], and the value of the shares has not been artificially depressed [ITEPA 2003, s446E(10)].

The taxable amount is UMV x IUP x (CD/AMV).

Therefore the chargeable amount is: £300 x 0.7 x (£30/£300) = £21.

12.3.4.13. Example Calculation 4: Multiple Chargeable Events

Here is an example of a calculation where there are three chargeable events:

Shares are offered to an employee at a **discount** and on the following terms:

- the shares are forfeitable if the employee leaves within three years;
- the shares have no dividend or voting rights for the first four years;
- the employee is unable to sell the shares for five years.

12.3.4.13.1. Acquisition date

IUMV is £100, the **unrestricted market value** of the shares on the **acquisition date**.

DA is £30, the amount the employee actually pays for the shares.

Therefore IUP is 0.7 [(£100-£30)/£100].

No election is made at the **acquisition date**, so no tax charge arises at that time.

12.3.4.13.2. First Chargeable Event

The first chargeable event is the third anniversary, when the shares cease to be forfeitable.

UMV on the third anniversary is £300

AMV on the third anniversary is £240

Therefore OP is 0.2 [(£300-£240)/£300]

The taxable amount is £300 x (0.7 – 0.2) = £150.

However, the employer and employee can at this time make a **Section 430 election** to ignore all the remaining restrictions.

If they do so, OP will be ignored, and the taxable amount will be £300 x 0.7 = £210.

12.3.4.13.3. Second Chargeable Event

The second chargeable event is the fourth anniversary, when the restrictions on dividend and voting rights fall away. Assume that no **Section 430 election** was made in relation to the first chargeable event.

UMV on the fourth anniversary is £400

AMV on the fourth anniversary is £360

Therefore OP is 0.1 [(£400-£360)/£400]

PCP is 0.5 [0.7-0.2].

The taxable amount is £400 x (0.7 – 0.5 – 0.1) = £40.

Again, the employer and employee could make a **Section 430 election** at this time.

12.3.4.13.4. Final Chargeable Event

The final chargeable event is the fifth anniversary, when the restrictions on sale fall away. Again, assume no **Section 430 election** was made on a previous chargeable event.

UMV on the fifth anniversary is £500

AMV is also £500, because there are no restrictions remaining.

Therefore OP is 0.

PCP is 0.6 [0.5 + 0.1]

The taxable amount is £500 x (0.7 – 0.6) = £50.

12.3.5. PAYE and NIC

PAYE applies if the securities are **readily convertible asset**s when the chargeable event occurs [ITEPA 2003, s698(1)(a)]. If the securities are not **readily convertible assets**, but the chargeable event is the disposal of the securities in return for a payment or an asset, then the amount of the payment, or value of the asset, is PAYE income [ITEPA 2003, s698(3) and (4)].

The employee must "make good" the PAYE within 90 days to avoid a further tax charge under ITEPA 2003, s222 (see section 3.7.3.14).

NIC also applies if PAYE applies [SSCR 2001, reg 22(7)]. Note however that, if the NIC liability has been passed to the employee, NIC is calculated on the amount before deducting the NIC liability, otherwise the calculation would be circular [ITEPA 2003, s428A(5)(a)].

Primary NIC can be recovered from the employee's salary or, by agreement, from a sale of the securities (see section 9.1).

The liability to pay secondary NIC can be passed to the employee either by agreement or transfer (see section 9.2).

12.3.6. Reporting

The employing company (and the company that issued the shares, if this is different) must notify HM Revenue & Customs when a reportable event occurs. The report must be filed before 7 July of the following tax year [ITEPA 2003, s421J(3)]. Any chargeable event under ITEPA 2003, s426 is a reportable event [ITEPA 2003, s421K(3)(b)]. See section 23.

12.3.7. Corporation Tax Relief

Corporation tax relief may be available under FA 2003, Sch23 (see section 17.4.4.1).

12.4. Convertible securities

12.4.1. Application of the Convertible Securities Rules

The **convertible securities** rules are contained in ITEPA 2003, Part 7, Chapter 3. This chapter applies to securities whenever acquired but only where the employee was **resident** and **ordinarily resident** in the UK on the **acquisition date** [ITEPA 2003, s421E(1)].

12.4.2. The Chargeable Event

The chargeable event is the earliest of the following events:

- the securities are converted, and an **associated person** is entitled to a beneficial interest in the securities both before the conversion and also in the securities into which they are converted [ITEPA 2003, s439(3)(a)];
- the securities are disposed of for consideration to someone who is not an **associated person** [ITEPA 2003, s439(3)(b)];
- the conversion right is released for consideration [ITEPA 2003, s439(3)(c)];
- an **associated person** receives some benefit in connection with the conversion right [ITEPA 2003, s439(3)(d)].

12.4.3. Exclusions from the Convertible Securities Rules

12.4.3.1. Employee-controlled company

If

- the company whose shares are used is employee-controlled by virtue of shares of the same class as the **convertible securities** and
- all the other shares of the same class are affected by an event similar to the chargeable event

then there is no charge to income tax in relation to this chargeable event [ITEPA 2003, s443(1)].

However, this exclusion does not apply if

- the **market value** of the **securities** was artificially increased by at least 10% during the period of seven years ending with the **acquisition date** [ITEPA 2003, s446NA(1)]; or
- something which affects the securities was done (at or before the time when the chargeable event would otherwise arise) as part of an arrangement of which one of the main purposes was the avoidance of tax or NIC [ITEPA 2003, s443(1A)].

12.4.3.2. *Open market shares*

If

- the majority of shares of the same class as the **convertible securities** are "**open market shares**" and
- all the other shares of the same class are affected by an event similar to the chargeable event

then there is no charge to income tax in relation to this chargeable event [ITEPA 2003, s443(1)].

However, this exclusion does not apply if the **CGT value** of the shares was artificially increased by at least 10% during the period of seven years ending with the **acquisition date** [ITEPA 2003, s446NA(1)].

12.4.4. Calculation of the Taxable Amount

The starting point is to calculate AG – CE, where

AG is the amount of the gain, which is calculated differently depending on the nature of the chargeable event, and

CE is the consideration given for the entitlement to convert the securities [ITEPA 2003, s440] (see section 12.4.4.5).

However, there is an adjustment if the arrangements were entered into to avoid tax or NIC, so that the value of the conversion entitlement was not ignored in determining any tax arising on the **acquisition date** (see sections 8.1.2.3, 8.4.6.4, and 11.1.2). In these circumstances, the taxable amount is reduced by the value that was brought into the earlier calculation to represent the conversion entitlement [ITEPA 2003, s440(3A)].

It is necessary to deduct from this any secondary NIC passed to the employee [ITEPA 2003, s442A].

12.4.4.1. *Amount of Gain on Conversion of Securities*

If the securities are converted, then AG is CMVCS – (CMVERS + CC) [ITEPA 2003, s441(2)].

CMVCS is the current **CGT value** of the converted securities, in other words the **CGT value** of the securities immediately after the conversion [ITEPA 2003, s441(6)].

CMVERS is the **CGT value** of the **employment-related** securities, in other words what the hypothetical value of the securities would have been immediately prior to conversion, if there were no conversion right [ITEPA 2003, s441(7)].

CC is the amount of any consideration given for the conversion (as opposed to CE, which is the consideration given for the right to convert) [ITEPA 2003, s441(8)].

12.4.4.2. Amount of Gain on Disposal of Securities

If the securities are disposed of, then AG is DC – CMVERS [ITEPA 2003, s441(3)].

DC is the sale proceeds for the securities [ITEPA 2003, s441(9)].

CMVERS is the **CGT value** of the **employment-related** securities, in other words what the hypothetical value of the securities would have been immediately prior to conversion, if there were no conversion right [ITEPA 2003, s441(7)].

12.4.4.3. Amount of Gain on Release of Conversion Right

If the conversion right is released, then AG is the consideration received for the release [ITEPA 2003, s441(4)].

12.4.4.4. Amount of Gain on Receipt of Benefit

If an **associated person** receives a benefit, then AG is the value of the benefit [ITEPA 2003, s441(5)].

12.4.4.5. Consideration Given for the Entitlement

CE is the amount, if any, given for the conversion right.

CE is ACS – NCMV, if that is a positive number; otherwise CE is zero [ITEPA 2003, s442(3)].

ACS is the acquisition consideration for the securities, i.e. the amount which was originally paid for the securities [ITEPA 2003, s442(4)].

NCMV is the non-convertible **CGT value**, i.e. what the hypothetical value of the securities would have been on the **acquisition date**, if there were no conversion right [ITEPA 2003, s442(5)].

12.4.5. PAYE and NIC

PAYE applies if the shares are **readily convertible assets** when the chargeable event occurs [ITEPA 2003, s698(1)(b)].

The employee must "make good" the PAYE within 90 days to avoid a further tax charge under ITEPA 2003, s222 (see section 3.7.3.14).

NIC also applies if PAYE applies [SSCR 2001, reg 22(7)]. Note however that, if the NIC liability has been passed to the employee, NIC is calculated on the amount before deducting the NIC liability, otherwise the calculation would be circular [ITEPA 2003, s442A(5)(a)].

Primary NIC can be recovered from the employee's salary or, by agreement, from a sale of the securities (see section 9.1).

The liability to pay secondary NIC can be passed to the employee either by agreement or transfer (see section 9.2).

12.4.6. Reporting

The employing company (and the company that issued the shares, if this is different) must notify HM Revenue & Customs when a reportable event occurs. The report must be filed before 7 July of the following tax year [ITEPA 2003, s421J(3)]. Any chargeable event under ITEPA 2003, s438 is a reportable event [ITEPA 2003, s421K(3)(c)]. See section 23.

12.4.7. Corporation Tax Relief

Corporation tax relief may be available under FA 2003, Sch23 (see section 17.4.3.2).

12.5. Artificially Depressed Securities

12.5.1. Application of the Artificially Depressed Securities Rules

The artificially depressed securities rules are contained in ITEPA 2003, Part 7, Chapter 3A. This chapter only applies to securities acquired on or after 1 September 2003 where the employee was **resident** (whether or not **ordinarily resident**) in the UK on the **acquisition date**[ITEPA 2003, s421E(2)]. No tax charge can arise under these rules in relation to securities acquired before 1 September 2003 [FA 2003, Sch22, para 5(3)].

12.5.2. Tax Charge on Acquisition

As mentioned in section 11.1.5, there can be a tax charge on the acquisition of artificially depressed securities.

12.5.3. Determining whether Securities are Artificially Depressed

12.5.3.1. Restricted securities forfeitable for a period of five years or less

If the exemption under ITEPA 2003, s425(2) applied when the securities in question were acquired (i.e. they were forfeitable for a period that could not exceed five years), then it is necessary to look at anything done otherwise than for genuine commercial purposes during the period of seven years ending with the acquisition [ITEPA 2003, s446E(3)(a)].

The tax charge will apply if the **CGT value** of the securities was reduced by at least 10% as a result of things done during this period [ITEPA 2003, s446E(2)].

12.5.3.2. Other Securities

If the exemption under ITEPA 2003, s425(2) did not apply when the securities in question were acquired, then it is necessary to look at anything done otherwise than for genuine commercial purposes during any period of seven years ending on any of the following events:

- an event which is a chargeable event in relation to the securities, as defined in ITEPA 2003, s427 [ITEPA 2003, s446E(3)(b) and s446E(4)(a)]
- the disposal or cancellation of the securities [ITEPA 2003, s446E(3)(b) and s446E(4)(b)]
- 5 April in any year in which the securities were **employment-related** [ITEPA 2003, s446E(3)(b) and s446E(4)(c)].

The tax charge will apply if the **CGT value** of the securities was reduced by at least 10% as a result of things done during this period.

12.5.4. Annual Tax Charge

If securities have been artificially depressed, then there will be a tax charge on 5 April in each year if the securities are **employment-related** on that date [ITEPA 2003, s446E(1)(b)].

12.5.5. Additional Tax Charges

If securities have been artificially depressed, then a tax charge will also arise:

- immediately after an event which is a chargeable event in relation to the securities, as defined in ITEPA 2003, s427 [ITEPA 2003, s446E(1)(a)] (see section 12.3.2), and
- immediately before the securities are disposed of, or are cancelled without being disposed of [ITEPA 2003, s446E(1)(aa)].

12.5.6. Calculation of the Taxable Amount

The taxable amount is calculated in broadly the same way as under ITEPA 2003, s428 (see section 12.3.4) but with some amendments as set out below.

- UMV is what would be the **CGT value** of the securities at the time of the chargeable event disregarding not only any restrictions on the shares but also disregarding the artificial depression and, if the shares are about to be disposed of or cancelled, that fact [ITEPA 2003, s446E(6) and (8)].
- If the securities are about to be disposed of or cancelled, OP is omitted from the calculation [ITEPA 2003, s446E(9)]
- If the securities are actually disposed of for less than UMV, they are treated as being disposed of for UMV [ITEPA 2003, s446E(10)].

12.5.7. PAYE and NIC

PAYE applies if the shares are **readily convertible asset**s when the chargeable event occurs [ITEPA 2003, s698(1)(c)].

The employee must "make good" the PAYE within 90 days to avoid a further tax charge under ITEPA 2003, s222 (see section 3.7.3.14).

If PAYE applies, then NIC also applies [SSCR 2001, reg 22(7)].

12.5.8. Reporting

When a tax charge arises under ITEPA 2003, s446E, this is a reportable event under ITEPA 2003, s421K, either because it actually is also a chargeable event under ITEPA 2003, s426, or because a chargeable event is treated as occurring under ITEPA 2003, s427(3)(a) by ITEPA 2003, s446E(5)]. See section 23.

12.6. Artificially Enhanced Securities

12.6.1. Application of the Artificially Enhanced Securities Rules

The artificial enhancement rules in ITEPA 2003, Part 7, Chapter 3B apply where the **CGT value** of **employment-related** securities been increased by 10% or more as a result of something done other than for genuine commercial purposes [ITEPA 2003, s446L].

The "relevant period" is the period over which the increase in value is measured. It starts with the later of:

- the previous 5 April and
- the **acquisition date** of the securities.

It ends with "the valuation date", which is the earlier of:

- the next 5 April and
- the date on which the securities cease to be **employment-related** [ITEPA 2003, s446O].

Note that there are special rules for shares (but not other securities) acquired before 1 September 2003 (see section 12.7).

12.6.2. Calculation of the Taxable Amount

12.6.2.1. Step 1 – Calculate IMV - MV

The starting point in determining the taxable amount is to calculate IMV – MV [ITEPA 2003, s446L(4)]:

- IMV is the actual **CGT value** of the securities on the valuation date [ITEPA 2003, s446L(5)], and
- MV is what the **CGT value** would have been if it had not been artificially enhanced ITEPA 2003, s446L(6)]

in each case ignoring any restrictions on the securities, and ignoring any artificial reduction in value that has occurred during the relevant period [ITEPA 2003, s446L(7)].

12.6.2.2. Step 2 – Adjustment for Relevant Restricted securities

However, there are provisions to prevent double charges to tax. If the securities are **restricted securities** on the valuation date, but are subject to either a **Section 430 election** or a **Section 431(1) election**, then IMV-MV must be multiplied by CP [ITEPA 2003, s446M(2)].

CP is 1 – OP, where OP is the amount that would be calculated under ITEPA 2003, s428(5).

This is because OP is the proportion of the value of the securities that is represented by the restrictions, and which has therefore already been taxed under Chapter 2 when the holder made the **Section 430** or **Section 431(1) election**. CP is therefore the proportion that has not been taxed under Chapter 2 and can be taxed under Chapter 3B [ITEPA 2003, s446M(3)].

If a **Section 431(2) election** has been made in relation to the securities, then appropriate adjustments are made so that the proportion of value subject to that election is not taxed again under Chapter 3B [ITEPA 2003, s446M(5)].

12.6.2.3. Step 3 – Adjustment where Chapter 2 charge has arisen during Relevant Period

If a chargeable event has occurred under Chapter 2 (the **restricted securities** rules) during the relevant period, then there is a further adjustment to prevent double taxation.

IMV-MV, as calculated under section 12.6.2.1 and, if relevant, multiplied by CP in accordance with section 12.6.2.2, is reduced by DA [ITEPA 2003, s446N(2)].

DA is the aggregate of (TA-ARTA) for each chargeable event that occurred during the relevant period [ITEPA 2003, s446N(3) and (4)].

TA is the taxable amount that was determined under ITEPA 2003, s428 [ITEPA 2003, s446N(5)].

ARTA is what the taxable amount would have been, if the calculation had ignored any artificial increases in value during the relevant period that occurred before the chargeable event [ITEPA 2003, s446N(6)].

Therefore the effect of this is that any artificial increase in value that has already been taxed under Chapter 2 during the relevant period will not be taxed again under Chapter 3B.

12.6.3. PAYE and NIC

PAYE applies if the shares are **readily convertible assets** when the chargeable event occurs [ITEPA 2003, s698(1)(d)].

The employee must "make good" the PAYE within 90 days to avoid a further tax charge under ITEPA 2003, s222 (see section 3.7.3.14).

If PAYE applies, then NIC also applies [SSCR 2001, reg 22(7)].

12.6.4. Reporting

The employing company (and the company that issued the shares, if this is different) must notify HM Revenue & Customs when a reportable event occurs. The report must be filed before 7 July of the following tax year [ITEPA 2003, s421J(3)]. The doing of anything that gives rise to a taxable amount under ITEPA 2003, s446L is a reportable event [ITEPA 2003, s421K(3)(d)]. See section 23.

12.7. Removal or Variation of a Restriction on Shares Acquired Before 1 September 2003

There is a chargeable event if the employee holds restricted shares that were originally acquired before 1 September 2003, and the restriction is varied or removed [ITEPA 2003, old s450(3)(a)]. This also applies to an interest in shares that is less than full ownership [ITEPA 2003, old s447(1)(a)].

12.7.1. Acquisition as a Director or Employee

This charge to tax only applies if the shares were originally acquired by the taxpayer as a director or employee [ITEPA 2003, old s447(1)(b)]. The enlarged definition of "**by reason of employment**" in ITEPA 2003, s421B does not apply. Instead, the tax charge will potentially apply if:

- he acquired the shares pursuant to a right conferred on, or an opportunity offered to, him by reason of his employment [ITEPA 2003, old s447(4)(a)];
- the right was originally conferred on some other person by reason of the employee's employment, and then assigned to the employee [ITEPA 2003, old s447(4)(b)];
- the shares were acquired by a person connected with the employee, pursuant to a right conferred on, or an opportunity offered to, the other person by reason of the employee's employment [ITEPA 2003, old s447(5)].

12.7.2. Cases Where the Charge does not Apply

The charge to tax does not apply in the following circumstances:

- If the employee was not **resident** and **ordinarily resident** in the UK on the **acquisition date** [ITEPA 2003, old s448(1)]
- If the shares were acquired through a public offer [ITEPA 2003, old s448(2)]
- If the restriction applies to all shares of the same class and, at the time is removed or varied,
    - the shares are **employee-control shares** [ITEPA 2003, old s450(4)(a)]
    - a majority of shares of that class are held by people who are not directors or employees of that company or any **associated company** [ITEPA 2003, old s450(4)(b)]
    - the company is a **51% Subsidiary** with only one class of shares [ITEPA 2003, old s450(4)(c)]
- If the shares are "only conditional" and the same event is also a chargeable event under ITEPA 2003, old s427 (see section 12.2.3) [ITEPA 2003, old s452(2)]

- If the event happens more than seven years after the employee terminates employment with the employing company, the company whose shares are involved, or any **associated company** of either [ITEPA 2003, old s452(3)].

12.7.3. The Taxable Amount

The taxable amount is the amount by which the value of the shares is increased by the chargeable event [ITEPA 2003, s451].

12.7.4. PAYE and NIC

PAYE applies if the shares are **readily convertible assets** when the chargeable event occurs [ITEPA 2003, s697].

The employee must "make good" the PAYE within 90 days to avoid a further tax charge under ITEPA 2003, s222 (see section 3.7.3.14).

If PAYE applies, then NIC also applies [SSCR 2001, reg 22(6)].

12.7.5. Reporting

The employing company (and the company that issued the shares, if this is different) must notify HM Revenue & Customs when a reportable event occurs. The report must be filed before 7 July of the following tax year [ITEPA 2003, old s446(1)]. See section 23.

12.8. Securities Acquired for less than Market Value

There is usually a general earnings charge when an employee acquires securities for less than their **money's worth value** (see section 11.1.2).

However, there can be circumstances where there is nothing that can be taxed as general earnings. Examples are:

- the **exercise** of an **option** by someone who was **resident**, but not **ordinarily resident**, in the UK on the **grant date** (see section 8.4.6). There is no general earnings charge possible here because the benefit derives from the **option** rather than the employment;
- where securities are issued nil-paid or partly paid, the employee benefits from full ownership of the securities without initially having made full payment. There is no general earnings charge in relation to the benefit of delaying the payment (see section 12.8.1);
- if the **CGT value** of unrestricted securities exceeded the **money's worth value**, then the general earnings charge would be calculated by reference to the money's worth value (see section 11.1.2) so conceivably there would be a benefit to the employee that could not be taxed as general earnings;
- the securities are **employment-related** as defined in ITEPA 2003, s421B, because of the expanded definition in that section; but were not acquired **by reason of employment** under general principles, so that there is no general earnings charge on acquisition.

12.8.1. Nil-Paid or Partly-Paid Securities

Here is an example of how an employee can benefit from acquiring nil-paid or partly-paid securities.

Imagine the employee is offered shares which have a **CGT value** of £12 and a nominal value of £1. The terms of the offer are that the employee has to pay £1 immediately and a further amount of £9 whenever the company calls for it.

This would give rise to a general earnings charge of £2, being the difference between the **CGT value** of £12 and the total price of £10 that the employee must pay (see section 11.1.3).

ITEPA 2003, Part 7, Chapter 3C imposes a tax charge in relation to the benefit of deferring payment of £9.

12.8.2. When a Chapter 3C liability arises

An employment income tax liability under ITEPA 2003, Part 7, Chapter 3C potentially arises whenever an employee acquires securities on or after 16 April 2003 without paying their **CGT value** at or before the **acquisition date** [ITEPA 2003, s446Q(1)].

In relation to securities acquired before 16 April 2003, the legislation is in ITEPA 2003, s192 to s197, and is effectively the same except where noted below.

The legislation also applies if the employee is under an obligation to make a further payment for the securities at a future date [ITEPA 2003, s446Q(2)].

- The full details of the calculation of the tax liability are set out in section 12.8.4
- There are exemptions for employee-controlled companies and transactions affecting shares of a class controlled by open market shareholders. There is also a *de minimis* exemption of £5,000. These are set out in section 12.8.3.

12.8.3. Exclusions

There are two exclusions which apply where all the securities of the same class are acquired for less than **CGT value**.

The first applies if the company is employee-controlled by virtue of shares of that same class on the **acquisition date** [ITEPA 2003, s446R(3)].

The second applies if the majority of shares of that class are open-market shares [ITEPA 2003, s446R(4)].

However, neither of these exclusions applies if

- the **CGT value** of the securities was artificially increased by at least 10% during the period of seven years ending with the **acquisition date** [ITEPA 2003, s446NA(1)]; or
- something has been done which affects the value of the securities (either before or at the **acquisition date**) as part of a scheme or arrangement, the main purpose of which is the avoidance of tax or NIC [ITEPA 2003, s446R(1A)].

The *de minimis* exemption of £5,000 also applies [ITEPA 2003, s180].

12.8.4. The Notional Loan

12.8.4.1. When the Notional Loan is deemed to be made

The employee is usually deemed to have received a notional loan on the **acquisition date** of the securities [ITEPA 2003, s446S(1)].

However, if the securities were covered by the exemption in ITEPA 2003, s425(2) on the **acquisition date**, i.e. they were **restricted securities** which were forfeitable and the maximum **forfeiture period** was less than five years, then the notional loan is deemed to be made on the first occurrence of a chargeable event under Chapter 2 (the **restricted securities** rules) [ITEPA 2003, s446Q(4)].

12.8.4.2. When the Notional Loan is deemed to be discharged

The notional loan remains outstanding until it is discharged.

It is discharged when

- the securities are disposed of to someone who is not an **associated person** [ITEPA 2003, s446U(1)(a)];
- if the obligation to pay up the balance of the **CGT value** is released, transferred or adjusted [ITEPA 2003, s446U(1)(b)]; or
- if something which affects the securities is done as part of a scheme or arrangement of which one of the main purposes is the avoidance of tax or NIC [ITEPA 2003, s446U(1)(c)].

It is also discharged if the employee pays the remaining amounts due on the securities, or dies [ITEPA 2003, s446T(4)].

12.8.4.3. The Amount of the Notional Loan

The amount of the notional loan is MV - DA [ITEPA 2003, s446T(1)].

12.8.4.4. Market value in the Notional Loan Calculation

The calculation of MV is set out in section 8.4.6.4.

12.8.4.5. The Deductible Amounts in the Notional Loan Calculation

DA are the deductible amounts. These include the following:

- Any amount actually paid for the securities [ITEPA 2003, s446T(3)(a)]
- Any amount charged to tax in relation to the acquisition of the securities [ITEPA 2003, s446T(3)(b)].
- If an election under ITEPA 2003, s425(2) was made on the acquisition of the securities, the amount charged to tax on the first subsequent chargeable event [ITEPA 2003, s446T(3)(c)].
- If the securities were acquired on the conversion of **convertible securities**, the amount taxed on the conversion [ITEPA 2003, s446T(3)(d)].

12.8.4.6. *Tax Charge on Discharge of Notional Loan*

If the notional loan is discharged for the reasons set out in ITEPA 2003, s446U(1), i.e. because the securities are disposed of to a non-**associated person**, or because the obligation to pay up the balance of the **CGT value** is released, transferred or adjusted, or because something is done as part of a tax or NIC avoidance scheme, then the employee is treated as receiving taxable income equal to the remaining balance of the notional loan [ITEPA 2003, s446U(2)]. However, note that if the securities are shares, and they are disposed of in a bargain at arm's length, and the company is a qualifying **trading company**, there may be an equal and opposite loss available under ICTA 1988, s574(1) (see section 12.12).

12.8.4.7. *PAYE on the Discharge of the Notional Loan*

If the notional loan was made on or after 16 April 2003, the income tax charge will arise under ITEPA 2003, s446U(2) and PAYE will be due [ITEPA 2003, s698(1)(e)].

However, if the notional loan was made before 16 April 2003, there is no PAYE requirement.

12.8.4.8. *NIC on Discharge of Notional Loan*

If the notional loan was made on or after 16 April 2003, then when the securities are sold, the amount of the notional loan will also be subject to Class 1 NIC [SSCR 2001, reg 22(7)]. This does not apply if the notional loan was made before 16 April 2003.

12.8.4.9. *Reporting the Notional Loan*

The employing company (and the company that issued the shares, if this is different) must notify HM Revenue & Customs when a reportable event occurs. The report must be filed before 7 July of the following tax year [ITEPA 2003, s421J(3)]. The discharge of a notional loan is a reportable event [ITEPA 2003, s421K(3)(e)]. See section 23.

12.9. Securities Disposed of for More than Market value

There will be an employment income tax charge if the employee sells **employment-related** securities for more than their **CGT value** to a non-**associated person**. The same applies if the securities are sold by an **associated person** of the employee [ITEPA 2003, s446X].

The taxable amount is the amount by which the sale proceeds exceed the **CGT value** of the securities and any disposal costs [ITEPA 2003, s446Y].

The disposal is a reportable event. See section 23.

The same disposal can give rise to a capital gains tax liability if the **CGT value** of the securities exceeds the allowable expenditure.

12.10. Post-Acquisition Benefits

ITEPA 2003, s447, imposes a charge to tax where an employee or **associated person** receives a benefit in connection withthe ownership of securities.

Senior HM Revenue & Customs officials have stated in meetings that they consider this section to be very wide in its application.

In particular, they believe that it applies in a VC downwards ratchet situation, where the value of an employee's shares is increased through the downwards conversion of shares held by an investor (see section 3.5.7.1.2).

It also applies to structures which set out to avoid tax or NIC by paying employment income as dividends. Generally, dividends will not be taxable under these provisions since they are already taxable under ITTOIA 2005, Part 4, Chapter 3, but this exclusion does not apply to dividends that are paid as part of an arrangement to avoid tax [ITEPA 2003, s447(4)]. This does not, however, mean that the dividends are taxed twice. Although the consolidation of ITTOIA 2005 removed the clear and unambiguous statement in ICTA 1988, s20(2) that distributions could not be taxed under any other provision, TMA 1970, s32 still operates to preclude a double charge to tax.

ITEPA 2003, s447 does not apply where the benefit is received by all shareholders of the same class, where either the shares are **employee-control shares**, or a majority of shares of the class are not **employment-related** securities [ITEPA 2003, s449]. However, even this exclusion is not available where something has been done to the securities on or after 2 December 2004 as part of an arrangement with a main purpose of avoiding tax or NIC [ITEPA 2003, s449(1A)].

The provision of a benefit is a reportable event. See section 23.

12.11. Capital Gains Tax

12.11.1. Disposal of Securities Acquired on Exercise of Option

When a shareholder disposes of securities that were originally acquired on the **exercise** of an **option**, the capital gains tax treatment depends on several factors.

- If the **option** was **exercise**d on or after 10 April 2003, and no income tax relief was given, then the calculation is in section 12.11.1.1.
- If the **option** was **exercise**d before 10 April 2003, and no income tax relief was given, then the calculation is in section 12.11.1.2.
- If income tax relief was given on the **exercise** of a **CSOP** or **SAYE** or EMI **option**, then the calculation is in section 12.11.1.3.

If the calculation results in an allowable loss, income tax relief may be available (see section 12.12).

12.11.1.1. *Option exercised on or after 10 April 2003; income tax relief not available*

Sale Proceeds	Less
Exercise price [TCGA 1992, s38(1)(a)]. NB TCGA 1992, s17 is disapplied by TCGA 1992, s144ZA	Less
Any amount which was a taxable amount in relation to the **exercise** of the **securities option** under ITEPA 2003, s476 [TCGA 1992, s119A(3)(d)]	Less
Any amount that constituted earnings when the **securities option** was acquired [TCGA 1992, s119A(5)]	Less
Any secondary NIC or special contributions paid by the employee in respect of the **securities option** [TCGA 1992, s119A(5)]	Less
Any amount that is taxed as employment income under ITEPA 2003, s446X (disposals at more than **market value**) [TCGA 1992, s37]	Less
Any amount that constituted employment income in relation to an earlier or simultaneous chargeable event under ITEPA 2003, s426 (**restricted securities**), s439(3)(a) (conversion of **convertible securities**), or s446U (discharge of notional loan) [TCGA 1992, s119A(3)]	Less
Grant price (if any)	Less
Taper Relief (if any)	Equals
Taxable Gain	

12.11.1.2. *Option exercised before 10 April 2003; income tax relief not available*

Sale Proceeds	Less
CGT value of shares on **exercise date** (NB - this is the effect of *Mansworth v Jelley*)	Less
Any amount on which the shareholder has paid income tax in relation to the **exercise** of the **option** under ITEPA 2003, s476 or the discharge of a notional loan under ITEPA 2003, s195(2), or under Chapters 2, 3, or 4 of Part 7 (manipulation of share rights, dependent subsidiary, sale at an overvalue, conditional shares and convertible shares)[TCGA 1992, s120]	Less
Grant price (if any)	Less
Taper Relief (if any)	Equals
Taxable Gain	

12.11.1.3. *CSOP, SAYE or EMI Option exercised with income tax relief*

Sale Proceeds	Less
Exercise price	Less
Grant price (if any)	Less
Taper Relief (if any)	Less
Taxable Gain	

NB – taper relief for an **EMI option** starts from the **grant date**, unless there has been a disqualifying event, in which case it starts from the **exercise date** [TCGA 1992, Sch7D, para 15](see section 8.2.4).

Note that if the optionholder acquires shares on the same day, some on the exercise of an option with tax relief, and others without tax relief, then the optionholder can elect to treat them as two separate acquisitions of shares for the purposes of the share identification rules [TCGA 1992, s105A]. This enables the optionholder to manage his capital gains tax exposure.

12.11.2. Disposal of Shares Following Release from SIP

When a shareholder disposes of shares following release from a **SIP**, the base cost is the **CGT value** of shares on the release date [TCGA 1992, Sch7D, para 5(1)] (see section 4.2.4.8.2).

12.11.3. Disposal of Restricted and/or Convertible securities

An employment income tax charge may arise on the disposal of restricted and/or **convertible securities** (see sections 12.3.2 and 12.4.2).

There are special identification rules for restricted securities [TCGA 1992, s104(4)].

Note also that HM Revenue & Customs believe that where **restricted securities** are acquired from an EBT, the period of ownership for capital gains tax purposes starts on the day the restrictions are lifted.[194]

If the calculation results in an allowable loss, income tax relief may be available (see section 12.12).

Capital gains tax on the subsequent disposal is calculated as follows:

Sale Proceeds	Less
The aggregate of the actual consideration given for the securities and any amount that constituted earnings in relation to the acquisition [TCGA 1992, s149AA(1)]	Less
Any amount treated as employment income in relation to the securities under ITEPA 2003, s446U (discharge of notional loan) [TCGA 1992, s119A(3)(c)]	Less
Any amount treated as employment income in relation to the securities under ITEPA 2003, s426 (**restricted securities**) [TCGA 1992, s119A(3)(a)]	Less
Any amount treated as employment income in relation to the securities under ITEPA 2003, s438 (**convertible securities**) [TCGA 1992, s119A(3)(b)]	Less
Any amount treated as employment income in relation to the securities under ITEPA 2003, s477(3)(a) (acquisition pursuant to **securities option**) [TCGA 1992, s119A(3)(b)]	Less
Any amount that is taxed as employment income under ITEPA 2003, s446X	Less

194 IR Tax Bulletin 51, February 2001 (http://www.hmrc.gov.uk/bulletins/tb51.htm#ctg)

(disposals at more than **market value**) [TCGA 1992, s37]	
Taper Relief (if any)	Equals
Taxable Gain	

12.11.4. Disposal of Securities Acquired At an Undervalue Before 16 April 2003

Where an employee acquired shares at an undervalue or for free by reason of his employment before 16 April 2003, the eventual capital gain on disposal is calculated as set out below.

If the calculation results in an allowable loss, income tax relief may be available (see section 12.12).

Sale Proceeds	Less
CGT value of shares on **acquisition date** [this is because **CGT value** is substituted for the actual acquisition cost under TCGA 1992, s17]	Less
Any amount that counted as employment income in respect of the shares under the original version of ITEPA 2003, Part 7, Chapter 4 (post-acquisition benefits) [TCGA 1992, s120(1A)]	Less
Any amount treated as earnings in relation to the shares under ITEPA 2003, old s195(2) (discharge of notional loan) [TCGA 1992, s120(3)]	Less
Any amount treated as employment income under the original version of ITEPA 2003, Part 7, Chapter 2 (conditional shares) [TCGA 1992, s120(5A)]	Less
Any amount treated as employment income under the original version of ITEPA 2003, Part 7, Chapter 3 (convertible shares) [TCGA 1992, s120(5B)]	Less
Any amount that is taxed as employment income under ITEPA 2003, s446X (disposals at more than **market value**) [TCGA 1992, s37]	Less
Taper Relief (if any)	Equals
Taxable Gain	

12.11.5. Disposal of Unrestricted, Non-Convertible securities Acquired On or After 16 April 2003

Where an employee acquires unrestricted, non-convertible **securities** for free, or for less than their **money's worth value**, there may be an income tax charge on the acquisition (see section 11.1.2). If the shares were disposed of on or after 16 April 2003, the capital gain on the subsequent disposal is calculated as set out below.

If the calculation results in an allowable loss, income tax relief may be available (see section 12.12).

Sale Proceeds	Less
CGT value of shares on **acquisition date** [this is because **CGT value** is substituted for the actual acquisition cost under TCGA 1992, s17]	Less
Any amount treated as employment income in relation to the securities under	Less

ITEPA 2003, s446U (discharge of notional loan) [TCGA 1992, s119A(3)(c)]	
Any amount that is taxed as employment income under ITEPA 2003, s446X (disposals at more than **market value**) [TCGA 1992, s37]	Less
Taper Relief (if any)	Equals
Taxable Gain	

12.11.6. Taper Relief

Business asset taper relief applies when an officer or employee of a company disposes of securities of that company, or in another company which has a "relevant connection" with it [TCGA 1992, SchA1, para 6(1)(b)(ii) for trading companies and para 6(1A)(b) for non-trading companies]. If the company is a non-**trading company**, or the **holding company** of a non-**trading group**, then business asset taper relief will not be available to a person who has a **material interest** in it [TCGA 1992, SchA1, para 6(1A)(c)].

Note that although the legislation refers to "shares", this is defined so as to include other securities of the company [TCGA 1992, SchA1, para 22].

Two companies have a relevant connection with each other if they are both members of the same **group of companies** or of the same **commercial association of companies** [TCGA 1992, SchA1, para 22(2)].

If the person owned the securities before 6 April 2000, the securities will not be "business assets" in relation to that period unless the company was a **trading company** or the **holding company** of a **trading group**, and:

- the person was a full-time working director or employee, and
- the person owned 5% or more of the voting rights in the company [TCGA 1992, SchA1, old para 6(3)].

If the person ceases to be an officer or employee, the securities may continue to be business assets if the company meets the relevant conditions.

To calculate the correct taper relief on the disposal, the gain has to be apportioned on a strict time basis between any period when the securities were business assets and any period when they were non-business assets [TCGA 1992, SchA1, para 3].

Table 6 shows the rates of business asset taper relief:

Table 6: Taper Relief for Business Assets

Period for which Securities Owned	Rate of Taper Relief	Effective Highest Rate of Capital Gains Tax
< 1 year	0%	40%
1 – 2 years	50%	20%
> 2 years	75%	10%

Table 7 shows the rates of taper relief for non-business assets:

Table 7: Taper Relief for Non-Business Assets

Period for which Securities Owned	Rate of Taper Relief	Effective Highest Rate of Capital Gains Tax
< 3 years	0%	40%
3 – 4 years	5%	38%
4 – 5 years	10%	36%
5 – 6 years	15%	34%
6 – 7 years	20%	32%
7 – 8 years	25%	30%
8 - 9 years	30%	28%
9 - 10 years	35%	26%
> 10 years	40%	24%

12.12. Income Tax Relief for Capital Losses

If the result of the calculation under section 12.11 is that the employee makes an allowable loss for capital gains tax purposes, then the employee may be able to set the loss against his taxable income.

This will be the case if the company is a qualifying **trading company**, and the employee originally subscribed for new shares [ICTA 1988, s574(1)]. The loss can be claimed either against the employee's income for the year in which the disposal takes place, or the previous year, but not against both. The definition of a qualifying **trading company** is found in ICTA 1988, s576(4), which refers to and qualifies the enterprise investment scheme legislation.

The relief is not available if the shares are disposed in a way that creates an artificial loss. If the shares are sold, then this must be by way of a bargain at arm's length for full consideration [ICTA 1988, s575(1)].

13. Corporate Transactions: Effect on Reward Plans

13.1. Change of Control of the Group

This section looks at the impact of a change of control of the group as a whole on rights under various reward plans. Section 13.2 looks at the sale of a subsidiary or a business out of the group.

13.1.1. Premature Exercise of CSOP and SAYE Options

The change of control of the group may trigger an accelerated **vesting** of **CSOP** and **SAYE options**.

In either case, the **optionholder** will be charged to income tax if the **exercise** takes place within three years of the **grant date**. The premature **exercise** of a **CSOP option** is taxed in these circumstances in exactly the same way as an unapproved **option** (see section 8.1.2). The same applies for an **SAYE option**, except that the tax is never withheld through PAYE and NIC does not apply (see section 8.4.2).

13.1.2. Disqualifying Event for EMI Options

A change of control will be a disqualifying event for an **EMI option** because the **relevant company** will cease to satisfy the independence requirement (see section 3.7.6.3.1). See section 8.2.1.2.4 for the implications of exercising an **EMI option** after a disqualifying event. To avoid a disqualifying event, it may be possible to have a qualifying rollover of the **EMI option** (see section 8.5.6.4).

13.1.3. Accelerated Exercise of Unapproved option

The change of control is likely to trigger the accelerated **exercise** of unapproved **option**s. This will be a chargeable event in the same way as normal (see section 8.1.2).

13.1.4. Rollover of Options

Income tax, capital gains tax and NIC can usually be deferred by rolling over the **option**s for **option**s over shares in the acquiring company. See the following sections:

Section 8.5.6.1 for income tax on unapproved **option**s

Section 8.5.6.2 for NIC on unapproved **option**s

Section 8.5.6.3 for **approved option**s

Section 8.5.6.4 for **EMI option**s and

Section 8.5.6.5 for capital gains tax.

13.1.5. Cancellation of Options

Often, the acquiring company will want to cancel the **option**s for a cash payment. This is taxable either as income or as a capital gain. See the following sections:

Section 8.2.1.3 for the cash cancellation of an **EMI option**

Section 8.3.1.3 for the cash cancellation of a **CSOP option**

Section 8.4.1.3 for the cash cancellation of an **SAYE option**

Section 8.5.1 for the income tax and PAYE treatment of an **option** cancellation

Section 8.5.2 for the NIC treatment of an **option** cancellation

Section 8.5.3 for the CGT treatment of an **option** cancellation

Section 17.8 for the corporation tax deductibility of a cash cancellation payment.

13.1.6. Exchange of Conditional Securities acquired before 16 April 2003

If an employee who holds "only conditional" securities that were acquired before 16 April 2003 exchanges them on a change of control for shares in the acquirer, the exchange will be a chargeable event [ITEPA 2003, old s427(1)(b)]. See section 12.2.3.

The securities acquired in exchange will be **employment-related** securities, and may be **restricted securities**. However, in most commercial arrangements it is unlikely that there will be any further taxable amount under ITEPA 2003, s428 because the value of the securities exchanged will be the same as the value of the securities received, so IUMV and DA will be equal.

13.1.7. Exchange of Restricted Securities

If an employee who holds **restricted securities** exchanges them on a change of control for shares in the acquirer, the exchange will be a chargeable event [ITEPA 2003, s427(3)(c)]. See section 12.3.2.

The securities acquired in exchange will be **employment-related** securities, and may be **restricted securities**. However, in most commercial arrangements it is unlikely that there will be any further taxable amount under ITEPA 2003, s428 because the value of the securities exchanged will be the same as the value of the securities received, so IUMV and DA will be equal.

13.1.8. Exchange of Convertible Securities

If an employee who holds **convertible securities** exchanges them on a change of control for shares in the acquirer, the exchange will be a chargeable event [ITEPA 2003, s439(3)(b)]. See section 12.4.2.

13.1.9. Sale or Exchange of SIP Shares

In most commercial circumstances, the acquirer will make a "general offer" that falls within ITEPA 2003, Sch2, para 37(5).

This means that the participant can direct the **SIP** Trustee to accept an offer for his Free or Matching Shares [ITEPA 2003, Sch2, para 37 and para 61].

If the participant directs the **SIP** Trustee to accept a cash offer, that will be a disposal of the shares and there will be a charge to income tax.

If the participant directs the **SIP** Trustee to accept shares or qualifying corporate bonds, this will be a "company reconstruction" as defined in ITEPA 2003, Sch2, para 86.

This means that there will be an effective rollover into the acquirer securities [ITEPA 2003, Sch2, para 87].

13.1.10. Loss of FA 2003, Sch23 deduction

If the acquirer is an unquoted company (or a **close company** that is quoted), then the shares will cease to be **corporation tax deductible shares** immediately after the change of control (see section 21.2). Therefore to preserve the entitlement to relief it is prudent to arrange for any **option**s to be **exercise**d before the change of control occurs, or to rollover the **option**s into acquirer shares if those shares are corporation tax deductible.

13.2. Sale of Business or Subsidiary

The sale of a business or subsidiary may be an event that triggers premature **exercise** of a share **option**, in which case see section 13.1.1 for **CSOP** and **SAYE** and section 13.1.3 for unapproved **options**. An approved rollover of **CSOP** and **SAYE option**s will not be possible because the requirements of the legislation will not be satisfied (see section 8.5.6.3).

It will also be a disqualifying event for **EMI**, because the **optionholder** will no longer meet the employment requirement (see section 3.7.6.4.1). A qualifying rollover will not be possible (see section 8.5.6.4).

It may also cause **option**s to lapse, in which case the employer may want to make a compensation payment. The tax treatment of such a payment is set out in section 13.1.5.

If the employee participates in a **SIP**, his shares will cease to be subject to the **SIP** because he will cease to be in **relevant employment**. However, in most commercial circumstances he will not be liable to income tax because of the exemptions in ITEPA 2003, s498(2)(c) on the sale of a business and ITEPA 2003, s498(2)(d) on the sale of a **subsidiary**.

13.3. Bonus Issues and Rights Issues

13.3.1. Adjustment of Options

When there is a bonus or rights issue, it is usual to adjust employee **option**s so that the **optionholder** is not adversely affected.

13.3.1.1. Bonus Issue

The adjustment formula for a bonus issue is simple:

Multiply the number of shares under **option** by A/B and multiply the **exercise price** by B/A, where A is the total number of shares in issue after the bonus issue, and B is the total number of shares in issue before the bonus issue.

Example: the ***optionholder*** *has an* ***option*** *to acquire 100 shares at an* ***exercise price*** *of £1 per share.*

There is a three for one bonus issue (i.e. a shareholder will receive three new shares for each share held making four shares in total), so A is 4 and B is 1.

The number of shares under ***option*** *is multiplied by 4 and the* ***exercise price*** *is divided by 4.*

Therefore the ***option*** *is adjusted so that it is an* ***option*** *to acquire 400 shares at an* ***exercise price*** *of 25p per share.*

The aggregate ***exercise price*** *the employee has to pay therefore is £100.*

13.3.1.2. Rights Issue

The adjustment formula for a rights issue is more complex. There is no single correct method, but the formula accepted by HM Revenue & Customs is as follows:

Multiply the number of shares under **option** by A/B and multiply the **exercise price** by B/A, where

A is the theoretical ex-rights price and

B is the value of the shares immediately before the rights issue, i.e. the last available cum-rights value.

The theoretical ex-rights price is

((B x N) + (R x P)) / (R + N)

where

N is the number of shares required to entitle the holder to the rights issue

R is the number of rights shares offered to a holder of N shares

P is the rights issue price

The following example is taken from HMRC Manual ESS29108[195].

Example:

An employee holds an ***option*** *over 1000 shares at an* ***exercise price*** *of 40p per share*

Company makes 1 for 4 rights issue at 50p per share (N=4; R=1; P=50p)

The last cum-rights value of a share (B) = 65p

Theoretical ex-rights price (A) =

((4 x 65p) + (1 x 50p)) / (1+4)

---

195 http://www.hmrc.gov.uk/manuals/essumanual/essu29000/essu29108.htm

= 62p per share

*Therefore the **exercise price** (40p) is multiplied by (62/65) = 38.153p*

*The number of shares under **option** (1000) is multiplied by (65/62) = 1048.4.*

13.3.2. Effect on "conditional shares" acquired before 16 April 2003

If an employee holds "conditional shares" that were acquired before 16 April 2003, and there is a bonus or rights issue, the shares acquired through the bonus or rights issue will not themselves be conditional shares. Therefore a potential tax charge under ITEPA 2003, old s427 can be mitigated by "swamping" the affected shares with a major bonus issue.

However, the new shares acquired through the bonus or rights issue will be **employment-related** securities, and since they are acquired on or after 16 April 2003, they may be subject to tax charges under the **restricted securities** rules (see section 13.3.3).

13.3.3. Bonus or rights issue shares as employment-related securities

New shares acquired by an employee through a bonus issue will be **employment-related** securities. However, this in itself does not create an additional tax charge except in the unlikely event that new value is conferred on the employees [HMRC Manual ERSM111100[196]].

A rights issue is technically the **grant** of an **employment-related securities option**. However, it is unlikely that any employment income tax charge will arise on the acquisition of new shares through the rights issue because of the adjustment in ITEPA 2003, s480(3). This is explained in HMRC Manual ERSM111000[197].

The acquisition of the bonus or rights issue shares will be a reportable event [ITEPA 2003, s421K(3)(a)] (see section 23). Although HM Revenue & Customs do not require a report in relation to bonus issues and rights issues by listed companies, they do expect a report in relation to unlisted and AIM companies (see Form 42 Guidance, p 11[198])

13.3.4. SIP

If there is a rights issue in respect of **SIP** shares, the participant has three choices:

- Provide the **SIP** Trustee with sufficient funds to exercise the rights. If he does this, the shares acquired through the rights issue will not be subject to the **SIP** [ITEPA 2003, Sch2, para 88(5)(a)]
- Instruct the **SIP** Trustee to sell sufficient of the rights shares to be able to subscribe for the balance, as permitted by ITEPA 2003, Sch2, para 77(1). If he

---

196 http://www.hmrc.gov.uk/manuals/ersmmanual/ERSM111100.htm

197 http://www.hmrc.gov.uk/manuals/ersmmanual/ERSM111000.htm

198 http://www.hmrc.gov.uk/shareschemes/form42-guidance.pdf

does this, the rights shares will be subject to the **SIP** and will be treated as having been acquired when the original shares were acquired and in the same way [ITEPA 2003, Sch2, para 88(2)]

- Instruct the **SIP** Trustee to sell the rights, in which case the sale proceeds will be a "capital receipt" [ITEPA 2003, s502(2)] (see section 4.2.4.7).

13.4. Demergers and Spinoffs

A demerger or spinoff is not considered by HM Revenue & Customs to be a **variation of share capital** [HMRC Manual ESS29084[199]]. Therefore, although it may be fair to adjust share **options**, they will lose their approved status (see section 3.7.8.8.1.8).

If an adjustment is made, the same formula should be used as for a rights issue adjustment (see section 13.3.1.2).

13.5. Earnouts

When a vendor sells a business in return for an "earnout" as part of the consideration, there are generally two reasons for this. The first is that the purchaser does not know how much the business is worth, so he wants to retain part of the consideration for a period of time to see how well it performs. The second is that the purchaser wants the vendor to continue working for the business in order for it to succeed, so payment of the deferred consideration is conditional on the vendor remaining employed.

In HM Revenue & Customs' view, if the deferred consideration takes the form of an issue of shares or loan notes of the purchaser, then the deferred consideration is itself a **securities option** [HMRC Manual ERSM110920[200]].

Insofar as all or part of the deferred consideration represents a reward for continued employment, HM Revenue & Customs will seek to tax it as general earnings.

There is, however, a safe harbour where HM Revenue & Customs will accept that the deferred consideration is not a reward for continued employment. This is where the arrangement has all the following characteristics:

- the sale agreement demonstrates that the earnout is part of the valuable consideration given for the securities in the old company;
- the value received from the earn-out reflects the value of the securities given up;

---

[199] http://www.hmrc.gov.uk/manuals/essumanual/essu29000/essu29084.htm

[200] http://www.hmrc.gov.uk/manuals/ersmmanual/ersm110920.htm

- if the vendor continues to be employed in the business, the vendor is fully remunerated for continuing employment;
- if the vendor continues to be employed, the earnout is not conditional on future employment, beyond a reasonable requirement to stay to protect the value of the business being sold – what is a reasonable requirement varies from one industry to another;
- if the vendor continues to be employed, there are no personal performance targets incorporated in the earn-out.

HM Revenue & Customs will also look at the following factors:

- negotiations between the seller and buyer as to the level of the earn out in relation to the value of the consideration given for securities in the old company;
- any clearance that might have been obtained demonstrating the bona fide nature of the transactions, and the level of the earn-out linked to profitability or other key performance indicators of the business;
- evidence that future bonuses were reclassified or commuted into purchase consideration would indicate that the earn-out was, at least partly, remuneration rather than consideration for the disposal of securities.

[HMRC Manual ERSM110940[201]].

201 http://www.hmrc.gov.uk/manuals/ersmmanual/ersm110940.htm

14. Structuring Management Equity Plans in Venture Capital Transactions

14.1. Loan Interest Relief

See section 16.5 for interest relief on loans to acquire shares in close companies and section 16.6 for interest relief on loans to acquire shares in employee-controlled companies.

14.2. Standard Ratchet (management shares convert upwards)

See section 3.5.7.1.1.

14.3. VC Reverse Ratchet (VC shares convert downwards)

See section 3.5.7.1.2.

14.4. Management Reverse Ratchet (management shares convert downwards)

See section 3.5.7.1.3.

14.5. "Flowering" Shares

See section 3.5.9.

15. Overview of Share Valuation for ITEPA 2003

There are, in effect, three different valuation standards used in ITEPA 2003.

First, there is the "money's worth" valuation that is found in ITEPA 2003, s62. This is used, for example, to determine the taxable value where an employee receives unrestricted shares. See section 15.1.

Second, there is the CGT valuation, which is used, for example, to determine the taxable amount on the **exercise** of a **securities option**. See section 15.2.

Third, there is the **unrestricted market value** or UMV, that is used, for example, to calculate the taxable amount on the **vesting** of **restricted securities** under ITEPA 2003, s428(2). See section 15.3.

15.1. Money's Worth Valuation

The "money's worth" value of an asset is its value in the hands of the employee. It is clear from the case law that this is a subjective test that takes account of any personal restrictions attaching to the asset, such as forfeiture conditions attached to shares. This is the case even if the restrictions are personal to the employee. In other words, it takes account of restrictions that would not apply to a purchaser of the shares. Relevant cases include *Tennant v Smith* 3 TC 158, *Wilkins v Rogerson* and *Heaton v Bell.*

The fact that the valuation is subjective also means that the purchaser is deemed to have access to all information about the company that the employee has, including price-sensitive information that is not in the public domain.

15.2. CGT Valuation Methodology

ITEPA 2003, s421(1) stipulates that market value, for the purposes of ITEPA 2003, Part 7, is the same as it is for capital gains tax purposes.

Using this methodology, the **CGT value** of a block of shares is the price which those shares "might reasonably be expected to fetch on a sale in the open market" [TCGA 1992, s272(1)].

There is no discount available for "flooding the market". In other words, it is not possible to reduce the estimated **CGT value** because of an assumption that all the shares are being placed on the market at the same time [TCGA 1992, s272(2)].

The prospective purchaser of the shares is deemed to have all the information that a prudent purchaser would reasonably require in a private arm's length sale [TCGA 1992, s273(3)].

The main difference between the **CGT value** and the **money's worth value** is that the CGT value is objective and does not take account of the personal situation of the vendor or the purchaser.

15.3. Impact of Personal Restrictions: Unrestricted Market Value

UMV, as used to determine the taxable amount under ITEPA 2003, s428, is the **CGT value** immediately after the chargeable event "but for any restrictions" [ITEPA 2003, s428(2)]. The restrictions that are relevant are ones that reduce the **CGT value** of the shares [ITEPA 2003, s423(1)(b)].

This has led some commentators to argue that the only restrictions that are relevant for determining whether shares are **restricted securities** are those which are inherent in the shares and would bind a prospective purchaser. Restrictions that are personal to the vendor are relevant in determining the **money's worth value** of the shares, but not in determining the **CGT value**. Since they are not relevant in determining the **CGT value**, they cannot reduce the **CGT value**.

HM Revenue & Customs do not agree with this argument [HMRC FAQ 1(k)[202] and HMRC Manual ERSM220020[203]] although their reasoning is far from clearly expressed.

The author disagrees with HM Revenue & Customs, but notes that this is a potentially dangerous line of argument to follow, as illustrated by the example below:.

An employee is **award**ed shares that are subject to personal restrictions that reduce their **money's worth value**.

If HMRC are wrong, then the correct technical position is as follows:

- There is a potential general earnings charge on the acquisition of the shares, based on the **money's worth value** less any price paid by the employee [ITEPA 2003, s62].
- The shares are not **restricted securities**, because the personal restrictions do not reduce the **CGT value** of the shares.
- Therefore the exemption in ITEPA 2003, s425(2) does not apply, and there can be no chargeable event under ITEPA 2003, s426.
- However, the employee has acquired the shares for less than their **CGT value**, so the "securities acquired for less than **market value**" rules apply (see section 12.8).

This means that the employee may actually pay more tax than if he had accepted HM Revenue & Customs' position. This will be the case if the value of the shares

[202] http://www.hmrc.gov.uk/shareschemes/faq_emprelatedsecurity-ch1.htm#k

[203] http://www.hmrc.gov.uk/manuals/ersmmanual/ERSM220020.htm

fails to increase sufficiently rapidly to cover the notional loan interest charge. If the share value actually falls, the employee may have a notional loan write-off tax charge under ITEPA 2003, s446U.

16. Employment-related Loans

This chapter discusses the implications when a company lends money, or procures a loan by a third party, to its employees to acquire its own shares.

16.1. Prohibition on Loans to Directors

See section 18.11.

16.2. Loans to a Corporate Trustee

It is illegal for a company to make a loan to a director in his capacity as a trustee of an EBT [CA 1985, s330].

It is, however, legal to make a loan to an EBT trustee or a pension scheme, even if directors are potential beneficiaries of the Trust [CA 1985, s346(3)(b)].

16.3. Tax on Cheap Loans to Directors and Employees

16.3.1. Affected Employees

The rules on the taxation of cheap loans are contained in ITEPA 2003, Part 3, Chapter 7. The rules apply to all directors, and to employees earning more than £8,500 per annum. The rules apply to employees who are **resident** in the UK, whether or not **ordinarily resident** [ITEPA 2003, s216].

The term "loan" includes an alternative finance arrangement to which FA 2005, s47 or s47A applies, or would do if one of the parties were a financial institution [FA 2006, s97].

16.3.2. Loans obtained by reason of employment

To determine whether a loan is made **by reason of employment**, it is necessary first to determine who is making the loan. Making the loan includes arranging, guaranteeing or in any way facilitating the loan [ITEPA 2003, s174(4)(b)]

The person who makes the loan must be:

(a) the employer [ITEPA 2003, s174(2)A];

(b) a company or partnership which the employer controls [ITEPA 2003, s174(2)B];

(c) a company or partnership that controls the employer [ITEPA 2003, s174(2)C];

(d) a company or partnership which is controlled by a person that controls the employer [ITEPA 2003, s174(2)D]; or

(e) a person who has a **material interest** in a **close company**, which is either the employer, controls the employer, or is controlled by the employer, or who has a **material interest** in a company that controls such a **close company** [ITEPA 2003, s174(2)E].

The legislation also applies to a loan that was originally made to the employee by a third party, and then assumed or taken over, or continued by any such person [ITEPA 2003, s174(4)(a)].

References to the employer include references to a prospective employer [ITEPA 2003, s174(3)].

16.3.3. How is the benefit calculated?

There are example calculations in the HMRC Manual at EIM26300[204]. Note that there is an exemption for loans up to £5,000 [ITEPA 2003, s180].

Note that "interest" includes alternative finance return from an alternative finance arrangement [FA 2006, s97(2)].

16.3.4. Position where interest is not actually paid during the tax year

The borrower must actually pay interest during the tax year at at least the official rate. If, instead, the interest is accumulated and added to the principal, it will not be treated as having been paid [HMRC Manual EIM26250[205]].

If the borrower actually pays the interest in a subsequent tax year, he can make a claim to have his tax returns for previous years adjusted and the tax repaid to him [ITEPA 2003, s191(2)]. However, any such claim must be made within six years of the end of the year of assessment in question [HMRC Manual EIM26255[206]].

16.3.5. Loans denominated in Foreign Currency

The official rate of interest is applied to loans in foreign currency as if they were denominated in sterling. The only two exceptions are for loans in Swiss Francs and Japanese Yen, for which separate official rates apply [HMRC Manual EIM26106[207]].

16.3.6. Loans to relatives

A loan that is made to a "relative"[208] of the employee will be taxable in the same way as if the loan has been made to the employee [HMRC Manual EIM26112[209]]. However, the employee can escape taxation if he can show that he actually derives no benefit from the loan [ITEPA 2003, s174(5) and HMRC Manual EIM26150[210]].

---

204 http://www.hmrc.gov.uk/manuals/eimanual/EIM26300.htm

205 http://www.hmrc.gov.uk/manuals/eimanual/EIM26250.htm

206 http://www.hmrc.gov.uk/manuals/eimanual/EIM26255.htm

207 http://www.hmrc.gov.uk/manuals/eimanual/EIM26106.htm

208 As defined in ITEPA 2003, s174(6)

209 http://www.hmrc.gov.uk/manuals/eimanual/EIM26112.htm

210 http://www.hmrc.gov.uk/manuals/eimanual/EIM26150.htm

16.3.7. Fixed rate loans made for a fixed period

If a loan is made for a fixed period of time at a fixed rate of interest, it is the official rate at the time the loan is made that is relevant in determining whether there is any taxable benefit. Even if the official rate is subsequently increased, this will not increase the taxable benefit for subsequent years. It is essential to be able to show that neither the term of the loan nor the interest rate can be altered under any circumstances [ITEPA 2003, s177 and HMRC Manual EIM26152[211]].

16.3.8. Interaction between Employment Income and Dividend Income where loan is written off

If any part of the loan is released or written off, that amount will be taxable as earnings [ITEPA 2003, s188].

But if the loan was made by a **close company** and the employee was a **participator**, the amount written off will also be taxable under ITTOIA 2005, s415 (see section 16.7.5). This charge has priority over the employment income charge [ITEPA 2003, s189 and HMRC Manual EIM21746[212]].

16.3.9. Death of Borrower

The employment income liability ends if the employee dies. There is no notional loan interest charge for periods following the death. There is no earnings charge if the loan is released or written off [ITEPA 2003, s190].

16.3.10. NIC

The notional loan interest charge is subject to Class 1A NIC. However, any release or write-off that is taxable as earnings is subject to Class 1 NIC [HMRC Booklet CWG5[213]].

16.3.11. Position where loan qualifies for interest relief

Interest relief on a "qualifying loan", e.g. to acquire shares in a **close company**, or an **employee-controlled company**, is offset against the notional interest charge [ITEPA 2003, s178]. See sections 16.5 and 16.6.

16.4. Consumer Credit Act 1974

Care must be taken in relation to a loan to an employee to make sure that it complies with the Consumer Credit Act 1974. In principle, the lender must obtain a consumer credit licence from the Director General of Fair Trading, unless an exemption is available.

---

211 http://www.hmrc.gov.uk/manuals/eimanual/EIM26152.htm

212 http://www.hmrc.gov.uk/manuals/eimanual/EIM21746.htm

213 http://www.hmrc.gov.uk/guidance/cwg5.pdf

In many cases, a loan to an employee to acquire shares will fall within the Consumer Credit (Exempt Agreements) Order 1989, reg 4(c). This covers loans with the following characteristics:

- the loan is made by an employer to an employee to be used to acquire shares from a third party (e.g. by purchasing shares from an EBT, or subscribing for shares in the employer's parent company);
- the loan is made available only to employees;
- the interest rate cannot be increased; and
- the APR of the loan is no more than 1% above base rate.

16.5. Loans to Acquire Shares in Close Companies

If an individual borrows money to acquire **ordinary shares** in a **close company**, tax relief may be available under ICTA 1988, s360 if all the following tests are met:

(a) the company must meet the requirements of ICTA 1988, s13A(2). This means that it must be a **trading company**, the **holding company** of a **trading group**, or a company that invests in land, apart from land that is let to someone **connected** with that company, or a relative or spouse or civil partner); and either

(b) the borrower holds a **material interest**[214] in the **ordinary share capital** of the company; or

(c) the borrower works for the greater part of his time in the "actual management or conduct"[215] of the company or an **associated company** - it is not sufficient just to be an employee.

The company must be close at the **acquisition date**. No relief is available if the company is not close at the **acquisition date** but subsequently becomes close.

On the other hand, the relief is not lost if the company is **close** when the shares are acquired, but subsequently ceases to be **close** [SP3/78].

See section 16.3.11 for the interaction with the taxing provisions for cheap employee loans.

16.6. Loans to Acquire Shares in an Employee-controlled company

If an individual borrows money to acquire **ordinary shares** in an **employee-controlled company**, tax relief may be available under ICTA 1988, s361 if all the following tests are met:

(a) full-time employees beneficially own more than 50% of both the issued **ordinary share capital** and the voting power in the company [ICTA 1988,

---

[214] A **material interest** for these purposes means more than 5% [ICTA 1988, s360A]

[215] RI62 discusses the meaning of "actual management or conduct"

s361(5)]. However, in applying this test, if any full-time employee holds more than 10% of the shares or voting power, it is necessary to ignore the excess over 10% [ICTA 1988, s361(6)]. This test must be satisfied either because the company became an **employee-controlled company** in the year in which the interest is paid, or for at least nine months in that year;

(b) the company must be a **trading company** or the **holding company** of a **trading group** [ICTA 1988, s361(4)(a)(ii)];

(c) the company must be resident in the UK and not resident elsewhere and its shares must not be listed on the London Stock Exchange [ICTA 1988, s361(4)(a)(i)];

(d) the borrower must be a full-time employee throughout the period between borrowing the money and paying the interest. If the borrower terminates employment, the relief remains available for interest paid during the next 12 months [ICTA 1988, s361(4)(d)].

See section 16.3.11 for the interaction with the taxing provisions for cheap employee loans.

16.7. Loans to Participators in Close Companies

If a **close company** makes a loan to a **participator**, or to an **associate** of a **participator**, there is a tax charge at 25% of the amount of the loan. This tax charge will be repaid when the loan is repaid.

16.7.1. What is an associate of a participator?

See ICTA 1988, s417(3) and HMRC Manual CT6115[216]. If the borrower is an EBT, it will be an **associate** of any individual who is a settlor or a beneficiary.

16.7.2. When is the tax due for payment?

The tax becomes payable nine months after the end of the accounting period in which the loan is made. [ICTA 1988, s419(3)].

16.7.3. Application to loan to EBT

This provision applies where the borrower is a corporate trustee [ICTA 1988, s419(6)] and also, in HM Revenue & Customs' view, to an individual trustee who receives a loan [HMRC Manual CT6650b[217]].

16.7.4. Loan to an EBT that is not a Participator

If the borrower is an EBT that already holds shares in the **close company**, or has an **option** to acquire shares, the Trustee will be a **participator** so the loan will be within these provisions.

---

216 http://www.hmrc.gov.uk/manuals/ct123manual/ct6115.htm

217 http://www.hmrc.gov.uk/manuals/ct123manual/ct6650b.htm

If the EBT does not hold shares at the time the loan is made, but later subscribes for new shares in the **close company**, the loan is not subject to ICTA 1988, s419.

If the EBT subsequently purchases shares from a **participator**, HM Revenue & Customs take the view is that this is a loan to that **participator** [ICTA 1988, s419(5)].

16.7.5. Release or Write-off of the Loan

If the loan is released or written off, rather than being repaid, the borrower is treated as having received a distribution equal to the amount written off, grossed up at the dividend ordinary rate [ITTOIA 2005, s416(2)].

16.7.6. The loan is repaid before the tax due date

The tax charge does not apply if the loan is repaid before the due date for payment of the tax. However, if the loan is repaid after the due date for payment of the tax, the company cannot claim repayment until nine months after the end of the accounting period in which the loan was repaid [ICTA 1988, s419(4A)].

16.7.7. Interaction with rules on cheap loans to employees

See section 16.3.8.

17. Corporation Tax Relief

17.1. General Principles

The general rules on corporation tax deductibility apply to employment costs. No deduction is available for employment costs unless they are properly charged to revenue account and incurred wholly and exclusively for the purposes of the trade [ICTA 1988, s74].

In the case of a company with investment business, expenditure is allowable if it constitutes "expenses of management of the company's investment business" [ICTA 1988, s75]. Although this term is not adequately defined in the legislation, such case law as there is indicates that expenditure which would, if incurred by a **trading company**, be deductible under general principles, will constitute expenses of management if incurred by an investment company [*Sun Life Assurance Society v Davidson* 37 TC 330].

The costs of establishing a new employee reward structure that is expected to last for a period of years may be regarded as capital and therefore not deductible [*Atherton v British Insulated and Helsby Cables Ltd* 10 TC 155]. However, there are special provisions to allow deductions for the costs of establishing certain approved schemes (see section 17.6).

A payment that is incurred by an employing company will usually be for the benefit of the trade. Sometimes, however, the costs of a scheme will be borne by a parent company. If so, they should be charged down to the employing companies to comply with transfer pricing rules (see section 17.9).

Payments that are made to substantial shareholders may be regarded by HM Revenue & Customs as having a duality of purpose and therefore be disallowed (see section 5.3.1).

There are special rules on the deductibility of termination payments (see sections 5.3.2 (**redundancy** payments), 5.3.3 (payments on **retirement**) and 5.3.4 (payments for post-termination restrictions)).

There are some cases where the corporation tax deduction can be deferred or denied. These are:

- FA 1989, s43 and FA 2003, Sch24 can operate to defer the corporation tax deduction (see sections 17.2 and 17.3).
- FA 2003, Sch23 can operate to deny a deduction for costs associated with shares and **option**s and replace it with a deduction based on the value delivered to the employee (see section 17.4).
- Exceptionally large pension contributions may be spread over a period of years (see section 3.3.7.2.2).

17.2. Deferral under FA 1989, s43

FA 1989, s43 applies where a company charges remuneration in its accounts for a year, but does not actually pay this to the employee until more than nine months after the end of the year.

This could happen, for example, if the employer has established a cash bonus plan where performance is measured over a period of years (see section 3.1). The employer would make a provision in its accounts at the end of each year for its expected costs relating to that year. However, if it did not actually pay the bonus to the employee during that year, or within the following nine months, the deduction would be deferred [FA 1989, s43(1)].

If the bonus is paid in a later accounting period, it will be deductible for that later period, assuming it meets the general tests of deductibility [FA 1989, s43(4)].

"Remuneration" for these purposes means anything that is earnings, or treated as earnings, under ITEPA 2003 [FA 1989, s43(7)].

Remuneration is treated as paid by the employer when it is treated as received by the employee [FA 1989, s43(6)] (see section 3.1.3.1).

17.3. Deferral under FA 2003, Sch24

17.3.1. Background

FA 2003, Sch24 was introduced when the Inland Revenue lost their case before the Special Commissioners and High Court in *Dextra v MacDonald*. In that case, an employing company made contributions to an EBT. HM Revenue & Customs had argued that the original wording of FA 1989, s43 deferred any corporation tax deduction for those contributions until employees received benefits from the EBT. This argument was rejected by the Special Commissioners and by Neuberger J. The case was appealed to the Court of Appeal and House of Lords on separate grounds.

FA 2003, Sch24 applies when an employer makes an "employee benefit contribution" [FA 2003, Sch24, para 1(1)]. The corresponding corporation tax deduction is deferred until either "qualifying benefits" are provided to employees or "qualifying expenses" are paid out of the contribution [FA 2004, Sch24, para 1(3)].

17.3.2. Employee Benefit Contribution

For FA 2003, Sch24 to apply, there must be an "employee benefit contribution".

A contribution to an **employer-financed retirement benefits scheme** made on or after 6 April 2006 is necessarily an employee benefit contribution [FA 2003, Sch24, para 2(1)(c)]. See section 3.4.6.1.

A transaction that has all the following elements will also be an employee benefit contribution:

- the employer must pay money or transfer an asset to a third party [FA 2003, Sch24, para 1(2)(a)];
- there must be an "employee benefit scheme" [FA 2003, Sch24, para 1(2)(b)]. This is widely defined to include any trust, scheme or other arrangement for the benefit of employees [FA 2003, Sch24, para 9(1)];
- the third party must be entitled or required, under the terms of the employee benefit scheme, to use the money or the asset for or in connection with the provision of benefits to current or former employees of the employer [FA 2003, Sch24, para 9(1)].

17.3.3. Qualifying Benefit

A qualifying benefit is a payment of money or the transfer of an asset to an employee, but does not include a loan to the employee [FA 2004, Sch24, para 2(1)].

This payment or transfer must either give rise to both an employment income tax liability and an NIC charge for the employee, or it must be made in connection with the termination of the recipient's employment [FA 2004, Sch4, para 2(1)].

A payment or transfer will still be a qualifying benefit even if it does not in fact give rise to an employment income tax liability or an NIC charge because the employee in question performed his duties outside the UK, or was **resident** outside the UK [FA 2003, Sch24, para 2(3)].

17.3.4. Qualifying Expenses

Qualifying expenses are any expenses incurred by the third party in operating the employee benefit scheme, which would have been deductible for the employer if it had incurred the expenses itself [FA 2003, Sch24, para 3].

17.3.5. Timing of Deduction

FA 2003, Sch24 does not in itself permit a deduction. It is still necessary to show that a deduction would be available for the employee benefit contribution on general principles [FA 2003, Sch24, para 1(1)(b)].

If the qualifying benefits or qualifying expenses are paid or provided in the same accounting period as the employer makes the employee benefit contribution, then the deduction is allowed for that accounting period. The same applies if the qualifying benefits or qualifying expenses are paid or provided within nine months of the end of the accounting period [FA 2003, Sch24, para 1(3)].

Otherwise, the corporation tax deduction arises in the accounting period in which qualifying benefits are provided out of the employee benefit contribution [FA 2003, Sch24, para 1(4)].

If the qualifying benefit is the provision of cash (except under an **employer-financed retirement benefits scheme** on or after 6 April 2006), it is treated as being provided by the third party when it is treated as received by the employee [FA 2003, Sch24, para 2(5)] (see section 3.1.3.1).

17.3.6. Amount of Deduction

If the qualifying benefit takes the form of the transfer of an asset to the employee, the deduction is limited to the lower of (a) the cost of the asset, or its value at the time it was transferred by the employer and (b) the amount charged to employment income tax on the employee [FA 2003, Sch24, para 5].

17.3.7. Exclusions

FA 2003, Sch24 does not apply to certain types of payment for which there are separate statutory rules on deductibility, such as payments into different types of pension scheme, payments into SIPs, and payments that qualify for relief under FA 2003, Sch23 [FA 2003, Sch24, para 8].

17.4. Relief under FA 2003, Sch23

FA 2003, Sch23 is intended to create symmetry between the employer's corporation tax deduction and the employee's employment income tax liability in relation to certain events where an employee acquires shares. The person who acquires the shares is referred to as "the recipient" [FA 2003, Sch23, para 1(3)].

The events that generate the tax deduction are:

- an acquisition of shares **by reason of employment**
- an acquisition of shares pursuant to an **option**
- a chargeable event in relation to conditional shares acquired before 16 April 2003
- a chargeable event in relation to restricted shares
- a chargeable event in relation to convertible shares

There are certain conditions that must be satisfied in all five cases, and others that relate only to the particular event.

17.4.1. Conditions Generally Applicable

17.4.1.1. Business within the charge to Corporation Tax

The **award** of the shares, or **grant** of the **option**, must originally have been made for the purposes of a business carried on by an employing company that is within the charge to corporation tax [FA 2003, Sch23, para 3]. This would include the overseas branch of a UK company, but not an overseas subsidiary.

17.4.1.2. Corporation tax deductible shares

The shares must be **corporation tax deductible shares** [FA 2003, Sch23, para 4] (see section 21.2). Note that shares in a subsidiary company, or a company controlled by a venture capital fund, will often not be **corporation tax deductible shares**.

The relief is not available where the employee acquires securities that are not shares, although it may be available where the employee converts **convertible securities** into shares. It is not available where the employee acquires cash.

17.4.1.3. *Company whose Shares are Acquired*

The company whose shares are acquired must meet at least one out of four conditions (or five conditions in the case of an **option**). However, the point in time when they have to meet each condition varies. The time when the condition has to be satisfied is not necessarily the same as when the corporation tax deduction arises.

17.4.1.3.1. Shares in the Employing Company

The first condition is that the recipient is a former or prospective employee of the employing company at the time the shares are acquired .

In relation to an **award** of shares, including restricted or convertible shares, this is tested at the **acquisition date** [FA 2003, Sch23, para 6(1)(a)]. Note however that an employment income tax charge may not arise at the **acquisition date**.

In relation to the **exercise** of an **option**, including an **option** to acquire restricted or convertible shares, this is tested at the **exercise date** [FA 2003, Sch23, para 12(a)].

17.4.1.3.2. Shares in a different company

If the company whose shares are acquired is not the employing company, the corporation tax deduction may still be available if it is:

- the **parent company** of the employing company [FA 2003, Sch23, para 6(1)(b) and para 12(b)]; or
- a member of a **consortium** that controls the employing company or its **parent company** [FA 2003, Sch23, para 6(1)(c) and para 12(c)]; or
- a different member of a **consortium** that forms part of the same **commercial association of companies** as the employing company [FA 2003, Sch23, para 6(1)(d) and 12(d)].

In relation to an **award** of shares, including restricted or convertible shares, the group relationship is tested at the **acquisition date** [FA 2003, Sch23, para 6(1)].

In relation to the **exercise** of an **option**, including an **option** to acquire restricted or convertible shares, this is tested at the **grant date** of the **option** [FA 2003, Sch23, para 12].

17.4.1.3.3. Shares in a qualifying successor company

FA 2003, Sch23, para 13 can apply where an **option** is rolled over by agreement in exchange for another **option** on a change of control. If it applies, then the company whose shares are subject to the new **option** is a qualifying successor company [FA 2003, Sch23, para 13(2)(a)] and the corporation tax relief is also rolled over until the **exercise** of the new **option** [FA 2003, Sch23, para 13(2)(b)].

The following conditions must be satisfied:

- the old **option** would have qualified under the tests in FA 2003, Sch23, para 12 (see section 17.4.1.3.2);
- the exchange of **options** is by agreement – the relief does not apply to a compulsory exchange [FA 2003, Sch23, para 13(1)(b)];
- the company whose shares are subject to the new **option** is the acquiring company or its **parent company**, or a member of a **consortium** that owns the acquiring company or its parent, or a different member of a **consortium** that forms part of the same **commercial association of companies** as the acquiring company [FA 2003, Sch23, para 13(4)].

17.4.2. Award of Shares (Not Restricted and Not Convertible)

17.4.2.1. Availability of Relief

The shares must have been **award**ed either to the employee or to some other person by reason of the employee's employment [FA 2003, Sch23, para 1(1)(a)].

Usually the employee must be subject to a charge to income tax under ITEPA 2003 in respect of the **award** of shares [FA 2003, Sch23, para 7(1)(a)].

However, the relief will also be available if the employee would have been subject to a tax charge under ITEPA 2003, if he had been **resident** and **ordinarily resident** in the UK, and performing the duties of the employment in the UK [FA 2003, Sch23, para 7(1)(b)].

The extension of the relief to employees who are not **resident** and **ordinarily resident** in the UK is not as wide as first appears. Given that the shares must have been **award**ed for the purposes of a business within the charge to UK corporation tax (see section 17.4.1.1), the most common situation where it applies is in relation to employees of the overseas branch of a UK company.

The relief is not available if there has been a charge under ITEPA 2003, s446UA (pre-acquisition avoidance) in relation to the shares [FA 2003, Sch23, para 7(3)]. For further information on this charge, see section 11.1.6.

17.4.2.2. Amount of Relief

The amount of relief is usually the same as the amount charged to income tax, that is it is the **CGT value** of the shares on the **acquisition date** less the consideration, if any, given by the employee [FA 2003, Sch23, para 8(1)]. There may be instances where the relief is different from the amount charged to income tax: this would be the case where the **money's worth value**, on which the income tax charge would be based, is different from the **CGT value** on which the corporation tax relief would be based.

17.4.3. Acquisition of Shares through Option

17.4.3.1. Availability of Relief

The **optionholder** must originally have obtained the **option** by reason of the employment, either of the **optionholder** or some other person [FA 2003, Sch23, para 1(1)(b)]. In other words the relief would not be available if the **option** was originally **grant**ed to one person by reason of that person's employment and then transferred to the **optionholder** for reasons unconnected with employment.

The **optionholder** must both obtain the **option** in that way and subsequently acquire the shares [FA 2003, Sch23, para 1(1)(b)].

Usually the acquisition of shares pursuant to the **option** must be a chargeable event under ITEPA 2003, s476. It does not matter if no tax is actually payable, for example because the **option** is a **CSOP, SAYE** or **EMI option** [FA 2003, Sch23, para 14(1)(a)].

However, the relief will also be available if the employee would have been subject to a tax charge under ITEPA 2003, s476 if he had been **resident** and **ordinarily resident** in the UK, and performing the duties of the employment in the UK [FA 2003, Sch23, para 7(1)(b)].

17.4.3.2. Amount of Relief

The amount of relief is effectively the same as the amount charged to income tax, that is it is the **CGT value** of the shares on the **exercise date** less the **exercise price** and the **grant price**, if any [FA 2003, Sch23, para 15(1)]. However, it does not include any secondary NIC paid by the **optionholder** [FA 2003, Sch23, para 15(2)(b)].

If the option is a **qualifying option** for EMI purposes, the amount of relief is effectively the amount that would have been relieved if the option had been non-qualifying [FA 2003, Sch23, para 21(4A)].

If the option has been rolled over, and the shares are in a qualifying successor company (see section 17.4.1.3.3) then the value of the old option is not taken into account as consideration for the new option. This is not clear from the legislation, but was confirmed by the Paymaster-General during the Committee Stage of FA 2003. See Hansard at
http://www.publications.parliament.uk/pa/cm200203/cmstand/b/st030612/pm/30612s03.htm

17.4.4. Conditional, Restricted and Convertible Shares

17.4.4.1. Availability of Relief

Corporation tax relief is also available:

- when an income tax charge arises under ITEPA 2003, old s427(1) in relation to conditional shares that were acquired before 16 April 2003 (see section 12.2) [FA 2003, Sch23, old para 20(2)];

- when a general earnings charge arises on the **award** of restricted shares, either because the shares are forfeitable for five years or more, or the employer and employee make a **Section 425 election** or a **Section 431 election** (see sections 11.1.3 and 11.1.4) [FA 2003, Sch23, para 21(2)(a)];
- when a general earnings charge arises on the **award** of convertible shares (see section 11.1.2) [FA 2003, Sch23, para 22C(2)(a)];
- when an employment income tax charge arises under ITEPA 2003, s476 in relation to the acquisition of restricted shares or convertible shares pursuant to an **option** (see section 8.1.2.1) [FA 2003, Sch23, para 21(2)(a) and para 22C(2)(a)];
- when an employment income tax charge arises under ITEPA 2003, s426 in relation to restricted shares (see section 12.3.2) [FA 2003, Sch23, para 21(2)(b)];
- when an employment income charge arises under ITEPA 2003, s439(3)(a) (see section 12.4.2) [FA 2003, Sch23, para 22C(2)(b) as qualified by FA 2003, Sch23, para 22C(11)];
- when an employee dies at a time when he, or an **associated person**, holds restricted shares or **convertible securities** acquired by reason of his employment [FA 2003, Sch23, para 21(1)(c) and para 22C(2)(c)].

Note that relief is available under the last two bullet points in relation to **convertible securities**, whether or not they are shares [FA 2003, Sch23, para 22B(2)], but only where the conversion is into **corporation tax deductible shares** that meet the requirements described in section 21.2 [FA 2003, Sch23, para 22C(11)].

17.4.4.2. Amount of Relief

The amount of relief is effectively the same as the amount charged to income tax. **Table 8** shows, for each section that charges income tax, what the corresponding paragraph is that determines the amount of corporation tax relief.

Table 8: Income Tax Charges and Corporation Tax Relief

Income Tax Charging Section in ITEPA 2003	**Amount of Corporation Tax Relief**	**Relevant Paragraph in FA 2003, Sch23**
Old s427(1)	**CGT value** of shares at time of chargeable event, less any consideration given for the shares or for their ceasing to be forfeitable	Old para 21(2)
S62 on **Award** of Restricted Shares	Amount of general earnings	Para 21(3)
S62 on **Award** of Convertible Shares	Amount of general earnings before any adjustment where something has been done to avoid tax or NIC	Para 22C(3)

Income Tax Charging Section in ITEPA 2003	**Amount of Corporation Tax Relief**	**Relevant Paragraph in FA 2003, Sch23**
S476 on Acquisition of Restricted Shares pursuant to **Option**	Amount of employment income,	Para 21(4)
S476 on Acquisition of Convertible Shares pursuant to **Option**	Amount of employment income before any adjustment where something has been done to avoid tax or NIC	Para 22C(4)
S476 on Acquisition of Convertible Shares pursuant to **Qualifying Option**	Amount of employment income before relief under EMI Code	Para 22C(4ZA)
S426	Amount of employment income	Para 21(6)
S439(3)(a)	Amount of employment income	Para 22C(6)

If the tax relief arises because the employee dies, there is no corresponding income tax charge.

17.4.4.2.1. Restricted Shares Held on Employee's Death

In relation to restricted shares, the amount of corporation tax relief is equal to what would have been the chargeable amount for income tax purposes under ITEPA 2003, s427(3)(c) if the employee had disposed of the restricted shares immediately before his death [FA 2003, Sch23, para 21(7)]. However, it is necessary to disregard:

- ITEPA 2003, s428(6) – so assume that the employee would not have incurred any disposal costs in relation to the shares; and
- ITEPA 2003, s428(9) – so assume that the employee would have sold the shares for **CGT value**.

17.4.4.2.2. Convertible securities held on Employee's Death

In relation to **convertible securities**, the relievable amount for corporation tax is equal to what would have been the chargeable amount for income tax purposes on the next chargeable event that arises under ITEPA 2003, s439(3)(a) after the employee's death [FA 2003, Sch23, para 22C(7)].

17.4.4.3. Interaction with Artificial Depression in Value Rules

There is no corporation tax deduction for amounts taxed through the artificial depression in value rules (see section 12.5).

FA 2003, Sch23, para 21(8) says that ITEPA 2003, s446E(6) is disregarded in calculating the amount of corporation tax relief. The effect of this is that the corporation tax relief is based on the value after the artificial depression, whereas the income tax charge ignores the artificial depression.

In relation to **convertible securities**, FA 2003, Sch23, para 22C(8) disapplies ITEPA 2003, s446G and s446H in determining the amount of corporation tax relief. The effect of this is to increase CE and reduce AG where there has been an artificial depression in value and thereby reduce the amount of corporation tax relief (see section 12.4.4).

17.4.4.4. *Interaction with Artificial Enhancement in Value Rules*

If the shares have been artificially enhanced in value, the amount of the enhancement is ignored in determining the amount of corporation tax relief in relation to **restricted securities** [FA 2003, Sch23, para 21(8)].

17.4.4.5. *Secondary NIC*

If the employee pays the secondary NIC arising, whether on the acquisition of restricted or convertible shares through an **option**, or on a subsequent chargeable event in relation to restricted shares or **convertible securities**, that is ignored in determining the amount of corporation tax relief [FA 2003, Sch23, para 21(4), 21(6), 22C(4) and 22C(6)].

17.4.4.6. *Employees outside scope of UK taxation*

The relief will also be available if the employee would have been subject to one of the tax charges listed in **Table 8**, if he had been **resident** and **ordinarily resident** in the UK, and performing the duties of the employment in the UK [FA 2003, Sch23, old para 20(3), para 20(4) and para 22C(10)].

The extension of the relief to employees who are not **resident** and **ordinarily resident** in the UK is not as wide as first appears. Given that the shares must have been **award**ed for the purposes of a business within the charge to UK corporation tax (see section 17.4.1.1), the most common situation where it applies is in relation to employees of the overseas branch of a UK company.

17.4.4.7. *Restricted and convertible*

Where an employee acquires shares that are both restricted and convertible, the relief is limited to the greater of the relief calculated under the restricted shares rules and the relief calculated under the **convertible securities** rules [FA 2003, Sch23, para 21(5) and 22C(5)].

17.4.5. Company that is Entitled to the Relief

The corporation tax relief is given to the company that was carrying on the business, for the purposes of which the shares were **award**ed, or the **option** was **grant**ed [FA 2003, Sch23, para 9(1) and 16(1)]. Difficulties arise where the **award** or **grant** was made for the purposes of more than one business, or where the business has been transferred within a group.

17.4.5.1. Award for purpose of more than one business

If the shares were **award**ed, or **option**s **grant**ed, for the purposes of more than one business, then the relief is apportioned between the different businesses on a just and reasonable basis [FA 2003, Sch23, para 9(4) and 16(4)].

17.4.5.2. Transfer of Business within a Group

The business for the purposes of which the **option**s were **grant**ed, or the shares were **award**ed, may cease to be carried on by the same company before the corporation tax relief arises. If that is because substantially the whole business (or the relevant part) is transferred to another group company, then the relief will follow the business, and can be claimed by the successor company [FA 2003, Sch23, para 23].

17.4.6. Relationship between Sch23 and other deductions

17.4.6.1. Priority of Deductions under SIP Code

Corporation tax deductions under the **SIP** code take priority over deductions under FA 2003, Sch23 (see section 4.2.4.17). Any amount deducted under the **SIP** code cannot be deducted again under FA 2003, Sch23 [FA 2003, Sch23, para 24].

17.4.6.2. Deductions claimed for periods beginning before 1 January 2003

If the employing company, or any other company, claimed deductions for the costs of providing the shares against its profits for an accounting period beginning before 1 January 2003, then the relief available under FA 2003, Sch23 will be reduced by the amount of those deductions [FA 2003, Sch23, para 33]. It is not clear how this is supposed to work where deductions were claimed over a number of years in relation to a pool of shares, perhaps held in an EBT, because it may be difficult or impossible to identify particular deductions with particular shares. In practice, it is understood that HM Revenue & Customs will agree to any reasonable method of identifying shares with deductions, such as averaging, or first in first out, provided that this is applied consistently.

17.4.6.3. Deductions for periods beginning on or after 1 January 2003

Where relief is available under FA 2003, Sch23 for any accounting period, no deduction can be claimed by the employing company (or any other company) in respect of the cost of providing the shares for that or any other period [FA 2003, Sch23, para 25(1)].

The problem with this is that, until the event occurs that triggers the relief, it is impossible to know for certain whether relief will be available under FA 2003, Sch23. The relief may be denied if, for example, the shares cease to be **corporation tax deductible shares** if the company is taken over by an unlisted company (see section 21.2).

This does not preclude a deduction for ancillary costs in relation to the share plan. FA 2003, Sch23, para 25(3) sets out certain expenses that are not regarded as part of the cost of providing the shares. These are: establishment costs; administration costs; borrowing costs; fees, commission, stamp duty and incidental costs.

For additional certainty that a deduction will eventually be available, the company should consider operating "symmetry" arrangements (see section 17.5). A claim for relief would be denied for the period in which the symmetry payment is made, both because of FA 2003, Sch23, para 25(1) and because of FA 2003, Sch24, para 1 (see section 17.3). However, if the FA 2003, Sch23 deduction is eventually denied, but the event that gives rise to the income tax charge is the provision of a qualifying benefit (see section 17.3.3), then relief should be available in that year, although it might be limited to the original symmetry payment (see section 17.3.6).

17.5. Symmetry Arrangements

Symmetry arrangements were widely used before 2003 to secure corporation tax deductions for the value of shares delivered to employees through **options**. They are still used by companies where relief will not or may not be available under FA 2003, Sch23 (see section 17.4).

Under symmetry, when an **option** was **exercised**, the employing company made a payment to an EBT equal to the **option gain**. The EBT used that payment, plus the **exercise price**, to subscribe for new shares in the parent company and deliver them to the **optionholder**.

This established a cost in the employing company for which it could claim a corporation tax deduction, subject to any disallowance under FA 2003, Sch23, para 25(1) or under FA 2003, Sch24, para 1 if the transfer of shares is not a qualifying benefit. It usually will be a qualifying benefit, but it may not be if the **option** was **granted** before 6 April 1999 so that there is no NIC charge.

However, the anti-arbitrage rules may apply if the payment from the employing company to the parent company is greater than the fair value of the option for accounting purposes (see section 17.9). Alternatively, HM Revenue & Customs may disallow part of the deduction under intra-UK transfer pricing rules on the basis that it is not seen as being at arm's length.

17.6. Establishment and Operation of Approved Schemes

There are specific reliefs for the costs of establishing approved share plans, which would otherwise be disallowable capital expenditure.

These are:

- ICTA 1988, s84A for **CSOP** and **SAYE**
- ICTA 1988, Sch4AA, para 7 for **SIP**.

17.7. Pension Contributions

See section 3.3.7.2.

17.8. Cash Cancellation Payments

If a company makes a payment to **optionholder**s to cancel existing **option**s, it may not be deductible under general principles. If the payment is made by the acquiring company on a takeover, it may be viewed by HM Revenue & Customs as part of the capital investment it is making. If the payment is made by the company that **grant**ed the **option**, it may be seen as the discharge of a capital obligation. If the payment is made by the employing company, it may fail the "wholly and exclusively" test, because it is hard to perceive a trading purpose. Nevertheless HM Revenue & Customs has allowed deductions in particular cases where the facts supported a deduction.

A deduction will not be available under FA 2003, Sch23, since no shares are acquired [FA 2003, Sch23, para 1(1)(b)].

In a takeover situation, it may be better to allow employees to **exercise** their **option**s and then sell the shares to the acquiring company, if this can be done with relief under FA 2003, Sch23, para 1(1)(b).

Alternatively, if symmetry arrangements (see section 17.5) were established when the **option**s were **grant**ed, it may be possible to obtain a corporation tax deduction for a payment to the EBT, which in turn makes a payment to the **optionholder** to cancel the **option**.

17.9. Transfer Pricing and Anti-Arbitrage Issues

There is a complex interaction between three pieces of legislation: the intra-UK transfer pricing rules in ICTA 1988, Sch28AA; the corporation tax deductions for share schemes in FA 2003, Sch23; and the anti-arbitrage rules in F(No.2) A 2005. The following section is a brief overview of how the rules affect a UK group with no overseas operations.

The transfer pricing rules do not generally affect small and medium-sized enterprises because of the exclusion in ICTA 1988, Sch28AA, para 5B.

Neither do they affect single company situations, where the employing company is the same entity as the provider of the shares.

The background is that, where a parent company operates a share scheme and provides shares to employees of a subsidiary company, that is the provision of a business facility by the parent to the subsidiary. The parent should charge an arm's length fee to the subsidiary for the facility; if it does not there may be a transfer pricing adjustment.

The problem this causes is that the receipt, or transfer pricing adjustment, may be taxable income for the parent but, the corresponding payment or adjustment may be disallowed for the subsidiary because of FA 2003, Sch23, para 25.

In December 2005, HM Revenue & Customs published revised guidance on this issue. This is on their website at http://www.hmrc.gov.uk/international/new-share-plan-guidance.pdf and applies to accounting periods beginning on or after 1 January 2005.

They confirm in the guidance that they will not make a transfer pricing adjustment on the parent company where the payment from the employing company to the parent company is no greater than the fair value of the shares or option. This is subject to the parent company treating the receipt as a capital item and not seeking a deduction for the cost of related share purchases [Share Plan Guidance, para 25].

Similarly, they will not apply the anti-arbitrage rules to the parent company if the payment from the employing company is limited to the fair value of the option or shares [Share Plan Guidance, para 30].

17.10. Termination Payments

17.10.1. Payments in Respect of more than one Employment

A termination payment will not be an allowable deduction for the employing company unless it is incurred "wholly and exclusively" for the purposes of its trade [ICTA 1988, s74].

If the employee concerned is employed by more than one company, then each company should pay its own share of the termination payment. Otherwise, the payment may fail the "wholly and exclusively" test for the company that pays it. This view is supported by case law [*Garforth v Tankard Carpets Limited* 53 TC 342, *Marshall Richards Machine Co Ltd v Jewitt* 36 TC 511 and *Watneys London Limited v Pike* 57 TC 372].

18. Company Law Issues

18.1. Public Offers of Securities

When a company offers shares or other securities to its employees, this may be considered an offer to the public. If it is an offer to the public, it is necessary to publish a prospectus, which must be approved in advance by the UK Listing Authority [FSMA 2000, s85(1)].

There are, however, two exemptions which are particularly relevant to smaller companies offering shares to employees. These are:

- securities where the total consideration of the offer is less than €2.5 million [FSMA 2000, Sch11A, para 9(1)]. At a meeting held with ifsProShare on 27 November 2005, representatives of the Financial Services Authority and the European Commission stated their views that it is not necessary to publish a prospectus in relation to free share awards or grants of options. A full note of this meeting is available at http://www.ifsproshare.org/eso/pdf/sub_group_meeting_note251105.pdf.
  It is important to note that these comments are not binding on either the Financial Services Authority or the European Commission and are for guidance only;
- securities offered to fewer than 100 persons, excluding qualified investors [FSMA 2000, s86(1)(b)]. It is unlikely that most employees will be qualified investors, although some may be. The definition of "qualified investor" is in FSMA 2000, s86(7).

Although there is a further exemption from the prospectus requirements for offers of shares to employees, this only applies to listed companies [Prospectus Rules 1.2.2 (5)].

18.2. Corporate Authority

The Memorandum of Association will generally contain power for the company to establish schemes for the benefit of its employees. It is important to check that this power exists.

The power to establish such a scheme will generally be vested in the Directors. However, there may be a requirement for the plan to be approved by shareholders; such a requirement might arise under a shareholders' agreement.

18.3. Auditor Notification of Written Resolution

If a private company proposes to seek a written resolution of its shareholders, the resolution must be notified to the auditors before it is sent to the shareholders [CA 1985, s381B].

18.4. Issuing Shares for less than Par

A company cannot issue new shares to any person for a consideration which is less than the nominal or par value of those shares [CA 1985, s100].

Note that what is relevant is the par value of the shares, not their market value.

If a company **grants** an **option** to subscribe for shares at less than their par value, it will be unable to satisfy the **option** unless it capitalises sufficient distributable reserves to issue the shares credited as fully paid.

Alternatively, the company could make a contribution to an EBT, which could subscribe for the shares at par and transfer them to the **optionholder** for no payment.

18.5. Restrictions on Allotment of Shares

The general rule is that a company cannot issue new shares without the prior approval of shareholders [CA 1985, s80]. However, this does not apply to allotments of shares through an **employees' share scheme**, since these are not "relevant securities" [CA 1985, s80(2)(a)]. It is therefore important to ensure that the share option plan does indeed constitute an **employees' share scheme** as defined in CA 1985, s743 (see section 18.8).

18.6. Pre-Emption Rights

When a company issues new shares, any existing shareholder has a general right to be allotted a proportionate part of that new issue [CA 1985, s89 to 95]. This right can be overridden by provisions in the Articles of a private company.

The statutory rules do not apply to the **grant** of an **option** to subscribe for shares to be held under an **employees' share scheme** or the allotment of shares under such a scheme [CA 1985, s89(5)].

18.7. Financial Assistance

It is illegal for a company to give financial assistance to a third party for the acquisition of its own shares [CA 1985, s151].

18.7.1. Prospective Financial Assistance

CA 1985, s151(1) prohibits prospective financial assistance. It applies where a person is acquiring or proposing to acquire shares in a company. It is unlawful for that company, or any of its subsidiaries, to give financial assistance directly or indirectly for the purpose of that acquisition.

18.7.2. Retrospective Financial Assistance

CA 1985, s151(2) prohibits retrospective financial assistance. It applies where a person has acquired shares in a company and a liability has been incurred (by that or any other person) for the purposes of that acquisition. It prohibits the company or any of its subsidiaries from giving financial assistance directly or indirectly for the purpose of reducing or discharging that liability.

18.7.3. Exemption for Employees' share scheme

There is an exemption if the financial assistance is provided by the company, in good faith in the interests of the company, for the purposes of an **employees' share scheme** [CA 1985, s153(4)(b)]. So, for example, a contribution to an EBT should be legal, assuming the directors are acting bona fide, i.e. there is no ulterior purpose.

18.7.4. Exemption for Transactions Between Employees

There is a further exemption for the provision of financial assistance which enables or facilitates transactions in the company's shares between employees, former employees and their spouses, civil partners, surviving spouses and surviving civil partners, children or step-children under the age of eighteen, if those transactions involve the acquisition of beneficial ownership of those shares by those persons [CA 1985, s153(4)(bb)].

18.7.5. Special Rules for Public Companies

The two exemptions mentioned in sections 18.7.3 and 18.7.4 are limited in how they apply to public companies.

Financial assistance given by a **public company** will only fall within one of the exemptions if and to the extent that, either the company's net assets are not reduced by the giving of the assistance (e.g. because the assistance takes the form of a loan or guarantee) or the assistance is provided from distributable profits [CA 1985, s154].

18.7.6. "Whitewash" Procedure for Private Companies

A private company can provide financial assistance if it is able to use the "whitewash" procedure set out in CA 1985, s155.

18.8. Definition of Employees' Share Scheme

If an arrangement is an **employees' share scheme**, it will be exempt from various provisions in CA 1985, FSMA 2000, and regulations issued under FSMA 2000.

For the purposes of CA 1985, an **employees' share scheme** is a scheme for encouraging or facilitating the holding of shares or debentures in a company by or for the benefit of:

(a) the bona fide employees or former employees of the company, the company's **subsidiary** or **holding company**, or a **subsidiary** of the company's **holding company**, or

(b) the spouses, civil partners, surviving spouses or surviving civil partners or children or step-children under the age of 18 of such employees or former employees.

[CA 1985, s743].

A wider definition is used in FSMA 2000 and the statutory instruments issued under it. This is because the definition of "group" for FSMA 2000 purposes includes a subsidiary undertaking in which a member of a group has a "participating interest", which includes a holding of 20% or more [CA 1985, s260(2)]. Therefore employees of joint venture companies can be regarded as within an employees' share scheme for FSMA 2000 purposes but not for CA 1985 purposes.

18.8.1. What is a "scheme"?

There is very little statutory or case law authority on what the word "scheme" means in this context.

The general view among practitioners is that it refers to an arrangement that is capable of covering more than one employee. So, for example, a contract between the company and a single employee would not be a "scheme".

18.8.2. Encouraging or Facilitating the Holding of Shares

The purpose of the scheme must be to encourage or facilitate the holding of shares. It would not be sufficient if the scheme was established for a different purpose, but held shares to achieve that purpose.

18.8.3. By or For the Benefit of

It is not necessary for the shares actually to be transferred into the hands of the employees. It would be sufficient if an EBT trustee acquired shares and held them for the benefit of the employees.

18.8.4. Bona Fide Employees

A non-executive director is not a "bona fide employee", and neither is a consultant.

18.9. Disclosure Requirements

An unlisted company must disclose all the following items of reward conferred on directors in the notes to its accounts:

1. the aggregate amount of emoluments [CA 1985, Sch6, para 1(1)(a)]
2. the aggregate amount of gains made by directors on the exercise of share **options** [CA 1985, Sch6, para 1(1)(b)]
3. the aggregate amount of money paid to directors under long-term incentive schemes [CA 1985, Sch6, para 1(1)(c)(i)]
4. the net value of assets, other than cash, shares and share **options**, provided to directors under long-term incentive schemes [CA 1985, Sch6, para 1(1)(c)(ii) as qualified by CA 1985, Sch6, para 1(2)(a)]
5. the aggregate of contributions made on behalf of directors to money purchase pension schemes [CA 1985, Sch6, para 1(1)(d)]

6. the number of directors who are accruing benefits under company-sponsored pension schemes [CA 1985, Sch6, para 1(1)(e)]
7. the number of directors who **exercised** share **options** [CA 1985, Sch6, para 1(2)(b)(i)]
8. the number of directors who have received, or may receive, shares under a long-term incentive scheme [CA 1985, Sch6, para 1(2)(b)(ii)]
9. if the aggregate of the amounts in paragraphs 1, 3 and 4 above exceeds £200,000, then the company must disclose how much of those amounts are attributable to the highest-paid director, and also the aggregate money purchase pension contributions made on behalf of the highest-paid director [CA 1985, Sch6, para 2(1)]
10. if the aggregate of the amounts in paragraphs 1, 3 and 4 above exceeds £200,000, then the company must disclose whether the highest paid director **exercised** any share **options** or received any shares under a long-term incentive scheme [CA 1985, Sch6, para 2(3)]
11. the aggregate amount of any compensation paid to a director for loss of office [CA 1985, Sch6, para 8]
12. any loans, **quasi-loans** or other dealings in favour of directors [CA 1985, Sch6, Part II]
13. the directors' interests in securities of the company [CA 1985, Sch7, para 2A]
14. details of any right to subscribe for shares **granted** to or **exercised** by a director or a member of his immediate family [CA 1985, Sch7, para 2B].

18.10. Financial Services and Markets Act 2000 (FSMA 2000)

18.10.1. Carrying on a Regulated Activity

It is an offence for any person to carry on a regulated activity in the UK unless they are authorised by the Financial Services Authority or are exempt from authorisation [FSMA 2000, s19]. There are several activities that a company, or an EBT trustee, might undertake in the course of establishing and operating an **employees' share scheme**.

18.10.1.1. Buying and Selling Shares as Principal or Agent

Where a company, or an EBT trustee, deals in shares as a principal for the purposes of an **employees' share scheme**, this is not a regulated activity [FSMA (Regulated Activities) Order 2001, article 71(1)]. The same applies if the company, or the Trustee, deals in shares as an agent for the purposes of an **employees' share scheme** [FSMA (Regulated Activities) Order 2001, article 71(3)].

18.10.1.2. Making Arrangements for Another Person to Buy, Sell, or Subscribe for Shares

If a company, or an EBT trustee, arranges deals in shares on behalf of an employee for the purposes of an **employees' share scheme**, this is not a regulated activity [FSMA (Regulated Activities) Order 2001, article 71(4)].

18.10.1.3. Safeguarding and Administering Investments

If a company, or an EBT trustee, safeguards and administers shares for the purposes of an **employees' share scheme**, this is not a regulated activity [FSMA (Regulated Activities) Order 2001, article 71(5)].

18.10.1.4. Advising on the merits of buying, selling and subscribing for shares.

There is no exemption where a company or an EBT trustee advises on the merits of participation in a share scheme. It is legal to explain the consequences of participation but not to 'sell' the scheme.

18.10.2. Financial Promotion

A person who is not authorised cannot communicate an invitation or inducement to engage in investment activity unless they obtain approval of the communication by an authorised person or fall within an exemption [FSMA (Financial Promotion) Order 2005].

Many activities inherent in launching and operating an **employees' share scheme** constitute "communication".

There is an exemption where the company, or an EBT trustee, communicates information for the purposes of an **employees' share scheme** [FSMA (Financial Promotion) Order 2005, article 67].

There is a further exemption for any communication which is made by an employer to an employee in relation to a group personal pension scheme or a stakeholder pension scheme [FSMA (Financial Promotion) Order 2005, article 81].

18.10.3. Misleading, False and Deceptive Statements

It is a criminal offence where a person knowingly or recklessly makes a misleading, false or deceptive statement, promise or forecast [FSMA 2000, s397].

There is no exemption from this, so any information that a company provides to employees must be carefully scrutinised to be sure of its accuracy.

18.11. Loans to Directors

It is illegal for a company to make a loan to a director of the company or of its **holding company** or to enter into a guarantee or provide security in connection with a loan to such a director [CA 1985, s330(2)].

It is illegal for a **public company**, or a company in the same group as a **public company**, to make a loan or a '**quasi-loan**' to a director or anyone connected with a director [CA 1985, s330(3)].

This does not prohibit a loan to a trustee of an **employees' share scheme** of which the director is a beneficiary [CA 1985, s346(3)(b)], unless the director himself is a trustee.

This does not prohibit the issue of shares partly paid.

There is an exemption for loans by a company to one of its directors (or a director of its **holding company**) not exceeding, in total, £5,000 [CA 1985, s334].

18.12. Interests in Contracts

Directors will often have a financial interest in a reward plan being considered at a Board meeting. They must declare this interest at the first meeting of the directors when the reward plan is discussed [CA 1985, s317].

The Articles of Association should specify how the Directors should make a decision if one of their own members is financially interested in the outcome of that decision. For example, if the company's Articles of Association follow Table A, a director who will be eligible to participate in a reward structure will not be able to vote at the Board meeting that establishes that structure [Table A, reg 94] or be counted in the quorum [Table A, reg 95]. This may mean that the Board cannot be quorate. In these circumstances it may be necessary to convene a shareholder's meeting to authorise a temporary suspension of that provision of the Articles.

18.13. Membership of Holding company

A company cannot hold shares in a company which is its **holding company** [CA 1985, s23].

However, if the **subsidiary** company is the trustee of a trust, such as an EBT or a pension scheme, it is excluded from this prohibition, unless the **holding company** or a **subsidiary** of the **holding company** is beneficially interested under the trust [CA 1985, s23(2)].

18.14. Frequently Asked Questions on Company Law

18.14.1. Can a director of the Company be a trustee of an EBT?

Yes, but this will make it illegal for the company to make a loan to the trustees [CA 1985, s330].

18.14.2. Can a company issue shares to its directors without requiring them to make immediate payment?

If this is achieved by way of a loan to the directors, it will be illegal [CA 1985, s330].

If the directors undertake to pay the cash to the company at a future date, this is a "credit transaction" [CA 1985, s331(7)]. This cannot be entered into with a director by a "relevant company" [CA 1985, s330(4)]. A relevant company is a **public company** or a member of a group that contains a **public company** [CA 1985, s331(6)].

Another possibility would be to issue partly paid shares to the directors.

19. Accounting Treatment

19.1. Accounting for Employment Costs – General

In many cases, employment costs will be clearly attributable to the accounts for one period and charged in that same period.

More complex accounting for employment costs is required in the following circumstances:

- in relation to costs of a defined benefit pension scheme, but this is outside the scope of this book;
- in relation to medium to long-term cash bonuses, including share appreciation rights, where the cost is incurred over a period of years (see section 19.2);
- in relation to **award**s of shares or share **option**s, where issues of valuation arise and where a cost is incurred over a period of years (see section 19.3);
- in relation to the secondary NIC arising in relation to costs incurred over a period of years (see section 19.4);
- in relation to the corporation tax deductions associated with bonuses, shares or share **option**s, where the cash benefit of the deduction may be deferred (see section 19.5);
- in relation to employee benefit trusts (see section 19.6.2).

19.2. Accounting for Cash Bonuses and Share Appreciation Rights

A cash bonus that is earned by performance over a period of years represents a contingent liability of the employing company. FRS 12 says that the company should recognise the liability by making a provision, but only in the following circumstances:

- where the company has a present obligation (legal or constructive) as a result of a past event – this will usually be the case where the company has granted the bonus rights before the balance sheet date;
- it is probable that a transfer of economic benefits will be required to settle the obligation – in other words it is more likely than not that the performance conditions will be satisfied; and
- a reliable estimate can be made of the amount of the obligation.

Where these conditions are met, the company should make its best estimate of what it would cost to pay out the bonus on the balance sheet date, and make a provision for this amount, less any amount already provided.

The accounting treatment of a share appreciation right is subtly different and is set out in FRS 20, paras 30 to 33. This is a share-based payment arrangement settled in cash.

If the share appreciation rights are fully **vested** immediately, which would be unusual, then the company has to recognise the rights as a cost immediately.

If the share appreciation rights do not **vest** unless the employee remains employed until the end of a **vesting period**, then the company has to recognise a liability to pay for the services as the employee renders the services during the period. In other words, the cost is spread over the **vesting period**.

In either case, except for companies that apply the Financial Reporting Standard for Smaller Entities (FRSSE), the liability has to be measured using an option pricing model (see section 19.3), at each reporting date until it is settled. Companies that apply the FRSSE do not have to use an option pricing model, but will nevertheless have to accrue the cost in accordance with FRS 12.

19.3. Accounting for Employment-related Securities and Options

19.3.1. General

Companies that apply the FRSSE do not have to recognise **award**s of shares or share **option**s as a cost in their accounts [FRS 20, para 1A].

Other companies do have to recognise any "share-based payment transaction" as a cost [FRS 20, para 1]. This includes the **grant** of a share **option** or the **award** of shares to an employee.

FRS 20, para 2 draws a distinction between equity-settled and cash-settled share-based payment transactions, and hybrid transactions. The distinction is whether the liability will be settled in shares, cash, or both.

Section 19.3.2 sets out the accounting treatment for equity-based share payment transactions.

Section 19.3.3 sets out the accounting treatment for cash-based share payment transactions.

Section 19.3.4 sets out the accounting treatment for hybrid transactions.

Section 19.3.5 sets out the effect of **vesting** conditions.

Section 19.3.6 shows how these accounting treatments apply to the forms of employee share plan and **option** plan described in this book.

19.3.2. Equity-Settled Share-Based Payment Transactions

19.3.2.1. Measurement Date

The company has to measure the fair value of the equity instruments **award**ed to employees on the **grant date** [FRS 20, para 11].

19.3.2.2. Period over which Costs are Recognised

If the employee is immediately entitled to the equity instruments, then the cost is recognised in full on the **award** date [FRS 20, para 14] with a corresponding entry to equity.

Where there is a **vesting period**, the cost is spread over the **vesting period** [FRS 20, para 15]. If the **vesting period** is a fixed period of time, the cost is spread over that period [FRS 20, para 15(a)]. If the **vesting period** ends when a performance condition is satisfied, then the company has to estimate how long it will take before that happens [FRS 20, para 15(b)].

19.3.2.3. Measuring the Fair Value of Shares

Where the company **award**s unlisted shares (or **option**s over unlisted shares) to employees, it is necessary to take an estimated market price [FRS 20, Appendix B, para B2]. This should take account of particular conditions on which the **award** is made, for example if the employee is not entitled to dividends during the **vesting period** or there are restrictions on saleability. It should not, however, take account of **vesting** conditions, which are treated separately (see section 19.3.5) [FRS 20, Appendix B, para B3].

19.3.2.4. Measuring the Fair Value of Options

The company should measure the fair value of **option**s using an option-pricing model, such as the Cox-Ross-Rubinstein model (sometimes called the binomial model) or the Black-Scholes-Merton model [FRS 20, Appendix B, para B5]. There are several examples of option-pricing models available; for example, a Black-Scholes-Merton calculator is at
http://www.numa.com/derivs/ref/calculat/option/calc-opa.htm
The model requires the following minimum inputs:

- **Exercise price**
- Expected Life (see section 19.3.2.4.1)
- **Market value** of Underlying Shares (see section 19.3.2.4.2)
- Expected Volatility (see section 19.3.2.4.3)
- Expected Dividends (see section 19.3.2.4.4)
- Risk-free Interest Rate (see section 19.3.2.4.5).

The model may also consider dilution (see section 19.3.2.4.6).

19.3.2.4.1. Expected Life

The company should estimate the expected life of the **option**, and can do so by, for example, looking at factors such as the average length of time that similar **option**s have remained outstanding in the past [FRS 20, Appendix B, para B16 et seq].

19.3.2.4.2. Market value of Underlying Shares

See section 19.3.2.3.

19.3.2.4.3. Expected Volatility

Expected volatility is a measure of the amount by which the value of a share is expected to fluctuate over a period. An unlisted company will not have historical information on this. It has to estimate volatility by looking at factors such as: actual transactions in its shares, particularly where there is an internal market; the volatility of listed companies in its sector; or volatility in a factor such as net assets or earnings [FRS 20, Appendix B, para B27 et seq].

The topic of volatility is discussed at: http://www.numa.com/ref/volatili.htm.

19.3.2.4.4. Expected Dividends

The company should estimate the expected dividend yield, or dividend payments, and input these into the model. If the company does not pay dividends, it should assume an expected dividend yield of zero [FRS 20, Appendix B, para B31 et seq].

19.3.2.4.5. Risk-free Interest Rate

The company should use the implied yield on zero-coupon gilts as the risk-free interest rate.

19.3.2.4.6. Dilution Impact

If the issue of new shares might have an impact on the fair value of the shares, then this can be inputted into the model [FRS 20, Appendix B, para B38 et seq].

19.3.3. Cash-Settled Share-Based Payment Transactions

The cumulative-to-date fair value of a cash-settled share-based payment has to be measured on each balance sheet date before and on the date of settlement. Any changes in the fair value of the liability should be recognised in the profit and loss account [FRS 20, para 30]. The eventual overall charge to the profit and loss account should equal the cash amount paid to the employee.

19.3.4. Hybrid Transactions

A hybrid share-based payment transaction is one that can be settled either in cash or in equity. The accounting treatment depends on whether the choice of how to settle is with the company or the employee.

19.3.4.1. Employee can choose between cash or equity

If the employee can choose to receive shares, or the same value in cash, then this should be treated in the same way as a cash-settled share-based payment transaction (see section 19.3.3) [FRS 20, para 38].

19.3.4.2. Employer can choose between cash and equity

If the company has the choice of settlement, the accounting treatment depends on whether it has a "present obligation" to settle in cash [FRS 20, para 41].

The company will have such a present obligation if:

- the choice of settlement in equity has no commercial substance;
- the company has a past practice or a stated policy of settling in cash; or
- the company generally settles in cash if the employee requests cash.

[FRS 20, para 41].

If the company does have such a present obligation then it should apply the accounting rules for cash-settled transactions (see section 19.3.3) [FRS 20, para 42].

If the company does not have such a present obligation, it should account in accordance with the rules for equity-settled transactions (see section 19.3.2). However, if the company actually settles in cash, the cash payment is accounted for as a repurchase of an equity interest. If the cash payment is higher than the value of the equity, then the excess is recognised as an additional expense. [FRS 20, para 43].

19.3.5. Vesting Conditions

FRS 20 draws a distinction between market and other **vesting** conditions.

19.3.5.1. Market Conditions

A market condition is one that looks at the share price. A market condition should be taken into account in determining the fair value of a share or **option** on the **grant date**. In other words, the amount charged to the profit and loss account should be discounted to reflect the difficulty of achieving the condition. If the market condition is not satisfied, it is not possible to adjust the cost to reflect this [FRS 20, para 21].

19.3.5.2. Non-Market Conditions

Vesting conditions that are not market conditions are not taken into account in determining the fair value of an individual share or **option** on the **grant date**. However, the cost in the accounts is adjusted to reflect the number of shares or **option**s that eventually **vest**. So there is a "truing-up" to reflect the real value delivered to employees [FRS 20, para 19]. An example of a non-market vesting condition is continued employment, or the occurrence of a listing or other exit event.

19.3.6. Application to Common Transactions

19.3.6.1. Award of Unrestricted Shares without vesting conditions

The company should charge the fair value of the shares in the year the **acquisition date** occurs, less the **acquisition price** if any [FRS 20, para 14].

19.3.6.2. Award of Restricted but not Forfeitable Shares without vesting conditions

The fair value of the shares should be reduced to reflect restrictions, such as no voting rights, no dividend rights, or restrictions on transferability. This amount, less the **acquisition price**, if any, should be charged in the year the **acquisition date** occurs [FRS 20, Appendix B, para B3].

19.3.6.3. Award of Restricted and Forfeitable Shares

A typical restricted share plan for an unlisted company involves the **award** of shares that are forfeitable if the employee terminates employment during the **vesting period** and/or the company fails to achieve certain non-market performance conditions.

The company should charge the fair value of the shares, reduced if necessary to reflect any restrictions that remain in place after **vesting**, such as continuing restrictions on transferability [FRS 20, Appendix B, para B3].

This amount, less the **acquisition price**, if any, should be spread over the **vesting period**, based on the company's best estimate of the number of shares that will actually **vest**. This should be trued up on the **vesting date**.

19.3.6.4. Management Downwards Ratchet

See section 3.5.7.1.3 for a description of this arrangement. It should normally be treated as subscriptions to share capital by employees. Any call or put options under which the company would buy back the shares held by employees should be considered separately, because there might be a separate instrument to be accounted for.

19.3.6.5. Share Options

A typical share **option** plan for an unlisted company involves the **award** of **options** with an **exercise price** equal to the **market value** of the shares. The **options** are forfeitable if the employee terminates employment during the **vesting period** and can only be **exercised** if the company achieves certain non-market performance conditions.

The company should charge the fair value of the **options** over the **vesting period**, based on the company's best estimate of the number of **options** that will actually **vest**. This should be trued up on the **vesting date**.

The company cannot make a correcting adjustment if **options vest**, but are not **exercised** [FRS 20, para 23].

19.3.6.6. SAYE Options

The accounting for **SAYE options** is the same as for standard share **options** (see section 19.3.6.5). However, under IFRIC D11, if an **optionholder** decides to stop saving, this is treated as the cancellation of the **option**, with the effect that the company needs to recognise immediately the amounts that would otherwise have been recognised over the remainder of the **vesting period**.

19.3.6.7. SIP

19.3.6.7.1. Free Shares and Matching Shares with no Forfeiture Period

See section 19.3.6.1.

19.3.6.7.2. Free Shares and Matching Shares with Forfeiture Period

See section 19.3.6.3.

19.3.6.7.3. Partnership Shares

The fair value of the Partnership Shares, less the amount of salary sacrificed by the employee, should be charged as equity-based compensation in the year the

acquisition date occurs. The charge is likely to be small. The salary itself should be charged as compensation expenses.

19.3.6.7.4. Dividend Shares

There should be no separate charge in relation to Dividend Shares because entitlement to these will have been included in the fair value of the underlying award. The dividend is treated in the normal way.

19.4. Accounting for Secondary NIC

The employing company should accrue for secondary NIC. The charge will be made in two phases: the **vesting period** and any period after **vesting** but before the NIC is paid, e.g. because a **vested option** has not been **exercise**d.

Example, an option is granted with a three-year vesting period followed by a seven-year exercise period.

One third of the expected secondary NIC liability should be charged in each of the first three years.

In subsequent years, the accrued liability should be adjusted upwards or downwards until the ***exercise date****, when the liability should be trued up to reflect the actual NIC cost.*

19.5. Accounting for Corporation Tax

As discussed in section 17, there can be corporation tax relief on events such as the **award** or **vesting** of shares or **exercise** of share **option**s.

FRS 19 is the accounting standard for deferred tax. It requires deferred tax assets to be recognised to the extent that it is regarded as more likely than not that they will be recovered.

Therefore, if the employer believes that it is more likely than not that, for example, an **option** will be **exercised**, it can recognise a deferred tax asset equal to the corporation tax relief that will arise when that **option** is in fact **exercise**d.

However, IAS 12, para 68C, limits the amount of the deduction that can be recognised in the profit and loss account to the corporation tax rate applied to the cumulative expense recognised since the **option** was **grant**ed, or when the shares were **award**ed. The ASB has stated that it will import this paragraph into FRS 19 when FRS 19 is revised to align it to international standards.

19.6. Accounting for Employee Benefit Trusts

19.6.1. EBT that holds Employer Shares

UITF Abstract 38 sets out the accounting treatment of EBTs that hold shares in the employing company or its parent. This does not apply to companies that account under FRSSE.

The text of UITF 38 can be downloaded from the ASB's website at: http://www.frc.org.uk/asb/uitf/pub0329.html

In these circumstances, the shares held by the EBT should be accounted for as a deduction from shareholders' funds rather than as assets.

The accounting treatment will depend in part on whether the sponsoring company of the EBT is the parent company or a subsidiary.

19.6.1.1. Acquisition of Shares where Parent company is Sponsoring Company

If the sponsoring company is the parent company, and the EBT goes out into the market and buys the parent's shares for £100,000, the accounting entries are:

Dr	Reserves	£100,000
Cr	Cash	£100,000

Shareholders' funds are reduced by £100,000. The notes to the accounts disclose that the shares are held in the EBT.

This is also the position following consolidation.

It is not clear which reserve account should be used.

19.6.1.2. Acquisition of Shares where Subsidiary is the Sponsoring Company

If the sponsoring company is a subsidiary, and the EBT goes out into the market and buys shares in the parent for £100,000 the accounting entries are:

Dr	Fixed asset: Shares in parent	£100,000
Cr	Cash	£100,000

This will get reclassified into equity in the consolidated financial statements.

19.6.1.3. During Holding Period

During the period while the EBT holds the shares, any dividend income on the shares should be excluded in arriving at profit before tax and deducted from the aggregate of dividends paid. The shares should be treated as cancelled for the purposes of calculating earnings per share.

19.6.1.4. Sale of Shares where Parent company is Sponsoring Company

If the sponsoring company is the parent company, and the EBT sells shares either to employees or to the market for £75,000, the accounting entries are:

Dr	Cash	£75,000
Cr	Reserves	£75,000

Shareholders' funds are increased by £75,000 and the notes to the accounts no longer show the shares being held by the EBT.

The overall effect is that the purchase by the EBT and subsequent sale creates a movement in reserves. The net effect is either an increase or a decrease equal to the profit or loss realised by the EBT.

19.6.1.5. Sale of Shares where Subsidiary is the Sponsoring Company

If the sponsoring company is a subsidiary, and the EBT sells shares in the parent either to employees or to the market for £75,000, the accounting entries are:

Dr	Cash	£75,000
Dr	Profit and Loss	£25,000
Cr	Fixed asset: Shares in parent	£100,000

19.6.2. Other Employee Benefit Trusts

If the EBT holds assets other than parent company shares, then these are treated as assets of the sponsoring company. Similarly, liabilities of the EBT should be recognised as liabilities of the sponsoring company. This is the effect of FRS 5, which requires companies to report the economic substance of transactions.

20. Anti-Avoidance

20.1. Background

On 2 December 2004, the Paymaster-General announced that the Government would take action to prevent what it regarded as unacceptable avoidance of income tax or NIC through **employment-related securitie**s or **securities options**, and that this could include retrospective legislation.

The first example of such retrospective legislation was introduced by FA 2006, which attempted to tackle avoidance schemes that used options. Previously, options were excluded from the definition of **securities** (although strangely, a warrant, which is a form of option, was a **security**).

FA 2006 amended the definition of **securities** so that an **option** was a **security** unless it was a **securities option**. The definition of **securities option** was also changed so that a right to acquire **securities** which was entered into for purposes of avoiding tax or NIC was not a **securities option**.

These changes were made with retrospective effect from 2 December 2004.

20.2. PAYE Implications

If PAYE arises as a result of retrospective legislation turning something which was previously not taxable into a notional payment, then that notional payment is deemed to have been made on the date the legislation is enacted [ITEPA 2003, s684(2)]. This means that an additional liability can arise under ITEPA 2003, s222, if the employee does not make good the PAYE within 90 days of the date the legislation is enacted.

The Treasury also has power to make regulations to collect NIC in relation to a transaction that becomes taxable as a result of retrospective tax legislation [SSCBA 1992, s4B].

21. Flowcharts and Checklists

21.1. Readily convertible asset

Use the following checklist to determine whether securities of an unlisted company are **readily convertible assets**:

	Question	Comment	Ref[218]
1.	Are the securities **ordinary share capital**?	If no, they cannot be **corporation tax deductible shares** and therefore must be **readily convertible assets**, If yes, go to question 2.	S702(5A)
2.	Were the shares acquired under an **SAYE** Plan?	If yes, go to question 5. If no, go to question 3	S701(2)(c)(i)
3.	Were the shares acquired under a **CSOP** in circumstances where tax relief is available?	If yes, go to question 5. If no, go to question 4	S701(2)(c)(ii)
4.	Were the shares acquired as a result of the **exercise** of an **option granted** before 27 November 1996, which was not **granted** or **exercised** as part of arrangements for the avoidance of tax or NIC?	If yes, go to question 5. If no, go to question 6	S701(2)(c)(iii)
5.	Are the shares in the employer company, a company that has **Section 840 control** of the employer company, or which is (or has **Section 840 control** of) a member of a **consortium** that has direct or indirect **Section 840 control** of the employer company?	If yes, these are not assets in relation to the **exercise** of the **option**, but may become assets in relation to subsequent events. If no, go to question 6	S701(3) and (3A)
6.	Are the shares **fully paid up**?	If no, they cannot be **corporation tax deductible shares** and therefore must be **readily convertible assets**. If yes, go to question 7	S702(5A)
7.	Are the shares **redeemable**?	If yes, they cannot be **corporation tax deductible shares** and therefore must be	S702(5A)

218 References in this column are to ITEPA 2003.

	Question	Comment	Ref[218]
		readily convertible assets. If no, go to question 8	
8.	Are the shares in a company that is under the **Section 840 control** of another unlisted company (or a listed but **close company**)?	If yes, they cannot be **corporation tax deductible shares** and therefore must be **readily convertible assets**. If no, go to question 9	S702(5A)
9.	Are there any trading arrangements in relation to the shares?	This includes an understanding that trading arrangements are likely to come into existence. If so, the shares are **readily convertible assets**. HM Revenue & Customs' views on the meaning of "trading arrangements" are set out in HMRC Manual EIM11908[219] et seq	S702(1)(c)

219 http://www.hmrc.gov.uk/manuals/eimanual/EIM11908.htm

21.2. Corporation tax deductible share

The concept of a **corporation tax deductible share** is important for two reasons:

- The statutory deduction in FA 2003, Sch23 is not available for shares that are not **corporation tax deductible** [FA 2003, Sch23, para 4] (see section 17.4); and
- Securities that are not **corporation tax deductible shares** are **readily convertible assets** [ITEPA 2003, s702(5A)] (see section 21.1)

Shares will not be **corporation tax deductible shares** unless they meet each of requirements A, B, C, D and E below, and at least one of requirements F, G and H [FA 2003, Sch23, para 4].

A: They are acquired by reason of employment with a company, or pursuant to an **option** granted by reason of employment with a company [ITEPA 2003, s702(5B)];

B That company is entitled to corporation tax relief under FA 2003, Sch23 in relation to the acquisition

C They are **ordinary share capital**

D: They are **fully paid up**

E: They are not **redeemable**

F: They are shares of a class that is listed on a **recognised stock exchange**

G: They are shares in a company that is not under the **Section 840 control** of another company

H: They are shares in a company that is under the **Section 840 control** of a company whose shares are listed on a **recognised stock exchange** and which is not close (or would not be close if it were **resident** in the UK).

21.3. Attribution of EBT shares to beneficiaries

There are provisions in the **SIP**, **SAYE**, **CSOP** and **EMI** codes and in the loan interest relief rules that provide that an EBT Trustee is not an **associate** of an individual, for the purpose of determining whether that individual has a **material interest** [ICTA 1988, s360A(4), ITEPA 2003, Sch2, para 23(2), Sch3, para 15(2), Sch4, para 13(2), Sch5, para 32(2). The following flowchart can be used to determine whether the EBT Trustee is an **associate**.

Step	Question	Comment	Statutory Reference
1.	Are all or most of the employees of the company eligible to benefit under the EBT?	If no, the EBT is an **associate**. If yes, go to step 2.	ICTA 1988, Sch8, para 7(5)(a), ITEPA 2003, s550(2)
2.	Has the EBT made any disposal of property after 13 March 1989 (NB disposal means a disposal by sale, loan or otherwise). For loan interest relief the relevant date is 27 July 1989	If no, the EBT is an **associate**. If yes, go to step 3	ICTA 1988, Sch8, para 7(5)(b) as varied by ICTA 1988, s360A(5), ITEPA 2003, s550(3) and (5)
3.	Was the disposal made in the ordinary management of the EBT?	If yes, it can be ignored. If this is the only disposal, the EBT is an **associate**. If no, or there are other disposals, go to step 4	ICTA 1988, Sch8, para 7(5)(b), ITEPA 2003, s550(4)(a)
4.	Did the disposal take the form of an application of **ordinary shares** in the company, or money, for the benefit of individual employees or former employees of the company or any other company of which the company has **Section 840 control**?	If yes, it can be ignored. If this is the only disposal, the EBT is an **associate**. If no, or there are other disposals, go to step 5	ICTA 1988, Sch8, para 7(6)(a), ITEPA 2003, s550(4)(b), s551(1), (2)(a), and (3)
5.	Did the disposal take the form of an application of **ordinary shares** in the company, or money, for the benefit of someone who has any of the following relationships to an individual employee or former employee of the company or	If yes, it can be ignored. If this is the only disposal, the EBT is an **associate**. If no, or there are other disposals, go to step 6	ICTA 1988, Sch8, para 7(6)(a), ITEPA 2003, s550(4)(b), s551(1), (2), and (3)

Step	Question	Comment	Statutory Reference
	any other company of which the company has **Section 840 control**? Those relationships are: spouse; former spouse; widow; widower; **dependant**, relative or spouse of relative. Relative means: parent; child; remoter ancestor; remoter issue; brother; sister; uncle; aunt; nephew; or niece.		
6.	Did the disposal take the form of an application of **ordinary shares** in the company, or money, for charitable purposes?	If yes, it can be ignored. If this is the only disposal, the EBT is an **associate**. If no, or there are other disposals, go to step 7	ICTA 1988, Sch8, para 7(6)(b), ITEPA 2003, s550(4)(b), s551(1) and (4)
7.	Did the disposal take the form of an application of **ordinary shares** in the company, or money, to another EBT, a **QUEST** or an approved profit sharing scheme?	If yes, it can be ignored. If this is the only disposal, the EBT is an **associate**. If no, or there are other disposals, go to step 8	ICTA 1988, Sch8, para 7(6)(c), ITEPA 2003, s550(4)(b), s551(1) and (5)
8.	Was there some other disposal?	If yes, it cannot be ignored and the EBT is an **associate**. If no, go to step 9	ICTA 1988, Sch8, para 7(5), ITEPA 2003, s550(3)
9.	It is now necessary to aggregate together all the following shareholdings or deemed shareholdings as set out in steps 10, 11, 12 and 13		
10.	Any shares which the individual or any **associate** has owned since 13 March 1989 (27 July 1989 for loan interest relief)		ICTA 1988, Sch8, para 7(8), ITEPA 2003, Sch2, para 23(2), Sch3, para 15(2), Sch4, para 13(2), Sch5, para 32(2)
11.	Any shares of which the individual or any **associate** has had direct or indirect **Section 840 control** since 13 March 1989 (27 July 1989 for loan interest relief)		ICTA 1988, Sch8, para 7(8), ITEPA 2003, Sch2, para 23(2), Sch3, para 15(2), Sch4, para 13(2), Sch5, para

Step	Question	Comment	Statutory Reference
			32(2)
12.	If, after 13 March 1989 (27 July 1989 for loan interest relief), the individual or any **associate** has received a payment from the EBT Trustee, and at any time within the previous three years ("the payment date") the EBT Trustee owned any part of the company's **ordinary share capital**, then the individual or **associate** is deemed to own the following percentage of the company:		ICTA 1988, Sch8, para 7(9), ITEPA 2003, s552
	(P x 100) / D where P is the lower of		ICTA 1988, Sch8, para 7(10), ITEPA 2003, s553(1)
	(i) the aggregate of all payments made to the individual and his **associates** by the EBT Trustee in the period of twelve months ending on the payment date; and		ITEPA 2003, s553(2)
	(ii) the aggregate of any distributions made by the company to the EBT Trustee in respect of its **ordinary share capital** in the three years ending on the payment date.		ITEPA 2003, s553(3)
	D is the aggregate of any distributions made by the company in respect of its **ordinary share capital** in the three years ending with the payment date, divided by the number of years in this period in which the company made distributions, or, if no distributions were made, D is 1.		ITEPA 2003, s553(4) and (5)
13.	If: • as a result of Step 12, the individual or an **associate** is deemed to own a percentage of the company's **ordinary share capital**, and • the individual or an **associate** has during the period of twelve months ending with the payment date, received any payment from any other trust that holds **ordinary shares** in the company, or which held **ordinary shares** within the period of three years ending with the payment date then it is necessary to perform the same calculation as in Step 12, but by reference to the payments received from the other trust.		ICTA 1988, Sch8, para 7(11), ITEPA 2003, s554
14.	If the aggregate of all the following shareholdings and deemed shareholdings from steps 10, 11, 12 and 13 exceeds 25% for **SIP**, **SAYE** and **CSOP** and loan interest relief, or 30% for EMI, then the EBT is an **associate** of the individual.		ICTA 1988, Sch8, para 7(8), ITEPA 2003, Sch2, para 23(2), Sch3, para 15(2), Sch4, para 13(2), Sch5, para

Step	Question	Comment	Statutory Reference
			32(2)

21.4. Rollover of Approved options

Use the following checklist to determine whether an approved rollover can take place:

	Question	Comment	SAYE[220]	CSOP[221]
1.	Do the Scheme Rules contain a rollover provision? If not, there cannot be an approved rollover.	HM Revenue & Customs will not approve a rollover unless it is provided for in the Scheme Rules [HMRC Manual ESSU 15012][222]		
2.	Is there a "**company reorganisation**" of the "**scheme company**"? If not, there cannot be an approved rollover.	The reorganisation must affect the **scheme company** itself. There cannot be an approved rollover where, for example, the **scheme company** disposes of a subsidiary or a business.	38(1)(a)	26(1)(a)
3.	Is the rollover mandatory? If so, there cannot be an approved rollover.	An approved rollover cannot be mandatory – it is the acquiring company's decision whether to offer it and the **optionholder** can choose whether to accept it.	38(1)	26(1)
4.	Did the rollover take place within six months of the **company reorganisation** or, in the case of a compulsory purchase of minority shareholdings, during the period while the acquiring company remains bound and entitled to purchase the shares?	The rollover must take place within these periods to be approved.	38(3)	26(3)
5.	Does the new **option** relate to shares in a different company from the **scheme company**?	An approved rollover cannot take effect in relation to different shares of the same company?	39(2)(a)	27(2)(a)
6.	Does the new **option** relate to	See section 3.7.8.2 for a	39(2)(b)	27(2)(b)

---

220 References in this column are to paragraphs in ITEPA 2003, Sch3.

221 References in this column are to paragraphs in ITEPA 2003, Sch4.

222 http://www.hmrc.gov.uk/manuals/essumanual/essu13000/essu15012.htm

	Question	Comment	SAYE[220]	CSOP[221]
	shares in the acquiring company or to another company that controls the **scheme organiser**, whether directly or indirectly or as a member of a **consortium** that directly or indirectly controls the **scheme organiser?**	more detailed analysis of this requirement.		
7.	Does the new **option** relate to shares that satisfy the conditions of ITEPA 2003, Sch3, paras 18 to 22 (for **SAYE**) or ITEPA 2003, Sch4, paras 16 to 20 (for **CSOP**)?	For a more detailed analysis of these provisions, see section 3.7.8.2 for **CSOP** and section 4.3.1.1 for **SAYE**.	39(4)(a)	27(4)(a)
8.	Is the new **option exercisable** in the same manner as the old **option** and subject to the original Plan Rules?	It is often mistakenly thought that the acquiring company can **grant** a new **option** under its own scheme to replace an old **option** under the original scheme, but this would not comply with the legislation. The **scheme company** remains the original company.	39(4)(b)	27(4)(b)
9.	Is the total **market value** of the shares subject to the new **option** the same as the total **market value** of the shares subject to the old **option**?	The values should be measured on the date the old **option** is released and the new **option** is **grant**ed and must be the same.	39(4)(c)	27(4)(c)
10.	Is the total **exercise price** payable under the new **option** the same as the total **exercise price** payable under the old **option**?	These must be the same.	39(4)(d)	27(4)(d)

21.5. Rollover of EMI Options

Use the following checklist to determine whether a qualifying rollover can take place:

	Question	Comment	Ref[223]
1.	Is there a transaction affecting shares in the **relevant company** whose shares are subject to the EMI **option**s ("Oldco")? If not, there cannot be a qualifying rollover. The following questions ask about the nature of the transaction.	The reorganisation must affect Oldco, i.e. the **relevant company** whose shares are subject to outstanding **EMI option**s. There cannot be a qualifying rollover where, for example, Oldco disposes of a subsidiary or a business.	39(2)
2.	Has another company ("Newco") obtained control of Oldco as a result of a general offer to shareholders, either to acquire the whole of the issued share capital or to acquire all the shares of the same class as those to which the **EMI option** relates?	This qualifies as a **company reorganisation.**	39(2)(a)
3.	Has Newco obtained control of Oldco as a result of a compromise or arrangement sanctioned by the court under CA 1985, s425?	This qualifies as a **company reorganisation.**	39(2)(b)
4.	Has Newco become bound or entitled under CA 1985, s428 to s430F to acquire shares of the same class as those to which the **EMI option** relates?	This qualifies as a **company reorganisation.**	39(2)(c)
5.	Is there a "qualifying exchange of shares"? Questions 6 to 11 below set out the determining factors of a qualifying exchange of shares?	A qualifying exchange of shares is a **company reorganisation.**	39(2)(d)
6.	Has Newco acquired **all** the shares of Oldco?	Newco must acquire all the shares for this to be a qualifying exchange of shares.	40(1)(a)
7.	Does the consideration for the Oldco shares consist entirely of Newco shares?	If any other consideration is given, this will not be a qualifying exchange of shares.	40(2)(a)
8.	Does Newco have any other shares in	If Newco has any other shares in	40(2)(b)

[223] References in this column are to ITEPA 2003, Sch5.

	Question	Comment	Ref[223]
	issue at the time of the exchange, except subscriber shares and shares already issued in exchange for Oldco shares?	issue, this will not be a qualifying exchange of shares.	
9.	Is any consideration given for Newco shares of any description except Oldco shares of the corresponding description [ITEPA 2003, Sch5, para 40(2)(c)]	This applies where Oldco has shares of more than one description. If so, then they must be exchanged only for Newco shares of the same description.	40(2)(c)
10.	Are the Newco shares of each description issued to holders of Oldco shares of the same description in the same proportions.	If the proportions are different, this will not be a qualifying exchange of shares.	40(2)(d)
11.	Does the exchange qualify as a rollover under the CGT capital reorganisation provisions?	The exchange must qualify under TCGA 1992, s127 as applied by TCGA 1992, s135(3).	40(2)(e)
12.	Is the rollover mandatory? If so, there cannot be a qualifying rollover	A qualifying rollover cannot be mandatory – it is the acquiring company's decision whether to offer it and the **optionholder** can choose whether to accept it.	41(2)
13.	Did the rollover take place within six months of the **company reorganisation** or, in the case of a compulsory purchase of minority shareholdings, during the period while Newco remains bound and entitled to purchase the shares?	The rollover must take place within these periods to qualify.	42
14.	Does the replacement **option** relate to shares in Newco?	The replacement **option** must relate to shares in the acquiring company.	41(2)
15.	Is the replacement **option grant**ed to the **optionholder** by reason of his employment with Newco or one of its subsidiaries?	The **optionholder** must have an employment relationship with Newco or one of its subsidiaries.	43(2)
16.	Is the replacement **option grant**ed for commercial reasons in order to retain the **optionholder**, and not as part of a scheme or arrangement to avoid tax?	There will not be a qualifying rollover if the replacement **option** is **grant**ed for any other reason.	43(3)(a)
17.	Does the total value of Oldco shares subject to the old **option**s being rolled over exceed £3 million?	If so, this will not be a qualifying rollover. It is necessary to measure the value of the Oldco shares immediately before the	43(3)(b) and 43(4)

	Question	Comment	Ref[223]
		rollover. Only those **option**s that are rolled over are taken into account.	
18.	Does the replacement **option** meet the requirements of ITEPA 2003, Sch5, Part 5?	If not, the replacement **option** will not qualify for EMI. These requirements are analysed in detail in section 3.7.6.7.1.	43(3)(c)
19.	Does Newco meet the independence requirement at the time of the release?	If not, the replacement **option** will not qualify for EMI. This requirement is analysed in detail in section 3.7.6.3.	43(5)(a)
20.	Does Newco meet the trading activities requirement at the time of the release?	If not, the replacement **option** will not qualify for EMI. This requirement is analysed in detail in section 3.7.6.3.5	43(5)(a)
21.	Is the **optionholder** an eligible employee in relation to Newco at the time of the release?	If not, the replacement **option** will not qualify for EMI. This requirement is analysed in detail in section 3.7.6.4.1.	43(5)(b)
22.	Are the **vesting** terms attached to the replacement **option** more favourable than those attached to the old **option**?	HM Revenue & Customs' view is that the conditions attached to the new **option** cannot improve the rights of the **optionholder**. This is not supported by the legislation. In relation to rollovers of **CSOP** and **SAYE** **option**s, this is clearly a requirement of Sch3, para 39(4)(b) and Sch4, para 27(4)(b). However there is no equivalent of those provisions in Sch5.	
23.	Is the total **CGT value** of the shares subject to the replacement **option** the same as the total **CGT value** of the shares subject to the old **option**?	The values should be measured on the date the old **option** is released and the new **option** is **grant**ed and must be the same.	43(6)
24.	Is the total **exercise price** payable under the new **option** the same as the total **exercise price** payable under the old **option**?	These must be the same.	43(7)

22. Restricted Securities Elections

This section summarises the elections that are available in relation to **restricted securities**, and the issues to be taken into account by employers and employees in deciding whether to make them.

22.1. The Elections

22.1.1. Section 425 election

A **Section 425 election** relates to restricted and forfeitable securities, where the risk of **forfeiture** lasts for less than five years. The default position is that there is no general earnings charge on the acquisition of such securities [ITEPA 2003, s425(2)] (see section 11.1.4).

If a **Section 425 election** is made, there is a general earnings charge on the restricted value of the securities [ITEPA 2003, s425(3)].

A **Section 425 election** must be made jointly by the employer and the employee within 14 days of the **acquisition date**. Specimen forms can be downloaded from HM Revenue & Customs' website at http://www.hmrc.gov.uk/shareschemes/s425-1-pe.rtf for a one-part election and http://www.hmrc.gov.uk/shareschemes/s425-2-pe.rtf for a two-part election.

22.1.2. Section 430 election

A **Section 430 election** can be made where there is a chargeable event in relation to **restricted securities**, but the securities remain restricted afterwards. The default position is that a proportion of the value of the securities is taxable at that time, and the remainder (OP) is taxable later. See section 12.3.4.6 for the definition of OP and section 12.3.4.13.2 for an example of the calculation of the taxable amount in these circumstances.

If a **Section 430 election** is made, the taxable amount is calculated as if OP were zero [ITEPA 2003, s430(1)]. The effect of this is to charge tax on any proportion of the value that has not already been taxed, and thereby preclude any further charge under the **restricted securities** provisions in relation to those securities.

A **Section 430 election** must be made jointly by the employer and the employee within 14 days of the chargeable event. Specimen forms can be downloaded from HM Revenue & Customs' website at http://www.hmrc.gov.uk/shareschemes/s430-1-pe.rtf for a one-part election and http://www.hmrc.gov.uk/shareschemes/s430-2-pe.rtf for a two-part election

22.1.3. Section 431(1) election

A **Section 431(1) election** can be made at the **acquisition date** of any **restricted securities**.

The effect is that all restrictions on the securities are disregarded, so that there is a general earnings charge on the IUMV of the securities, which precludes any further charge under the **restricted securities** provisions in relation to those securities [ITEPA 2003, s431(1)].

A **Section 431(1) election** must be made jointly by the employer and the employee within 14 days of the **acquisition date**. Specimen forms can be downloaded from HM Revenue & Customs' website at
http://www.hmrc.gov.uk/shareschemes/s431-1-pe.rtf for a one part election and http://www.hmrc.gov.uk/shareschemes/s431-2-pe.rtf for a two-part election.

There are special forms for use where the shares have been acquired through an **EMI option**. These are at

http://www.hmrc.gov.uk/shareschemes/emi_one_part_election_under_section_431_itepa_2003.pdf for the one part election and

http://www.hmrc.gov.uk/shareschemes/emi_two_part_election_under_section_431_itepa_2003.pdf for the two part election.

22.1.4. Section 431(2) election

A **Section 431(2) election** can be made at the **acquisition date** of any **restricted securities**.

The effect is that certain specified restrictions on the securities are disregarded in determining the amount charged to tax as general earnings charge. There may still be a further charge under the **restricted securities** provisions in relation to those securities, but it will ignore any increase in value as a result of the specified restrictions being lifted [ITEPA 2003, s431(2)].

A **Section 431(2) election** must be made jointly by the employer and the employee within 14 days of the **acquisition date**. Specimen forms can be downloaded from HM Revenue & Customs' website at
http://www.hmrc.gov.uk/shareschemes/s431-1-pe.rtf for a one_part election and http://www.hmrc.gov.uk/shareschemes/s431-2-pe.rtf for a two-part election.

22.2. Deciding to Make an Election

22.2.1. Employee

In deciding whether to make an election the employee has to take account of the following factors:

- The amount of tax payable immediately as a result of making the election (t).
- The cost of funding t for the period before the securities can be disposed of (t multiplied by interest rate i for period p).
- The proportion of the IUMV of the securities that would be taxed immediately as a result of the election (v%).
- The expected gain on the securities (g).

- His marginal rate of capital gains tax (c).
- His expected marginal rate of income tax and NIC when the chargeable event occurs (r) - this depends on whether the securities are **readily convertible asset**s and whether the employee pays the secondary NIC.
- The amount of tax deferred if the election is not made (t2). Normally t and t2 will be the same, but they could be different if, for example, the securities are not **readily convertible asset**s when the election is made, but will be **readily convertible asset**s when the chargeable event occurs.
- The likelihood of a chargeable event occurring (l).

It is worth making an election if:

$t2l + vlgr > t + tip + vlgc$

Here is a simple example.

Assume that:

- There is certainty that a chargeable event will occur, so l is 1.
- The employee's marginal rate of tax and NIC is and will continue to be 41%, so r is 0.41.
- The effect of the first two assumptions is that t and t2l are the same.
- The chargeable event will be a sale of the securities after two years with full business asset taper relief, so c is 0.1.
- The election being considered is a **Section 431(1) election**, so that v is 100%.

This resolves to:

$0.41g > tip + 0.1g$

This can be simplified as $0.31g > tip$ or $g > 3.23\ tip$

So in this simple example, it will be worth making an election if the expected growth in value of the securities is more than 3.23 times the cost of funding the upfront tax payment.

22.2.2. Employer

The decision for the employer is less complex than for the employee. If the securities are **readily convertible asset**s, then by making the election, the employer crystallises an immediate secondary NIC liability. By not making the election, the employer defers any secondary NIC liability, but the eventual liability may be greater or smaller.

Similarly, if the securities are **corporation tax deductible shares** and the conditions for relief are fulfilled, then, by making the election, the employer crystallises an immediate corporation tax deduction (see section 17.4.4). By not making the election, the employer defers the deduction, but the eventual deduction may be greater or smaller.

22.3. Reporting

The signed election form does not have to be sent to HM Revenue & Customs, but the employer must enter a note on Form 42 stating whether an election has been made and, if so, which election (see section 23).

23. Form 42 Reporting

ITEPA 2003, s421J sets out the statutory reporting requirements in relation to events that may potentially give rise to tax charges under ITEPA 2003, Part 7. Form 42 is the prescribed HM Revenue & Customs form for reporting these events. A copy of the 2006 version can be downloaded from

http://www.hmrc.gov.uk/forms/form42.pdf.

It is sent by HM Revenue & Customs to companies that they think are likely to have to report relevant events. It is not obligatory to use Form 42 itself; companies can use a substitute form which is in the same format and contains the same information. There is a separate simpler form for companies that were incorporated in the relevant year and have only issued unrestricted shares to employees. HM Revenue & Customs have published guidance on completing Form 42. This is available from their website at http://www.hmrc.gov.uk/shareschemes/form42-guidance.pdf.

The reporting obligations are imposed both on employing company and the company that issued the shares, if this is different. However, a report filed by one of them discharges the obligations of the other [ITEPA 2003, s421J(7)].

If HM Revenue & Customs issue Form 42 to a company, it must return it by 6 July of the tax year following the reportable event. Even if the company has nothing to report it must make a nil return.

A company that has events to report but is not issued with Form 42 should download a copy from the website and return it to HM Revenue & Customs by 6 July of the tax year following the reportable event.

Table 9 sets out the events that must be reported, the section of ITEPA 2003 that imposes the obligation, the section of ITEPA 2003 that creates the chargeable event, the section of Form 42 (2006) where the event must be reported, and the section of this book where the event is discussed.

Table 9: Reporting Obligations

Reportable Event	Reporting obligation[224]	Charging Provision	Form 42	Where discussed
Grant of **securities options**	(a)	S62[225]	1a	8.1.1
Acquisition of securities in connection with **securities options**	(a)	S477(3)(a)	1b	8.1.2.1
Assignment and release of **securities options**	(h)	S477(3)(b)	1c	8.5.1
Receipt of benefit in connection with **securities option**	(i)	S477(3)(c)	1c	8.5.1
Acquisition of un**restricted securities**	(a)	S62	2 (Type A)	11.1.2
Acquisition of securities with an artificially reduced **market value**	(a)	S446B	2 (Type F)	11.1.5
Acquisition of **restricted securities** without a **forfeiture** provision	(a)	S62	2 (Type D)	11.1.3
Acquisition of **restricted securities** with a **forfeiture** provision	(a)	S62	2 (Types B and C)	11.1.3 and 11.1.4
Chargeable event on **restricted securities** acquired after 15 April 2003	(b)	S427	3a	12.3.2
Chargeable event on shares subject to **forfeiture** acquired before 16 April 2003	Old S432	Old S427	3a	12.2.3
Variation of restrictions for shares acquired before 1 September 2003	Old S465	Old S450	3b	12.7
Conversion of securities on or after 6 April 2003	(c)	S439(3)	3c	12.4.2
Discharge of notional loans	(e)	S446U	3d	12.8.4
Receipt of other benefits from securities	(g)	S447	3e	12.10
Securities sold for more than **market value**	(f)	S446X	3f	12.9

224 References are to sub-paragraphs of ITEPA 2003, s421K(3), unless otherwise specified

225 NB – no charge to tax if the **optionholder** is **resident** and **ordinarily resident** in the UK on the **grant date** [ITEPA 2003, s475(1)] (see section 8.1.1)

Reportable Event	**Reporting obligation[224]**	**Charging Provision**	**Form 42**	**Where discussed**
Artificial enhancement of **market value**	(d)	S446L	3g	12.6.1
Shares with artificially reducedf **market value**	(b)	S446E	3a	12.5.4 and 12.5.5

24. Glossary

Term	Meaning
51% Subsidiary	A company is a "51 per cent **subsidiary**" of another body corporate if and so long as more than 50 per cent of its **ordinary share capital** is owned directly or indirectly by that other body corporate [ICTA 1988, s838].
Acquisition date	The date on which the acquisition occurs.
Acquisition price	The price per share that an employee must pay to acquire the underlying shares .
Alternatively secured pension	A form of **income withdrawal** payable to a member who has reached the age of 75 [FA 2004, Sch28, para 5].
Alternatively secured pension fund	The member's **alternatively secured pension fund** consists of the money and assets which were held in his **unsecured pension fund** immediately before his 75th birthday, and which have not been applied towards the provision of a **scheme pension** [FA 2004, Sch28, para 11(2)]. The **alternatively secured pension fund** also includes any amount which became held in the member's fund on or after his 75th birthday or which was previously held in a hybrid arrangement that has now become a money purchase arrangement [FA 2004, Sch28, paras 11(3) and (4)].
Approved option	A **CSOP** or **SAYE** option
Approved plan	A **CSOP, SAYE** or **SIP**
Associate (Close company – ICTA definition)	The following are the **associate**s of a **participator** in a **close company**: • a relative (meaning a spouse, civil partner, parent or remoter forebear, child or remoter issue, brother or sister) • a partner • the trustee of any settlement in relation to which the **participator** or any relative was a settlor • the trustee of any settlement or estate which holds shares in the company in which the **participator** is interested [ICTA 1988, s417(3)]
Associate (Close company – Benefits code)	This is the same as for ICTA, except that the term "relative" is widened to include a spouse's parent or remoter forebear, child or remoter issue, brother or sister, and any spouse of any such person [ITEPA 2003, s68(5)]
Associate (EMI code)	The following are the **associate**s of an individual for the purposes of determining whether he has a **material interest** for the EMI code: • a relative (meaning a spouse, parent or remoter forebear, or child or remoter issue) • a partner

Term	Meaning
	• the trustee of any settlement in relation to which the individual or any relative was a settlor • the trustee of any settlement or estate which holds shares in the company in which the individual is interested [ITEPA 2003, Sch5, para 31(1)] However, it does not include: • the Trustee of certain EBTs – use the flowchart in section 21.3 to determine whether shares held in an EBT should be attributed to the individual [ITEPA 2003, Sch5, para 32] • the Trustee of a discretionary trust of which the individual was once a potential beneficiary if the individual (a) has been irrevocably excluded from benefit ; (b) no **associate** of the individual has an interest in shares or obligations of the company and (c) neither the individual nor any **associate** received any benefit from the trust during the twelve months prior to his being excluded [ITEPA 2003, Sch5, para 33]
Associate (**SIP**, **SAYE** and **CSOP** codes)	This is the same as for the EMI code, except that the term "relative" includes a brother or sister [ITEPA 2003, Sch2, para 22, Sch3, para 14 and Sch4, para 12]
Associate (Interest Relief)	The following are the **associates** of an individual for the purposes of determining whether he has a **material interest** for the purposes of claiming loan interest relief: • a relative (meaning a spouse, parent or remoter forebear, or child or remoter issue, brother or sister) • a partner • the trustee of any settlement in relation to which the individual or any relative was a settlor • the trustee of any settlement or estate which holds shares in the company in which the individual is interested [ICTA 1988, s360A(2)] However, in relation to loans made on or after 27 July 1989, it does not include the Trustee of certain EBTs – use the flowchart in section 21.3 to determine whether shares held in an EBT should be attributed to the individual [ICTA 1988, s360A(4)]
Associated company (ICTA)	A company is to be treated as another's **associated company** at a given time if, at that time or at any other time within one year previously, one of the two has control of the other, or both are under the control of the same person or persons [ICTA 1988, s416].
Associated company (Company law)	A director of a company is associated with a body corporate if, but only if, he and the persons connected with him, together (a) are interested in shares comprised in the equity share capital of that body corporate of a nominal value equal to at least one-

Term	Meaning
	fifth of that share capital (excluding any shares in the company held as treasury shares); or (b) are entitled to exercise or control the exercise of more than one-fifth of the voting power at any general meeting of that body (excluding any voting rights attached to any shares in the company held as treasury shares). [CA 1985, s346(4)].
Associated person (ITEPA)	All the following people are "**associated persons**" in relation to **employment-related** securities: 1. the person who acquired the **employment-related** securities 2. the employee by reason of whose employment the securities were acquired 3. any **connected person** of either 1 or 2 above 4. the domestic staff of either 1 or 2 above 5. the guests of either 1 or 2 above But excluding any company which is: ● the employer ● the person from whom the shares were acquired ● the person who made the right or opportunity available ● the person who issued the securities [ITEPA 2003, s421C]
Award	An **award** of shares
Awardholder	An individual, usually an employee, who has been **grant**ed an **award** of shares.
Benefit crystallisation event	An event where a person crystallises an entitlement to a lump sum or benefit from a **registered pension scheme**. A full list of **benefit crystallisation event**s is in FA 2004, s216.
Blocking period	A period during which the shareholder is not permitted to sell the shares.
Bonus date	The date on which a bonus is payable under a **certified SAYE savings arrangement** linked to an **SAYE Option**. This will be the third, fifth or seventh anniversary of the start of the savings [ITEPA 2003, Sch3, para 30(3)]
By reason of employment	For the purposes of ITEPA 2003, Part 7, the term "**by reason of employment**" has an enlarged definition contained in ITEPA 2003, s421B. For all other purposes, whether securities are acquired **by reason of employment** is a matter of fact. HM Revenue & Customs have published a list of circumstances in which they will accept that

Term	Meaning
	securities are not acquired **by reason of employment** [HMRC Manual SSM4.4[226]] and this is reproduced in Chapter 25 on page 407.
Cash balance plan	A **cash balance plan** is a type of pension scheme where the employer promises that a certain amount of money will be made available to the employee on **retirement**. The amount of money can be calculated according to a formula based on, for example, length of service and final salary. In a **cash balance plan**, the value of the fund on **retirement** does not depend on the amounts contributed by the employer or the employee or any other person [FA 2004, s152].
Certified SAYE savings arrangement	A savings contract linked to an **SAYE option** [ITTOIA 2005, s703(2)]
CGT value	See section 15.2
Close company	A company which is under the control of five or fewer **participators** [HMRC Manual CT6110[227]], or any number of **participators** if those **participators** are directors. A company is also close if more than half of its assets would be distributed to five or fewer **participators**, or to **participators** who are directors, in the event of the winding up of the company [HMRC Manual CT6302[228]]. For more detailed commentary see HMRC Manual CT6100[229].
Commercial association of companies	A company together with such of its **associated companies** as carry on businesses which are of such a nature that the businesses of the company and the **associated companies**, taken together, may be reasonably considered to make up a single composite undertaking [TCGA 1992, SchA1, para 22(1) and FA 2003, Sch23, para 29(2)]
Company reorganisation	This term is used in ITEPA 2003, Sch3, para 38(2) and Sch4, para 26(2). It includes a change of control following a general offer to shareholders, and a change of control that follows a scheme of arrangement under CA 1985, s425. It also includes a situation where an acquiring company becomes bound or entitled to buy in minority shareholdings under CA 1985, s428 to 430.

226 http://www.hmrc.gov.uk/manuals/ssmmanual/HTMl/SSM04/04_0004_SSM4.4.htm

227 http://www.hmrc.gov.uk/manuals/ct123manual/ct6110.htm

228 http://www.hmrc.gov.uk/manuals/ct123manual/ct6302.htm

229 http://www.hmrc.gov.uk/manuals/ct123manual/ct6100.htm

Term	Meaning
Connected company (**SIP** code definition)	Company A and Company B are connected if Company A has **Section 840 control** of Company B, or if both are under the **Section 840 control** of Company C, or if Company A is a member of a **consortium** that has **Section 840 control** of Company B [ITEPA 2003, Sch2, para 18(3)]
Connected person (CA 1985 definition)	For company law purposes, a person is connected with a director of a company if, but only if, he (not being himself a director of it) is— (a) that director's spouse, civil partner, child or step-child; or (b) except where the context otherwise requires, a body corporate with which the director is **associate**d; or (c) a person acting in his capacity as trustee of any trust the beneficiaries of which include— (i) the director, his spouse, civil partner, or any children or step-children of his, or (ii) a body corporate with which he is **associate**d, or of a trust whose terms confer a power on the Trustee that may be **exercise**d for the benefit of the director, his spouse, or any children or step-children of his, or any such body corporate; or (d) a person acting in his capacity as partner of that director or of any person who, by virtue of paragraph (a), (b) or (c), is connected with that director; or (e) a Scottish firm in which— (i) that director is a partner, (ii) a partner is a person who, by virtue of paragraph (a), (b) or (c) above, is connected with that director, or (iii) a partner is a Scottish firm in which that director is a partner or in which there is a partner who, by virtue of paragraph (a), (b) or (c) above, is connected with that director. A reference to the child or step-child of any person includes an illegitimate child of his, but does not include any person who has attained the age of 18; and paragraph (c) does not apply to a person acting in his capacity as trustee under an **employees' share scheme** or a pension scheme [CA 1985, s346].
Connected person (IHTA definition)	The ICTA 1988 definition applies for IHT purposes, except that the term "relative" includes uncles, aunts, nephews and nieces [IHTA 1984, s270].
Connected person (ICTA, ITEPA and TCGA definition)	For the purposes of ICTA 1988, TCGA 1992 and ITEPA 2003, an individual is connected with: • his/her spouse or civil partner; • any relative of the individual (i.e. brother, sister, ancestor and lineal descendant);

Term	Meaning
	• any relative of the individual's spouse or civil partner; • any person with whom he/she is in partnership; • any relative of any person with whom he/she is in partnership; • any spouse or civil partnerof any of the above; • any person with whom the individual acts to secure or **exercise** control of a company; • any company the individual controls either alone or jointly with **connected persons**. A Trustee is connected with: • any individual settlor of the settlement; • any person connected with that individual; • any body corporate connected with the settlement. A company is connected with: • any other company under the control of the same person or group of **connected persons**; • a person who controls it either alone or jointly with **connected persons**. A body corporate which is close is connected with a settlement of which the trustees include its **participators**, and so is any other body corporate that it controls [ICTA 1988, s839, TCGA 1992, s286, and ITEPA 2003, s718].
Consortium	A **group of companies**, which between them own 75% of another company's **ordinary share capital**, and each of which beneficially owns at least 5% [ITEPA 2003, s701(5), Sch2, para 99(3), Sch3, para 48(2), Sch4, para 36(2),].
Constituent company	A company whose employees participate in a group **SAYE** Plan [ITEPA 2003, Sch3, para 3(3)].
Convertible securities	Securities are **convertible securities** if— (a) they confer on the holder an entitlement (whether immediate or deferred and whether conditional or unconditional) to convert them into securities of a different description, (b) a contract, agreement, arrangement or condition authorises or requires the **grant** of such an entitlement to the holder if certain circumstances arise, or do not arise, or (c) a contract, agreement, arrangement or condition makes provision for the conversion of the securities (otherwise than by the holder) into securities of a different description [ITEPA 2003, s436].
Corporation tax deductible share	See section 21.2
CSOP	A Company Share Option Plan (see section 3.7.8)

Term	Meaning
Defined benefits plan	This is a type of pension plan where the benefits available to the member on **retirement** do not depend on the amounts contributed to the plan, but instead on the earnings or service of the member [FA 2004, s152].
Dependant	The following persons are **dependant**s of a member of a **registered pension scheme** at the date of the member's death: • the member's spouse or civil partnre • a child of the member who is under 23 • a child of the member who is 23 or over, but who is dependent on the member because of physical or mental impairment • a person who was financially dependent on the member • a person whose financial relationship with the member was one of mutual dependence • a person who was financially dependent on the member because of physical or mental impairment. [FA 2004, Sch28, para 15]
Dependants' annuity	This is the equivalent of a **lifetime annuity**, but payable to the **dependant** of a member. The member or **dependant** must have had the opportunity to select the insurance company. If the **dependant** is not the member's child, the annuity can be payable until the **dependant**'s death, or until the earlier of the **dependant**'s marriage or death. If the **dependant** is the member's child, the annuity can be payable until the earlier of the child's dying or ceasing to be a **dependant**, or until the earliest of the child's marriage, ceasing to be a **dependant**, or dying [FA 2004, Sch28, para 17]
Dependants' income withdrawal	**Income withdrawal** payable to a **dependant** of a member [FA 2004, Sch28, para 21]
Dependants' scheme pension	This is the equivalent of a **scheme pension**, but payable to the **dependant** of a member. If the **dependant** is not the member's child, the pension can be payable until the **dependant**'s death, or until the earlier of the **dependant**'s marriage or death. If the **dependant** is the member's child, the pension can be payable until the earlier of the child's dying or ceasing to be a **dependant**, or until the earliest of the child's marriage, ceasing to be a **dependant**, or dying [FA 2004, Sch28, para 16]
Discount	The difference between the fair **market value** of the shares at the **acquisition date** and the **acquisition price**.
Discount at grant	The difference between the fair **market value** of the underlying shares at the **grant date** and the **exercise price**.
EMI	An Enterprise Management Incentive (see section 3.7.6)
Employee-controlled	A company which is controlled by the holders of shares of a

Term	Meaning
company	particular class if— (a) the majority of the company's shares of that class (other than any held by or for the benefit of an **associated company**) are held by or for the benefit of employees of the company or a company controlled by the company, and (b) those employees are together able as holders of the shares to control the company. For these purposes, an "employee" includes a person who is to be or has been an employee [ITEPA 2003, s421H].
Employee-control shares	Shares in a company are **employee-control shares** if (a) the persons holding those shares, by virtue of their holding, together have **Section 840 control** of the company and (b) those persons are or have been employees or directors of the company or of any other company of which it has **Section 840 control** [ITEPA 2003, Sch3, para 22(2), Sch4, para 20(2)]
Employees' share scheme	See section 18.8
Employer-financed retirement benefits scheme	See section 3.4.1
Employment-related	Securities, or **securities option**s, are **employment-related** if they are acquired by a person where the right or opportunity to acquire them is available by reason of an employment of that or any other person [ITEPA 2003, s421B(1) and s471]. "Employment" includes a former or prospective employment [ITEPA 2003, s421B(2)(b) and s471(2)] and the holding of an office such as director [ITEPA 2003, s5]. A right or opportunity that is made available by a person's employer, or by a person connected with a person's employer, will be regarded as available **by reason of employment** [ITEPA 2003, s421B(3) and s471(3)] Two exceptions are: • acquisitions through public offers [ITEPA 2003, s421F] • transfers of shares by individuals through domestic, family or personal relationships [ITEPA 2003, s421B(3) and s471(3)].
Excluded employment	For the purposes of the benefits code, a person is in **excluded employment** if their annual earnings rate is less than £8,500 and either (a) the person is not a director or (b) the person is a full-time working director of a non-profit-making or charitable company

Term	Meaning
	[ITEPA 2003, s63(4) and s216(1)].
Exercisable	Describes a **securities option** whose **vesting period** has ended and which may now be **exercise**d by the **optionholder**.
Exercise	The act of acquiring the underlying securities subject to an **option** by paying the **exercise price**.
Exercise date	The date on which the **exercise** occurs.
Exercise period	The period which starts when the **option** first becomes **exercisable** and ends when the **option** expires.
Exercise price	The price per share that an **optionholder** must pay to acquire the underlying shares at the time of **exercise**.
Forfeiture	An **awardholder** forfeits an **award** if it is taken away from him, or if he is forced to sell the shares subject to the **award** for less than their **market value**.
Forfeiture period	The period during which Free or Matching Shares acquired through a **SIP** are forfeitable, which cannot be more than three years beginning with the **award** date [ITEPA 2003, Sch2, para 32(5)]
Fully paid up	Shares to be used for EMI, **CSOP**, **SAYE** or **SIP** must be **fully paid up**. For an **option** plan, this means that if the **option** is satisfied by another shareholder selling shares to the **optionholder**, the shares must be **fully paid up** in the hands of the selling shareholder. If the **option** is satisfied by issuing new shares, this means that the **optionholder** must pay the shares up in full when he subscribes for them.
Good leaver (SIP and **SAYE)**	An employee who terminates employment due to • injury or disability • **redundancy** • the company that employs him ceases to be an **associated company** • **retirement** on reaching the Specified Age • death In relation to **SAYE**, this also means someone who terminates employment because the business or part of a business that employs him is transferred to a person that is not **associate**d with the **scheme organiser.** In relation to **SIP**, this also means someone who terminates employment by reason of a **TUPE transfer.** [ITEPA 2003, Sch2, para 32(2) and Sch3, para 34]
Grant	The making of an **award** or **grant** of an **option** under a share plan.
Grant date	The date on which the **grant** occurs.

Term	Meaning
Grant price	The price, if any, which the **optionholder** must pay in order to receive the **option**.
Group of companies	A company which has one or more 51% subsidiaries, together with those subsidiaries [TCGA 1992, SchA1, para 22].
Holding company (Company Law)	A company is a "**holding company**" of another company if it: (a) holds a majority of the voting rights in the other company, or (b) is a member of the other company and has the right to appoint or remove a majority of its board of directors, or (c) is a member of the other company and controls alone, or pursuant to an agreement with other shareholders or members, a majority of the voting rights in it, or if it is a **holding company** of a company which is itself a **holding company** of the other company. The other company is the "**subsidiary**" of the **holding company** [CA 1985, s736 and 736A].
Holding company (Interest Relief)	A company whose business (disregarding any trade carried on by it) consists wholly or mainly of the holding of shares or securities of one or more companies which are its 75% subsidiaries [ICTA 1988, s361(8)].
Holding company (Taper Relief)	A company whose business (disregarding any trade carried on by it) consists wholly or mainly of the holding of shares in one or more companies which are its 51% subsidiaries [TCGA 1992, SchA1, para 22].
Ill health condition	An employee meets the **ill health condition** if he is no longer capable of carrying on his occupation because of physical or mental impairment [FA 2004, Sch28, para 1].
Income withdrawal	If the member is under the age of 75, this means an amount payable from the member's **unsecured pension fund**. If the member is 75 or over, this means an amount payable from the member's **alternatively secured pension fund** [FA 2004, Sch28, para 7].
Interest in securities	An **interest in securities** is an interest that is less than full beneficial ownership. It includes an interest in the proceeds of sale, but not include a right to acquire securities [ITEPA 2003, s420(8)].
Jointly owned company (**SIP**)	A **jointly owned company** is one of which 50% of the issued share capital is owned by one person, and 50% by another, and which is not under the **Section 840 control** of any person [ITEPA 2003, Sch2, para 91(5)].
Jointly owned company (**CSOP** and **SAYE**)	A **jointly owned company** is one of which 50% of the issued share capital is owned by one person, and 50% by another, or which is otherwise under the **Section 840 control** of two persons acting

Term	Meaning
	together [ITEPA 2003, Sch3, para 46(5), Sch4, para 34(5)].
Lifetime annuity	An annuity payable by an insurance company to the member. The member must have had the opportunity to select the insurance company. The amount of the annuity either cannot decrease or is determined in accordance with HM Revenue & Customs regulations. The annuity must be payable until the member's death, or until the later of a fixed period of up to ten years or the member's death [FA 2004, Sch28, para 3].
Long term incentive scheme (Company Law)	any agreement or arrangement under which money or other assets may become receivable by a director and which includes one or more qualifying conditions with respect to service or performance which cannot be fulfilled within a single financial year; and for this purpose the following shall be disregarded, namely: (a) bonuses the amount of which falls to be determined by reference to service or performance within a single financial year; (b) compensation for loss of office, payments for breach of contract and other termination payments; and (c) **retirement** benefits. [CA 1985, Sch6, para 1(4)]
Lump sum death benefit	A lump sum payable on the death of a member [FA 2004, s168(2)].
Market value	See Valuation section
Material interest (registered pensions and benefits code)	A person has a **material interest** in a company for the purposes of the benefits code, and the **registered pension scheme** rules, if either Condition A or Condition B below is met: Condition A is that he and all his **associates** together own, or have direct or indirect **Section 840 control** of, more than 5% of the company's share capital [ITEPA 2003, s68(2)]. Condition B is that he and all his **associates** together have a right to receive more than 5% of the assets of the company on a winding up or other distribution [ITEPA 2003, s68(3)].
Material interest (EMI code)	A person has a **material interest** in a company for the purposes of the EMI code if Condition A below is met or (if the company is close) Condition B below is met: Condition A is that he and all his **associates** together own, or have direct or indirect **Section 840 control** of, more than 30% of the company's share capital [ITEPA 2003, Sch5, para 29(2)] Note that the person or his **associate** is treated as having **Section 840 control** of any shares that he or the **associate** has a right to acquire [ITEPA 2003, Sch5, para 30(2)] but not shares that are subject

Term	Meaning
	to an unexercised **qualifying option** [ITEPA 2003, Sch5, para 30(3)]. However, if the individual or an **associate** has a right to acquire shares that have not yet been issued, the share capital of the company is treated as being increased by the number of those shares in determining whether he controls more than 30% [ITEPA 2003, Sch5, para 30(5)]. Note also that an interest in unallocated **SIP** shares is ignored for these purposes [ITEPA 2003, Sch5, para 30(7)] Condition B only applies to a **close company**. The individual and all his **associates** together must have (or be entitled to acquire) a right to receive more than 30% of the assets of the company on a winding up or other distribution [ITEPA 2003, Sch5, para 29(3)]
Material interest (**SIP**, **SAYE** and **CSOP** codes)	A person has a **material interest** in a **close company** for the purposes of the **SIP**, **SAYE** and **CSOP** codes if either Condition A or Condition B below is met: Condition A is that he and all his **associates** together own, or have direct or indirect **Section 840 control** of, more than 25% of the company's share capital [ITEPA 2003, Sch2, para 20(2), Sch3, para 12(2), Sch4, para 10(2)]. Note that the person or his **associate** is treated as having **Section 840 control** of any shares that he or the **associate** has a right to acquire [ITEPA 2003, Sch2, para 21(2), Sch3, para 13(1), Sch4, para 11(1)]. However, if the individual or an **associate** has a right to acquire shares that have not yet been issued, the share capital of the company is treated as being increased by the number of those shares in determining whether he controls more than 25% [ITEPA 2003, Sch2, para 21(4), Sch3, para 13(3), Sch4, para 11(3)]. Note also that an interest in unallocated **SIP** shares is ignored for these purposes [ITEPA 2003, Sch2, para 21(6), Sch3, para 13(5), Sch4, para 11(5)]. Condition B is that the individual and all his **associates** together must have (or be entitled to acquire) a right to receive more than 25% of the assets of the company on a winding up or other distribution [ITEPA 2003, Sch2, para 20(3), Sch3, para 12(3), Sch4, para 10(3)].
Material interest (Taper Relief)	A person has a **material interest** in a company for the purposes of taper relief if he possesses, or has direct or indirect control of: • more than 10% of any class of the company's share capital or • more than 10% of the voting rights in the company or • rights to more than 10% of the income or

Term	Meaning
	• rights to more than 10% o the assets on a winding up [TCGA 1992, SchA1, para 6A(1)]. Note that the person is treated as having control of any shares that he has a right to acquire [TCGA 1992, SchA1, para 6A(2)]. This includes a conditional or unconditional present or future right to acquire shares [TCGA 1992, SchA1, para 6A(3) and (4)]. However, if the individual has a right to acquire shares that have not yet been issued, the share capital of the company is treated as being increased by the number of those shares in determining whether he controls more than 10% [TCGA 1992, SchA1, para 6A(5)].
Material interest (Loan Interest Relief)	A person has a **material interest** in a **close company** for the purposes of loan interest relief if either Condition A or Condition B below is met: Condition A is that he and all his **associate**s together own, or have direct or indirect **Section 840 control** of, more than 5% of the company's share capital [ICTA 1988, s360A(1)(a)]. Condition B is that the individual and all his **associate**s together must have (or be entitled to acquire) a right to receive more than 5% of the assets of the company on a winding up or other distribution [ICTA 1988, s360A(1)(b)]. There are special rules for loans made before 14 November 1986 [ICTA 1988, s360A(8)].
Members of a person's family or household	The following are the **members of a person's family or household**: • The person's spouse or civil partner • The person's children and their spouses or civil partners • The person's parents • The person's **dependant**s • The person's domestic staff • The person's guests [ITEPA 2003, s721(5) and FA 2004, s173(11)]
Money purchase plan	This is a type of pension scheme where the amount of benefits provided on **retirement** depends on the amount of funds contributed by the employer and/or the employee. Normally these funds will be invested and the investment returns will be available to provide benefits on **retirement**. A **cash balance plan** is a form of **money purchase plan.**
Money's worth value	See section 15.1
Normal minimum pension age	Before 6 April 2010, age 50; on or after 6 April 2010, age 55 [FA 2004, s279(1)]

Term	Meaning
Open market shares	This term is used in the **SAYE** code [ITEPA 2003, Sch3, para 22] and in the **CSOP** code [ITEPA 2003, Sch4, para 20]. There is also a subtly different concept is used in determining whether certain exemptions apply under ITEPA 2003, Part 7 [ITEPA 2003, s429(4), s443(4), s446R(4), and s449(3)]. For the purposes of the **SAYE** code and **CSOP** code, **open market shares** are shares that are held by people who are NOT • people who acquired shares **by reason of employment** (except as a result of an offer to the public) • trustees holding shares on behalf of people who acquired their interests in the shares **by reason of employment** • companies which have **section 840 control** of the company whose shares are concerned • **associated companies** of the company concerned For the purposes of the exemptions in ITEPA 2003, Part 7, **open market shares** are shares that are held by people who are NOT • employees or directors of the company or an **associated company** • another person who acquired shares by reason of the employment of an employee or director of the company or an **associated company** • any person connected with such an employee, director or other person and who acquired the shares from the employee or such other person unless he acquired the shares in a bargain at arm's length • **associated companies** of the company concerned.
Option	A right to acquire or dispose of an asset. This is a narrower term than "**securities option**"
Option period	The period which starts with the **grant date** and ends when the **option** expires.
Optionholder	An individual, usually an employee, who has been **grant**ed a securities **option**.
Ordinarily resident	A person will be **ordinarily resident** in the UK once he has been **resident** in the UK for three or more years, or if he takes an action which indicates that he will be **resident** in the UK for three or more years. Examples include: • acquiring a freehold or long leasehold property • signing a contract of employment for more than two years • deciding to stay for at least three years
Ordinary shares	Shares which carry either

Term	Meaning
(Inheritance Tax)	(a) a right to dividends not restricted to dividends at a fixed rate, or (b) a right to conversion into shares carrying such a right as is mentioned in paragraph (a) above [IHTA 1984, s13(5)].
Ordinary share capital (ICTA 1988)	All of the company's share capital other than that whose holders have a right to a fixed rate dividend but have no other right to share in the profits of the company [ICTA 1988, s832(1)]. See also HMRC Manual ESS10020[230].
Parent company	This term is used in FA 2003, Sch23. A company is the "**parent company**" of any company that is its **51% Subsidiary** [FA 2003, Sch23, para 28(c)].
Parent scheme company	The **scheme organiser** of a group **SAYE** Plan [ITEPA 2003, Sch3, para 3(1)].
Participator	This term is defined in ICTA 1988, s417. Further commentary is in the HMRC Manual CT6110[231].
PAYE Settlement Agreement	An agreement between an employer and HM Revenue & Customs to account for income tax on general earnings of the employer's employees in a particular way, rather than in accordance with the strict regulations [IT (PAYE) Regulations 2003, reg 105(3)].
Pension Death Benefit	A pension payable on the death of a member (except a pension payable to his estate) [FA 2004, s167(2)].
Property Investment LLP	A limited liability partnership whose business consists wholly or mainly in the making of investments in land and the principal part of whose income is derived therefrom [ICTA 1988, s842B(1)(b)].
Public company	A company limited by shares or limited by guarantee and having a share capital, being a company (a) the memorandum of which states that it is to be a **public company**, and (b) in relation to which the provisions of CA 1985 or the former Companies Acts as to the registration or re-registration of a company as a **public company** have been complied with on or after 22nd December 1980. [CA 1985, s1(3)]
Qualifying option	An EMI option
Qualified plan	An EMI Plan
Quasi-loan	A **quasi-loan** is a transaction under which one party ("the creditor")

230 http://www.hmrc.gov.uk/manuals/essumanual/essu10000/essu10020.htm

231 http://www.hmrc.gov.uk/manuals/ct123manual/ct6110.htm

Term	Meaning
	agrees to pay, or pays otherwise than in pursuance of an agreement, a sum for another ("the borrower") or agrees to reimburse, or reimburses otherwise than in pursuance of an agreement, expenditure incurred by another party for another ("the borrower")— (a) on terms that the borrower (or a person on his behalf) will reimburse the creditor; or (b) in circumstances giving rise to a liability on the borrower to reimburse the creditor. [CA 1985, s331(3)]
Qualifying Employee Share Ownership Trust	A qualifying employee share ownership trust ("QUEST") is a special kind of EBT that had tax advantages granted by FA 1989 and subsequent legislation. Those advantages were removed by FA 2003 but many QUESTs still exist.
Readily convertible asset	See section 21.1
Recognised stock exchange	The current list of "**recognised stock exchange**s" is in the HMRC Manual at CT6211e[232].
Redeemable	Shares to be used in a **CSOP**, **SIP**, EMI or **SAYE** plan must not be **redeemable**. It is not entirely clear what "**redeemable**" means in this context. In one sense, all shares in a UK company are "**redeemable**", since the company has the power to buy them back for cancellation in certain circumstances. "**Redeemable**" must therefore have a more limited meaning. In the author's view, "**redeemable**" securities are ones where, according to their terms of issue, either the issuer or the holder or both have the power to cause the issuer to redeem them in certain circumstances for payment of an amount which is fixed or calculated according to a formula, but which is not directly related to the **market value** of the shares at that time.
Redundancy	**Redundancy** is when an employee is terminated and the reason for the dismissal is wholly or mainly attributable to: 1. The fact that his employer has ceased or intends to cease: (a) to carry on the business for the purpose of which the employee was employed by him, or (b) to carry on that business in a place where the employee was so employed, or 2. The fact that the requirements of that business have ceased or

[232] http://www.hmrc.gov.uk/manuals/ct123manual/ct6211e.htm

Term	Meaning
	diminished or expected to cease or diminish: (a) for the employees to carry out work of a particular kind, or (b) for the employees to carry out work of a particular kind in the place where the employee was employed by the employer [ERA 1996, s139]. An employee will not be made redundant if, before the contract has ended, he is offered a renewal of his contract of employment, or a re-engagement under a new contract of employment which takes effect either immediately on or after an interval of not more than four weeks after the end of his employment [ERA 1996, s141].
Registered pension scheme	See section 3.3.1
Relevant company (EMI)	The company whose shares are used in an EMI plan [ITEPA 2003, Sch5, para 2].
Relevant employment	For the purposes of the **SIP** code, this means employment by the original employing company or any **associated company** [ITEPA 2003, Sch2, para 95(2)].
Relevant UK earnings	Employment income, income from a trade, profession or vocation [FA 2004, s189(2)].
Relevant UK individual	An individual who has **relevant UK earnings**, or who is **resident** in the UK, or who became a member of a **registered pension scheme** while he was UK **resident** and was UK **resident** within the last five years [FA 2004, s189(1)].
Resident	A person is **resident** in the UK if • he comes to the UK for a specific purpose (e.g. employment) which means he will remain in the UK for at least two years; • he is present in the UK for 183 days in a tax year; • he is present in the UK for an average of 91 days per tax year over four tax years.
Restricted securities	**Restricted securities** are **employment-related** securities in relation to which there is any provision (contract, agreement, arrangement or condition) which reduces their **market value** and which is one of the three types listed below [ITEPA 2003, s432(1)]: the holder could, in certain circumstances, be compelled to dispose of the securities, and he would not necessarily receive at least their UMV in exchange [ITEPA 2003, s423(2)] • the holder is restricted in his ability to dispose of the securities, or to retain the securities or their proceeds of sale, or in relation to any other right conferred by the securities [ITEPA 2003, s423(3)] • there is a provision that could cause a disadvantage to the

Term	Meaning
	holder, the employee, or any person connected to either of them [ITEPA 2003, s423(4)] However, there are the following exclusions: • where the securities are unpaid or partly-paid, and the holder can forfeit them if he fails to pay any call on the shares, as long as there is no restriction preventing him from paying the call • where the holder can be compelled to sell the shares if the employee concerned is dismissed for misconduct [ITEPA 2003, s424(1)]. Even so, neither of these exclusions apply to securities acquired on or after 2 December 2004 if one of the main purposes of the arrangements under which the right or opportunity to acquire the securities was made available was the avoidance of tax or NIC [ITEPA 2003, s424(2)]. In addition to the above exclusions, redeemable securities acquired before 2 December 2004 cannot be restricted securities [ITEPA 2003, old s424].
Retirement	HM Revenue & Customs will look at several factors to determine whether an employee's employment is terminated due to **retirement**. These include: • the age of the employee; • if he was dismissed, the reasons for dismissal; • whether the employee makes himself available for subsequent full-time work. If an individual is unfairly dismissed, HM Revenue & Customs will not treat him or her as having retired.
SAYE	A Save As You Earn share option plan (see section 4.3)
Scheme chargeable payment	See section 3.3.6.5
Scheme company	The company whose shares are used in a **CSOP** or **SAYE** [ITEPA 2003, Sch3, para 38(1)(a) and Sch4, para 26(1)(a)] In this book, this term is also used to describe the company whose shares are used in a **SIP**
Scheme organiser	This term is used in the **SAYE** code and the **CSOP** code to refer to the company which establishes the scheme. This may be different from the **scheme company**. [ITEPA 2003, Sch3, para 2(2) and Sch4, para 2(2)]. In this book, this term is also used to describe the company that establishes a **SIP**
Scheme pension	See section 3.3.4.5.1
Scheme sanction	See section 3.3.6.5

Term	Meaning
charge	
Section 416 control	Actual control (or entitlement to actual control) over the affairs of a company, whether • control through voting power • control through share capital or through issued share capital • control over the income of the company or • control over the assets of the company [ICTA 1988, s416] These tests are considered in detail in HMRC Manual CT6201 et seq[233].
Section 425 election	See section 22.1.1
Section 430 election	See section 22.1.2
Section 431(1) election	See section 22.1.3
Section 431(2) election	See section 22.1.4
Section 840 control	A person has **Section 840 control** of a company if he has the power to secure— (a) by means of the holding of shares or the possession of voting power in or in relation to that or any other body corporate; or (b) by virtue of any powers conferred by the articles of association or other document regulating that or any other body corporate, that the affairs of the company are conducted in accordance with his wishes [ICTA 1988, s840].
Securities option	A **securities option** is a right to acquire **securities**. However, a right to acquire **securities** is not a **securities option**, if it was acquired on or after 2 December 2004 pursuant to a right or opportunity made available under arrangements the main purpose (or one of the main purposes) of which is the avoidance of tax or national insurance contributions [ITEPA 2003, s420(8)]. Although the term "right to acquire" is generally understood to refer to situations where the employee has some degree of choice, HM Revenue & Customs have a more extensive interpretation. In their view, any arrangement whereby securities will or may be delivered to the employee in future, regardless of whether the employee has a choice, will be a **securities option** (see HMRC FAQ 5(d)[234] and 5(i)[235]).

[233] http://www.hmrc.gov.uk/manuals/ct123manual/ct6201.htm

[234] http://www.hmrc.gov.uk/shareschemes/faq_emprelatedsecurity-ch5.htm#d

[235] http://www.hmrc.gov.uk/shareschemes/faq_emprelatedsecurity-ch5.htm#i

Term	Meaning
Security	Virtually any financial asset is a "**security**" for the purposes of ITEPA 2003, Part 7. One major exception to this is that a **securities option** is not a **security** [ITEPA 2003, s420(5)(e)]. Other kinds of option can be **securities**. For example, put options which give a right to sell shares are themselves **securities**. The full definition is in ITEPA 2003, s420.
SIP	A Share Incentive Plan (see section 4.2.4)
Option gain	The **market value** of the underlying share at the time of **exercise**, less the **exercise price**.
State retirement pension	Retirement pension under SSCBA 1992 or graduated retirement benefit under NIA 1965 [FA 2004, Sch28, para 2(5)].
Subsidiary (Company Law)	A company is a "**subsidiary**" of another company if the other company: (a) holds a majority of its voting rights, or (b) is one of its members and has the right to appoint or remove a majority of its board of directors, or (c) is one of its members of the other company and controls alone, or pursuant to an agreement with other shareholders or members, a majority of its voting rights, or if it is a **subsidiary** of a company which is itself a **subsidiary** of the other company. The other company is the "**holding company**" of the **subsidiary** [CA 1985, s736 and 736A].
Trading company (Interest Relief)	A company whose business consists wholly or mainly of the carrying on of a trade or trades [ICTA 1988, s361(8)].
Trading company (Taper Relief)	A company which is either (a) a company existing wholly for the purpose of carrying on one or more trades ; or (b) a company that would fall within paragraph (a) above apart from any purposes capable of having no substantial effect on the extent of the company's activities [TCGA 1992, SchA1, para 22].
Trading group (Interest Relief)	A group the business of whose members taken together consists wholly or mainly of the carrying on of a trade or trades, and for this purpose "group" means a company which has one or more 75% subsidiaries together with those subsidiaries [ICTA 1988, s361(8)].
Trading group (Taper Relief)	A **group of companies**, the activities of which (if all the activities of the companies in the group are taken together) do not, or not to any substantial extent, include activities carried on otherwise than in the course of, or for the purposes of, a trade [TCGA 1992, SchA1, para

Term	Meaning
	22(1)].
TUPE transfer	A transfer of a business to which the Transfer of Undertakings (Protection of Employment) Regulations 1981 apply.
Unauthorised borrowing	See section 3.3.6.4.2
Unauthorised member payment	Any payment to or in respect of a member of a **registered pension scheme** that is not authorised [FA 2004, s160(2)(a)].
Unrestricted Market Value	See section 12.3.4.1
Unsecured pension	A short-term annuity or **income withdrawal** [FA 2004, Sch28, para 4].
Unsecured pension fund	The member's **unsecured pension fund** consists of the money and assets held in the fund, which have been designated for payment of **unsecured pension**, and have not been applied towards the provision of a **scheme pension** [FA 2004, Sch28, para 8(1)].
Variation of share capital	It is not possible to adjust an approved share **option** except to take account of a "**variation of share capital**" [ITEPA 2003, Sch3, para 28(3), Sch4, para 22(3)]. The following corporate events constitute variations of share capital: Capitalisation or bonus issues; [HMRC Manual ESS29082[236]] Rights issues; [HMRC Manual ESS29082] Consolidation of share capital; [HMRC Manual ESS29082] Sub-division of share capital; [HMRC Manual ESS29082] Reduction of share capital; [HMRC Manual ESS29082] Vendor placings with clawback; [HMRC Manual ESS29083[237]] Vendor rights offers; [HMRC Manual ESS29083] Cash open offers; [HMRC Manual ESS29083] However, the following events do not constitute variations of share capital, in the view of HM Revenue & Customs: Demergers or spin-offs; [HMRC Manual ESS29084[238]] Stock dividends.
Vest	Shares or options **vest** in the holder when he becomes fully entitled to them, i.e. they can no longer be forfeited.
Vesting date	The date on which the **vesting period** ends.
Vesting period	In relation to an **option**, means the time period during which the

236 http://www.hmrc.gov.uk/manuals/essumanual/essu29000/essu29082.htm

237 http://www.hmrc.gov.uk/manuals/essumanual/essu29000/essu29083.htm

238 http://www.hmrc.gov.uk/manuals/essumanual/essu29000/essu29084.htm

Term	Meaning
	individual is not permitted to **exercise** the **option**. In relation to a share award, means the time during which the employee can forfeit the shares.

25. SSM 4.4 (From HMRC's Share Scheme Manual, now withdrawn)

Where shares are acquired by a director or employee in the following circumstances, you may accept that they are acquired in another capacity and that no [general earnings charge] arises.

a) Where additional shares are issued or offered to all shareholders, including directors and employees, on the occasion of a bonus or rights issue, unless

- a director or employee acquires shares on a rights issue in which other shareholders do not take up all the rights to which they are entitled, or
- a director or employee acquires additional shares in a rights issue in respect of a particular class of shares when there has been no corresponding issue to holders of other classes of shares in the same company.

b) Where shares are allotted, on the formation of a company, to the individuals who are to be the directors of the company unless

- the shares are being offered to such individuals as an inducement to join the company, or
- the bulk of the finance for the new company is being supplied by another company or companies (other than in the normal course of a banking business).

c) Where new shares are issued to the founder shareholders (whether or not in proportion to their existing shareholdings) and the reason for the new issue of shares is to raise additional finance for the purposes of the company's business.

d) Where the issue or transfer of shares among the shareholders of a company (including the directors) is in the nature of a family arrangement.

Examples include

- the introduction of sons or daughters into the business when they reach a suitable age
- the transfer of shares to relatives by a director who is reducing his active participation in the business, perhaps due to inheritance tax considerations.

e) Where shares or securities are made available to directors or employees under public offers for sale of share capital, unless

- the public offer does not satisfy the requirements of *[ITEPA 2003, s542]*, or
- the directors or employees are offered shares at a discount to the public offer price.

f) Where, as part of a capital reorganisation, all holders of the ordinary share capital of a company receive, in exchange for their shares, shares which

- are of another class, or
- have different rights, or
- are in another company (for example on a merger or takeover)

unless the employee shareholders are being treated more favourably than the other shareholders.

26. Table of Authorities

Cases

Web Sites

HMRC Material

Statutes

Regulations

Other Material

27. Index